W9-DFY-265

The African American Experience

The African American Experience

VOLUME I

Through Reconstruction

JOE WILLIAM TROTTER, JR.
Carnegie Mellon University

HOUGHTON MIFFLIN COMPANY
Boston   New York

〜

To my students, past and present

Carnegie Mellon University
Pittsburgh, Pennsylvania

University of California
Davis, California

University of Minnesota
Minneapolis–St. Paul, Minnesota

Tremper Senior High School
Kenosha, Wisconsin

Editor in Chief: Jean L. Woy
Senior Development Editor: Frances Gay
Senior Project Editor: Christina M. Horn
Production/Design Coordinator: Jodi O'Rourke
Senior Cover Design Coordinator: Deborah Azerrad Savona
Manufacturing Manager: Florence Cadran
Senior Marketing Manager: Sandra McGuire

Cover design: Nina Wishnok/Dynamo Design
Volume I cover image: William Brown, *Hauling the Whole Week's Picking.*
Historic New Orleans Collection.

PART OPENER PHOTO CREDITS: *Part I:* New York Public Library; *Part II:* Library of Congress; *Part III:* Chicago Historical Society; *Part IV:* Harper's Weekly.

Copyright © 2001 by Houghton Mifflin Company. All rights reserved.

No part of this work may be reproduced or transmitted in any form or by any means, electronic or mechanical, including photocopying and recording, or by any information storage or retrieval system without the prior written permission of Houghton Mifflin Company unless such copying is expressly permitted by federal copyright law. Address inquiries to College Permissions, Houghton Mifflin Company, 222 Berkeley Street, Boston, MA 02116-3764.

Printed in the U.S.A.

Library of Congress Catalog Card Number: 00-1338859

ISBN: 0-618-07196-2

2 3 4 5 6 7 8 9-QF-05 04 03 02 01

BRIEF CONTENTS

CONTENTS

Appendix

BOXES

MAPS AND ILLUSTRATIONS

TABLES

PREFACE

T**he African American Experience** is rooted in the recent maturation of African American studies as a scholarly field. Over the past three decades, scholars have revamped our understanding of race, class, culture, and power in U.S. and African American history. Yet popular perceptions of African Americans reflect certain enduring stereotypes and erroneous notions about African American life and history. In the mainstream media, portraits of African Americans continue to revolve around images of poor and working-class blacks as economically improvident, culturally impoverished, devoid of viable family life, isolated from community, and largely passive in the face of dehumanizing social conditions. In contrast, this book shows how African Americans developed their own notions of work, family, culture, and power and forged their own distinct community. The black poor, working-class, and business and professional people created a broad range of multiclass institutions that not only fueled the African American struggle for cultural autonomy but also established a foundation for the ongoing struggle for political freedom and economic emancipation.

While this study rejects portraits of the black community as internally fragmented and incapable of acting in its own best interests, it rejects the idea that racism overwhelmed difference, transformed the black population into a homogeneous mass, and suppressed internal dissent. This book builds on research in African American social, working-class, and women's history and probes both class and gender conflicts within the black community. Poor and working-class blacks were by no means passive participants in middle-class or elite-led community-building activities. They challenged the moral injunctions of their elite counterparts and pioneered in the development of unique cultural forms such as the blues and gospel. Similarly, black women questioned the most blatant manifestations of gender inequality within the black community. They built their own auxiliaries and pushed for change within black civic, religious, civil rights, and political organizations. By showing how black life unfolded within diverse groups and regions and how it changed over time, this book also treats the black experience as a dynamic, multifaceted, historical process from its African beginnings through the onset of the twenty-first century.

As African Americans navigated internal social conflicts and forged collective responses to class and racial inequality, they also gained the support of a small but influential roster of white allies. These included abolitionists during the antebellum years, radical Republicans during the emancipation period, and freedom marchers during the modern civil rights era, to name a few. Such recurring patterns of interracial cooperation offered hope that America could create a more just and inclusive society. Still, both the promise and limits of American democracy persist as the curtains open on a new century.

This book is divided into six interrelated parts, each covering a major phase in African American life and history. Part I (Chapters 1–2) traces the black experience from its African roots to enslavement in the Latin American and Caribbean colonies of Portugal, Spain, France, and England. By discussing the multiracial nature of slavery in the Old World, Part I concludes that the rise of race-based slavery was the product of historical developments on a global scale. Focusing on the enslavement of blacks in British North America, Part II (Chapters 3–6) describes the transition from a relatively flexible system of indentured servitude during the early seventeenth century to bondage "for life" during the late seventeenth and eighteenth centuries. It also analyzes regional differences and concludes with a discussion of the promise and limits of the American Revolution and life in the new republic for African Americans.

The development of African American life in the antebellum South is the subject of Part III (Chapters 7–10). This section discusses work, housing, and living conditions in a variety of urban and rural settings; the development of slave culture, family, community, and forms of resistance; and the growth of a free black population, the rise of abolitionism, and the coming of the Civil War. Part III also describes how African Americans helped to transform the Civil War into a struggle for their own liberation.

Part IV (Chapters 11–14) discusses the triumphs and disappointments of emancipation. It shows how newly emancipated blacks won and then lost the franchise; won and then lost a measure of control over their own land and labor; and won and then lost a coterie of white allies. At the same time, these chapters show how African Americans forged new forms of culture, community, and political activism and resisted the rise of Jim Crow, disfranchisement, and mob violence.

The African American struggle for freedom escalated during the era of the Great Migration, the Great Depression, and the two world wars, which are the subjects of Part V (Chapters 15–19). African Americans built new institutions and launched new cultural, civil rights, and political movements. The NAACP, the National Urban League, the Garvey movement, the Communist Party, and the Congress of Industrial Organizations all helped to establish a foundation for the modern civil rights movement and the rise of the Second Reconstruction during the 1950s and 1960s, as discussed in Part VI (Chapters 20–23). Part VI explores not only the rise of massive nonviolent direct action struggles but also the Black Power movement, the decline of the Second Reconstruction, and the emergence of new African American movements for social change during the 1990s. By the turn of the twenty-first century, African Americans struggled to redefine what it meant to be black in an increasingly multiracial nation and world.

Reinforcing the foregoing treatment of black life and history, *The African American Experience* includes special features designed to deepen the reader's understanding of the subject. Distributed at appropriate points throughout the text are more than one hundred photographs; statistical tables, maps, and charts; special full-color inserts displaying artifacts and artwork; and boxed excerpts of primary sources. The Appendix contains tables that show population growth, urbanization, and suburbanization, as well as excerpts from more than a dozen documents—key civil rights laws, executive orders, and Supreme Court decisions. By providing a visual image of African American life over time and by telling the story in the voices and language of the people who lived during different periods of the nation's history, these documents and artwork enable readers to imagine times and experiences quite different from their own. An extensive Chronology of significant events also appears at the end of the book, to enable readers to review the sequence of events. These pages are tinted at the edges for ease of reference.

Because historical knowledge and interpretation require an understanding of diverse viewpoints, this book provides brief historiographical critiques of available scholarship. These "Changing Historical Interpretations" boxes pinpoint areas of controversy on key topics, issues, and periods in African American history—the origins of African slavery, the emergence of African American culture, Reconstruction, the rise of Jim Crow, the development of black urban communities, and the origins of the modern civil rights movement. By introducing readers to major controversies in African American life and history, these succinct essays encourage students to ponder how and why commonly agreed-on facts often produce widely divergent interpretations. This unique feature allows students to explore how historians think, conduct their research, and interpret the black experience.

As always, I am indebted to numerous institutions, staff, colleagues, friends, and relatives for helping to make this book possible. At Carnegie Mellon University, I wish to thank Steve Schlossman, head of the Department of History; Peter Stearns, former dean of the College of Humanities and Social Science; Gail Dickey, business manager; Elaine Burrelli, administrative assistant; Robin Dearmon Jenkins, Ph.D. candidate; colleagues Tera Hunter and Joel Tarr; members of the advisory board of the Center for Africanamerican Urban Studies and the Economy (CAUSE); and the offices of the president and provost. For encouraging my research, writing, teaching, and work with CAUSE, I also appreciate the current and past support of the Mellon Bank Foundation, the Maurice Falk Medical Fund, the Ford Foundation, and collaborative schools and colleagues in the Midwest Consortium for Black Studies.

Moreover, this book was completed while I was a Fellow at the Center for Advanced Study in the Behavioral Sciences (CASBS), Stanford, California. I am grateful for the financial support provided by the Andrew W. Mellon Foundation. At CASBS, I benefited from the critical insights of Center Fellows Portia Maultsby, Michael Fultz, Edward Ayers, Michael Johnson, Sara Berry, and Jitka Maleckova. For providing a forum for the discussion of my ideas for the book, especially Chapter 10, I am indebted to James Grossman and participants in the Newberry Library Seminar in Social History in Chicago.

At other universities, I am indebted to friends Earl Lewis, University of Michigan, Ann Arbor; Quintard Taylor, University of Washington, Seattle; Julie Saville, University of Chicago; Elias Mandala, University of Rochester; Laurence Glasco, University of Pittsburgh; Stephanie Shaw, Ohio State University, Columbus; Henry Louis Taylor Jr., State University of New York, Buffalo; James and Lois Horton, George Washington University, Washington, D.C.; Clarence Walker, University of California, Davis; Irwin Marcus, Indiana University, Pennsylvania; Darlene Clark Hine, Michigan State University; and Nellie McKay and other members of the Midwest Consortium for Black Studies. And I would like to thank the following reviewers who gave very helpful critiques and advice on the manuscript at various stages in the process: Mia Bay, Rutgers University; Nemata Blyden, University of Texas at Dallas; Stephanie Cole, University of Texas at Arlington; Selika Ducksworth-Lawton, University of Wisconsin—Eau Claire; Roy E. Finkenbine, University of Detroit—Mercy; Thelma Wills Foote, University of California, Irvine; Paul Harvey, University of Colorado; Larry E. Hudson Jr., University of Rochester; Ben Keppel, University of Oklahoma; Elias Mandala, University of Rochester; Edna Greene Medford, Howard University; Tiffany Ruby Patterson, Binghamton University; W. Bryan Rommel-Ruiz, Colorado College; Clarence E. Walker, University of California, Davis; and Michael R. West, College of the Holy Cross.

I also wish to extend a special thanks to the editors and staff of Houghton Mifflin Company for the careful attention given to this book. I am especially grateful to Jean Woy, Vice President and Editor in Chief, and her predecessor, Sean Wakeley, for their firm confidence in this project. For effectively steering this book through various phases of the production process, I also thank Frances Gay, Senior Development Editor; Christina Horn, Senior Project Editor; and Sharon Donahue, photo researcher. Indeed, it has been a real pleasure working with and learning from these publishing professionals.

For providing inspiration as well as community-based forums, documents, books, and memories of the postindustrial North-to-South migration, I thank my brothers and sisters, and nieces and nephews, especially Otis and his wife, Dotsie; my sister, Voncille Hines; my niece, Marva Ann Williams; and my nephews, Greg Harris and Carson Trotter III. Most important, however, I am indebted to my wife, LaRue. In addition to her love and ongoing spiritual support, LaRue offered unyielding faith and confidence in this book. Finally, for inspiring my teaching, challenging my ideas, and sustaining my faith in the educational enterprise, I am grateful to my students. These include not only undergraduate students and the high school students whom I first taught, but also numerous graduate students— Steve Tripp, John Hinshaw, Ancella Livers, Donald Collins, Liesl Miller Orenic, Matthew Hawkins, Trent Alexander, Charles Lee, Susannah Walker, Tywanna Whorley, and Robin Dearmon Jenkins, to name only a few. To them, I dedicate this book with a great deal of appreciation and respect for sharing their remarkable insights into the human condition.

Joe William Trotter Jr.
Pittsburgh, Pennsylvania

PART I

The African American Experience in Global Perspective:
Prelude to a New World

The African American experience had its roots in the gradual globalization of the world's people. Like Asian, Latino, and European immigrants, African Americans were part of the great transatlantic migration of people from the Old World. Unlike other ethnic and nationality groups, however, African Americans entered the New World in chains. Yet their enslavement was by no means inevitable. Before the arrival of Europeans on the west coast of Africa during the fifteenth and sixteenth centuries, Africans had developed their own independent economic, social, and political systems. In addition to the ancient kingdoms of Egypt and Ethiopia in North and East Africa, the medieval kingdoms of Ghana, Mali, and Songhay had emerged in West Africa. Although the spread of the Sahara Desert in ancient times had disrupted the geographical unity of the continent and stimulated the emergence of sharp regional differences, the development of trans-Saharan transportation and trade networks joined Africans together across regions and promoted the vigorous transfer of goods, people, and ideas, including the spread of Islam into West Africa and the export of gold and human captives to North Africa and the Mediterranean.

In the meantime, during the medieval crusades, Europeans gained knowledge of sugar production following their capture of the Islamic territories of the eastern Mediterranean and North Africa. On their Mediterranean sugar plantations, Europeans initially enslaved Arabs, Africans, and eastern and southern Europeans. Only gradually did the plantation system spread to the islands off the northwest coast of Africa and then to the New World, where Europeans acquired a predominantly African labor force. Despite the heroic efforts of Africans to resist enslavement and retain their freedom, Europeans gradually instituted a color- or race-based system of human bondage and set the principal context for the first four hundred years of black life in the New World. As a backdrop for understanding this process in British North America, Part I analyzes the development of independent precolonial African societies; the rise of a multiracial system of bondage in the Mediterranean world; and finally the emergence of African bondage in the New World colonies of the Caribbean and Latin America.

CHAPTER 1

⌒

Before the Atlantic Crossing

Western images of Africa have changed tremendously over time, but certain perceptions endure. Despite the remarkable, though tedious and slow, climb of African nations toward independence and democracy during the late twentieth century, no contemporary image of Africa is more pervasive than the portrait of starving men, women, and children in the drought- and civil war–stricken countries of East Africa and the Sahel. The image of Africa as a land of economic hardship, starvation, and political turmoil has a long history. Between 2500 and 2300 B.C., the major rivers of the Sahara gradually evaporated, forcing inhabitants of the river valleys to move farther north and south. As Europeans entered Africa in search of a better life and riches for themselves during modern times, they often seized on these harsh conditions as a rationale for their enslavement and colonization of African peoples. They argued that an even worse fate had confronted blacks in their own land and at their own hands. In short, Europeans denied that Africans could come to grips with their own problems. On the contrary, as this chapter will demonstrate, precolonial Africans adapted to changing social, cultural, and environmental conditions by creating numerous states and social systems—Egypt and Ethiopia in the northeast, the trans-Saharan trade network in the northwest, and a succession of West African kingdoms from Lake Chad in the east to the Atlantic Ocean in the west. By assessing the transformation of African societies during the ancient period, we will be able to better understand the many forces that gave rise to the African American experience in the New World.

NORTHEAST AFRICA

Before 2500 B.C., the Sahara was a highly fertile land capable of supporting a variety of plant, animal, and human life. The Sahara river system flowed unbroken from Lake Chad in the east, southwest into the Benue-Niger Rivers, and thence to the Atlantic Ocean. Moreover, from west to east, numerous mountainous rivers replenished this inland system of waters, giving rise to vibrant Stone Age fishing communities. Remains of harpoons, fishhooks, and decorative wavy-line clay pottery offer evidence of a thriving culture in this region. Farther east, Sahara tributaries added to the river systems of the Nile Valley and Ethiopian highlands. Given the pre–Saharan Desert history of this continent, it is no wonder that recent archaeologists have located some of the most impressive early remains of human life in Africa.

Ancient Egypt

The emergence of the Sahara Desert presented Africans with new and enduring challenges to human survival and development. As the wet phase of the Sahara came to an end, settlements on the edge of the Nile Valley gradually moved inland along the naturally irrigated floodplains of the Nile River. Egyptians depended increasingly on the annual overflow of the Nile River, which owed its existence to its tributaries, the White Nile and Blue Nile (and Atbara), the latter originating in the highlands of Ethiopia (see map). Each year, heavy rains and floods inundated these rivers, bringing into the Nile Valley new dark, fertile soils. All along the Nile Valley, farming communities depended on these annual deposits of fresh land and water from thousands of miles away. It was this remarkable phenomenon that led the Greek historian Herodotus to describe Egypt as the "miracle" or "gift" of the Nile River.

The fertility of the Nile Valley gave rise to a series of small agricultural communities along its banks. These small communities soon developed into a number of local states, which in turn formed the foundation for the emergence of the Upper and Lower kingdoms of Egypt. Under the leadership of Narmer, or Menes, Upper and Lower Egypt united into a single kingdom sometime between about 3000 B.C. and 2850 B.C., setting in motion one of the longest-lasting cultures in human history.

Several overlapping periods of stability and instability punctuated ancient Egyptian history: the Old Kingdom (3100–2180 B.C.); the First Intermediate period (2180–2080 B.C.); the Middle Kingdom (2080–1640 B.C.); the Second Intermediate period (1640–1570 B.C.); and the New Kingdom (1570–1090 B.C.). During the New Kingdom era, Egypt established a large standing army and extended its territorial control over Palestine and Syria in the northeast, to parts of Nubia in the south, and to key trade routes down the Red Sea into the "Land of Punt" on the Somali coast of East Africa.

Closely interconnected with the rise of the centralized Egyptian state were significant developments in religion, culture, and science. Ancient Egyptians believed in many gods, each of which had its own shrine or temple. Egyptian gods represented different aspects of nature, including the sun god, Re; the god of wind, Amun; and others representing different forms of animal life. During the Middle Kingdom, the gods of wind and sun were combined into Amun-Re, the official

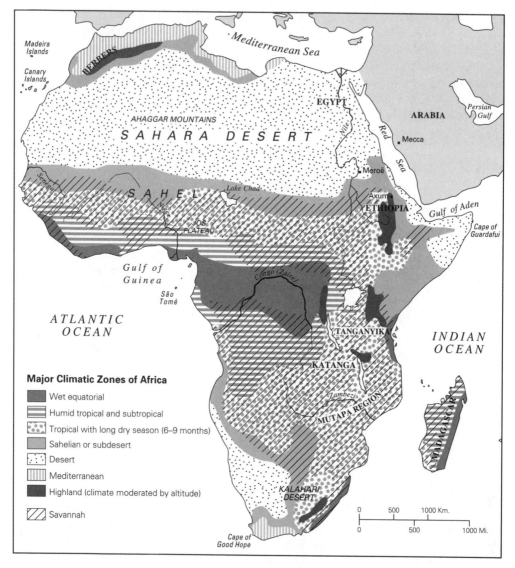

Vegetation Zones, Modern Africa. Before the emergence of the Sahara Desert between 2500 and 2300 B.C., West and East Africa were connected by a system of inland waterways. The spread of the Sahara created conditions for the emergence of significant regional differences in modern Africa.

state god. Over time, the pharaohs, or rulers, of ancient Egypt claimed power over the rains and floods and increasingly linked their authority to the gods themselves. At the same time, Egyptians created the world's first annual twelve-month calendar of 365 days, as well as an instrument for measuring the rise and fall of the Nile and the techniques that underlay the building of the pyramids. Moreover, hieroglyphics (a combination of pictures and sound symbols inscribed on papyrus, a form of paper) and hieratics (a cursive form of hieroglyphics) recorded the political and administrative activities of the kings and bureaucrats and constituted the earliest written history of Africa and of the world.

Nile Valley farmers, workers, and slaves or captives provided the basis of Egyptian wealth, political influence, and cultural development. Referred to as the "living dead," captives made up between 10 and 13 percent of the total population during ancient times. Because Egyptian bondage was not tied to skin color or race, captives included dark-skinned Nubian peoples from the south and light-skinned Semitic and Mediterranean people from the north. Nile Valley farmers and workers—captive and free—produced food surpluses for royal and noble households and labored on huge irrigation projects, temples, and royal tombs. Over a period of 1500 years, Egyptian pharaohs directed the building of over seventy pyramids. Khufu, or Cheops, the Great Pyramid, was the largest and most renown of the royal tombs, built for the first pharaoh of the 4th Dynasty. In the fifth century B.C., the Greek historian Herodotus described the human costs of pyramid making:

> Cheops . . . drove them [the Egyptian people] into the extremity of misery. . . . To some was assigned the dragging of great stones from the stone quarries in the Arabian mountains as far as the Nile; to others he gave orders, when these stones had been taken across the river in boats, to drag them, again, as far as the Libyan hills. . . . The people were afflicted for ten years of time in building the road along which they dragged the stones. . . . The pyramid itself took twenty years in the building.

The pharaohs also employed craftsmen and artists to adorn the walls and columns of their palaces and tombs. During the 1920s, archaeologists uncovered the tomb of King Tutankamun, still preserved with its various contents after over thirty centuries. By contrast, the poor were buried in simple graves with few worldly possessions to speed them on their journey.

Although rural peasants and captives faced inequality and exploitation, they did not accept their position without protest and appeals for social justice. In "The Tale of the Eloquent Peasant," a text from the First Intermediate period, a peasant appealed to the king for justice. After a large landowner had seized his property through illegal means, the farmer wrote:

> Leader free of greed, great man free of baseness, destroyer of falsehood, creator of rightness, who comes at the voice of the caller! When I speak, may you hear! Do justice, oh praised one, who is praised by the praised; remove my grief, I am burdened. Examine me, I am in need.

The pharaoh recognized the justice of the man's cause and recompensed him with the goods of the dishonest steward.

Poor people also expressed their dissatisfaction with inequality by raiding the tombs of the elites, by making appeals for freedom and release from bondage, and by running away. Records from the late ancient period show how owners of run-away bondsmen and -women employed agents authorized to imprison, beat, and return their possessions, but the problem persisted.

Egyptian women were subordinated to their men, but their position also re-flected their class and social status. Some women in royal families became powerful figures and made an indelible imprint on Egyptian history. Queen Hatshepsut (c. 1504–1482 B.C.), for example, was at first named regent on behalf of her stepson, but she soon took power by skillfully manipulating the gender system. Claiming to be the son of the god Amun, she received the crown as "king" of Egypt. During her reign, she selected able military and administrative advisors and built an elaborate temple at Thebes. Cut deep into rock walls, the temple included multiple rooms of artistic carvings and writings that celebrated her reign. Although existing historical scholarship is clearer on the role of Queen Hatshepsut and women in royal house-holds, we must not assume that peasant and captive women were passive.

Beginning around 1100 B.C., Egypt faced increasing attacks from outside. In succession, the Greeks (332 B.C.), Romans (30 B.C.), and Arabs (after A.D. 622) conquered Egypt and helped to reorient its culture toward Greco-Roman, Christ-ian, and then Islamic ideas and social practices. By the early tenth century A.D., Egypt had become a predominantly Islamic country. Islamic unity in Egypt and on the Arabian Peninsula was short-lived, however. The Shi'ites, an Islamic reform group in Baghdad, criticized established groups for corruption and violation of the principles of the Koran. Under the influence of Shi'ites in North Africa, the Fa-timid dynasty, aided by a small army recruited from a group of people in northwest Africa called Berbers, gained control of Egypt and much of North Africa in A.D. 950. As the so-called Berber soldiers left the army and became part of Egyptian so-ciety, Islamic rulers replenished their ranks by importing Turkish captives from north of the Mediterranean (around the Black Sea region) and blacks from south of the Sahara. Whereas the black bondsmen served as foot soldiers, the Turkish cap-tives, called Mamluks, became part of a highly disciplined cavalry of horsemen armed with bows, arrows, and iron swords.

With the end of the Fatimid dynasty in A.D. 1171, the Turkish soldier Salah al-Din ibn Ayyub (known as Saladin in European history) ascended to power and founded the Ayyubid dynasty. Under the Ayyubid dynasty, the Mamluks received extensive opportunities to earn their freedom, become army commanders, and ac-quire land. In A.D. 1250, the Mamluks established two dynasties that governed Egypt until the Ottoman Turks conquered Egypt in 1517. The Ottomans over-powered the Mamluk horsemen with new instruments of warfare, including firearms and cannon.

Nubia

Egyptian history unfolded in close connection with the Nubian peoples to the south and east. Under direct Egyptian rule between 1500 and 1000 B.C., Nubians adopted many aspects of Egyptian language, religion, and writing and in turn influenced the Egyptian institution of kingship/pharaohs. After 1000 B.C., Nubians developed a politically independent state known by the Egyptians as Kush. As the power of Kush increased, however, in 730 B.C. the state invaded and conquered Egypt, establishing what became known as the 25th, or Ethiopian, Dynasty.

Nubian control of Egypt came to an end with the Assyrian invasion of Lower Egypt in about 678 B.C. Kushite leaders abandoned Egypt and established a new kingdom farther south along the upper Nile, first at Napata and then permanently on the island of Meroe, between the Nile and Atbara Rivers. At Meroe, the interplay of Egyptian and indigenous cultural influences created a unique culture. Meroites developed their own writing script, added their own local gods to the pantheon of Egyptian gods, and modified their pyramids and burial tombs to reflect their own perspectives (Meroite pyramids were small and flat topped, rather than large with pointed tops).

In A.D. 350, the kingdom of Aksum on the Eritrean coast invaded Meroe and promoted the spread of Christianity in the region. However, by A.D. 800, under the impact of Islam, Aksum had lost control of its trade to the Indian Ocean, and the capital was moved deep into the interior of the Ethiopian central highlands. During the twelfth century, a new Zagwe dynasty displaced the old Aksumite line of kings and ushered in an aggressive period of expansion. The Zagwe kings extended

Pyramids of Meroe. Unlike the Egyptian pyramids, the pyramids of Meroe were small with flat tops rather than large with pointed tops. *Werner Forman Archive/Art Resource, N.Y.*

Ethiopia's influence farther south of Lake Tana to Gojjam and the Shoan Plateau, where it came into conflict with the Muslim states of the Awash Valley. At the Battle of Shimbra-Kure in 1529, Muslims defeated the Ethiopian army and controlled southern Ethiopia for the next six years.

In the meantime, Ethiopian rulers not only had maintained contacts with the declining Christian, or Coptic, church of Egypt but also had reestablished linkages with Mediterranean Christendom. Building on these contacts with European Christendom, the Ethiopian emperor eventually appealed to Christian Europe for help in dispelling the Muslims. Portugal responded with a small, well-armed contingent of troops. Although scholars now doubt that Portuguese support was necessary, in 1543 the combined Ethiopian-Portuguese armies defeated the Muslims, and Ethiopia regained its footing as a Christian nation on the African continent.

The history of ancient Ethiopia and Egypt suggests that African societies were always in flux. They were the products of ongoing interactions between peoples of diverse regions, cultures, and institutions. Such interactions were constantly formed and reformed to meet new needs and circumstances. It is also clear that changes in the natural and man-made environment helped to shape the ongoing formation and re-formation of African societies. Although the emergence of the Sahara Desert would hamper interactions between different parts of the continent and foster distinct regional differences, Africans retained contacts with each other and other parts of the world by developing innovations in agriculture, manufacturing, transport, and trade. The history of northwest Africa and the rise of the trans-Saharan trade reflected these processes.

NORTHWEST AFRICA AND THE TRANS-SAHARAN TRADE

Like Egypt and Ethiopia, northwest Africa experienced the impact of Christendom and Islam. Although the original inhabitants of this area referred to themselves as Imagzighen, meaning "the noble" or "freeborn," the Greeks called them Libyans, and the Romans and later the Arabs referred to them as Berbers, the term that is now most commonly used.

In 146 B.C., the Romans conquered Carthage, the most significant independent state in this region, and renamed it "Africa," a name that would eventually refer to the entire continent. The Romans soon extended their control over the North African kingdoms of Numidia and Mauritania to the west. By A.D. 711, however, the Arabs had gained control of North Africa from Egypt in the east to Morocco on the Atlantic coast. In the coastal towns and cities such as Carthage (later renamed Tunis), Arabs set up farms using war captives from northern, central, and southern Africa. At the same time, the Islamic state levied tribute, or taxes, on peoples in the highlands and along the edges of the desert to the south.

Even as Arabs conquered and enslaved African peoples, however, they carried out an aggressive program to convert subject peoples to Islam and consolidate their hold over the region. Arab leaders recruited North Africans into the military, exposed them to the Islamic faith, and provided opportunities for movement up in the hierarchy of the empire. North Africans slowly adopted the Muslim faith, but they did so on their own terms. Islam gained its strongest and most orthodox foothold in the cities, whereas rural inhabitants slowly incorporated Islam into their traditional religious beliefs and practices. Even in the coastal cities and towns, North Africans reshaped Islam to fit their own circumstances. In the conflict between Baghdad and rival factions of Islam, for example, North Africans sided with the dissenting Shi'ite movement and resisted centralized authority.

North Africa served as the major conduit for the spread of Islam into West Africa south of the Sahara. As North Africans converted to Islam in rising numbers, they perceived their non-Muslim black West African neighbors as culturally inferior. Advocating strict observance of Islamic law and holy war against "infidels," the Almoravids, a new Islamic state in northwest Africa, launched holy wars against their rivals to the north and south. By A.D. 1054, the Almoravids not only had taken Awdaghust from the West African kingdom of Ghana but also had conquered the desert town of Sijilmasa, much of the northern coast, and southern Spain. Although the Almoravid empire would collapse under the weight of internal and external conflicts during the thirteenth century, it helped to spread Islamic culture, mosques, and centers of learning throughout North and West Africa.

In addition to conquest, the expansion of the trans-Saharan trade network stimulated the spread of Islam into West Africa. Before about A.D. 300, the trans-Saharan trade was largely a regional affair. It involved the exchange of desert salt, donkeys, and horses for food from the agricultural regions to the north and south. During the third and fourth centuries A.D., the introduction of the camel among nomads of the northern Sahara by the Romans transformed the trans-Saharan trade into an international trade network. The camel's capacity to store fat and water enabled it to travel twice the time and distance of short pack-oxen and horses. Under the impact of this new form of desert transport, new trading settlements emerged north and south of the Sahara, and products from sub-Saharan Africa entered the Mediterranean world in growing numbers.

By the early sixteenth century, several major caravan routes accounted for the bulk of this trade. One route stretched from Timbuktu to Sijilmasa via Taghaza near the Atlantic coast; a second reached the Mediterranean from Gad via Tadmekka; another route connected the Lake Chad and Kanem-Bornu area to Tunis via the desert town of Ghat; and still another extended from Lake Chad to Tripoli and Cairo via the Fezzan (see map). Although North Africans (mainly the Sanhaja in the west and Tuareg in the central and southern Sahara) controlled transport across the desert, trading communities on each end of their routes exercised decisive power. The principal West African import was salt from Saharan salt mines like the one at Taghaza in the center of the western Sahara. Other imports included a variety of manufactured products from Europe via the Mediterranean—cloth, metal, cooking utensils, jewelry, copper, and weapons. Conversely, West Africans exported gold from mines at Bambuk, Bure, and the Akan forests; agricultural,

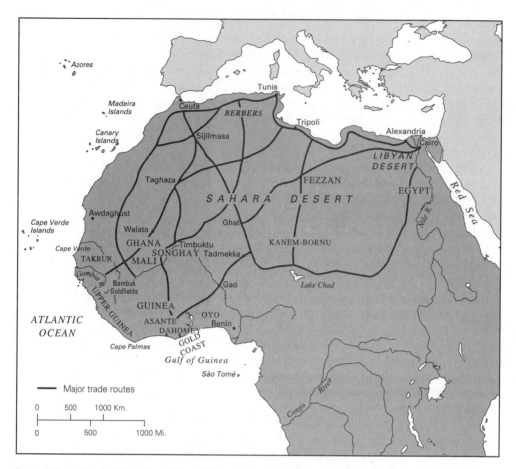

Trans-Saharan Trade Network and West African States. Although the Sahara Desert hampered the flow of trade and ideas among parts of the African continent, the introduction of the camel during the third and fourth centuries A.D. stimulated the rise of an extensive international trade network, which linked West and southern Africa to East and northern Africa.

animal, and forest products, including ivory, gum, and kola nuts; and growing numbers of human captives taken in wars with neighboring ethnic groups.

Between A.D. 900 and 1400, nearly 3.4 million African captives entered the markets of North Africa and the Mediterranean (see table). Many of these slaves were women headed for the harems and households of the Muslim world. Others, in substantial numbers, were young boys targeted for service as eunuchs in the same Islamic lands. Still others, as we will see in Chapter 2, were bound for European sugar plantations in the Mediterranean. Until the sixteenth century, whites from European countries also became captives in Islamic households, serving alongside

Estimated Numbers of the Trans-Saharan Slave Trade		
Period	Annual Average	Total
650–800	1,000	150,000
800–900	3,000	300,000
900–1100	8,700	1,740,000
1100–1400	5,500	1,650,000
1400–1500	4,300	430,000
1500–1600	5,500	550,000
1600–1700	7,100	710,000
1700–1800	7,100	715,000
1800–1880	14,500	1,165,000
1880–1900	2,000	40,000
Total		7,450,000

Source: William D. Phillips, Jr., *Slavery from Roman Times to the Early Transatlantic Trade* (Minneapolis: University of Minnesota Press, 1985), p. 87. Reprinted with permission.

Africans as eunuchs, concubines, and domestics. More so than Christians and Europeans, it was Muslims, Arabs, and diverse African nationality groups themselves who controlled the trans-Saharan trade and determined the course of West African history during the medieval period.

WEST AFRICA

Although the long-term spread of the Sahara Desert had undercut farming communities in the region, a thriving agricultural economy had emerged by the medieval period. In the savannah grasslands just below the Sahel (the Arabic word for "border,") on the southern edge of the Sahara Desert, farmers not only raised sheep, goats, and a few cattle, but also produced cereal crops like millet and sorghum, as well as cotton and sesame. Farther south, in the forest zone, hunters, gatherers, and fishermen pursued earlier forms of making a living. They collected their food from wild leaves, roots, and berries and hunted small animals. At the same time, the forest people built on their knowledge of the growing cycles of certain root, fruit, and tree crops and pioneered in the development of vegeculture. They gradually domesticated various types of gourds and calabashes, as well as oil and sophia palms. Cereal production and cattle herding played little role in the agricultural development of the forest region because of the tsetse fly, which transmitted the cattle-killing disease called *nagana*. A form of "sleeping sickness," *nagana* made it difficult for cows and horses to survive in the region.

Along with the expansion and diversification of the agricultural sector, West Africans developed centers of cotton and cotton textiles, sheep raising and woolen cloth, and iron production. Until recently, scholars assumed that iron-making techniques spread into West Africa from the kingdom of Meroe, south of Egypt. Although most scholars now seem to believe that such processes reached West Africa via Carthage, some argue that West Africans discovered iron-making processes independently of outside influence. In any case, ironworks arrived early in West Africa. Remains from the Nok culture of central Nigeria (c. 280–180 B.C.) suggest the earliest and most advanced use of iron-making technology in West Africa. Building on their earlier history of clay modeling, the Igbo-Ukwo developed the fine art of bronze casting. Over the next millennium, ironworks spread widely through West Africa and formed the basis for more efficient agriculture, warfare, and hunting techniques, which in turn stimulated population growth, new artistic forms, and large territorial and political units.

Iron making represented a major technological achievement. Although metals like copper and tin required a relatively simple process of smelting or melting metal from its ore (that is, metal-bearing rock), iron extraction entailed a complex chemical process. Because the iron was chemically intermixed with its ore, craftsmen had to carefully execute a number of steps in the production of iron. First, as suggested by archaeological evidence, mainly large slag heaps and metal products from ancient times, West Africans constructed two types of iron-smelting furnaces—one a trench dug below the ground and the other a circular clay structure built several feet above the ground. Second, they carefully selected the proper proportions of ore, crushed hardwood, charcoal, and sometimes a flux substance such as lime to aid the smelting process; workers meticulously layered these ingredients in the oven. Third, iron workers then fired the furnace, using bellows to pump air into the structure, which increased the heat and facilitated the chemical process necessary for smelting. Fourth, after a certain number of hours, workers opened the furnace and raked out red-hot iron (crude iron). Finally, after the crude iron had been extracted, the product required frequent reheating and hammering to remove impurities and prepare it for forging into useful weapons, tools, or implements.

West Africans became not only skilled iron workers but also leather, cloth, wood, copper, brass, gold, and, to some extent, silver craftsmen. Over time, these craftsmen concentrated in specialized villages where they intermarried with each other and passed their skills on from one generation to the next. Among the various crafts, the metal workers were most revered, while the leather workers seemed least valued. Some scholars describe these occupational specialties as "castes," midway in status between free persons and slaves. As we will see below, the various craft workers played a key role in the development of West African religious and cultural life.

The intensification of agriculture, manufacturing, and the trans-Saharan trade stimulated the political, social, and cultural transformation of West African society. Small, village-based, West African communities increasingly united to form larger state systems. In turn, Ghana, Mali, and Songhay emerged as the major kingdoms of medieval West Africa. The development of these kingdoms reveals not only the impact of technological, economic, and political change but also patterns of ethnic diversity, conflict, and cooperation among West African peoples.

State Formation, Politics, and the Economy

The rise of West African kingdoms coincided with the expansion of the trans-Saharan trade from about the fourth century A.D. through the medieval period. The kingdom of Ghana, the first of these centralized states to gain prominence, had its roots in the expansion of the Soninke peoples. Well-armed with iron swords and spears and mounted on horses received from Saharan traders, the Soninke expanded their dominion over less-organized neighboring groups and resisted the onslaught of Islamic North Africans. By the mid-eleventh century, as alluded to earlier, Ghana had enclosed Awdaghust, one of the most important Islamic trading centers in the southwestern Sahara, and had extended its boundaries from just east of Takrur and Bambuk to the upper Niger River in the west (see map on page 10).

Situated midway between desert sources of salt and the goldfields of Bambuk on the upper Senegal River, the Soninke served as middlemen in the trans-Saharan trade. Soninke merchants bought gold from the Bambuk miners in exchange for salt, linen, and other manufactured items from northwest Africa. They then sold gold to Muslim traders at the capital city of Kumbi-Saleh, where they received new supplies of salt and goods for another round of trade with the gold miners farther south. The Ghanaian king not only extracted agricultural surplus from the outlying rural areas but also imposed double duties on salt: once when it entered the area from the Sahara and again on re-export to the goldfields. The king also extracted all the large gold nuggets for the royal treasury and permitted only the remainder to enter the trade network.

Taxation of the salt trade and the extraction of gold nuggets not only enriched West African rulers but also stimulated the emergence of new merchant groups. The Wangara and Dyula, for example, facilitated the integration of the far-flung empires into a tightly interconnected West African trade network. These merchants traveled throughout West Africa and stimulated intraregional as well as international trade. Closely related to the trade activities of the Wangara and Dyula was the increasing use of the cowrie shell from the Indian Ocean as a medium of exchange in the West African economy. Although use of the cowrie shell strengthened intraregional trade and taxation, international trade continued to revolve around salt, gold, and, to some extent, war captives.

As Islam penetrated deeper into West Africa and as Ghana in turn conquered Islamic outposts, the king employed literate Muslim administrators to systematize tax collection and oversee international trade. Muslims instituted elaborate accounting procedures and helped royal officials extract enormous surplus from the African peasantry. As we will see, Islamic officers would influence not only the economic life of West African kingdoms but its religious and cultural life as well.

The Ghanaian king exercised substantial direct and indirect control over the population. Partly by holding the sons of local leaders hostage at his court, the king gained compliance from local elites. Although Ghana did not have a standing army, for example, the king could raise an army of over two hundred thousand men on short notice. The Ghanaian army sometimes raided neighboring ethnic groups and sold captives to Muslim traders. A late-eleventh-century report described such raids by the kingdom of Ghana: "The people of Ghana make raids on the land of Barbara [probably Bambara] and Anima. . . . These people have no iron and fight only with clubs of ivory. For this reason the people of Ghana overcome them, for they fight with swords and spears."

Although Ghana incorporated Muslims into its administrative structure, the Islamic Berbers resented Soninke domination. Under the leadership of Yahya ibn Umar and his brother Abu Bakr, the Sanhaja joined the Almoravid movement and waged war against Ghana. The Almoravids reconquered Awdaghust during the 1050s, as noted above, and plundered the Ghanaian capital of Kumbi-Saleh in A.D. 1076. Soon thereafter, Ghanaians converted to Islam in rising numbers, and the kingdom gradually declined. By A.D. 1300, as new trans-Saharan trade routes emerged to the east and the new Bure goldfields opened to the south and west, Ghana lost its control of the trans-Saharan gold trade from the western Sudan.

Closely related to the decline of Ghana was the rise of Mali as the second great West African kingdom. Mali had its origins in the same forces that led to the decline of Ghana, namely the opening up of the new Bure goldfields in the woodland savannah country to the south, and the development of new trans-Saharan trade routes farther east of Awdaghust. The opening of new goldfields and trade routes enabled the Soninke and Malinke peoples of the south to assert their independence. During the early 1200s, the Sosso, a branch of Soninke, established a new state independent of former Ghana and extended their influence over most of old Ghana as well as their southern neighbors the Malinke.

Under the leadership of Sundiata (also called Sundjata), several small Malinke lineages formed an alliance and resisted the authority of the new Soninke-based Sosso state. The Malinke defeated the Sosso army at Kirina near modern Bamako and brought several Soninke peoples under their control. Shortly thereafter, the Malian empire built its capital at Niani, located in the savannah country of the upper Niger Valley near the Bure goldfields. The empire of Mali soon extended from the edges of the forest zone in the southwest, through the savannah territories of the Malinke and southern Soninke, to the Sahel of the ancient Ghanaian kingdom. Mali incorporated and moved well beyond the boundaries of the old Ghanaian kingdom. At its height in the 1300s, Mali stretched from the Atlantic Ocean south of Senegal to the Songhay capital of Gao on the east side of the middle bend of the Niger River, including the city of Timbuktu, originally established by northwest Africans as a trading center and grazing settlement for livestock. To the south, Mali incorporated the goldfields of Bure and Bambuk, and along the Sahel, it extended from the Atlantic east to Walata and Tadmekka.

Like Ghana, Mali relied on literate Muslims to administer the kingdom. Unlike Ghana, however, Mali established a large standing army to facilitate defense as well as compliance from peoples in outlying areas. More so than Ghana, Mali exploited its broader, more fertile, and diverse farming communities, which produced sorghum and millet in the savannah, rice in the regions of the Gambia and Niger

Rivers, and camels, sheep, and goats in the more arid Sahelian grasslands. As long as local rulers collected and forwarded tribute to the capital, Malian kings allowed traditional rulers to maintain their authority, which they claimed as an entitlement for themselves and their descendants.

Following a series of internal dynastic struggles, Mali declined during the late fifteenth century. By the early 1500s, Mali had lost most of its non-Malinke population and was composed mainly of its small original Malinke homelands. Located on the eastern bend of the Niger River, the Songhay posed the most formidable challenge to the Malian state. As early as the ninth century, Songhay had emerged as a single state, with its capital at Kukiya. Although farmers, hunters, and fishermen of diverse ethnic groups inhabited the area, the Sorko fishermen dominated the region. Using their mastery of the river, these people developed trading routes along the territory upstream toward the Niger bend, including the city of Gao, which emerged as the chief trans-Saharan trade route of the central and eastern Sahara.

As Mali declined during the fifteenth century, Songhay expanded its cavalry and increasingly transformed its trading vessels into war canoes. Under the leadership of Sonni Sulayman Dandi and his successor, Sonni Ali the Great (1464–1492), Songhay captured Timbuktu and extended the empire's control north to the desert town of Taghaza, east to Agades, west to the Senegal River, south to below the Niger River, and deep into Mossi territory, where Songhay forces launched periodic raids and sold war captives to Muslim traders. Songhay reached its peak under the reign of Muhammad Ture, also known as Askiya Muhammad (1493–1528). Unlike Mali and Ghana, whose territory spread widely from west to east, the kingdom of Songhay extended more narrowly north and south along the Niger River. Its authority revolved around control of the Niger River and its surrounding peasant communities. Songhay replaced local traditional rulers with royal officials. These officials could not claim hereditary rights to their posts and were dependent on the king for their authority. The centralization of authority in turn put more distance between the king and the masses of the people.

Although Ghana, Mali, and Songhay represented the chief West African kingdoms during the medieval period, other important states came to prominence at the same time. Located near the Atlantic coast in the Senegal Valley, Takrur was one of the earliest of these West African states. Some scholars suggest that Takrur may have antedated Ghana as an early trading state. At about the same time that Takrur expanded in the Senegal Valley, the state of Kanem emerged in the region northeast of Lake Chad. Beginning around A.D. 900, several Kanuri-speaking pastoralist groups banned together under a single dynasty known as the Sefawa. Early on, the state exhibited Islamic influences, and by the late eleventh century, the Kanuri-speaking Sefawa had set up a new Islamic dynasty in Kanem. As Kanem fell during the fourteenth century, one of its principal tributaries, Borno, exerted its independence. Located to the southwest of the empire, Borno established its own trade networks across the Sahara and succeeded in transforming Kanem into a tributary state. Although a series of peasant revolts hampered the expansion of Borno, the state strengthened its position by importing enough horses and firearms from

North Africa to outfit a cavalry of three thousand troops. Armed with new weapons, Borno undercut the volume of trade flowing through the kingdom of Songhay and retained its position in the region through the eighteenth century.

Important West African kingdoms and states also emerged west of Borno and south of the savannah grasslands. Between A.D. 1000 and 1200, the Hausa city-states developed west of the kingdom of Borno. Based on a combination of agriculture, manufacturing, and trade, the principal Hausa states were Gobir, Katsina, Zazzau, and Kano. Although all of these states were important trade centers, Kano craftsmen became especially well known for their weaving, cloth dyeing, and leatherworks. Kano products not only reached other parts of West Africa but also entered the Mediterranean trade of North Africa and Europe. Although no single Hausa state emerged and consolidated the others into a single empire, these states nonetheless represented key links in the trans-Saharan trade and the spread of Islam into West Africa. Similarly, the principal forest states, the Yoruba kingdoms of Ife and Benin, emerged during the eleventh and twelfth centuries A.D. Extending from the borders of the savannah into the region to the south, Ife and Benin produced a substantial agricultural surplus—a range of root and cereal crops as well as domestic animals—that supported ruling elites, court craftsmen and artists, and significant urbanization. By the fifteenth century, Benin had evolved into a large walled city.

Although a large number of highly organized states had emerged in West Africa by the eve of the Atlantic slave trade, other metalworking agricultural communities remained small and less formally organized. Some analysts have referred to these as "stateless" societies. Small, family-based villages of subsistence farmers were widespread in the savannah and forest regions of West Africa. These communities cultivated crops for home consumption and local or intervillage trade rather than for long-distance trade. As such, they escaped taxes levied on products that entered the international trade network. Unlike the large states, these small communities settled internal difficulties locally, usually in family groups without bureaucratic structures. These small communities also developed mechanisms for banding together to defend themselves from external attacks but usually disbanded after such dangers had subsided. Although the so-called stateless societies had their own ideas about governance, they were not completely isolated from international influences. Such communities provided an initial lineage foundation for ethnic-based states like the early Soninke and Malinke, which in turn spearheaded the rise of Ghana, Mali, and Songhay.

Social, Religious, and Cultural Life

Socioeconomic and cultural life in West African states was highly stratified. Most kingdoms were comprised of three major groups: nobles, freeborn or commoners, and captives. Kings, administrators, merchants, and army commanders inhabited the best residences, wore the best clothing, and adorned themselves with the most expensive jewelry. Moreover, on their death, their graves were often marked by imposing tombs.

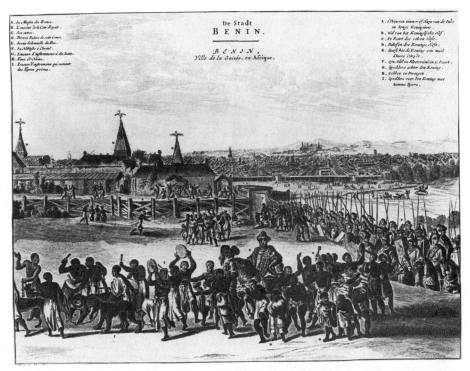

By the fifteenth century, the Yoruba kingdom of Benin had evolved into a large walled city. Here a Dutch artist captures the city in the seventeenth century. *Corbis*

Social stratification was most pronounced in the urban centers. The capital of ancient Ghana, Kumbi-Saleh, was divided between its Islamic center and its royal African sector. The former received Arab and North African merchants and housed Muslim mosques, whereas the latter housed the king and his court, about six miles away. In between were the stone and wooden structures of the Soninke people; outlying residents apparently lived mainly in houses of less durable construction. In Mali and Songhay, patterns of social inequality were even more pronounced than they were in Ghana.

Mali and Songhay maintained large standing armies, and army officials became important residents at the royal court. Composed of a small elite corps of horsemen and contingents of foot soldiers, the army not only played a role in securing the empire against external attacks but also collected taxes on trade, extracted monetary tribute from surrounding rural provinces, and maintained farms with the forced labor of captives. Merchants also figured prominently at the king's court, trading their products and enriching themselves in the process. During the reign of Askiya Muhammad, the Moroccan Leo Africanus observed life at Gao, the capital of Songhay, accenting the place of merchants and soldiers:

The houses there are very poor, except for those of the king and his courtiers. The merchants are exceedingly rich. . . . Here is a certain place where slaves are sold, especially on those days when the merchants are assembled. . . . The king of this region has a certain private palace where he maintains a great number of concubines and slaves; and for the guard of his own person he keeps a sufficient troupe of horsemen and footmen.

The various royal pilgrimages to Mecca also symbolized the concentration of wealth at the top of West African society. Mansa Musa, Mali's most renowned ruler, made his famous pilgrimage to Mecca in 1324–1325. He arrived in Egypt with a hundred camel loads of gold, which he distributed so freely that the value of gold in Cairo dropped precipitously. During his pilgrimage to Mecca, Askiya Muhammad's caravan included an escort of five hundred cavalry and one thousand infantry, as well as three hundred thousand pieces of gold, a third of which were distributed as gifts in Islamic cities along the way.

Scholars are reluctant to generalize about gender differences in West African societies because there were significant differences in the roles of men and women from place to place and from one ethnic group to another. Some societies were matrilineal and conferred important power on women. Other societies, probably most, were not only patrilineal but also polygynous, with men empowered to take more than one wife and to exercise fundamental control. In matrilineal systems, the offspring belonged to the family of the mother, whose oldest brother served as the head of the family. Conversely, in patrilineal arrangements, the father served as head of the family and exercised parental authority and responsibility for the children. The arrival of Islam reinforced patrilineality and polygyny but limited the number of wives to four. Support for polygyny was widespread, although in practice only the elite could afford to support multiple wives.

Despite significant variations in gender practices from one society to another, salient gender differences were apparent in the economic and social life of West Africa during the period. Men normally cleared the land and cultivated crops for the market and international trade, whereas women raised food crops for family and communal subsistence. Even in the practice of skilled crafts such as weaving, men produced such goods largely for the wider regional and international market, whereas women produced for home consumption. Thus, women invariably dominated local trade markets, whereas men traveled widely and controlled international trade. Moreover, as in so many societies elsewhere, women shouldered the bulk of domestic work, tending children, cooking, and cleaning.

Along with the gender division of labor, most societies linked state power closely to military service and excluded women. Still, women in West African societies devised ways for influencing the state, politics, and culture of the region. Most African states placed considerable power in the hands of royal families. Specifically, they established the practice of designating "electing families" and "enthroning families." The former decided who within the royal household should be enthroned, whereas the latter could accept or veto the selection. Thus, women in royal families were in an excellent position to voice their opinions and to influence the affairs of state, including arranging succession to the throne. Since queen mothers and queen sisters had intimate knowledge of the king's health and were the first to know of his death, they played important roles in matters of succession to the throne. Succession often precipitated crises and heated struggles among the elite and required delicate handling.

Enslavement was no doubt the most important manifestation of inequality in West African society. West African societies not only exported bondsmen and -women but also used them in the regional economy as domestics, concubines, soldiers, and agricultural workers. Captives also served as skilled labor on construction projects, in the manufacture of cloth, and in the mining and processing of gold, copper, and salt. In the salt-mining town of Taghaza, captives constructed the principal buildings of the town from blocks of salt secured from the mines. Moreover, bondsmen took on great symbolic as well as practical value. West African kings sometimes gave captives as gifts to secure "loyal" subjects, and to Islamic officials to indicate piety and commitment to the Koran. When the first Muslim missionary arrived in the kingdom of Kanem, for example, the ruler showered him with gifts of one hundred captives, camels, and silver coins.

Like other aspects of West African society, slavery was a highly gendered experience. The large North African demand for women in their harems and as domestics led to large numbers of women in the trans-Saharan trade. Yet it was men who were usually designated for sale outside West Africa; women and children were used in households within the area. On one occasion, the Arab scholar Ibn Battuta described bondswomen in West African households: "During Ramadan I saw many of them . . . in the house of the sultan, each one brings his food carried by twenty or more of his slave girls, they all being naked." The practice of selling men far away from their region of origin and enslaving their women and children hampered resistance movements, but captives nonetheless sought freedom by running away, self-purchase, and service in the army or state bureaucracy.

Although West African societies were stratified along class and cultural lines, they developed some beliefs and practices that helped to mitigate conflict, ease tensions, and create unity. Through ongoing historical and cultural interactions, West Africans of diverse ethnic and cultural backgrounds developed a core of beliefs and practices that helped to distinguish and unify them as a region. Certain underlying understandings and perspectives on the natural and spirit worlds characterized their world view. Although they might not agree on the precise significance of twin births, for example, most imbued such births with supernatural significance. Despite the payment of tribute by agricultural villages, to take another example, land was a community resource and could not be alienated or owned outright by an individual.

West African bondsmen and -women gained access to freedom and a level of upward mobility. Some of the provincial governors of the kingdom of Mali were slaves. When disputes weakened the dynasty, slave men sometimes occupied the throne, as did Sakura the freed slave (c. 1300) and Sandiki (1387–1388). Such opportunities for people at the bottom of society, particularly slaves, led some contemporary Arab observers to comment on and exaggerate the sense of justice among African rulers.

The Negroes possess some admirable qualities. They are seldom unjust, and have a greater abhorrence of injustice than any other people. The sultan (the musa) shows no mercy to any one guilty of the least act of it. There is complete security in their country.

The Spanish Muslim al-Sharishi also painted an idyllic portrait of captive women in royal households:

God has endowed the slave girls there with laudable characteristics, both physical and moral, more than can be desired: their bodies are smooth, their black skins are lustrous, their eyes are beautiful, their noses well shaped, their teeth white, and they smell fragrant.

African religious traditions played a key role in bridging as well as fomenting social cleavages. West Africans believed in one god, the creator, but their ideas differed from Islam and Christianity. They held that the original mover was no longer active in shaping human affairs. Rather than an ongoing moral force for good or evil, God set the stage for human action, retired from active duty, and allowed human beings to shape their own destinies. Supernatural forces did play a role in day-to-day life, but they were not intrinsically good or evil.

West Africans recognized at least two distinct sets of supernatural beings. One group included the spirits of the ancestors who watched over the descendants of specific lineages or ethnic groups. Africans believed that the spirit of a deceased relative could influence the life of the family. The spirits of the dead had to be handled with care through prayer, sacrifice, and ritual. Since the spirits of the ancestors would live on after death, funeral rites also figured prominently in religious practices. Such rites served to create solidarity within families, lineages, and ethnic groups. A second group of spirits were more universal in their work. These spirits were not the property of any one family, ethnic, or lineage group. By controlling aspects of nature—thunder, lightning, death, and disease, for example—their duties cut across ethnic, class, and social lines. The number of such spirits varied from one West African society to another, but almost everywhere professional or semi-professional religious leaders, both men and women, emerged to provide instructions on how to press these "gods" into service.

Several forms of ritual observance emerged as the principal way to put the individual or congregation in touch with the gods. Rituals included sacrifice (of animals and sometimes humans), spirit possession, music, dance, and prayer. Along with such rituals, most West African societies used divination. This religious practice was different from those attached to specific gods or spirits. Employing amulets, talismans, and other magical devices, the diviners advised individuals on the spirit world and answered questions about the future, misfortune, death, sickness, and witchcraft.

Malinke religious traditions illustrate the close connection between the material and spiritual worlds of West African peoples. The Malinke believed that the "spirits of the land" determined the success of their harvests. According to their origin story, the earliest farmers in the area negotiated with the spirits to ensure successful

The West African city of Timbuktu became a major center of Islamic education and learning during the reign of Mali's Mansa Musa. Following a period of decline, it was also revitalized under Songhay's Askiya Muhammad. *New York Public Library. Astor, Lenox and Tilden Foundations*

crops. The village head, *mansa* in Malinke, represented the most direct descendant of the first generation of farmers and thus the most viable link to the ancient "spirits of the land." Thus, the *mansa* combined both spiritual and secular authority and power. By persuading local *mansas* to cede their power to him, Sundiata, the first emperor of Mali, became the *mansa* of all the Malinke people. He combined at an even higher level of organization both spiritual and secular authority.

Following Sundiata's reign, most of the Malian rulers were Muslim. Islam had a powerful influence on the culture of royal officials and merchants in the towns and cities. In Egypt, on his pilgrimage to Mecca, Mansa Musa recruited a Muslim architect who returned to Mali and designed mosques. Mansa Musa also sent Sudanese scholars to North African universities to study, and by the end of his reign, the West African city of Timbuktu had itself become a major center of Islamic education and learning. Although Timbuktu would decline during the fall of Mali, it was revived and expanded under the control of Songhay during the reign of Askiya Muhammad. The Moroccan Leo Africanus described the city of Timbuktu during its period of revival:

The rich king of Tombuto [governor of Timbuktu] has many articles of gold, and he keeps a magnificent and well furnished court. When he travels anywhere he rides upon a camel which is led by some of his noblemen. . . . Here there are many doctors, judges, priests, and other learned men, that are well maintained at king's cost. Various manuscripts and written books are brought here out of Barbarie and sold for more money than any other merchandise.

Even as rulers like Mansa Musa and Askiya Muhammad made pilgrimages to Mecca and promoted Islamic culture, they recognized the need to adapt Islam to African conditions. Most Africans lived in the countryside and maintained their traditional beliefs, which challenged certain Islamic ideas about marriage and the family. Islam permitted men up to four wives, for example, but indigenous African societies allowed as many as a man could attract. Whereas the Islamic rulers of Songhay accepted marriage between a free man and a slave woman, or between a slave man and a free woman, as legitimate, most West African peasant societies accepted the former but rejected the latter. Moreover, although Islam promoted literate culture, most Africans continued to pursue and enrich their own oral traditions.

Art, music, dance, and storytelling permeated West African society and culture. African metal, cloth, wood, and leather workers not only were skilled in fashioning material culture but also were key communicators of oral traditions, beliefs, and ideas. The crafts themselves were invariably imbued with deep religious significance. Among the Bambara, for example, only blacksmiths or woodworkers could cut down large old trees, believed to be inhabited by the gods. More importantly, archaeological evidence suggests that West African craftspeople and artists developed their own aesthetic principles. Their decorative, ornamental, and intricate designs of furniture, jewelry, cloth, tombs, and buildings convey unique ideas about beauty.

West African artistic practices withstood the new designs ushered in by the arrival of Islam. The most outstanding evidence of artwork from the ancient period comes from the kingdom of Benin. The bronze and terracotta heads from Ife and Benin offer powerful evidence of African aesthetics. Such art also reflects African beliefs about the social order, including the notion that the king represented the fusion of both divine and earthly power. The cultural productions of Ife and Benin are best known because the British looted Benin City in 1897 and shipped its massive artworks back to England.

Integral to each craft were musicians, storytellers, and griots. Craftsmen not only made a variety of musical instruments—the drum, guitar, harp, flute, zither, and xylophone—but also used instruments to accompany an even wider variety of songs—religious, work, dance, recreational, and others. Described as "antiphonal" and highly "rhythmic," songs with or without instrumental accompaniment represented the major form of African music. African songs and dances served a variety of purposes, both religious and secular, although the line between the religious and worldly was quite blurred in West African culture.

Oral traditions contained the most outstanding literary achievements of West Africans during the period. The epic bards—the "griots," or oral historians—

This seventeenth-century bronze plaque from Benin City shows the Oba and his assistants. © *The British Museum, London*

emerged at the center of West African literary and cultural life. As a group, they were well regarded and ranked high with the metal workers in status. It was the griots who gave life to one of the most famous epics in West African society—the Sundiata *fasa* ("praise song in honor of jata"). Named after the Malian king, the jata epic recalls the struggle between the Malinke and the Soninke states, which gave rise to the kingdom of Mali. According to Ibn Battuta, Malian bards regularly recited the story honoring the great deeds of the king and his predecessors. Over twenty versions of the epic exist, but all agree on the basic ordering of events. Rich with folklore and tales relating to jata's childhood as well as his exploits as a leader of the nation, the jata epic helped to reinforce important aspects of West African ideas, beliefs, and social practices (see box).

Written nearly a century after Sundiata's reign during the Islamic era, the epic also demonstrates the way that West Africans sought to reconcile their beliefs in the "spirit of the land" with the spread of Islam. In some versions of the epic, for example, the character Bilali Bounama heads the descent lists of ancestors. Bounama is described as both a companion of the prophet Muhammad and the original founder of the Manding lineage—that is, Sundiata's branch of the Keitas, the direct descendants of the Prophet's helpers. Some griots even suggest that Muhammad himself was born just one day before Bilali.

SOURCES FROM THE PAST

Griot Djeli Mamoudou Kouyaté Narrates the Sundiata Fasa, n.d.

We are now coming to the great moments in the life of Sundiata. The exile will end and another sun will arise. It is the sun of Sundiata. Griots know the history of kings and kingdoms and that is why they are the best counsellors of kings. Every king wants to have a singer to perpetuate his memory, for it is the griot who rescues the memories of kings from oblivion, as men have short memories.

Kings have prescribed destinies just like men, and seers who probe the future know it. They have knowledge of the future, whereas we griots are depositories of the knowledge of the past. But whoever knows the history of a country can read its future.

Other peoples use writing to record the past, but this invention has killed the faculty of memory among them. They do not feel the past any more, for writing lacks the warmth of the human voice. With them everybody thinks he knows, whereas learning should be a secret. The prophets did not write and their words have been all the more vivid as a result. What paltry learning is that which is congealed in dumb books!

I, Djeli Mamoudou Kouyaté, am the result of a long tradition. For generations we have passed on the history of kings from father to son. The narrative was passed on to me without alteration and I deliver it without alteration, for I received it free from all untruth.

Listen now to the story of Sundiata, the Na'Kamma, the man who had a mission to accomplish.

At the time when Sundiata was preparing to assert his claim over the kingdom of his fathers, Soumaoro was the king of kings, the most powerful king in all the lands of the setting sun. . . . But Soumaoro was an evil demon and his reign had produced nothing but bloodshed. Nothing was taboo for him. His greatest pleasure was publicly to flog venerable old men. He had defiled every family and everywhere in his vast empire there were villages populated by girls whom he had forcibly abducted from their families without marrying them. . . .

. . . Soumaoro proclaimed himself king of Mali by right of conquest, but he was not recognized by the populace and resistance was organized in the bush. Soothsayers were consulted as to the fate of the country. The soothsayers were consulted as to the fate of the country. The soothsayers were unanimous in saying that it would be the rightful heir to the throne who would save Mali. This heir was "The Man with Two Names." The elders of the court of Niani then remembered the son of Sogolon. The man with two names was no other than Maghan Sundiata.

Source: D. T. Niane, *Sundiata: An Epic of Old Mali* (London: Longmans, 1965), pp. 40–45. The abridged version of *Sundiata: An Epic of Old Mali* is published by joint permission of Pearson Education Limited and Présence Africaine, owners of the original copyright. All rights reserved.

On the other hand, West African bards invoked the name of Surakata as their own collective progenitor and reinforced the effort to blend Islamic and indigenous African beliefs. According to oral traditions, Surakata was initially an infidel who pursued Muhammad with the intent to kill him. After failing his mission on several occasions, Surakata had a change of heart. Impressed by Muhammad's extraordinary power, he converted to Islam and became a staunch believer and supporter of the Prophet. Surakata soon accompanied Muhammad into battle with his enemies. At the Battle of Kaybura, one of Muhammad's most renowned campaigns, Surakata became the father of later bards by singing the praises of Muhammad and encouraging victory over his enemies.

As suggested by the translation of the Sundiata epic, only slowly did Africans and their Islamic allies collaborate in the translation of African oral traditions into written form. Although the technical difficulties of translating the varieties of African tongues into written symbols were formidable, other examples of this effort include Es Sadi's history of the Sudan, *Tarikh-es-Soudan,* and Kati's *Tarikh-El-Fettach.* By undertaking the difficult and often painful task of reconciling Islam with their own indigenous beliefs, West Africans demonstrated their ability to forge new cultural forms that gave unity and cohesiveness to their lives.

THE AFRICAN EXPERIENCE WAS DEEPLY rooted in the transformation of the Sahara from a rich agricultural land of many rivers into a desert covering about one-third of the continental landmass. Although the desert would not bar interactions between different parts of the African continent, it did help to create distinct regional differences between West Africa south of the Sahara, Egypt, and northwest Africa. The history of these regions not only reveals the immense contributions, strengths, and achievements of diverse African peoples and cultures but also highlights the myriad challenges that they faced before the advent of European expansion and the emergence of the international slave trade. Although war, exploitation, and even human bondage were integral aspects of African history, these forms of inequality and social conflict would take on new and different meanings in the confrontation with European traders, armies, and nation-states. Driven as they were by a strong capitalist ethos, Europeans would heighten indigenous forms of inequality and usher in new ones. These issues are explored in Chapter 2.

CHAPTER 2

ↄ

Transatlantic Trade, the Plantation System, and Black Labor

D uring the fifteenth century, the rise of unified states, wealth, capital, and innovations in sailing technology transformed the role of Europeans in international trade networks. The new technology enabled Europeans to sail around the west coast of Africa, dispense with North African middlemen, and sell their products directly to West Africans in exchange for gold. Although Europeans initially sought the riches of West African gold mines and the luxury goods of the Indian Ocean trade, they soon realized that the new maritime technology produced other possibilities. Their position on the West African coast provided opportunities to sell shipping services to Africans, establish coastal settlements, and gain access to new labor supplies. European merchants not only transported goods from one continent to another but also soon carried goods from one part of the West African coast to another, including bound labor for their own sugar plantations in the Mediterranean and on islands off the coast of northwest Africa.

As sugar plantations spread across the Atlantic Ocean to the New World, the demand for Africans escalated and soon supplanted indigenous and European sources of labor. After rising slowly during the sixteenth century, the number of Africans rapidly increased and became the predominant labor force during the seventeenth and eighteenth centuries. African labor fueled the production of the major cash crops as well as the mining of precious metals. Sugar, tobacco, rice, coffee, cotton, silver, and gold figured prominently in the lives of New World blacks, who faced harsh working conditions, constraints on family and cultural life, and stiff punishment for infractions of plantation discipline and rules of comportment. Although the forces unleashed by the imperatives of capitalist production curtailed their choices, African peoples would nonetheless play a key role in shaping their own experiences over time and space. Focusing on Caribbean and Latin American societies, this chapter examines the Old World origins of New World bondage, the transition from a mixed to an African labor force, and the development of enslaved African American communities, cultures, politics, and forms of resistance.

26

THE OLD WORLD ROOTS OF NEW WORLD BONDAGE

The Atlantic system of bondage had its roots in the development of Mediterranean sugar plantations. During the medieval crusades, Europeans adopted sugar-producing techniques when they conquered the Islamic countries of the eastern Mediterranean and North Africa. Following their expulsion from these areas by the Muslims, Europeans carried their knowledge of sugar to the islands of Cyprus and Sicily and to southern Spain and Portugal. Sugar production required a combination of agricultural and manufacturing skills, huge amounts of capital, and a large labor force for planting, weeding, harvesting, and refining. European merchants and manufacturers provided capital and managerial knowledge, but the local population proved inadequate to meet the labor demands of the crop.

The Mediterranean Model

Unable to secure a free labor force among regional farmers, the Mediterranean sugar industry gradually turned toward bound labor. Sugar planters purchased Europeans from the northern and eastern seaports of the Black Sea, captives from wars between Christians and Muslims, and Africans from the trans-Saharan trade. Notably, although northern European slaves had made the transition to various forms of serfdom by the late medieval era, enslaved whites from southern and eastern Europe continued to supply the labor needs of sugar plantations alongside Africans, Arabs, and Muslims. Sugar planters developed techniques of closely supervised gang labor, attention to profits, and social subordination that would later inform the spread of the plantation system along the west coast of Africa and in the New World.

The decision to import Africans to the New World was partly a product of past practices and conditions in Europe as well as on the Mediterranean sugar islands. The English word *slave* soon developed cognates in all western languages: *esclave* in French, *esclavo* in Spanish, *escravo* in Portuguese, *schiavo* in Italian, and *Sklave* in German. As early as 1479, the Spanish government authorized Portugal to sell slaves within its borders. The port at Seville soon emerged as the primary center for the sale of humans to European countries. On the Spanish mainland, the trading cities of Cádiz, Málaga, Cartagena, and Granada also imported significant numbers of captives. Although Africans were the predominant group, the Spanish enslaved Arabs, mainly Muslims, and after 1500, a few Amerindians. Some contemporaries compared enslaved Africans and Muslims in Seville to "a giant chessboard containing an equal number of white and black chessmen." These cities employed blacks in a wide range of common labor and domestic service jobs as well as in silver mines. Other Africans worked in soap factories and municipal granaries and as longshoremen, retail sellers, and assistants for shopkeepers and merchants. Although Africans worked in a variety of jobs on the European mainland, the Mediterranean sugar industry claimed the bulk of their labor.

The plantation system spread slowly outward from the Mediterranean to the islands off the coast of northwest Africa. As early as 1335, the Genoese merchant Lanzaroto Malocello aroused European interest in the Canary Islands. The Pope assigned the islands to the crown of Castile (later Spain) in 1344, and the Treaty of Alçacovas in 1479 further confirmed the Spanish claim. More importantly, in the Treaty of Tordesillas, two years after Columbus's first voyage to America, Portugal and Spain agreed to a line of demarcation that ceded to Spain control of all land in the New World (with the exception of Brazil), and to Portugal, dominion over West Africa and islands of the Atlantic Ocean (except the Canaries). The Canary Islands provided not only an environment for the profitable production of dyestuffs such as orchil and another popular dye called "dragon's blood," but also captives for sale in the Mediterranean slave markets and for a nascent Canary Island sugar industry. Europeans subsequently used the Canaries as a staging ground for occupying other islands, such as Madeira and the Azores, and establishing beachheads on the coastal mainland of West Africa itself.

The Mediterranean sugar islands established a model for the development of the plantation system and helped to set in motion the largest forced migration of human beings in world history. The Portuguese and Spanish took the lead in peopling the coastal islands with African labor. Between 1433 and 1488, Portuguese mariners used ocean wind patterns to navigate the western coast of Africa. Such knowledge—mainly recognition that ocean wind patterns tended to be circular—soon enabled them to inch their way along the west coast of Africa and in time sail around the Cape of Good Hope to East Africa as well. After reaching the Senegal River in 1444, the Portuguese established trade relations with the gold-producing portion of the Guinea Coast called the Gold Coast, a fort at El Mina, and sugar plantations on the islands of Madeira, Príncipe, and São Tomé. As Europeans opened up new plantations off the coast of Africa, they turned increasingly toward labor from sub-Saharan Africa. Before the turn of the sixteenth century, Portugal imported to its island colonies some 500 to 1,000 Africans per year.

During the sixteenth century, the sugar industry spread across the Atlantic to the New World. In 1502, the Spanish imported their first Africans to work on sugar plantations in Hispaniola (later named Saint-Domingue under the French and called Haiti following independence). The crown limited this early trade in human beings to Christians born in Spain or baptized or naturalized there. In 1518, the Spanish government reversed this policy and granted *ascientos* (licenses) for the transport and sale of people directly from Africa to the New World; but only in 1595 would the crown limit its contract to one carrier, the Portuguese. The annual number of Africans rose from about 2,000 in the sixteenth century to an average of about 80,000 in the 1780s. After declining during the 1790s, the number rose to a new peak in the 1840s. Despite American and European legislation outlawing the international slave trade after 1808, it persisted through the 1870s. Although historians disagree on the precise figures, they agree that no less than 10 million Africans landed alive in the Americas during the era of the slave trade (see figure). Another 2 million Africans died in the so-called Middle Passage (see page 36) en route to the New World.

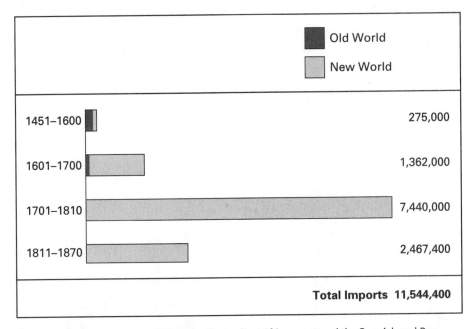

		Old World
		New World
1451–1600		275,000
1601–1700		1,362,000
1701–1810		7,440,000
1811–1870		2,467,400
		Total Imports 11,544,400

Imports of Africans by Time and Region. The earliest Africans entered the Spanish and Portuguese colonies of the New World during the sixteenth century, but the numbers remained relatively small until the seventeenth and eighteenth centuries. By the end of the international slave trade, over 11 million Africans had entered the Americas, but only about 5 percent of these reached British North America. *Source: Data from Orlando Patterson,* Slavery and Social Death: A Comparative Study *(Cambridge, Mass: Harvard University Press, 1982), p. 162. Adapted from* Time on the Cross: The Economics of American Negro Slavery, *by Robert William Fogel and Stanley L. Engerman. Copyright © 1974 by Robert William Fogel and Stanley L. Engerman. Used by permission of W. W. Norton & Company, Inc.*

The Portuguese dominated the initial phases of trade with West Africa, but the Spanish, English, French, and Dutch soon made legal and extralegal inroads on Portuguese interests. With three thousand miles of African coastline, however, most countries could not police the huge West African trade, and monopolistic efforts soon broke down. By the eighteenth century, independent shippers carried the bulk of slaves to the New World, and piracy against the shipping of other nations steadily increased. Using their base on the Canary Islands, the Spanish regularly conducted secret raids on Portuguese strongholds. During the 1560s, before the British became major actors in the slave trade, the Englishman John Hawkins launched three raiding expeditions against the Portuguese in West Africa (see map). Hawkins not only forcibly seized Africans from rival ships but also fomented war between indigenous factions to increase the number of bondsmen and -women at his disposal.

Portugal faced its most serious threat from the Dutch. During the 1630s and 1640s, the Dutch took the Portuguese ports of São Jorge da Mina, Angola, and Arguin. Although Portugal would regain much of its colonial territory, including Angola, it permanently lost Mina and other Gold Coast ports. After 1650, the English

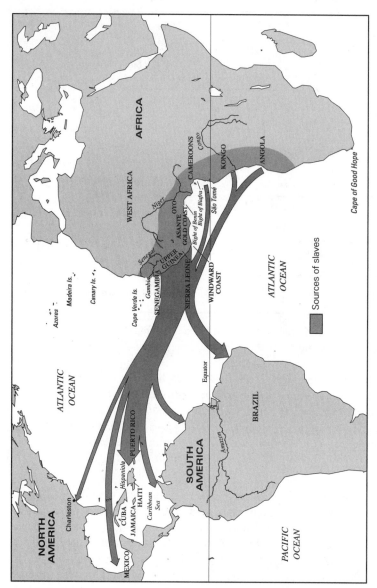

Origins and Destinations of Africans Enslaved in the New World. Blacks arrived in the Americas from a variety of West African locations—including Senegambia, Upper Guinea, and the so-called Gold Coast—but the Niger Delta region (and Cameroons) became the most consistent source of captives shipped to the New World over time.

and French would undermine both Portuguese and Dutch influence. As early as 1677, the French captured Gorée (the former Portuguese El Mina) from the Dutch, and the English established a series of forts and made inroads on Dutch control of the Gold Coast. Sweden, Denmark, and Germany followed suit with their own drives for a piece of the West African trade.

European Traders, African States, and Captives

Wherever Europeans gained a foothold in the African trade, they initially deferred to African heads of state and merchant elites for both health and military reasons. Although Africans and Europeans shared similar diseases and immunities, yellow fever and certain strains of malaria were especially deadly for Europeans. New arrivals to the West African coast suffered mortality rates as high as 25 to 50 percent in the first few months. When the Portuguese sent a fleet of twenty ships to enforce its will on the Jolof state in 1590, disease undercut its force, and resistance from African peoples defeated the effort. The heavy mortality cost of conducting business on the west coast of Africa, along with proud, independent, and determined African peoples, discouraged European forays inland.

European raids on African peoples also met staunch and determined military resistance. When a Portuguese war ship arrived in the Senegambian region in 1446, African ships met and attacked the vessel, killing most of its crew. A year later, a Danish sailor and most of his contingent lost their lives when an African ship intercepted their craft near the island of Gorée. When the Portuguese sought to impose their handpicked successor on the kingdom of Kongo, the people rose up and drove the Portuguese south toward Angola. Europeans of different national backgrounds soon recognized the power of indigenous residents and sought to arrange lucrative trading agreements with their leaders.

African states placed a number of legal and technical constraints on European traders. According to a Dutch commercial guide from the mid-seventeenth century, European traders provided gifts and taxes to African leaders in a variety of states along the so-called Slave Coast area. At Allada, for example, prospective European buyers presented offerings not only to the king and merchants but also to entertainers, food venders, and interpreters. Once Europeans met such gift-giving requirements, African officials opened the market to them with the promise of protection.

The sources of African captives varied from place to place and over time. Some areas supplied few people to the European market; others faced drastic depopulation; and still others supplied captives for a period and then dropped out of the slave trade network altogether. Although the kingdom of Benin first attracted the attention of Europeans and became well known on the continent, it supplied relatively few people for the international trade. Between 1516 and the late 1600s, the king of Benin restricted the sale of captives and then banned the export of humans entirely. The embargo was lifted during the early 1700s, when the kingdom faced internal disputes and civil war, but the trade from Benin remained small, even during the height of the slave trade during the late eighteenth century. By the early nineteenth century, Benin no longer supplied captives to the international market, although human exports from the larger area called the Bight of Benin continued.

During the sixteenth century, Senegambia emerged as one of the earliest and most important exporters of people from Africa. Located on the shores of the Senegal and Gambia Rivers, this area supplied nearly one-third of all human exports during the period. Senegambia also represented a pointed example of how Europeans diverted the earlier trans-Saharan trade in people to the Atlantic coast. As soon as the Portuguese reached the Senegal region, they tapped northward-bound caravans for bondsmen and -women, exporting some 700 to 1,000 per year. With the opening of markets north of the Gambia River, such exports rose after about 1456 to an estimated 1,200 to 2,500 per year. Closely associated with the breakup of the Jolof empire into a number of smaller states, captives from the Senegambia would decline as the region regained political, military, and social stability during the seventeenth century.

Upper Guinea and Sierra Leone were also important sources of black labor during the sixteenth century. Like Senegambia, these areas supplied about one-third of the total exports. In the southern part of the region, around the present-day Sierra Leone, ancestors of the Bullom, Temne, Limba, and other ethnic groups referred to by Europeans as Sape were inundated by a people called Mane. The conflict between the Mane and the Sape resulted in the sale of many people until the early seventeenth century. Once social relations between the Mane and Sape stabilized,

Enslaved Africans march overland to forts on the West African coast. *The Library Company of Philadelphia*

however, this area contributed even fewer captives than the Senegambia. To the east of Sierra Leone and Upper Guinea was an area known to Europeans as the Windward Coast. Subdivided into what Europeans called the Grain Coast on the east and the Ivory Coast on the west, this area produced few bondspeople for sale in the international trade network.

The so-called Gold Coast had the highest concentration of European trading posts and military personnel. The Portuguese, Dutch, English, Danes, Swedes, and Germans all built forts along the Gold Coast. Yet until the end of the seventeenth century, Europeans valued the area more for its gold than its labor. Indeed, the Dutch and Portuguese sometimes discouraged the trade in humans, fearing interference with the gold trade, but several developments slowly converged to transform European interest in the area from gold to people: the increasing labor demands of sugar plantations in the Old and New World; the spread of interethnic warfare among West African peoples; and the emergence of new coastal slave-trading states. Together the Gold Coast state of Asante and the Bight of Benin states of Dahomey and Oyo emerged as key suppliers of humans to European traders.

Under the leadership of Osei Tutu, the Asante kingdom was founded in the 1670s. By the early 1700s, Asante had conquered the Akan states of Denkyera and Akwamu, among others, and had pushed the boundaries of the Asante nation, an area covering most of present-day Ghana, from the forest on the coast to the savannah on the north. Initially, Asante's ruling elites depended on unfree labor to produce gold for sale in exchange for European firearms and North African salt, cloth, and other products. By the 1680s, however, the trade in people had increased to 75 percent of the total value of exports from the region. Organized into a centralized state around 1650, Dahomey also gradually turned toward the sale of captives as a means of territorial expansion. Under the leadership of King Agaja, Dahomey captured the coastal states of Allada and Quidah during the 1720s and increased its contacts with Europeans and the human trade. In exchange for firearms from Europeans over the next two decades, Dahomey provided increasing numbers of captives for the international trade. Before Dahomey could fully consolidate its hold over conquered territories, the state of Oyo to the north became a major supplier of captives, reaching its peak as an exporter during the 1780s. Yet to exert its independence of Oyo and to strengthen its hand as a state, Dahomey intensified its involvement with the trade in people. Under the leadership of Tegbesu (1740–1774) and other rulers, the Dahomean armies systematically raided neighboring peoples for sale to Europeans.

The Niger Delta and the Cameroons provided the most continuous supply of captives over time. Beginning around the late seventeenth century, Africans in this area devised an elaborate commercial organization that increased the number of bondspeople. According to recent scholars, this area, also known as the Bight of Biafra, supplied more captives per mile of African coastline or rural hinterland than any other part of the continent. In the Niger Delta and Cameroons, the Ijo and Efik increased their regional trade activities, but they depended on other groups to establish connections with long-distance trade and transport of people from the interior. The Akwa and the Aro, both trading groups with strong religious credentials

SOURCES FROM THE PAST

1785

Diary of Antera Duke, an Efik Slave Trader

26.9.1785

About 6 a.m. at Aqua Landing; it was a fine morning so I went down to the landing and after 5 o'clock Esin and I went on board the Opter but Esin went away before me. . . .

27.9.1785

About 6 a.m. at Aqua Landing; it was a fine morning. We hear that Tom Salt or Captain Andrew's people are fighting with Combesboch's long boat. Captain Opter, the Captain of the tender, and Combesboch's Captain of the tender went down the river in the long boat to look for the boat which the Combesboch people had taken from his mate, and they got away with goods for fifteen slaves. So Tom Salt or Captain Andrew fought with the Captains and the people got the Captain out of the boat (?). One captain took thirty-two men and one woman from them and brought them back. . . .

3.10.1785

. . . so I got together goods for Calabar Antera to go to Cameroons. Soon after that we three put our heads together and settle what we think to do and at 7 o'clock at night I put the things in Egbo Young's big canoe and at midnight I sailed to go to Curcock. . . .

10.10.1785

At about 5 a.m. in Curcock town; it was a fine morning so I went down to the landing. I gave Andam Curcock goods for one slave to live at his place. At three o'clock after noon I saw our Boostam canoe come down with five slaves and yams. At the same time I sailed away home with the slaves in my canoe and there were three small canoes besides mine. . . .

14.12.1785

About 5 a.m. at Aqua Landing; there was a great morning fog; I went down to the landing to put yams in [my] canoe. After 8 o'clock we went down in three big canoes, I, Esin, and Egbo Young with 32 slaves. So he kept 25 slaves and about 6,000 yams. He dashed (gave) us three great guns. Some time after 8 o'clock at night we went aboard Captain Fairweather whose tender went away with 250 slaves and two tons [of palm-oil].

Source: Daryll Forde, ed., *Efik Traders of Old Calabar: Containing the Diary of Antera Duke.* Copyright © 1956. Published by Oxford University Press for the International African Institute.

as diviners, emerged as the principal suppliers of people from the interior. When their spiritual pronouncements as keepers of the famous Aro-chuku Oracle called for punishment by sacrifice to the gods, victims were often spared for sale into human bondage (see box).

Although Europeans depended on developing trade relations with African traders and heads of state to meet their demand for unfree labor, they did not forgo opportunities to raid African villages, aggravate internal rivalries, and increase the number of captives. Portuguese behavior in the Kongo and Angola offers an extreme illustration of this process. Early on, the Portuguese launched their own raiding parties and deliberately fomented interethnic strife to gain their objectives. When the Portuguese landed in the area in 1483, they initially deferred to the authority of King Nzinga Nkuwu, who converted to Christianity and was baptized into the Catholic church. Moreover, the king solicited and received Portuguese support in driving back a challenge from the surrounding Tio peoples. Within a decade, however, in order to man their sugar plantations on the island of São Tomé, the Portuguese slowly and then rapidly launched slave raids on Kongo villages. In 1493, the king of Portugal authorized settlers on São Tomé to engage in the human trade. By 1507, an estimated 2,000 captives worked on the island's sugar plantations, and another 5,000 to 6,000 were held for reexport elsewhere. Although some of these people came from other parts of West Africa, 50 percent or more came from the Kongo region of central Africa.

Portuguese slave-raiding activities soon ensnared members of the royal family and weakened the king's authority. As a result of Portuguese influence, first the Kongo, then Angola, and later Matamba and Kasanje became the principal suppliers of people to the Portuguese New World plantations in Brazil. Although some scholars suggest that these areas were already involved in internal slave-trading operations before the arrival of the Portuguese, only the coming of Europeans incorporated these Africans into the international slave trade network.

Integral to the rise of the trade in human beings was the emergence of Afro-European communities on the west coast of Africa. Mixed Afro-Portuguese communities emerged in Upper Guinea, in Sierra Leone, and on the Cape Verde Islands. Although the Portuguese government used Cape Verde Islands as a base for organizing trade with Senegambians, many Portuguese individuals defied official policy and moved onto the mainland, then intermarried with Africans. Although they retained their identity as Portuguese and Catholics, their descendants were mixed in appearance and Luso-African in culture. By the early 1600s, the Afro-Portuguese made up the principal trade community on the coast and up the Gambia River. These people slowly developed a new lingua franca, or creole, that permitted communication between Europeans and a wide range of African language groups. Similarly, on the Senegal River, an Afro-French community developed at St. Louis. Unlike the Afro-Portuguese, however, these people were the product of intense language and cultural interactions more than of actual intermarriage between Africans and the French. A similar process of linguistic and cultural interchange took place in the English areas of influence. The African Philip Quaque of Cape Coast, for example, was educated in England. Later ordained as an Anglican priest, he married an Englishwoman and returned to Cape Coast Castle, where he served as the fort's official chaplain. For his part, the Englishman Richard Brew spent thirty years among Africans on the Gold Coast and established a prominent Anglo-African family in the area. The emergence of mixed communities suggested that European notions of African or black inferiority would become most pronounced in the New World as human bondage itself escalated.

The Process of Enslavement

Enslavement was a dehumanizing and painful process. It involved capture and movement to the Atlantic coast, the ocean passage to the Americas, and disembarkation and settlement in the New World. The journey began with capture on the West African coast, where men and women were chained together and forced to make the trip along inland waterways and overland to the European forts and trading ships. Captives were often passed on from one group of indigenous traders to another until they reached the coastal slave-trading states. Usually victims of wars deep in the interior, such people had already suffered what one recent scholar calls "social death," the loss of connection to their original community. Since war captives were traditionally put to death, captivity created a new status that ensured physical survival but divorced people from their place in a culture that confirmed their existence as human beings.

The historical record is replete with stories of escape attempts and mutinies, but few were successful. Upon reaching the coast, survivors were housed together with others from diverse locations within West Africa. Invariably overcrowded and disease ridden, these holding areas, maintained by African heads of states, merchants, and European trading firms, served as the staging ground for international shipment. Following intense and demeaning physical inspection, European slave traders made their selections, settled on a price with African middlemen, and marked their charges with hot branding irons. An eighteenth-century observer described the procedure in the kingdom of Dahomey:

> As the slaves come down to Fida [Dahomey] from the inland country, they are put into a booth or prison, built for that purpose, near the beach, all of them together; and when the Europeans are to receive them, they are brought out into a large plain, where the [ships'] surgeons examine every part of every one of them, to the smallest member, men and women being all stark naked. Such as are allowed good and sound, are set on one side [and] . . . marked on the breast with a red-hot iron, imprinting the mark of the French, English or Dutch companies, that so each nation may distinguish their own.

It often took several days and sometimes weeks to secure a sufficient number of captives to embark for the Americas. In the meantime, captives had to endure an additional round of indignities and poor living conditions. They were either returned to holding areas on shore or brought on board European ships to await the arrival of new shipments. Depending on how far afield the traders had traveled, new arrivals sometimes brought diseases and epidemics, causing sickness and even death for those already selected as fit for the transatlantic voyage. When the ship had reached its quota of cargoes, human and material, it embarked on the journey to the Americas, the so-called Middle Passage, the most destructive aspect of the trade in human beings. The ocean passage received its Eurocentric name from the second leg of an intercontinental trade network that included, first, movement from Europe to Africa and, finally, return to Europe after dispatching human cargoes in the colonies of America. For Africans, of course, it was the "first passage" from their continental home.

In preparation for the overseas trip, people were stripped naked, chained together, and tightly packed in highly confining compartments. Although some slavers, as such ships were called, utilized "loose packing" techniques, most followed the principal of maximum capacity. People were chained close together and forced to lie down on layers of shelving with little room for sitting up straight or moving about. For the next several weeks, bondsmen and -women suffered some of the most inhumane conditions known in human history. In the hot, humid, cramped, foul-smelling holds of ships, those positioned on the lower decks had to endure not only their own vomit, urine, and feces but the trickling down from others above them. Seeking to ensure the maximum number of survivors, ship captains often stocked a variety of foods for the voyage, but such supplies often proved insufficient beyond bare survival.

Although colonial authorities placed limits on the number of human beings each ship could carry, captains routinely ignored such regulations. Contemporary accounts repeatedly described the maladies or "fevers" that accompanied the slave ships, including yellow fever, smallpox, and dysentery. Epidemics sometimes broke out and decimated an entire cargo. More often, as much as a third of human exports lost their lives at sea. As the Portuguese cleric Alonso de Sandoval put it, the African bondsmen and -women were

> packed so closely in such disgusting conditions, and so mistreated, as the very ones who transport them assure me, that they come by six and six, with collars around their necks, and these same ones by two and two with fetters on their feet, in such a way that they come imprisoned from head to feet, below the deck, locked in from outside, where they see neither sun nor moon, [and] that there is no Spaniard who dares to stick his head in the hatch without becoming ill, nor to

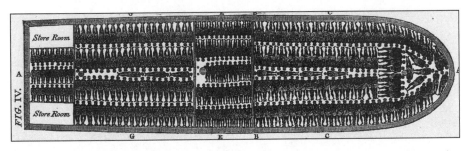

This detailed sketch of a slave ship demonstrates the tight, unsanitary, and dehumanizing packing methods. *Peabody Essex Museum, Salem*

SOURCES FROM THE PAST

1756

The Enslavement of Olaudah Equiano

I have already acquainted the reader with the time and place of my birth. My father, besides many slaves, had a numerous family, of which seven lived to grow up, including myself and a sister, who was the only daughter. As I was the youngest of the sons, I became, of course, the greatest favourite with my mother, and was always with her; and she used to take particular pains to form my mind. . . . One day, when all our people were gone out to their works as usual, and only I and my dear sister were left to mind the house, two men and a woman got over our walls, and in a moment seized us both; and, without giving us time to cry out, or make resistance, they stopped our mouths, and ran off with us into the nearest wood. Here they tied our hands, and continued to carry us as far as they could, till night came on, when we reached a small house, where the robbers halted for refreshment, and spent the night. . . . The next day proved a day of greater sorrow than I had yet experienced; for my sister and I were then separated, while we lay clasped in each other's arms: it was in vain that we besought them not to part us: she was torn from me, and immediately carried away, while I was left in a state of distraction not to be described. . . .

The first object which saluted my eyes when I arrived on the coast was the sea, and a slaveship, which was then riding at anchor, and waiting for its cargo. . . . I now saw myself deprived of all chance of returning to my native country, or even the least glimpse of hope of gaining the shore, which I now considered as friendly; and I even wished for my former slavery, in preference to my present situation, which was filled with horrors of every kind, still heightened by my ignorance of what I was to undergo.

Source: The Interesting Narrative of Olaudah Equiano, or Gustavus Vassa, the African (London, 1789), I:46–48.

remain inside for an hour without the risk of great sickness. So great is the stench, the crowding and the misery of that place . . . that most arrive turned into skeletons.

Captured and sold into slavery in 1756, the African Olaudah Equiano (Gustavus Vassa), from the Niger Ibo region of West Africa, left a vivid description of his feelings on reaching the coast and entering the slave ship (see box). His description also demonstrates how the pain of separation from home led some Africans to desperate responses—refusal to eat and efforts to end their lives by jumping overboard:

Quite overpowered with horror and anguish, I fell motionless on the deck and fainted. . . . I now saw myself deprived of all chance of returning to my native country. . . . I became so sick and low that I was not able to eat. . . . One day

Olaudah Equiano. This engraving was printed in his 1789 autobiography. Equiano left one of the earliest and most detailed descriptions of the enslavement of Africans in the Americas. *Library of Congress*

when we had a smooth sea and a moderate wind, two of my wearied countrymen who were chained together . . . preferring death to such a life of misery, somehow made through the nettings and jumped into the sea, immediately another quite dejected fellow . . . also followed.

Once Africans reached America, another round of indignities ensued. When the ships anchored, they were met by colonial merchants, slave traders, and government officials charged with inspecting the cargo to determine if any illegal goods were aboard. In Spanish America, the government set limits on the number of people allowed on a ship, depending on the size and condition of the ship. Although officials charged with such duties invariably took bribes and overlooked infractions of the law, they routinely met slave ships and conducted a perfunctory inspection. They required the unloading of captives into small boats waiting alongside the ship, counted the slaves, and then reloaded them on board the seagoing vessel. Following the legal inspection, the captain took charge of the cargo and arranged the transfer of captives to local wholesalers. These agents conducted their own minute inspection of the Africans' physical conditions, paying close attention to their eyes, teeth, limbs, and sexual organs, with particular interest in signs of venereal disease. After completing this inspection, merchants transferred captives to nearby warehouses or encampments, where they were allowed to eat, clean up, receive some medical attention, and rest in preparation for sale locally. Survivors of the Middle Passage were about to embark on their new lives in a new world.

THE CARIBBEAN AND LATIN AMERICA

The African American experience in the New World unfolded within the larger context of European colonization of America. In 1492, the Genoese mariner Christopher Columbus landed in America and claimed the land for the Spanish empire. Two years later, the Spanish initiated colonization of the Caribbean on the island of Hispaniola. Within less than four decades, Spain also conquered the Aztec empire in the high-lying valley of Mexico and extended Spanish dominion over Incan peoples of Peru on the mainland of South America. The Portuguese soon followed suit with the exploration of Brazil around 1500, although Portugal's colonization of the area would not begin in earnest until 1532. Before long, the Dutch, French, and English also colonized portions of the New World in their own interests. Yet on the basis of linguistic, archaeological, and historical evidence of African artistic styles, facial features, and words in ancient Amerindian cultures (such as the Olmec of Mexico at Laventa), such scholars as Leo Wiener and, more recently, Ivan Van Sertima have forcibly argued that Africans came to the New World before Christopher Columbus and the aggressive expansion of Europe. These scholars accept that African boat-making skills and knowledge of ocean currents were considerable and that some of their crafts were durable enough to make the Atlantic crossing. Even so, most Africans entered the New World with Europeans.

Transition to African Labor

From the outset, African labor, knowledge, and skills helped to advance the European conquest of the New World. Although scholars now doubt that Pedro Alonzo Nino, a pilot on Columbus's first voyage, was black, Africans did accompany Columbus on his second voyage in 1493–1494 and also accompanied Balboa to the Pacific Ocean in 1513, Cortez to Mexico in 1519–1520, and Pizarro to Peru in the 1530s. More important, as on the west coast of Africa, gold and labor propelled the initial European settlement of America. Beginning in 1495, the Spanish government required Hispaniola's indigenous Arawak ages fourteen through seventy to pay tribute in gold and agricultural produce. When Amerindians deserted their villages in large numbers rather than deliver payments to Spanish officials, indigenous farmlands deteriorated, malnutrition spread, and Native Americans died in growing numbers. The Dominican friar Bartolomé de Las Casas estimated that more than 3 million original inhabitants of Hispaniola died through starvation, over-work, and disease between 1494 and 1508. In his report on the declining Arawak population, de Las Casas reported: "Who of those born in future centuries will believe this? I myself who am writing this and saw it and know most about it can hardly believe that such was possible."

As the population declined, the demands on survivors escalated, adding to the mortality rate in a vicious circle. The cycle repeated itself as Europeans moved from one island to the next. In 1511, the Arawak and Caribs in Puerto Rico responded to forced labor in the mines by rising up and killing nearly eighty Spanish settlers. In the Bahamas, where no precious metals could be found, Europeans focused on the indigenous Lacayans as a source of slave labor for Hispaniola and to some extent Puerto Rico. According to one contemporary observer, Peter Martyr (1493–1525), the Bahamas lost 40,000 inhabitants in less than five years. Although the sea crossing was quite short, many died en route. Spanish ships, Martyr wrote, could sail "without compass or chart, merely by following for the distance between the Lacayan Islands and Espaniola . . . the trace of those Indian corpses floating in the sea, corpses that had been cast overboard by earlier ships."

Although the colonists were especially preoccupied with gold, they soon discovered the promise of profits in agriculture, particularly sugar production. In 1500, the Spanish crown sponsored an expedition of over three thousand men, charging them with stimulating Spanish settlement in the Caribbean islands. In 1515, the surgeon Ganzalo de Vellosa employed sugar planters from the Canary Islands to set up a sugar mill on Hispaniola. Two years later, the first full-fledged sugar mill opened in Spanish America. By 1527, Hispaniola had twenty-five working mills, which exported increasing volumes of sugar to Europe.

Following its establishment in Hispaniola, sugar production soon spread to Puerto Rico, Jamaica, Barbados, and Brazil. As early as 1624, the Dutch directed their trade activities toward the Portuguese sugar region of northeastern Brazil. Between 1636 and 1645, Dutch traders took control of the Pernambuco region and introduced sugar-producing techniques based on the Madeira model from the northwest coast of Africa. Under Dutch control, Brazil became the leading producer of sugar for the European market and replaced the sugar islands off the west coast of Africa in importance. Like the Spanish, the Portuguese initially exploited the labor of indigenous residents, and, like the Spanish, they faced staunch Amerindian resistance. After defeating the Tupinamba in Bahia around 1549, the Portuguese pressed these people into work on the sugar plantations. By the late sixteenth century, Brazil's bound workers were mostly Tupinamba and other rural indigenous peoples.

Under the impact of European colonization, diseases, and sugar production, the indigenous population continued to decline. The cleric de Las Casas became a staunch reformer on behalf of Amerindians. Emphasizing the suffering of indigenous inhabitants, he recommended the substitution of African for Amerindian slave labor. Indeed, the Spanish government outlawed the use of Amerindians in the sugar-refining houses by the late 1500s, emphasizing the large numbers of deaths that occurred among indigenous workers. As a consequence of the declining Amerindian population, planters turned toward alternative sources of labor. European indentured servants (called *engagés* in French) partly filled the labor needs of the Caribbean islands during the early years but proved insufficient and difficult to retain over the long haul. The number of servants shipped from the single port of Bristol to the West Indies rose from nearly 1,500 in 1654–1659 to about 1,800 in 1660–1669. Thereafter, the numbers dropped to a little more than 700 in the 1670s, and to less than 450 during the 1680s.

A variety of factors militated against the large-scale employment of white servants. First and most importantly, European servants had legally enforceable agreements for a specified term of service, usually three to four years in English colonies and thirty-six months in French settlements. When they ended their term of service, they were also entitled to a portion of land and resources for establishing themselves as free men. Thus, their obligations to work on sugar plantations were limited. European indentured servants also faced abuses from their employers, which in turn undermined efforts to recruit additional workers. Moreover, as the sugar industry expanded, large planters took increasing amounts of the best land out of circulation, leaving free workers fewer opportunities to carve out farms for themselves and their families.

As planters found it increasingly difficult to exploit European and Amerindian labor, the importation of Africans increased dramatically. Stretching from Cuba in the northwest to Trinidad near the Venezuelan coast, the Caribbean islands imported an estimated 4 million Africans, about 40 percent of all Africans brought to the Americas during the entire transatlantic slave trade. African imports soon transformed the major sugar-producing islands into black majorities. By 1560, an estimated 12,000 to 13,000 Africans inhabited Hispaniola, compared with about 1,000 whites. Hispaniola had also become the major port for the transshipment of blacks to other islands.

As early as 1530, Puerto Rico had some 2,292 Africans, compared with only 327 Europeans. In 1645, before the transition from tobacco to sugar in Barbados, there were 5,680 blacks to 18,130 whites, mostly indentured servants looking forward to gaining access to their own land and bound labor. By the 1670s, Africans had become a majority; and by 1690, they made up 60,000 of the colony's 80,000 inhabitants. Over the next century, the enslaved black population would outnumber free whites by four to one.

Jamaica's transformation was even more dramatic than that of Barbados. The African population rose from 1,300 in 1658, to 40,000 in 1698, and to over 200,000 during the eighteenth century. This represented an increase from less than 25 percent to over 90 percent of the total population. By the mid-eighteenth century, huge black majorities also existed on the islands of Antigua, Montserrat, St. Thomas, and Guadeloupe. Although it would be later and less complete than elsewhere, during the nineteenth century Cuba would experience a similar transformation.

In smaller numbers, Africans also reached the mainland of Spanish America. During the colonial era, from the sixteenth through the early nineteenth century,

Africans played a prominent role in the economies of Mexico (New Spain), Panama, and Peru. The Spanish imported an estimated 100,000 Africans into New Spain during the entire colonial period. Most of these Africans came between 1570 and 1610 and worked in a variety of jobs: on sugar plantations in Morelos, Pueblo, and Veracruz; in the silver mines of the northern region; and in the urban centers of Mexico City, Guadalajara, Querétaro, Valladolid, Antequera, and Puebla. By the end of the colonial period, Africans and their descendants made up 60 percent of the inhabitants of Panama, where they worked in the transshipment of goods between the Atlantic and Pacific Oceans. According to available evidence, the number of Africans probably equaled the number of whites in Peru in 1604; however, by the late eighteenth century, the number of Africans had dropped to less than 1 percent. Quito and New Granada (now Ecuador and Colombia) also imported African labor.

Only the Portuguese colony of Brazil surpassed the Caribbean islands in the number of Africans imported to the New World. Brazil imported an estimated 5 million Africans between the 1530s and the mid-nineteenth century. Its annual slave imports rose from an average of about 2,000 during the sixteenth century; to 13,000 a century later; and to a peak of 60,000 during the eighteenth century. African imports into Brazil remained high through the mid-nineteenth century. In relatively rapid succession, Brazil employed enslaved blacks to produce first sugar, then gold, and finally coffee.

As the sugar boom peaked in the first half of the seventeenth century, the discovery of gold in the Brazilian highlands stimulated new demands for African labor. Mine owners imported over 1 million Africans into the mining districts of Minas Gerais, Mato Grosso, and Goias. Although some blacks came from the declining sugar regions of Pernambuco, imports directly from Africa reached an estimated 7,000 to 15,000 per year. In all, nearly 2 million Africans entered Brazil during the mining boom, which peaked by the mid-eighteenth century. During the 1780s, the Brazilian economy rebounded from a hard recession and grew steadily for nearly 150 years. Although mining never recovered, sugar production rebounded, and coffee emerged during the nineteenth century as the new boom crop. Located south of the mining district in the rural hinterlands of Rio de Janeiro, coffee producers imported the largest percentage of new Africans. During this period, African imports peaked at about 38,000 per year during the 1840s. Following the country's ban on slave imports in 1850, the old sugar areas of the northeast became principal suppliers of black labor to the coffee growers.

Work and Social Conditions

New World bondsmen and -women deployed a range of skills that greatly enhanced their value to owners. In Brazil, for example, large numbers of skilled miners arrived from the Portuguese-influenced Costa da Mina (located between the Bight of Benin and the Windward Coast), where they had acquired knowledge of pick-and-shovel methods for working in dangerous gold-mine pits. In Mexico, too, the Spanish imported Africans to work in the most skilled as well as common laborer jobs in the mining and refining of silver.

More important, sugar was the mainstay of Caribbean and much of Latin American economies, and it built directly on the skills that Africans had acquired in their homelands. Planters carefully selected captives from the sugar-producing Canary Islands and São Tomé. Africans not only supervised Amerindian field hands, instructing them in the clearing, planting, weeding, harvesting, and transporting of cane to the mills and refinery plants, but also played a key role in setting up machinery, constructing buildings, and carrying out the technical operations in the refining process. In the mills, skilled hands placed the plant between rollers, which squeezed juice from the cane into large containers. The juice was then poured into large cauldrons and boiled down to separate impurities from the syrup. After extensive boiling in rooms that became extremely hot and steamy, the syrup was poured into clay molds, where it dried into the standard sugar loaf. The final step involved crating and shipping to market.

Sugar, coffee, and mining did not exhaust the range of jobs that captives occupied. They also worked on cattle ranches and cultivated ginger, indigo, cacao, and tobacco. Moreover, throughout the Caribbean and Latin America, blacks lived in the major cities and worked as carpenters, blacksmiths, barbers, and retail sellers as well as laborers in household, commercial, and governmental establishments and on public works. As suggested by the history of blacks in Brazil, the work experiences of captives also varied considerably over time. When sugar production declined in the northeast, for example, blacks gained greater access to skilled jobs as artisans and opportunities to earn income. Some of these Africans and Brazilian-born blacks gained sufficient resources to purchase their freedom. As sugar planters lost their edge in the market, bondsmen and -women also seized more control over their time, including opportunities to tend their own subsistence crops and sell surpluses in nearby towns or to neighboring plantations.

Enslaved men and women shared some but not all work experiences. From the beginning to the end of the transatlantic trade, plantation owners purchased disproportionately more men than women and children. Available statistics suggest that men outnumbered women three to one. During the entire period, women made up only 36 to 38 percent of Africans entering the Caribbean on Dutch, Danish, and British ships. The sex ratio for grown men and women was about 187 males to every 100 females. For children the ratio was an estimated 193 boys per 100 girls. Planters and colonial officials frequently alleged that women were "useless in field labor," but recent scholarship undermines this proposition. Planters invariably purchased women with an eye for their use in field or common labor, whereas they purchased men with both skilled and unskilled work in mind. Even when they captured women from other ethnic groups outside their own district, West African states emphasized keeping women and children at home. Between 1791 and 1798, women made up only about 38 percent of all adult Africans transported from West Africa in English ships. An almost identical ratio characterized the numbers of male and female children on such ships (see table).

Age and Sex of Africans Carried from the West Coast in English Ships, 1791–1798				
African Region	Men	Women	Boys	Girls
Senegambia	4,319	2,143	817	519
Sierre Leone	517	243	55	29
Windward Coast	4,526	2,414	383	215
Gold Coast	2,539	1,321	188	117
Bight of Biafra	14,375	10,971	435	384
Bight of Benin	304	189	9	10
Congo-Angola	11,596	6,144	968	509
Unknown	10,113	5,822	992	556
Total	48,289	29,247	3,847	2,339

Source: Claire C. Robertson and Martin Klein, eds., *Women and Slavery in Africa* (Madison: University of Wisconsin Press, 1983), p. 31. Reprinted by permission of The University of Wisconsin Press.

As we will see, given the actual burdens that planters placed on black women as workers, had the market produced more women, certainly planters would have purchased them. When the prices of men and women are compared without regard to skill levels, the prices of males average about 10 to 20 percent more than for women. Conversely, when analysts control for skills, the price differential virtually disappears, suggesting that planters valued men and women about equally as general field hands. Indeed, because men were widely dispersed in skilled and miscellaneous laboring jobs, contemporary scholarship shows that women were overrepresented in the field labor forces of most New World plantations. In Jamaica, for example, women made up 54 percent or more of field hands on sugar and coffee plantations during the late eighteenth and early nineteenth centuries. Women worked extensively clearing, planting, weeding, and harvesting the key staple crops.

Gender differences were closely linked to emerging color and cultural cleavages within the enslaved population. Even before blacks left the west coast of Africa, they had witnessed the slow spread of mulatto populations among the coastal traders. In America, interracial mixing continued and even intensified over time. A small elite, mainly the product of unequal and exploitive sexual relations between white men and black women, gained increasing status among slaves as well as free blacks. In Brazil and Haiti, for example, a large middle strata of mixed peoples—mulattos, mestizos, and others—stood between enslaved blacks and European ruling elites. Within the middle tier, the color line per se blurred as education, money, family background, occupation, and other criteria took on significance. Some free blacks could move among whites of the same class background on a relatively equal basis. To explain this phenomenon, the Portuguese coined the term *dinheiro embranquece,* or "money whitens," and one recent historian has called the color dimension of this process the "mulatto escape hatch." To be sure, such terms exaggerate the privileges of color and economic position among blacks, enslaved and free alike, but they nonetheless underscore the rise of socioeconomic and cultural differences within the African American population.

As the plantation system spread through the New World colonies, the distinction between American-born and African-born blacks also slowly emerged. Almost everywhere, over time, planters favored American-born, or "seasoned," blacks over African-born, or "saltwater," blacks. In Brazil, new Africans from abroad were called *bocal* (*bozal* in Spanish). Whites perceived the *bocal* as ignorant of European culture and backward looking. Compared with American-born Creoles (*crioulo* in Portuguese; *criollo* or *ladino* in Spanish), who were knowledgeable and relatively trusted components of the enslaved labor force, the newcomers faced greater restrictions on their movement and expressions. Indeed, the old Africans and African Americans frequently looked down on and ridiculed the new blacks.

Despite the emergence of significant internal distinctions within the enslaved population, African and African American men, women, and children shared the horrors of slavery together. With the transition to an all-African labor force, malnutrition, disease, and death took a rising toll on all blacks. Once planters made the decision to use enslaved Africans, they believed that it was cheaper to import new workers than to maintain the health and longevity of existing ones. Although sugar planting and refining required important skills and knowledge, it was difficult, dangerous, and life-threatening work. A mistake in the sugar-refining process not only would ruin the product but also could result in a serious injury, a loss of limbs, or severe burns. With temperatures sometimes soaring to over 120 degrees Fahrenheit, the mill houses exposed captives to lung disorders and other infectious diseases. Available statistics show that young Africans who arrived in the American sugar regions died at a rate nearly twice that of those who stayed at home.

Working conditions in the mining districts were even more hazardous than those in sugar production. Miners who worked in the placer mines in river streams stood for long periods of time in cold water, whereas pick-and-shovel miners faced the dangers of cave-ins, rock slides, and rising water. Although contemporary observers sometimes referred to domestics as pampered servants, life in the big house was also difficult. Household workers were on call around the clock and were frequently whipped for minor infractions. When they resisted harsh conditions in the house, domestics were often condemned to hard labor in the field. When two Bahia female house slaves challenged their master's authority, they were demoted from domestics to field hands and repeatedly whipped until they both died a short time later.

Planters and their overseers and managers imposed a strict regimen on all blacks. As noted earlier, harsh conditions on plantations in the Caribbean and Latin American colonies prevented Africans from becoming a self-reproducing population until the nineteenth century. Physical brutality for minor and major infractions was also common. Although the government specified offenses and penalties, planters could easily sidestep regulations and punish captives well beyond the letter of the law. In Spanish and Portuguese law, penalties for runaways escalated with each of-

Whipping of a female slave in the Caribbean. The portrait was titled "Flagellation of a Female Samboe Slave"—that is, a slave with one black and one white parent. *James Ford Bell Library/University of Minnesota*

fense, ultimately leading to the death sentence. A four-day absence brought fifty lashes; eight days brought one hundred lashes and "an iron shackle of twelve pounds, on one foot for two months"; four months' absence and evidence of involvement with *cimarrónes* (organized communities of fugitives) brought two hundred lashes; and "absence of more than six months and the committing of some offense, whether or not with the *cimarrónes,* was punishable by death." Punishment for runaways also included hangings, castration, and other forms of mutilation, including the pouring of hot molten fat or pitch on a captive's naked body. To paraphrase one commentator, the captive's life was often "nasty, brutish, and short."

Although the transition to sugar and Africans produced similar conditions from one colony to the next, it would be a mistake to assume that there were no differences among the colonies. Indeed, there were important legal and cultural differences between the Iberian and British colonies. In the Iberian colonies, blacks could legally marry, own property, purchase their freedom, and even seek redress against abusive owners before the church and state. Moreover, Portuguese and Spanish colonies seemed less riveted to a racially divided world based on skin color. Some people of color would gain access to the government, society, and culture of the dominant groups. Conversely, British colonial law defined bondsmen and -women as chattel without any rights that owners were bound to respect. Still, in practice, the treatment of captives tended to converge across national boundaries, based on particular demographic, economic, and social factors. Wherever captives touched down in the New World, they experienced a hard life. In Spanish, British, and Portuguese America, bondage was a tough form of inequality. It created super-profits for white elites and helped to underwrite the economic development of Europe and the Americas. Within this exceedingly exploitative and inhumane context, however, Africans would forge a New World culture that would enable them to survive, maintain their dignity, and devise new forms of resistance.

SLAVE CULTURE, POLITICS, AND RESISTANCE

Africans responded to bondage by creating new cultures, families, communities, and forms of resistance. As noted earlier, when Africans arrived in the New World, they shared certain underlying understandings and perspectives on the human, natural, and spirit worlds. Based on centuries of interactions between African peoples of diverse ethnic and nationality backgrounds, these understandings helped to lay the foundation for the development of new African American cultures. Although the large numbers of Europeans and Amerindians would curb this process on the mainland, it would emerge clearly and forcefully in the Caribbean and Brazil, where Africans made up huge majorities and successfully blended their Old World cultures with New World ideas and beliefs.

Beginning with the Middle Passage, people from diverse backgrounds forged new bonds. "Shipmates," survivors of the overseas journey, acquired a new sense of kinship and began the arduous process of rebuilding their lives in the New World. Recognition of their common experience helped to link men, women, and children of African descent to each other throughout the New World spiritually, culturally, and physically. As discussed earlier, on the west coast of Africa, diverse ethnic and language groups had already made the transition to a creole lingua franca that enabled them to communicate with different groups of Europeans as well as each other. This language was especially well developed in Portuguese areas and had moved forward in Dutch, English, and French zones. Whereas in Africa, the lingua franca was a second language, in America the new Creole language became the principal tongue, which blacks passed on to their children.

At the same time that Africans struggled to build a new system of communication through language, they also developed New World music, songs, dance, dress, and other forms of aesthetic expression. Contemporary observers frequently commented on black music as part of festivals and funerals. Hans Sloane, a visitor to Jamaica in 1688, recorded the lyrics and music of songs in Koromanti and Angolan. When colonial officials sought to limit the captives' practice of their own language in Brazil, Africans petitioned the crown to permit them to sing songs in "the Angolan idiom." Although authorities condemned and outlawed drums in some colonies as subversive instruments, blacks refashioned new percussion instruments out of New World materials and adapted their dance traditions to the new environment and music. In the 1640s, for example, the Dutch artist Ekhout painted a dancing scene that included a band with African percussion instruments, some with designs identified with line and lozenge motifs from central Africa.

Closely intertwined with their growing ability to communicate with each other and forge new cultural forms across nationality lines, Africans took their first steps toward creating new families and communities. Despite the unequal sex ratios, the number of black children born and raised in New World societies gradually increased, adding to the Creole population. On certain plantations, conditions were more favorable for family and community life than others. In the French colony of Guadeloupe, for example, a 1680 survey revealed that over 70 percent of enslaved people lived in family groups, either formally or informally. Similarly, during the seventeenth century, Barbados planters imported equal numbers of men and women, which enabled Africans to form families early on. Moreover, enslaved people often gained access to provision grounds to grow their own food and to modest materials to construct their own houses, which provided additional opportunities to structure their family and community life. Although this so-called peasant breach was designed to help planters defray the costs of maintaining captives, Africans took hold of these opportunities and turned them into perquisites that planters would later find difficult to deny.

The development of African American culture drew on both African and European ideas. Few planters could avoid importing large blocs of Africans from the same ethnic or nationality group. With an estimated 15,000 imports a year arriving from Angola between 1620 and 1623, Brazil offers the most pointed example of this process. But other places also received ethnic clusters. On the well-documented Remire estate of French Guiana, the largest group came from Allada, with the remainder almost equally divided between Angola and the northern part of Senegal. Out of twenty-four married couples on the Remire estate, twelve came from the same nationality group and two from the same village. Some were already married before they reached the Americas. The Kalabari bondsman Quanbom and his wife, Aunon, were bought and sold together and remained together on the Remire estate. Without formal sanction by church or state, enslaved men and women developed familial commitments to each other, to their children, and to extended kin. When planters respected such unions, these relationships endured over long periods of time. Within these family units, men and women defined roles for themselves and their children and instilled values, attitudes, and knowledge that would enable them to build broader and more inclusive communities.

Religion played a key role in African efforts to build families and sustain their New World culture. Contrary to popular and some scholarly perceptions, some Africans had already confronted the Christian challenge to their indigenous beliefs before arriving in America. Although Africans and Europeans had different systems of religion, they shared some key elements, particularly the notion that there existed two worlds—this material one and a spiritual, otherworldly one, knowledge of which required divine revelation. The close correspondence between African cosmologies, emphasizing multiple "gods," and Catholicism, stressing multiple saints, facilitated the adoption of Christianity. Still, as with their earlier response to Islam, Africans adapted Christianity to their own world views.

Rather than simply adhering to European gods, Africans found ways to retain beliefs associated with their own deities—from Senegambia, Reboucou; from Allada, Boudou, or Vodu; and from Angola, Gambi, or Nzambi. The emergence of an informal African priesthood helped to give substance to their faith. Under the guidance of their own spiritual leaders, African Americans rejected European beliefs in ancient or limited revelations based on biblical scriptures. On the contrary, perhaps even more so than their forebears, they believed that God was repeatedly revealed to living human beings.

Europeans sometimes accepted African ideas but more often condemned and feared them as the work of Satan. Colonial officials often questioned the work of African diviners as "an implicit or explicit pact with the devil." Although some blacks would create a new religion out of African and Catholic forms, others would virtually reconstruct their Old World religion on American soil. In Brazil, for example, the heavy and sustained importation of Yoruba people into northeastern Brazil enabled Africans to develop a distinctive Afro-Brazilian religion called Candomble. By the early nineteenth century, some free blacks regularly returned to Africa to renew their contacts with the ancestral spirits that characterized their New World beliefs. In Angola, as Europeans gained a strong foothold, they condemned some indigenous priests to captivity in the New World for challenging certain Euro-Christian beliefs. Portuguese church officials sentenced the head priest of Matamba to slavery in Brazil during the late 1600s. In a sense, even before leaving home, some Africans had already worked to remake European gods in their own image. On arrival in America, for example, the same Matamba priest mentioned above was condemned for spreading the same beliefs among blacks in Brazil and ordered back to Africa. Throughout large parts of the Caribbean and Latin America, Africans insisted on the integrity of their beliefs as diviners and people possessed by the spirit of God.

As their familial, religious, and communal bonds with each other grew, Afro–New World blacks also gave their ideas broader institutional expression. By the early seventeenth century, African Americans had formed organizations that buried their members, staged festivals and celebrations, and held informal elections of officials to preside over enslaved black communities. In Brazil, blacks elected kings and queens over the larger community and governors and lesser officials to help administer the affairs of each nation (or ethnic group). Although Brazilian authorities withheld formal recognition of these structures, their informal influence on Brazilian and African American society was considerable. These efforts informed African participation in mainstream organizations like the Catholic broth-

Family of Negro Slaves from Loango, c. 1792. Although the illustration reflects certain idealistic and stereotypical notions about slaves in the Caribbean, it nonetheless shows that Africans built new families in the Americas. *James Ford Bell Library/ University of Minnesota*

erhoods, especially the well-known Brotherhood of Our Lady of the Rosary. As early as 1693, a Colombian captive expressed surprise that a colonial official would ask him

if he knew that the Negroes of the Arara, Mina, and other newly arrive[d] [*bozales*] nations [*castas*] have their kings, governors, and captains, and if they meet in their councils [*cabildos*] to deal with the problems of their nation or caste, and have their parties and festivities in which they join together.

Although most captives resisted bondage within the context of the plantation system, others sought permanent and immediate release from the slavery regime. Throughout the Americas, Africans escaped as individuals and as groups. Fugitives offered planters their most common problem. In a study of criminal cases in Peru between 1560 and 1650, running away was the largest single category of offenses

(270 cases), with theft (81), assault (72), and murder (36) comprising the next three most common infractions of colonial slave codes. Although some blacks absconded for short periods of time, seeking to gain concessions for better treatment, others resolved to be free or die.

The mountainous topography of the Caribbean and Latin American colonies provided ample opportunities for escape. Runaway communities emerged almost everywhere in the Caribbean and Latin America: in Jamaica, Hispaniola, Cuba, Mexico, Panama, Puerto Rico, and Brazil, to name a few. Variously called Maroon, *cimarrón, quilombo,* and *mocambo* communities in English, Spanish, and Portuguese America, respectively, these communities of escaped slaves were especially prominent in Jamaica and Brazil. As early as the seventeenth century, Jamaican Maroons controlled outposts in the eastern and western mountains of the colony. Despite repeated attempts of the Spanish and the English (after 1655) to destroy these enclaves, the Maroons not only retained their autonomy but also launched raids on nearby plantations, freed captives, and in general kept colonial authorities and owners on edge. Conceding defeat in 1739, English officials signed a peace treaty with the runaways. The treaty recognized the freedom of Maroons, granted them title to the land, and exempted them from taxes. For their part, the runaways agreed to cease raids on plantations and to return further fugitives to owners. Hispaniola, Cuba, Mexico, and Surinam authorities also signed peace treaties with powerful Maroon communities.

Maroon settlements offered Africans opportunities to recreate their own beliefs, culture, and notions of community. African ideas and social organization informed Palmares, the largest and most renown Brazilian *quilombo.* Established in the backlands of Pernambuco in northeastern Brazil, Palmares persisted for nearly the entire eighteenth century. Runaways installed a king, raised their own food, developed extensive fortifications, and deployed a large military force to protect the establishment from outside attack. Although Brazilian authorities overpowered and destroyed the settlement in 1794, such establishments persisted elsewhere in Brazil and the Caribbean until the advent of emancipation.

Rebellions emerged as the most overt and violent form of resistance. In 1522, the earliest recorded African revolt erupted on the island of Hispaniola, on the plantation of the governor, Admiral Diego Columbus (son of the explorer). Some forty Africans killed nine whites before a mixed force of Amerindians and Spanish put the revolt down. Spanish authorities blamed the revolt on *ladinos* (Christianized blacks from Spain) and *gelofes* (Islamized Africans, who also came to Hispaniola via Spain). The Spanish government decreed that no more *ladinos* or *gelofes* would be sent to America.

As the black population increased, colonial authorities frequently reported "plots," real and imagined, to overthrow their rule: in Mexico City (1537 and 1609), in Cartagena (1693), and in Barbados (1649, 1675, and 1692), to name a few. Following the brutal suppression of the 1692 plot, authorities reported few conspiracies in Barbados during the eighteenth century. Then, in 1813, enslaved Barbadians launched a desperate attack. During three days of violence, some fifty whites lost their lives. For their part, nearly a thousand blacks died in the fighting and the mass executions that followed. At the same time, Jamaican bondsmen escalated their attacks on the plantation system. Their efforts culminated in the famous Christmas Revolt of 1831, which precipitated passage of the general Emancipation Act in 1833. Although planters and other colonial elites no doubt exaggerated certain plots to revolt, the ubiquity of resistance suggests widespread planter insecurity as well as the African Americans' determination to free themselves from bondage.

The most renowned and successful revolt occurred in the French colony of Saint-Domingue (formerly Hispaniola under Spanish authority), where blacks outnumbered whites nearly fourteen to one. As elsewhere, black culture, community, and religious traditions informed the revolt. Under the initial leadership of a bondsman named Boukman, described as a voodoo priest and Maroon from Jamaica, enslaved blacks assembled at the Mourne Rouge, a mountain overlooking a heavily forested area. Boukman urged captives to return to their own god of liberation and social justice:

> The God who created the sun which gives us light, who rouses the waves and rules the storm, though hidden in the clouds, he watches us. He sees all that the white man does. The God of the white man inspires him with crime, but our god calls on us to do good works. Our god, who is good to us, orders us to revenge our wrongs. He will direct our arms and aid us. Throw away the symbol of the god of the whites, who has so often caused us to weep, and listen to the voice of liberty, which speaks in the hearts of us all.

Blacks rose up against their French captors on August 22, 1791. After Boukman's death early on in the struggle, Toussaint L'Ouverture, a former overseer, took up the banner. Following nearly twelve years of bloody warfare, blacks declared their independence and changed the island's name from Saint-Domingue to Haiti. Blacks gradually gained control over the island, adopted a new constitution, and extended citizenship to all residents without regard to race or color, but only after the French lured Toussaint into a trap and shipped him off to prison in France did blacks declare their independence. Following Toussaint's imprisonment, African Americans completed the work of independence under the leadership of Jean Jacques Dessalines. They pushed Napoleon's troops off the island and became the second republic in the Western Hemisphere. Although Haiti inspired fear and hatred in planters, it inspired hope among captives throughout the Americas.

≈

THE ENSLAVEMENT OF AFRICAN PEOPLES was a complicated and difficult process. Europeans discovered that slave raids on African villages were perilous undertakings. Both the military might of African states and the West African disease environment posed formidable obstacles to European designs. Rather than risk alienating indigenous inhabitants and endangering their own lives, Europeans initially confined their activities to the coast and negotiated with African peoples and their leaders for material and human cargo. Before falling prey to European slave raiders themselves, African statesmen and commercial elites sold people captured in interethnic wars with their enemies rather than members of their own nationality groups. Still, the enslavement of Africans in the New World was not a foregone conclusion. It was accompanied and even preceded by the coerced labor of indigenous Indian people and white indentured servants, but these sources of forced labor were relatively short-lived. Although the transition to enslaved African labor varied from place to place and over time, Africans gradually forged New World families and communities and resisted human bondage. This process gained its most powerful expression in Brazil and the Caribbean, but it also characterized life in Mexico, Peru, and other places on the Spanish mainland. Although Africans in British North America would share much with their Latin and Caribbean counterparts, their experiences and responses to bondage would take on unique characteristics. The beginnings of African American life in North America are examined in Chapter 3.

PART II

Enslavement, Revolution, and the New Republic

1619–1820

Part I discussed the rise of an enslaved African labor force in the European colonies of the Caribbean and Latin America. Part II explores similar but contrasting developments in British North America. In 1619, when the first Africans landed in Jamestown, Virginia, indentured servitude rather than enslavement for life defined the system of labor in British North America. Some of the earliest black residents gained their freedom and imported their own black and white servants under the colonies' "headright system," which encouraged settlement by offering free men fifty acres of free land for each new worker brought into the colony. By the late 1600s and early 1700s, however, this labor system came to a close when the British colonies instituted new laws condemning Africans to servitude *durante vita*—"for life." Borrowing from the Caribbean experience, colonial legislators also instituted "black codes" and sought to redefine Africans as property, or "things," by excluding them from the "rights of Englishmen."

Like their Caribbean and Latin American counterparts, African Americans in British North America resisted enslavement in myriad ways. Before making the shift to perpetual enslavement, blacks often joined forces with white indentured servants and sought to escape from servitude together. As the colonies defined blacks as bondspeople in perpetuity, African Americans intensified their efforts to build families and communities as a foundation for diverse forms of resistance, including flight, rebellion, and plots to rebel. In the wake of the American Revolutionary War, African Americans heightened their struggle for freedom by participating in mass demonstrations and protests leading to the break with England and the creation of the new republic.

Although the American Revolution failed to abolish human bondage, it stimulated the growth of the free black population and established a new philosophical context for the African American struggle for freedom. Part II examines the arrival of African Americans in the British colonies; their shift from a somewhat fluid system of servitude to a color-conscious system of bondage for life; the development of African American culture and changing forms of resistance to enslavement; and the growth of the free black population in the wake of the American Revolution and the rhetoric of the "rights of man."

∽

CHAPTER 3

The Transition to African Labor

As suggested in Chapter 2, a variety of international and local forces shaped the African experience in the New World. These forces represented the complicated interaction of historical changes in Europe, America, and Africa. The results, however, were never predetermined. They depended on the volition, culture, and politics of African peoples, as well as the vagaries of international relations, geography, and economics during the expansion of commercial capitalism. African peoples in Latin America and the Caribbean played a key role in shaping their own experience over time and space, but the forces unleashed by the imperatives of capitalist production limited their choices. This chapter examines similar though quite different processes in British North America, where black life also had its earliest beginnings in Spanish conquest and settlement of the region.

AMBIGUOUS BEGINNINGS

The first Africans came to North America with Spanish-speaking explorers who pushed northward from the Caribbean into the Gulf of Mexico, Florida, and the south Atlantic coast. As early as 1526, Africans were part of Lucas Vásquez de Ayllón's settlement of nearly five hundred people on the future site of South Carolina. Two years later, another contingent of blacks entered the Tampa Bay region with Pánfilo de Narváez. When the indigenous people violently resisted their settlement, the Spanish-speaking African Estebanico (Estebán, or Stephen) was one of the few survivors. A skilled linguist, Estebán played a major role in the small party's escape and remarkable eight-year transcontinental journey across the southwest from Florida to Mexico City, the capital of New Spain. As the Spanish officer Alvar Núñez Cabeza de Vaca later recalled, Estebán "was constantly in conversation [with indigenous peoples], finding out about routes, towns, and other matters we wished to know." In search of the fabled Seven Cities of Cíbola, which were reputed to have streets and houses adorned with gold, Estebán later died on a return expedition to the area around Arizona and New Mexico.

Other Africans accompanied Francisco Vásquez de Coronado into the southwest and Hernando de Soto into the southeast. By 1565, Africans also helped the Spanish establish St. Augustine, Florida, the first permanent non-Indian settlement in North America. Before the British established their settlement at Jamestown in 1607, nearly 100 Africans inhabited St. Augustine, which served as an outpost to protect Spanish ships from European pirates. Although most of these Africans were men, the wealthiest settlers reported a handful of African and mulatto women among their servants and slaves.

From the beginning of Spanish settlement of North America, Africans resisted enslavement by running away and joining forces with the indigenous peoples. Ayllón's

Although most Africans arrived in British North America, the first settlement emerged in Spanish America. This is a modern illustration of the free black settlement of Gracia Real de Santa Teresa de Mose, located about two miles north of St. Augustine. *Courtesy of Florida Museum of Natural History, Fort Mose Exhibition*

SOURCES FROM THE PAST

1619

John Rolfe Describes the First Africans to Arrive in Virginia

In May [1619] came in the *Margaret of Bristoll*, with foure and thirty men, all well and in health; and also many deuout gifts: and we were much troubled in examining some scandalous letters sent into *England*, to disgrace this Country with barrennesse, to discourage the aduenturers, and so bring it and vs to ruine and confusion. Notwithstanding, we finde by them of best experience, an industrious man not other waies imploied, may well tend foure akers of Corne, and 1000. plants of Tobacco; and where they say an aker will yeeld but three or foure barrels, we haue ordinarily foure or fiue, but of new ground six, seuen, and eight, and a barrell of Pease and Beanes, which we esteeme as good as two of Corne, which is after thirty or forty bushels an aker, so that one man may prouide Corne for fiue; and apparell for two by the profit of his Tobacco. . . .

The 25. of *Iune* [1619] came in the *Triall* with Corne and Cattell all in safety, which tooke from vs cleerely all feare of famine; then our gouernour and councell caused Burgesses to be chosen in all places, and met at a generall Assembly, where all matters were debated [that were] thought expedient for the good of the Colony, and Captaine *Ward* was sent to *Monahigan* in new *England*, to fish in May, and returned the latter end of May, but to small purpose, for they wanted Salt. The *George* also was sent to *New-found-land* with the Cape Merchant: there she bought fish, that defraied her charges, and made a good voyage in seuen weekes.

About the last of August [1619] came in a dutch man of warre that sold vs twenty Negars: and *Iapazous* King of *Patawomeck*, came to Iames towne, to desire two ships to come trade in his Riuer, for a more plentifull yeere of Corne had not beene in a long time, yet very contagious, and by the trechery of one *Poule*, in a manner turned heathen, wee were very iealous the Saluages would surprize vs.

Source: Captain John Smith, *Works*, 1608–1631, ed. Edward Arber (Westminster, U.K.: Archibald Constable and Co., 1895), Part II: 540–543.

colony in the southeast collapsed soon after blacks set fire to several buildings and escaped into surrounding Indian territory. Because Africans ran away and allied with Amerindians, Spanish authorities frequently complained that blacks were the "worst enemies we can have."

Black life in North America originated in the non-English parts of the continent, but the British colonies absorbed the vast majority of Africans and their descendants. England also set the principal socioeconomic, political, and cultural parameters of African American life during the colonial era. The first Africans entered the region via ships engaged in piracy against the Spanish colonies in the Caribbean. In 1619, a "Dutch man-of-war" dispatched the initial group of 20 Africans in the English settlement of Jamestown, Virginia (see box). Over the next two decades, the black population increased slowly, rising to no more than 170 by 1640.

SOURCES FROM THE PAST

1655

The Virginia Court Awards Anthony Johnson, a Former Slave, Custody of His Slave Property

The deposition of Captain Samuel Goldsmith taken (in open court) 8th of March Sayth, That beinge at the howse of Anthony Johnson Negro (about the beginninge of November last to receive a hogshead of tobacco) a Negro called John Casor came to this Deponent, and told him that hee came into Virginia for seaven or Eight yeares (per Indenture) And that hee had demanded his freedome of his master Anthony Johnson; And further said that Johnson had kept him his servant seaven yeares longer than hee ought. . . . Further this deponent saith That mr. Robert Parker and George Parker they knew that the said Negro had an Indenture (in on Mr. Carye hundred on the other side of the Baye) And the said Anthony Johnson did not tell the negro goe free The said John Casor would recover most of his Cowes of him; Then Anthony Johnson (as this deponent did suppose) was in a feare. Upon this his Sonne in lawe, his wife and his 2 sonnes perswaded the said Anthony Johnson to sett the said John Casor free. more saith not

Samuel Goldsmith

This daye Anthony Johnson Negro made his complaint to the Court against mr. Robert Parker and declared that hee deteyneth his servant John Casor negro (under pretence that the said Negro is a free man). The Court seriously consideringe and maturely weighinge the premises, doe fynde that the said Mr. Robert Parker most unjustly keepeth the said Negro from Anthony Johnson his master as appeareth by the deposition of Captain Samuel Goldsmith and many probable circumstances. It is therefore the Judgement of the Court and ordered That the said John Casor Negro forthwith returne unto the service of his said master Anthony Johnson, And that mr. Robert Parker make payment of all charge in the suit, also Execution.

Source: Warren M. Billings, ed., *The Old Dominion in the Seventeenth Century: A Documentary History of Virginia, 1660–1689* (Chapel Hill: University of North Carolina Press, 1975), pp. 155–156.

Although 1619 marked the beginnings of African life in British North America, the arrival of blacks also signaled the rise of a multiracial, but unfree, labor force. Merchant elites sought labor from a variety of sources, including Amerindians, Europeans, and Africans. Thus, the first generation of Africans shared a subordinate status with white indentured servants and substantial ambiguity in their social status. Some could demand payment for their labor, gain their freedom, legally marry, own property, and even import servants of their own, including white ones (see box). Anthony Johnson arrived in the colony in the 1620s. Two decades later, Johnson had imported five servants for his own use and owned 250 acres of land under the colony's headright system, which rewarded with fifty acres of free land persons who brought workers into the colony. Another black man, Richard Johnson, apparently no relation to Anthony, imported two white servants and received one hundred acres of land. Another black received five hundred acres for importing a total of eleven people. These early Africans used their access to land and freedom to initiate the building of black families. By the 1650s, for example, Anthony Johnson had married Mary, described as "a Negro woman" who had entered the colony in 1622. The couple's household soon included no fewer than four children, who later inherited the family's wealth.

Early colonial Africans also gained substantial access to English courts of law, partly because of the Africans' conversion to Christianity and growing familiarity with European culture. In 1624, for example, John Phillip, described as "a negro Christened in *England* 2 years since," testified in the Virginia court against a white man. At about the same time, the Virginia court mandated that the "negro caled by the name of *brase* [apparently a sailor] shall belonge to *Sir Francis Wyatt, Governor etc.,* As his servant"; the court also ordered that another black, possibly the same "brase," receive "monthly for his labor forty pownd waight of good marchantable tobacco for his labor and service so longe as he remayneth" with Lady Yeardley, wife of the former colonial governor. Such evidence suggests that Africans who entered North America during the first years were not "slaves for life." Some apparently arrived as free men and remained so. Others served a period of years and then gained their freedom. Still others faced a long period of servitude that covered the balance of their lives, but this fate also greeted some white servants as well.

Although indentured servitude offered opportunities for freedom, it was nonetheless a form of unfree labor marked by unequal class relations and economic exploitation. Earlier forms of European labor exploitation conditioned the rise of indentured servitude in England and later in North America. Until the onset of European expansion overseas, English society had recognized a condition known as villeinage. Defined as hereditary servitude passed on from father to son by law, villeinage deprived Englishmen of their freedom and subjected them to the arbitrary will of the "lords of the land." The villein (servant) and his family had few property or contractual rights and could be bought and sold with or without the land on which they worked. Once the legal, hereditary, or customary practice of villeinage declined, however, the British government instituted the system of indentured servitude, which reinforced old patterns of inequality. Although the system represented a voluntary agreement between free people, indentured servants could also be bought and sold to the highest bidders and "transferred like movable goods or chattels."

Indentured servitude in America was even harsher than its English counterpart. Separated by distance from relatives, friends, and English law, New World servants faced substantial abuse. Whereas servants entered annual or short-term contracts in England, most contracted for as much as seven years in the colonies of North America, where they often served for more than seven years and sometimes for life. Colonial law permitted masters to increase the length of service for a variety of offenses, particularly running away and theft. In Lancaster County, Virginia, for example, a white servant, Christopher Adams, escaped from his master for six months. When later captured by authorities, the man received a stiff penalty in the Virginia court: three years' additional service—one year for the time away, another for the crop that he would have produced, and another for the expenses involved in his recovery. Since white indentured servants frequently stole food and held communal feasts in the woods near plantations, persons found guilty of hog killing faced a year of additional service to the owner and a year of service to the informer. A third offense could result in death. Women servants often had additional years added to their term for pregnancy during the period of their indenture. In one case, when a woman became pregnant and delivered a child, the colonial court added two years' service to her contract.

Colonial court records are replete with cases of mistreatment of white servants by white masters. In 1623, one white Virginia servant, Thomas Best, wrote: "My master Atkins . . . hath sold me for a £150 sterling like a damnd slave." As early as 1614, John Rolfe reported that: this "buying and selling of [white] men and bodies" had already become a scandal in the colony. Captain John Smith also protested the "extortion and oppression" of men who sold "even men, women and children for who will give most." An extreme case involved John and Alice Proctor and their servants Elizabeth Abbott and Elias Hinton, who died after a series of beatings, administered by the Proctors as well as by other servants. A colonial official counted five hundred lashes inflicted on the girl at one time and warned Proctor that he might as well kill her and be done with it. A woman, Alice Bennett, examined the girl's body and found it riddled with holes and sores. Witnesses said that Proctor beat Hinton to death with a rake. Yet there is no evidence that the perpetrators of these abuses were punished by law.

Indentured servitude subordinated whites as well as blacks, but the system took its greatest toll on Africans. From the outset of British settlement in North America, most whites arrived with written contracts and recourse to courts of law, whereas the first Africans were literally "sold" to the colonists in exchange for "vitualles." Colonial records regularly reported ships arriving in Virginia to sell Africans in exchange for commodities like tobacco as well as food. Although whites lay legal claim to better treatment and specified periods of service, Africans soon confronted laws and social practices that permitted servant holders to claim their labor for an indefinite period of time. In 1640, for example, Maryland passed a statute specifying that "all persons who were imported without indentures [are] to serve four years (slaves [that is, blacks] excepted)." Thus, despite fluidity in their early encounter with the Chesapeake labor system, blacks faced the brunt of new and existing European forms of labor exploitation.

As early as the mid-1620s, the exploitation of African labor took on increasingly racial overtones. In 1624 and 1625, Virginia conducted two censuses that revealed the subordination of Africans within a larger context of unfree labor. In 1624, none of the twenty-two blacks enumerated had last names, and almost 50 percent had no names at all. The 1625 census offered more complete data for whites than the earlier one, including age and date of arrival of ships, but failed to record similar information for Africans. Moreover, blacks were usually placed at the end of such lists along with Amerindians. By 1627, the will of George Yeardley, governor of Virginia (1619–1621, 1626–1627), offered an even clearer separation of blacks from whites. Yeardley equated Africans and European servants with things rather than persons, but he further identified blacks as a separate category: to his heirs, he left "goode debts, chattels, servants, negars, cattle or any other thing." In Yeardley's mind, blacks occupied a status just above cattle and just below other white servants.

The increasing legal and social separation of black and white laborers escalated over time. In 1639, a Maryland civil rights statute reflected the gradual emergence of extended servitude and even slavery for Africans: "All the inhabitants of the province of Christian standing (slaves excepted) to enjoy full liberties and rights of Englishmen." A year later, the Virginia court sentenced white and black fugitives to different terms of service for running away from their master. A Dutchman and a Scotsman received an added year of service, whereas the African, John Punch, received a sentence of servitude for life. Until the 1630s and 1640s, the colonial statutes usually dealt with all persons defined as "unfree" or servant labor. Now such laws started to recognize distinctions between enslaved Africans and other unfree workers. Moreover, until this time, the terms used to describe unfree labor ("Irish Slave," "Negro Servants," and "Negars") were quite ambiguous.

Changing gender and sexual relations also underscored the increasing racialization of servitude. By the 1630s, the Chesapeake colonies had started to tax the field labor of black women, whereas before, the state had taxed all male labor, excluding that of both black and white women. At the same time, Virginia and Maryland instituted new constraints on interracial sex and marriage. On 17 September 1630, the Virginia court sentenced a white man, Hugh Davis, to a sound whipping "before an assembly of Negroes and others for abusing himself to the dishonor of God and shame of Christians, by defiling his body in lying with a negro" (presumably a woman). In 1640, another white man had "to do penance in church according to laws of England, for getting a negroe woman with child and the woman whipt." During the early 1650s, a white man won a slander suit for the statement that "he had a black bastard in Virginia."

Despite growing social restrictions on interracial sexual relations, such relationships persisted. Indeed, since black children took the status of their fathers in early colonial Chesapeake society, for awhile the free black and mulatto population increased faster than the white population. Some whites feared and sought to reverse this process. In the meantime, however, the number of children resulting from the unions of free and servant white women and black men also markedly increased. Because these children took the status of their fathers, who were invariably servants or slaves, some planters actually sanctioned and even encouraged these interracial relations. They gained not only access to the future labor of young children but also an extension of the mother's term of service, ostensibly to cover the labor lost during pregnancy.

The enslavement of Africans was also related to the impact of Europeans on Amerindian society. As in the Caribbean and Latin America, the arrival of the English provoked widespread resistance among the indigenous people. In Virginia, for example, Europeans encountered a powerful "confederacy" of some six indigenous ethnic groups. In 1622 and again in 1644, Amerindians attacked the Virginia colony, killing some eight hundred people. In the second attack, however, the war dragged on for two years, and the colonists turned the tide. By 1646, the Virginia assembly was describing the Indians as "driven from the townes and habitations, lurking up & downe the woods in small numbers." Warfare, combined with the onslaught of European diseases, particularly smallpox, reduced the indigenous population from an estimated eight or nine thousand in 1607 to fewer than two thousand during the 1660s. Coupled with growing restrictions on the exploitation of white labor, the declining indigenous population offered an additional rationale for the enslavement of African people. Over the next half century, British North America would define Africans as "slaves for life."

EXPANSION AND CONSOLIDATION OF AFRICAN SLAVERY

As resistance, warfare, and disease undermined the labor potential of indigenous people, and as white indentured servants gained their freedom and occupied their own land, the British colonists intensified their search for African labor. By the onset of the American Revolution in 1775, nearly 300,000 Africans had entered the British colonies of North America. Most of these blacks came from the Senegambia, Sierra Leone, Windward Coast, Gold Coast, Bight of Biafra, and Angola regions of West and central Africa (see table). During the first third of the eighteenth

Africans Imported into British North America, by Origin				
	Percent of Slaves by Identifiable Origin Imported By—			
Coastal Region of Origin	(1) Virginia 1710–1769	(2) South Carolina 1733–1807	(3) British Slave Trade 1690–1807	(4) Speculative Estimate, All Imported into North America (%)
Senegambia	14.9	19.5	5.5	13.3
Sierra Leone	5.3	6.8	4.3	5.5
Windward Coast	6.3	16.3	11.6	11.4
Gold Coast	16.0	13.3	18.4	15.9
Bight of Benin	—	1.6	11.3	4.3
Bight of Biafra	37.7	2.1	30.1	23.3
Angola	15.7	39.6	18.2	24.5
Mozambique- Madagascar	4.1	0.7	*	1.6
Unknown	—	—	0.6	0.2
Total	100.0	100.0	100.0	100.0

*Included in Angola figure.
Source: Philip C. Curtin, The Atlantic Slave Trade: A Census (Madison: University of Wisconsin Press, 1969), p. 157. Reprinted by permission of The University of Wisconsin Press.

century, these Africans experienced a preponderance of men over women, widespread disease, and high death rates. Thereafter, however, as the ratio of women to men gradually improved and the death rate declined, the black population rose from less than 70,000 in 1720, to an estimated 236,400 in 1750, to nearly 500,000 in 1770. The tobacco- and rice-producing regions of the Upper and Lower South, respectively, claimed the vast majority of these Africans. In rapid succession, between 1660 and the early 1700s, the British colonies codified the enslavement of Africans and their descendants as *durante vita,* or "slaves for life."

The Chesapeake Region

The legal transformation of Africans into slaves for life gained its first and sharpest articulation in the Upper South, or Chesapeake, region—in the colonies of Virginia and Maryland, both of which border the Chesapeake Bay (see map). Virginia passed its statute in 1661, followed by Maryland three years later:

> Bee itt Enacted . . . That all Negroes or other slaues already within the Prouince And all Negroes and other slaues to bee hereafter imported into the Prouince shall serue Durante Vita[.] And all Children born of any Negro or other slaue shall be Slaues as their ffathers were for the terme of their liues [.]

At the same time, the colonies blocked earlier avenues to freedom, including conversion to Christianity, mastery of European language and culture, and access to land and labor through the headright system. In 1670, the Virginia legislature prohibited blacks from importing white servants. "No negro . . . though baptised and enjoyed their own freedom shall be capable of any such purchase of Christians [that is, whites]." By the early 1700s, colonial legislators also redefined offspring of blacks by the status of their mother, rather than the status of their father. Although white women gained some protection from unscrupulous efforts to enslave their children, black women now faced the prospects of unwanted children by free white men. Such practices enabled planters to retain access to black women while curtailing interracial sexual relations among their wives and daughters. The Maryland statute explicitly stated that the new law aimed at "divers freeborne English women forgettfull of their free Condicon and to the disgrace of our Nation doe intermarry with Negro Slaues."

Once the Chesapeake codified Africans as slaves for life, the importation of Africans dramatically increased. In 1680, about 4,600 blacks lived in the Chesapeake. Two decades later the black population had trebled, rising to 13,000, almost all of whom were enslaved people. By 1770, Africans and their descendants numbered about 200,000. They made up about a third of the total population, more than two-thirds of all laborers, and nearly all agricultural workers. Whereas the first generation of blacks had arrived primarily from the West Indies and included substantial numbers of women as well as men, the new wave came directly from Africa and was predominantly male. Between 1700 and 1740, for example, African-born men made up about 50 to 75 percent of the estimated 54,000 blacks imported into

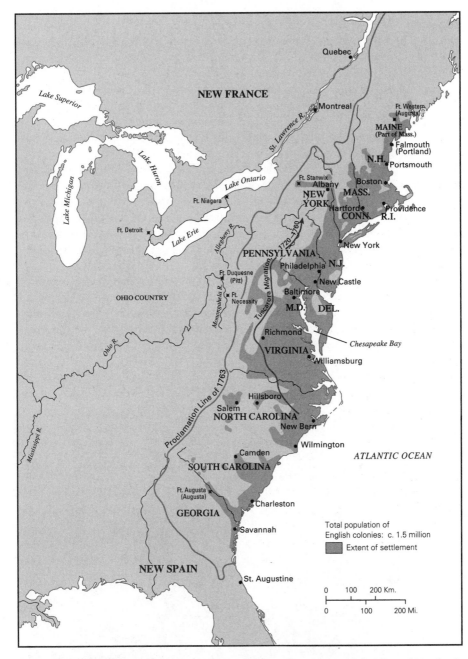

British North America, Eighteenth Century. The Chesapeake colonies of Virginia and Maryland claimed the largest concentration of Africans by the 1770s. Although blacks constituted about a third of the total Chesapeake population and only about 5 percent of the northern colonies, they made up a much larger percentage of the total in the Deep South, where they became a majority in South Carolina and in the low-country areas of Georgia.

Virginia and Maryland. Men outnumbered women by a ratio of nearly two to one, and black women found it impossible to sustain the African American birthrate. Only during the 1740s would African Americans gradually overcome the sexual imbalance and develop a self-sustaining population.

As in the Caribbean, once Africans survived the Middle Passage and arrived in the Chesapeake, they faced the rigors of New World bondage. They were sold to the highest bidders, stripped of their African names, and dispersed across work units of various sizes. As in other New World slave societies, life in the Chesapeake revolved around staple production, namely tobacco. A delicate crop, tobacco required strenuous labor and meticulous care. Under the strict supervision of overseers, gangs of slaves sowed the seeds during late winter or early spring in specially prepared beds. Thereafter, they tended the small plants until they were ready for transplanting to the tobacco fields. At the appropriate moment, when a spring or early summer rain occurred, the plants were carefully removed from their beds and transplanted. Blacks had to work feverishly to complete the job before the ground dried and destroyed the small seedlings.

Following transplanting, tobacco cultivation entered its peak growing season between June and August. Most new Africans arrived in the Chesapeake during this period, when the crop demanded consistent hoeing, weeding, and plowing. Workers then confronted the difficult chores of harvesting and preparing the plant for market. These processes involved cutting stalks close to the ground and transporting

Shipping tobacco along the shores of the Chesapeake, Virginia Tobacco Wharf, 1775. *Yale University Art Gallery*

bundles to well-ventilated tobacco houses, where plants were hung for curing. After curing, Africans carefully sorted the cured stalks by quality and then stripped the tobacco leaves from the stalk. Finally, they bound, pressed, and prepared the crop for shipping. Tobacco cultivation was a difficult and arduous process that frequently strained "every nerve" of the bondsmen and -women, but life and labor were even more difficult in the Lower South, where rice production predominated during the colonial era.

The Lower South

African labor emerged later in the Deep South colonies of South Carolina and Georgia than it did in the Chesapeake. In 1670, the first Africans entered the British Lower South with planters who migrated from the island of Barbados. The Lower South bypassed the period of ambiguity that marked the rise of slavery in the Upper South. From the outset, the proprietors used Barbados as a model for the establishment of plantation labor in South Carolina. As one spokesman put it, "Negroes and other servants" were "fitt for such labor as wilbe there required." Between 1706 and the coming of the American Revolution, South Carolina imported an estimated 95,000 blacks. Unlike in the Chesapeake, however, South Carolina's black population became a majority. As early as 1708, Africans made up over 50 percent of the colony's total population of 9,580. In 1720, the number of Africans reached an estimated 12,000, compared with about 7,000 whites. By the 1750s, blacks made up nearly 40,000 of the colony's 65,000 people.

Although African bondage emerged from the beginning of South Carolina's history, the character of slavery and the use of black labor nonetheless changed over time. Until the 1720s, life for Africans and African Americans was less rigid than it would become. Since most of these early arrivals came in small groups from the West Indies, some were already American born and had mastered elements of the English language, customs, and culture. On arrival in early colonial South Carolina, blacks lived on small farms and worked closely with landowners, who produced mainly for the West Indian market. Since black and white men frequently found themselves on opposite ends of a sawbuck, one historian has described early colonial South Carolina as years of "sawbuck equality."

South Carolina whites acknowledged the value of Africans to the development and protection of the land. They depended on Africans for understanding of the local geography, climate, and topography, all of which resembled West Africa more than the English countryside. Africans identified useful flora and fauna, accenting what to avoid as poisonous and what to use for food, beverage, and medicine. Since the colony feared invasion by the Spanish, French, and Indians, colonial officials also drafted bondsmen during war times and regularly enlisted them into the militia. Black soldiers fought in every major war that faced the early colony. As late as 1708, the colonial governor reported on

the whole number of the militia of this province, 950 white men, fit to bear arms . . . to which might be added a like number of negro slaves, the captain of

As suggested by this advertisement, South Carolina planters took special care to import Africans knowledgeable in rice cultivation. Although Lower South slaves died in disproportionately large numbers until the late eighteenth century, this ad also reveals efforts to prolong the life of bondsmen. *Library of Congress*

TO BE SOLD. on board the Ship *Bance-Iſland*, on tueſday the 6th of *May* next, at *Aſhley-Ferry*; a choice cargo of about 250 fine healthy NEGROES, juſt arrived from the Windward & Rice Coaſt. —The utmoſt care has already been taken, and ſhall be continued, to keep them free from the leaſt danger of being infeated with the SMALL-POX, no boat having been on board, and all other communication with people from *Charles-Town* prevented.
Auſtin, Laurens, & Appleby.

N. B. Full one Half of the above Negroes have had the SMALL-POX in their own Country.

each company being obliged by act of Assembly, to enlist, train up, and bring into the field for each white, one able slave armed with a gun or lance, for each man in his company.

Moreover, another contemporary observer wrote that the law "gives every one of those his freedom, who in time of an invasion kills an enemy." When Virginia offered to send white soldiers to South Carolina in exchange for black women, South Carolina authorities rejected the offer, saying that it would be "impracticable" to deprive black men of their women. Such an act, they believed, "might have occasioned a Revolt."

During the early to mid-eighteenth century, South Carolina made the transition from a mixed economy of small farming and cattle raising for the West Indian market to increasing dependence on rice production and international trade. As in the pioneer phase, African knowledge of rice cultivation as well as their labor played key roles in the success of the Deep South economy. Many Africans entered the low country of colonial South Carolina with knowledge of rice planting, hoeing, processing, and cooking techniques. They planted rice in the spring by creating a hole in the ground with the heel of their foot, planting the seed, and then covering it with their foot. Africans also influenced the use of the mortar-and-pestle method of cleaning and processing rice. Like their West African counterparts, South Carolina blacks, usually women, placed small amounts of grain in a wooden mortar (made from the upright trunk of a pine or cypress tree). They then beat the grain with long wooden clubs or pestles "with a sharp edge at one end for removing husks and a flat tip at the other for whitening the grains."

As rice plantations rapidly expanded, the colony entered a new and more intense era of labor exploitation, and the quality of black life deteriorated. Even more so than for tobacco, rice cultivation required grueling labor in unhealthy surroundings. From the beginning, blacks worked in damp swamplands, but the introduction of floodgates for irrigating the rice fields intensified the health hazards that they faced. Irrigation required extensive ditch digging and long periods of standing and work in stagnant water. Yet unlike tobacco planters, rice producers adopted the task, rather than the gang, system of labor and permitted blacks to set their own pace, as long as they performed a set number of specified tasks. Moreover, rice planters allotted small parcels of land to bondsmen and -women for their own subsistence use and gave them limited access to marketing outlets for their goods. Africans and their American-born descendants would later elaborate the system of tasks and access to small plots of land into important instruments of resistance against the system of slavery itself. By completing their tasks early, they managed to carve out time for themselves for cultivating their own crops, participating in the market economy, and increasing their level of autonomy.

The task system, small garden plots, and marketing opportunities were insufficient to allay the harsh impact of rice production. South Carolina blacks experienced not only intense suffering through the imposition of rice cultivation but also greater demographic imbalance, disease, and mortality than their Chesapeake counterparts. African men outnumbered women, reaching nearly 130 men to every 100 women in some places by the late 1720s. Moreover, although planters imported 15,000 new Africans between 1734 and 1740, the black population rose from about 26,000 to only 40,000 during the same period, suggesting a high death rate among the slave population. This pattern resembled the Caribbean, where planters often "worked slaves to death" because they could rely on cheap sources of new workers from the transatlantic slave trade. Only slowly would South Carolina's black population become self-sustaining, as we will see, following the imposition in 1741 of a prohibitive tax on the importation of new Africans after the Stono Rebellion of 1739.

The rapid growth of rice plantations also shaped the early history of Georgia. Although the colony of Georgia emerged during the early 1730s, it did not adopt slave labor until the mid-1750s. Georgia had its origins as a "philanthropic enterprise," designed by English elites to reform elements of the nation's "criminal classes." The trustees believed that slavery would compromise efforts to create a class of virtuous, hard-working, small landholders. Thus, colonial statutes initially prohibited the importation and use of slaves. Following the failure to attract white workers in sufficient numbers during the 1740s and under growing pressure from South Carolina planters who wished to expand their area of rice cultivation, the British Parliament permitted the introduction of human bondage. After passage of the new law in 1750, planters from neighboring South Carolina flooded into Georgia to set up rice plantations using enslaved African labor. By the eve of the

As rice plantations rapidly expanded during the early eighteenth century, the Lower South entered an intense period of labor exploitation. This photo shows slaves at work in rice fields. *Library of Congress*

Revolution, the colony's black population had increased to about 15,000, roughly 50 percent of the total (see box).

Africans not only played a role in the Deep South colonies of British North America but also accompanied the French settlement of Louisiana. As the British pronounced blacks slaves for life, the French colonized the Louisiana territory with African labor. By 1718, a French company under the leadership of the Scotsman John Law laid out the city of New Orleans and encouraged the importation of slave labor. By 1750, the colony had a population of about 10,000, nearly 50 percent enslaved blacks. Owing primarily to African labor, Louisiana would become a major sugar-producing region with a decidedly Caribbean pattern of African bondage.

Although tobacco and rice dominated the working lives of blacks in the mid-eighteenth-century colonial south, African slaves worked in a variety of occupations. Alongside rice cultivation, Deep South planters also produced indigo as a major cash crop. In North Carolina, the production of turpentine, pitch, and other naval stores from the rich pine forests represented major profits in the employment of black labor. For its part, the Chesapeake became an important source of slave-produced wheat crops as well as tobacco. Similarly, despite its growth as a sugar-producing area, from the outset Louisiana employed Africans to produce indigo,

CHANGING HISTORICAL INTERPRETATIONS

The Controversy over the Origins of Slavery

The enslavement of Africans in the Americas is a subject of ongoing scholarly and popular debate. Although current scholarship shows how African bondage emerged from a complicated series of global demographic, economic, social, cultural, ideological, and political developments, the debate initially churned around a set of sharply but narrowly drawn issues: Was African slavery the consequence of racist attitudes and behavior among Europeans? Was it a result of economic necessity in a New World of bountiful land and natural resources but few workers? Did it emerge from the time that Africans first set foot on British/Amerindian soil? Did it develop later? Did it represent continuity with a similar status among Africans on the continent?

Until about the mid-twentieth century, most professional historians, mainly whites, followed the lead of U. B. Phillips, the leading scholar on African bondage in the United States. In the view of these historians, American slavery rescued blacks from an even harsher bondage in their own land. In the meantime, African American scholars like W. E. B. Du Bois and Carter G. Woodson countered the racist interpretation of black bondage. In books, and in articles published in magazines and journals like the *Crisis* and the *Journal of Negro History*, these scholars emphasized the role of whites and white racism in establishing and perpetuating human bondage. With the advent of the modern civil rights movement during the 1950s and 1960s, these scholars' ideas and interpretation gained increasing support among white historians, culminating in Winthrop Jordan's *White over Black* (1968). Jordan concluded that racial prejudice and cultural and psychological factors interacted with certain material forces to set in motion "a cycle of Negro debasement"—that is, a race-based system of human bondage. The debate nonetheless continued, albeit on somewhat different terrain.

As early as the 1940s, the West Indian historian Eric Williams foreshadowed the rise of a different interpretation. In 1944 Williams wrote his path-breaking study of African bondage, *Capitalism and Slavery.* He complained that scholars too often equated slavery with black people, racism, and the existence of color prejudice. In his view, this correlation was wrong: "Slavery was not born of racism: rather, racism was the consequence of slavery. Unfree labor in the New World was brown, white, black, and yellow; Catholic, Protestant and pagan." In other words, Williams forcefully argued that slavery had economic roots. Although Williams's book gained few adherents in the early aftermath of World War II, his emphasis on economic factors experienced a revival in the wake of Jordan's *White over Black.*

Several historians of Africa and the African American experience—the late Guyanese scholar Walter Rodney, John Thornton, Peter Wood, Daniel Littlefield, and most recently Ira Berlin, among others—not only emphasized the role of European capitalism but also demonstrated how African bondage varied from place to place, over time, and by gender. Most importantly, however, these studies accent the hand that Africans took in shaping the institution of human bondage on the continent as well as in the New World. By emphasizing the interplay of people from Europe, Africa, and the Americas, this scholarship has important implications for current efforts to understand the multiracial nature of inequality in our own times. Research on the enslavement of blacks reminds us again that the African American experience opened on a global stage.

tobacco, rice, cotton, and forest products. In addition to the lowliest labor-intensive jobs in the colonial economy—collectors and dispensers of refuse, loaders and haulers of all kinds of commodities, builders of roads and canal passages—African Americans occupied a variety of skilled positions on plantations and farms as well as in cities. As noted in the table, Robert Carter's Chesapeake plantations employed enslaved blacks in a wide range of skilled occupations.

Virginia landowner George Mason also employed bondsmen as carpenters, coopers, sawyers, blacksmiths, tanners, curriers, shoemakers, spinners, weavers, knitters, and even whiskey makers. Mason's huge plantation provided timber and charcoal for the carpenters, coopers, and blacksmiths while his cattle, sheep, and orchards supplied skins, hides, wool, and fruit for his tanners, curriers, shoemakers, weavers, spinners, and distillers. As Mason's son later recalled, "It was very much the practice with gentlemen of landed and slave estates . . . to employ and pay but few [free white] tradesmen." White craftsmen, however, would gain a stronger foothold in the North, where blacks made up only a small percentage of the total population. Nonetheless, as we will see, northern blacks concentrated disproportionately in the port cities of Philadelphia, Boston, and New York, where they also entered a relatively broad range of occupations.

Occupations of Male Bondsmen on Robert Carter's Chesapeake Plantations, 1733	
Agricultural	
Field hands	74
Drivers	13
Family farmers	0
Total	87
Semiskilled	
Servants	0
Sawyers	3
Carters	2
Boatsmen	1
Total	6
Craftsmen	
Carpenters and coopers	6
Others	1
Total	7
Grand Total	**100**

Source: Adapted from Allan Kulikoff, *Tobacco and Slaves: The Development of Southern Cultures in the Chesapeake, 1680–1800* (Chapel Hill: University of North Carolina Press, 1986), p. 385. Copyright © 1986 by the University of North Carolina Press. Used by permission of the publisher.

The North

As the African American population reached a majority in the Deep South and an estimated one-third in the Chesapeake, it also gradually increased in the New England and middle colonies. As late as 1770, Africans and their descendants made up less than 5 percent of the total population in the northern colonies. Yet slavery emerged earlier in the North than in the Deep South. In 1626, the Dutch initiated the institution of African slavery in the North when New Amsterdam landowners imported enslaved Africans from the Dutch West Indian colony of Curaçao. After the British took over the colony and renamed it New York in 1664, they sanctioned and extended the institution of human bondage. The number of blacks in the colony increased from 2,000 during the early 1700s to about 10,000 (10 to 15 percent of the total) on the eve of the American Revolution.

Although New York contained the largest concentration of Africans and their American descendants in the North, other middle colonies and New England augmented the number of blacks in the region. Almost from the beginning of their arrival in New England, Africans faced the prospects of legal enslavement. Indeed, the New England colonies legalized slavery earlier than their southern counterparts. In 1641, Massachusetts enacted its Body of Liberties, which sanctioned both slavery and indentured servitude:

> There shall never be any bond slaverie, villinage or captivitie amongst us, unless it be lawfull Captives taken in just warres, and such strangers as willingly sell themselves or are sold to us. And these shall have all the libertieis and Christian usages which the law of God established in Israell concerning such persons doth morally require. This exempts none from servitude who shall be Judged thereto by Authoritie.

Until relatively recently, scholars assumed that a strong abolitionist sentiment undercut the growth of slavery in the North. As early as February 1688, the Germantown, Pennsylvania, Mennonites issued their historic protest against the African slave trade. During the eighteenth century, the New Jersey Quaker John Woolman would emerge as perhaps the most renowned of the Quaker advocates of abolition. Yet Massachusetts, Rhode Island, Connecticut, New Jersey, and, despite its early antislavery pronouncements, Quaker Pennsylvania enslaved significant numbers of blacks. Although relatively few blacks entered the northern colonies as compared with the South, the number of northern blacks nonetheless increased from under 2,000 in 1690, to just over 14,000 in 1720, to nearly 50,000 by 1770. The port cities of Philadelphia, Boston, Portsmouth (New Hampshire), and Newport attracted disproportionate numbers of blacks in their respective states: about 20 percent of Pennsylvania's total black population; 30 percent of that of Massachusetts and New Hampshire; and 50 percent of Rhode Island's.

By the 1770s, the wealthiest urbanites belonged to the slaveholding class—nearly 70 percent in Boston and Philadelphia. Small shopkeepers and artisans also owned a handful of slaves, giving one contemporary visitor the impression that "every" house in Boston had "one or two" slaves.

Engraving of enslaved blacks at work in New Amsterdam, c. 1642–1643. *I. N. Phelps Stokes Collection, Miriam and Ira D. Wallach Division of Art, Prints and Photographs, New York Public Library, Astor, Lenox and Tilden Foundations*

As elsewhere in British North America, the first wave of blacks entered the northern colonies from the West Indies. This pattern persisted until the 1740s, when wars on the continent limited the supply of white indentured servants. The number of white laborers also declined as earlier servants completed their indentures, moved west, and sought land of their own. Consequently, for the first time in the history of the northern colonies, landowners and merchants imported large numbers of blacks directly from Africa. Before 1741, for example, 70 percent of New York's black population came from the West Indies or other mainland sources. By 1750, the pattern had reversed itself—an estimated 70 percent of blacks now came directly from Africa, whereas only 30 percent arrived from the West Indies or other places in British America. From the outbreak of the Seven Years' War in 1756 through the early 1760s, Quaker merchants also imported rising numbers of Africans into Pennsylvania. In 1762 alone, some 500 enslaved blacks entered the Philadelphia region.

As the northern colonies increased their reliance on African labor, the earlier demographic balance between men and women broke down. Sex ratios shifted from a relatively equal distribution of black men and women to nearly two or three men to every woman. Black death rates also escalated, rising during the 1750s and

1760s to an estimated 60 per 1,000 persons in Boston and Philadelphia, compared with less than 30 per 1,000 for whites. Despite increasing northern participation in the international trade in human beings, however, this phenomenon was short-lived and involved far fewer people than those imported into the plantation economies of the Upper and Lower South. By the 1770s, northern whites turned again to European labor, and the African-born population declined.

Although their numbers were small compared with those of the Upper and Lower South, enslaved blacks nonetheless played an important role in the economy of New England and the middle colonies. They lived and worked on small farms, in coastal cities, and on large commercial farms, where they sometimes made up 50 percent of the labor force. The densest areas of black settlement included southern New England, Long Island, and northern New Jersey. The area around Narragansett Bay in Rhode Island and northern New Jersey included substantial estates with twenty or more bondsmen and -women, used to provide meat and agricultural crops for the West Indian sugar islands. Whereas black women worked as dairy maids and domestics of various kinds, these large estates employed black men in a wide variety of jobs, including work as stock minders, herdsmen, or "cowboys."

In some areas of northern New England, the Hudson Valley, and Pennsylvania, blacks made up as much as 25 percent of the work force. They worked not only in the wheat fields but also in the houses of their masters as domestics. However, since white indentured servants made up an estimated 75 percent of the total work force, some scholars argue that Africans were valued as much as status symbols as for labor in the wheat fields and houses of the colonial North. In their wills, for example, landowners often listed "slaves" among expensive clocks, jewelry, carriages, and other luxury goods of high value, rather than among livestock, implements, or farm tools. Few southern plantations recorded blacks in this way.

Other northern blacks worked in highly capitalized rural and urban industries. Located in the northern hinterlands, colonial tanneries, saltworks, and iron furnaces employed significant numbers of captive black workers. In these rural industries, Africans often made up the majority of workers classified as skilled and unskilled. Iron masters, the largest employers of industrial slaves, were sometimes the largest slaveholders in parts of Pennsylvania, New York, and New Jersey. As early as 1727, Pennsylvania iron masters expressed their dependence on black labor when they petitioned the colonial legislature to reduce the tariff duties on slaves so that they could keep their furnaces in operation.

In addition to doing housework (cooking, cleaning, tending gardens, and running errands for their owners), enslaved urban blacks labored in a wide range of general labor and manufacturing pursuits as teamsters, stockmen, dock workers, draymen, and sailors, on the one hand, and as shipyard, sail factory, and rope walk workers on the other. Although some employers supplemented bound labor with free white hands, others relied entirely on wage-earning slaves. According to William Penn, enslaved blacks were better than white servants, "For then . . . a man has them while they live"—that is, for life.

Although urban elites were the principal slaveowners in the North, urban bondsmen and -women lived in the least desirable, overcrowded, and unhealthy urban quarters. Seaport bondsmen and women occupied back rooms, lofts, closets, and back alleys. As a result of such overcrowding, some northern owners discouraged childbearing among blacks. One New Yorker advertised the sale of a cook, "because she breeds too fast for her owners to put up with such inconvenience." Others considered children of black women an added expense and sometimes gave them away. Such pressures on black women to curtail childbearing placed a severe strain on black urban families, which included few children.

Partly because of limitations on space, northern blacks gained opportunities to live outside the master's household and to hire their own time in the wage labor market. In exchange for a fixed amount of their earnings, slaveowners allowed them to dispose of a portion of their income as they saw fit. Self-employed slaves not only filled a variety of occupations in a diversified economy but also gained substantial control over their work, including the selection of employers and the opportunity to save money toward the purchase of their own freedom. As we will see, urban slavery also stimulated the rise of a small free black population. Still, although a disproportionate number of northern blacks worked in urban areas and in rural industries, most lived and labored on northern farms.

LEGAL DIMENSIONS

As the enslavement of Africans expanded in practice and in law, colonial officials adopted systematic "slave codes." Chesapeake legislators borrowed from the Caribbean slave codes and became a model for other colonies. Based on color and African origins, the slave codes played a key role in colonial efforts to control the movement and behavior of Africans and later African Americans. Such codes suppressed the human and civil rights of Africans and redefined them as property. The new laws eliminated the right of Africans to bear arms, engage in commerce, own property, move from place to place, or seek legal redress of their grievances in courts of law. Other provisions prohibited enslaved people from beating drums, assembling in large groups, or gaining legal sanction for their marriages, family, and community life.

The new colonial slave codes also covered a variety of specific offenses and established levels and types of punishment. Chesapeake legislators defined murder, rape, and repeated cases of theft as capital offenses for bondsmen, punishable by hanging. For robbing a house or store, blacks could receive sixty lashes by the sheriff and be placed in the pillory—with their ears nailed to posts and even severed from their heads. Lying, disobedience, or intransigence resulted in whipping, maiming, or branding. Such laws supported the master's right to implement strict disciplinary measures, including the killing of slaves deemed intransigent. In 1669, for example, Virginia passed "An act about the casual killing of slaves." The law stated:

> Be it enacted and declared by this grand assembly, if any slave resist his master (or other by his masters order correcting him) and by the extremity of the correction should chance to die, that his death shall not be accompted Felony, but the mas-

ter (or that other person appointed by the master to punish him) be acquit from molestation, since it cannot be prepensed malice (which alone makes murther Felony) should induce any man to destroy his own estate.

As the size of the black population increased in the Deep South, whites feared the growth of a black majority and soon passed some of the most stringent slave codes known to British North America. South Carolina planters and colonial officials repeatedly complained that the growing numbers of blacks enabled them "to drink, quarrel, fight, curse and swear, and profane... resorting in great companies together, which may give them an opportunity of executing any wicked designs." Accordingly, the South Carolina assembly not only deprived

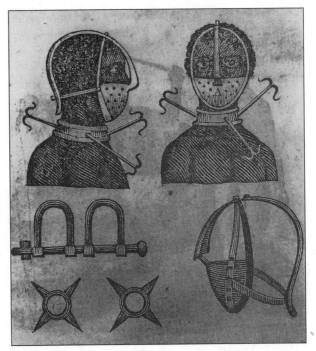

Plantation owners sometimes employed muzzles to control the communication of slaves with each other. Such devices also deprived the slave of food and water. *Library of Congress*

blacks of the right to bear arms, assemble, and move from place to place but also subjected them to the close regulation of their personal lives, including forms of dress. In the Negro Act of 1735, the South Carolina assembly limited the types of clothing that blacks could wear, arguing that African Americans wore "clothes much above the condition of slaves, for the procuring whereof they use sinister and evil methods." In order to enforce these restrictions, the colonial legislature strengthened the slave patrols, making it mandatory that every able-bodied white male take responsibility for regulating the behavior of blacks. South Carolina planters also provided a model for Georgia's legal and extralegal discipline of black labor. Southerners reinforced the slave codes with the whip, leg irons, chains, and even muzzling devices designed to control the slaves' communication with others as well as to restrict their intake of food and drink.

Although the African population of the North was smaller than that of the South, northern statutes also limited African people's movement and their ability to peaceably assemble, bear arms, and defend themselves from attacks by hostile whites. As early as 1656, Massachusetts excluded blacks from militia service. By 1705, New York had enacted the death penalty for any slave caught traveling alone forty miles from Albany. In 1705–1706, New England colonies prohibited blacks from "striking a white person." Violators could be whipped severely at the discretion of local magistrates. In 1730, Connecticut passed a similar but more stringent law that permitted the whipping of blacks who "attempted to strike" a white person. At the same time, municipalities reinforced colonial statutes by passing their own supplementary measures. Boston prohibited blacks from carrying a stick or cane or "any other thing of that nature" that might "be fit for quarrelling or fighting," and South Kingstown, Rhode Island, supplemented the colony's ban on the sale of "spirits" to slaves by prohibiting the sale of "cider" to bondsmen and -women as well.

Northern slave codes were nonetheless somewhat less stringent than those of the Upper and Lower South, where the law more often prescribed the death sentence, maiming, and dismemberment for certain slave offenses. Indeed, as early as 1656, New England legislatures prescribed the death penalty for any slaveowner who "willfully killed his servant or slave," although there is little evidence of convictions under the law. Among northern colonies, only Massachusetts instituted a law prohibiting interracial sexual relations. As the historian Lorenzo J. Greene noted, the Puritan colonies of New England promoted marriages and stable family among slaves:

> All the New England colonies required that wedding banns be read either at three public meetings or be posted in a public place at least fourteen days before the wedding. These regulations applied to black as well as white persons, slaves as well as freemen.

Moreover, northerners also prohibited the emancipation of old or infirm bondspeople without the posting of bonds to ensure their social welfare, but it does not follow that the law was uniformly upheld in practice.

Despite differences between the North and South, slave codes underscored a central paradox of human bondage—that is, how to treat human beings as property and at the same time recognize their humanity and make them responsible for their own behavior. The system of slavery posed problems because it sought to combine "things" and "humans" into a single category. Despite the legislative definition of Africans as property or chattel and the legalization of their sale in a commercial economy, the law recognized Africans as moral beings capable of discriminating between right and wrong. As such, the law burdened blacks with the liabilities and responsibilities of life in a human and civil society but denied them the immunities and privileges of membership in such communities. In other words, unlike bondage in West Africa, the European system of bondage recognized the enslaved person's humanity as a means of punishment and discipline, designed to reinforce the property rights of slaveholders. This irreconcilable paradox would mark the black experience from the rise of human bondage in the colonial period through the emancipation era of the mid-nineteenth century.

⤺

BY THE EVE OF THE AMERICAN REVOLUTION, the enslavement of Africans had expanded and consolidated on mainland British America. Although Africans initially shared a subordinate status with Native Americans and white indentured servants, they soon faced the full brunt of racial inequality. After a period of ambiguity in the Chesapeake region, colonial authorities defined Africans as slaves "for life." Virginia and Maryland not only systematically deprived Africans of human and civil rights in their own territory but also provided a precedent for the subsequent expansion of the plantation system and African labor into the Deep South. Although the northern colonies failed to develop an extensive plantation system, they gradually increased their participation in the buying and selling of human beings and used African labor in a variety of rural and urban pursuits. They also instituted slave codes and intensified the extralegal control of Africans and their American descendants. Such laws and social practices demonstrated certain continuities in the experience of bondsmen and -women across regional, generational, and class lines, but they were more severe in the South than in the North. Although African knowledge, technology, and labor enabled Europeans to survive and later profit from New World plantations, Africans and their American descendants would also use their African culture, beliefs, and ideas to resist social injustice in the new land.

CHAPTER 4

~

Responses to Bondage

D espite the enactment of stringent slave codes and forms of labor discipline, Africans and their American descendants were by no means passive in the face of enslavement. From their settlement at Jamestown in 1619 through the late seventeenth century, blacks in the Chesapeake region responded to bondage within the context of indentured servitude. During this period, Africans frequently ran away with white indentured servants, but the escalation of the international slave trade and the transformation of Africans into slaves for life disrupted this earlier pattern of cooperation and changed the context of black resistance. By the mid-eighteenth century, increasing numbers of blacks worked on large diversified plantations that housed owners, overseers, and a mixture of American- and African-born blacks. Building on both their African background and American experience, blacks gradually developed a new culture and forms of resistance. The emergence of New World families and communities not only enabled blacks to survive the rigors of bondage but also established the foundation for individual and collective struggles against the system of slavery itself. The development of African American culture and acts of resistance were by no means unproblematic, however. In addition to navigating the rough terrain of intercolonial and European-Amerindian wars, African Americans had to overcome their own internal cleavages and social conflicts.

THE EMERGENCE OF AFRICAN AMERICAN CULTURE AND COMMUNITIES

Key to the rise of African American culture and communities was the emergence of new modes of communication and new beliefs about the spirit and material worlds. North American blacks elaborated on a process of language and culture formation that had its beginnings on the west coast of Africa. Certain underlying characteristics of West African languages facilitated the emergence of New World linguistic and cultural forms. As the captive Olaudah Equiano revealed in his recollections, blacks from different language groups could understand each other: "One of my fellow prisoners spoke to a countryman of his, about the horses, who said they were the same kind they had in their country. I understood them, though they were from a distant part of Africa."

Language and Religion

A distinctive African American language emerged most clearly in the South Carolina and Georgia Sea Islands, where blacks made up a majority of the colonial population. In 1740, a South Carolina woman offered a reward for return of "a Negro fellow named Pierro but commonly stiles himself Peter." Pierro, or Peter, the owner claimed, "spoke English, French, and Dutch." Fifteen years later, a group of South Carolina runaways "spoke English, French, Spanish, and German." Arabic was also spoken by some blacks in the Carolinas. Some captives, such as the Muslim Job Ben Solomon, were literate in Arabic. Solomon has been called "the

Job Ben Solomon, the Islamic slave who gained his freedom and returned to his home in West Africa. *By permission of the Houghton Library/Harvard University*

SOURCES FROM THE PAST

1734

Job Ben
Solomon
Writes His
Way Out of
Slavery (as
described by
Thomas
Bluett)

Job, who is now about 31 or 32 years of age, was born at a town called Boonda [Bondu] in the county of Galumbo (in our maps Catumbo) in the kingdom of Futa in Africa; which lies on both sides the River Senegal, and on the south side reaches as far as the River Gambia.

In February, 1730, Job's father hearing of an English ship at Gambia River, sent him, with two servants to attend him, to sell two Negroes, and to buy paper, and some other necessaries; but desired him not to venture over the river, because the country of the Mandingoes, who are enemies to the people of Futa, lies on the other side. Job not agreeing with Captain Pike (who commanded the ship, lying then at Gambia, in the service of Captain Henry Hunt, brother to Mr. William Hunt, merchant, in Little Tower-street, London) sent back the two servants to acquaint his father with it, and to let him know that he intended to go farther. Accordingly having agreed with another man, named Loumein Yoas, who understood the Mandingoe language, to go with him as his interpreter, he crossed the River Gambia, and disposed of his Negroes for some cows. As he was returning home, he stopped for some refreshment at the house of an old acquaintance; and the weather being hot, he hung up his arms in the house, while he refreshed himself. Those arms were very valuable; consisting of a gold-hilted sword, a gold knife, which they wear by their side, and a rich quiver of arrows, which King Sambo had made him a present of. It happened that a company of the Mandingoes, who live upon plunder, passing by at that time, and observing him unarmed, rushed in, to the number of seven or eight at once, at a back door, and pinioned Job, before he could get to his arms, together with his interpreter, who is a slave in Maryland still. They then shaved their heads and beards, which Job and his man resented as the highest indignity; tho' the Mandingoes meant no more by it, than to make them appear like Slaves taken in war. On the 27th of February, 1730, they carried them to Captain Pike at Gambia, who purchased them. . . .

. . . By him he was carried to Maryland, and sold to a planter, with whom Job lived about a twelve month . . . ; at the end of which time he had the good fortune to have a letter of his own writing in the Arabic tongue conveyed to England. This letter coming to the hand of Mr. Oglethorpe, he sent the same to Oxford to be translated; which, when done, gave him so much satisfaction, and so good an opinion of the man, that he directly ordered him to be bought from his master, he soon after setting out for Georgia. Before he returned from thence, Job came to England; where being brought to the acquaintance of the learned Sir Hans Sloane, he was by him found a perfect master of the Arabic tongue, by translating several manuscripts and inscriptions upon medals: he was by him recommended to his Grace the Duke of Montague, who being pleased with the sweetness of humour, and mildness of temper, as well as genius and capacity of the man, introduced him to court, where he was graciously received by the Royal Family, and most of the nobility, from whom he received distinguishing marks of favour. After he had continued in England about fourteen months, he wanted much to return to his

CONTINUED

native country, which is Bundo (a place about a week's travel over land from the Royal African Company's factory at Joar, on the River Gambia) of which place his father was High-Priest, and to whom he sent letters from England. Upon his setting out from England he received a good many noble presents from her most Gracious Majesty Queen Caroline, his Highness the Duke of Cumberland, his Grace the Duke of Montague, the Earl of Pembroke, several ladies of quality, Mr. [Samuel] Holden, and the Royal African Company, who have ordered their agents to show him the greatest respect.

Source: Thomas Bluett, *Some Memoirs of the Life of Job, the Son of Solomon the High Priest of Boonda in Africa* (London: Richard Ford, 1734), pp. 9–53. Also appears in Philip D. Curtin, ed., *Africa Remembered: Narratives by West Africans from the Era of the Slave Trade* (Madison: The University of Wisconsin Press, 1968), pp. 33–55.

fortunate slave" because he was able to draft a letter in Arabic explaining his predicament, a letter that resulted in his being bought out of bondage and returned to his West African home (see box).

British slaveowners deliberately withheld aspects of their language from blacks. They viewed "proper" English as an "emblem of civilization" and white superiority. They camouflaged its secrets from bondsmen by "accent, tone, diction, and vocabulary." Thus, eighteenth-century Chesapeake advertisements for runaways frequently emphasized the inability of Africans to understand English. Moreover, as early as 1740, South Carolina prohibited the teaching of slaves to write, and Georgia later prohibited the teaching of slaves to read or write. Such prohibitions, however, strengthened the resolve of some blacks to learn to "talk to books," as they perceived many whites could do.

As Africans from different regions interacted with each other and Europeans, their New World language gradually emerged as the first, or "creolized," language of American-born blacks. Early Africans spoke a pidgin comprised of words from English, African, and to some extent Spanish, Portuguese, and Amerindian languages. By the mid-eighteenth century, fugitive ads revealed the slow growth of black English in the region. In 1745, a Virginia advertisement declared that "Sambo" could speak English "so as to be understood." Ten years later, another Virginian reported that his "Angola Fellow" spoke "very good English, as he was imported young." In the Sea Islands, blacks perfected the Gullah language of South Carolina and the Geechee dialect of Georgia. After the 1730s and 1740s, the Gullah language became the dominant language of Sea Island blacks. It also became the language through which new Africans gained access to English, while reinforcing Gullah's indigenous roots. In varying degrees, African American culture influenced language formation in the Upper South and North as well as the Deep South. Indeed, African terms like *goober, tote, gumbo, banjo, yam, okra,* and *juke,* among others, entered the language of the region and nation. Whites increasingly made the distinction between the Africans' acquisition of "good standard English" on the one hand and "good black English" on the other. As one historian notes, however, black English was a product of "ingenuity," not of ignorance, "and it served its function well."

Early African American English was largely a spoken rather than a written language. When asked if he could read, one South Carolina bondsman remarked that he "would rather choose hereafter to practice the good he could remember." As in Africa, folklore played a key role in the language training of black children, who learned not only ways to survive the system of bondage but also certain subtle and not so subtle means to resist the harsh demands of the slave regime. Folk tales clarified and confirmed the social and cultural values of African Americans, instilled a sense of morality, and painted a picture of proper behavior. Conversely, the process of curtailing the slave's access to literacy and formal English inadvertently facilitated the use of an alternative strategy of resistance—that is, the deliberate misapprehension of instructions. Captives regularly evaded orders under the pretense that they did not understand English. In short, blacks who failed to learn formal English as well as those who mastered English used language as weapons of resistance.

Despite the difficulties of acquiring access to formal English, a few blacks gradually gained recognition for their literary skills. Africans gained greater access to education and literacy in the northern than in the southern colonies and gradually made an impact on the literature of the region. In 1760, the slave Jupiter Hammon of Long Island, New York, wrote "An Evening Thought: Salvation by Christ with Penitential Cries." Although Hammon's verse is regarded as the earliest known poem of an American-born black, Phillis Wheatley would become the most renown of the early black writers in British North America. Born in Senegal around 1753–1754, Wheatley was sold to the Boston merchant and tailor John Wheatley in 1761. Seven years later, at about age fourteen, she wrote "An Address to the Atheist." Five years later, a London publishing house released her *Poems on Various Subjects, Religious and Moral.* Her writings demonstrated not only her facility with the English language but also her firm commitment to Christianity. In perhaps her most famous verse, she wrote:

> Twas mercy brought me from my *Pagan* land,
> Taught my benighted soul to understand
> That there's a God, that there's a *Saviour* too:
> Once I redemption neither sought nor knew.

Unlike Phillis Wheatley and Jupiter Hammon, most African Americans expressed themselves through oral communication. Moreover, their language reflected the blending of African and European words and linguistic styles.

African American language and oral traditions facilitated the spread of New World black culture. As in Africa, religion occupied a pivotal place in this process. Seventeenth-century West Africans came from a variety of religious backgrounds, including Islam and Christianity as well as various indigenous religions. Yet, as in language, they shared core ideas about the spirit, natural, and social worlds. As noted in Chapter 1, West African blacks believed that spirits inhabited the bodies of human beings. At death, the spirit left the body for a broader spiritual realm

A N

Evening THOUGHT.

SALVATION BY *CHRIST*,

WITH

PENETENTIAL CRIES:

Compofed by Jupiter Hammon, a Negro belonging to Mr Lloyd, of Queen's-Village, on Long-Ifland, the 25th of December, 1760.

SALVATION comes by Jefus Chrift alone,
  The only Son of God ;
Redemption now to every one,
  That love his holy Word.
Dear Jefus we would fly to Thee,
  And leave off every Sin,
Thy tender Mercy well agree ;
  Salvation from our King.
Salvation comes now from the Lord,
  Our victorious King ;
His holy Name be well ador'd,
  Salvation furely brig.
Dear Jefus give thy Spirit now,
  Thy Grace to every Nation,
That han't the Lord to whom we bow,
  The Author of Salvation.
Dear Jefus unto Thee we cry,
  Give us thy Preparation ;
Turn not away thy tender Eye ;
  We feek thy true Salvation.
Salvation comes from God we know,
  The true and only One ;
It's well agreed and certain true,
  He gave his only Son.
Lord hear our penetential Cry :
  Salvation from above ;
It is the Lord that doth fupply,
  With his Redeeming Love.
Dear Jefus by thy precious Blood,
  The World Redemption have :
Salvation comes now from the Lord,
  He being thy captive Slave.
Dear Jefus let the Nations cry,
  And all the People fay,
Salvation comes from Chrift on high,
  Hafte on Tribunal Day.
We cry as Sinners to the Lord,
  Salvation to obtain ;
It is firmly fixt his holy Word,
  Ye fhall not cry in vain.
Dear Jefus unto Thee we cry,
  And make our Lamentation :
O let our Prayers afcend on high ;
  We felt thy Salvation.

Lord turn our dark benighted Souls ;
  Give us a true Motion,
And let the Hearts of all the World,
  Make Chrift their Salvation.
Ten Thoufand Angels cry to Thee,
  Yea louder than the Ocean.
Thou art the Lord, we plainly fee ;
  Thou art the true Salvation.
Now is the Day, excepted Time ;
  The Day of Salvation ;
Increafe your Faith, do not repine :
  Awake ye every Nation.
Lord unto whom now fhall we go,
  Or feek a fafe Abode ;
Thou haft the Word Salvation too
  The only Son of God.
Ho ! every one that hunger hath,
  Or pineth after me,
Salvation be thy leading Staff,
  To fet the Sinner free.
Dear Jefus unto Thee we fly ;
  Depart, depart from Sin,
Salvation doth at length fupply,
  The Glory of our King.
Come ye Bleffed of the Lord,
  Salvation gently given ;
O turn your Hearts, accept the Word,
  Your Souls are fit for Heaven.
Dear Jefus we now turn to Thee,
  Salvation to obtain ;
Our Hearts and Souls do meet again,
  To magnify thy Name.
Come holy Spirit, Heavenly Dove,
  The Object of our Care ;
Salvation doth increafe our Love ;
  Our Hearts hath felt thy fear.
Now Glory be to God on High,
  Salvation high and low ;
And thus the Soul on Chrift rely,
  To Heaven furely go.
Come Bleffed Jefus, Heavenly Dove,
  Accept Repentance here ;
Salvation give, with tender Love ;
  Let us with Angels fhare.

F I N I S.

Jupiter Hammon's "An Evening Thought" is considered the earliest poem by an American-born black. *New-York Historical Society* where it combined with those of the ancestors. Spirits, including those of the ancestors, were quite active and could influence the course of life on earth. Since West Africans believed that spirits inhabited not only the bodies of human beings but inanimate objects as well, they employed a variety of ritual and magical practices—the wearing of amulets or charms, for example—to gain favor. Such beliefs gave rise to a plethora of African American healers, conjurers, priests, and magic workers who served as intermediaries between the spirits, the individual, and the group.

Although the international slave trade disrupted the institutional structures of West African religious traditions, the memory of African beliefs and social practices influenced New World black culture and forms of resistance. During the early colonial years, black religion reflected the interplay of African beliefs and white resistance to the conversion of slaves. Many slaveholders believed that Christianity would bestow human rights on blacks and undermine the system of bondage, whereas others believed that the religious instruction of bondsmen and -women would require valuable time away from labor in the fields, shops, and households of their masters. Converts to Christianity would no longer be able to work on Sunday, depriving masters of material returns on their investment.

Other Christian slaveowners opposed slave conversion on racial grounds. In 1748, for example, the Swedish botanist Peter Kalm traveled through the British colonies and reported:

> They [masters] are partly led by the conceit of its being shameful, to have a spiritual brother or sister among so despicable a people, partly by thinking that they should not be able to keep their Negroes so meanly afterwards; and partly through fear of the Negroes growing too proud, on seeing themselves upon a level with their masters in religious maters.

In South Carolina, some white Anglican parishioners "resolved never to come to the Holy Table" while slaves were "rec[eive]d there." A white woman was even more direct. She asked her minister: "Is it possible that any of my slaves could go to heaven, & must I see them there?"

The rise of Afro-Christianity was not only hampered by white resistance to slave conversion but also undercut by the reorientation of Christian precepts to justify the enslavement of Africans. In New England and the northern colonies no less than in the Upper and Lower South, Christian ministers repeatedly exhorted blacks to be obedient to their masters. In 1727, for example, Bishop Gibson of London assured slaveholders that conversion to Christianity did not alter the status of slaves:

> The Freedom which Christianity gives, is a Freedom from the Bondage of Sin and Satan, and from the Dominion of Men's Lusts and Passions and inordinate Desires; but as to their *outward* Condition, whatever that was before whether bond or free; their being baptized and becoming Christians makes no manner of change in it.

White ministers not only preached obedience, discipline, and hard work in the interests of slaveowners but also segregated black members, refused them a voice in church governance, and adopted the belief that slavery was part of "God's plan" for the conversion of "African heathens."

As religious thinkers, theorists, and theologians sanctioned the holding of human property, growing numbers of planters permitted the proselytization of their slaves. In 1724, in the Chesapeake, three Anglican clergymen in Prince George's County, Maryland, reported that they preached to the enslaved people and baptized both children and adults, particularly the American born. In 1731, another Prince George's minister emphasized that he not only baptized blacks "where perfect in their catechism" but also "visit[ed] them in their sickness and married them when called upon." In 1706, the Anglican Francis Le Jau embarked on his ministry among the poor whites, Indians, and Africans of Charlestown, South Carolina. In New England, the Congregationalist ministers John Eliot and Cotton Mather spearheaded the movement to convert Africans to the Puritan faith. Eliot warned masters to attend to their duty of Christianizing the slaves "lest the God of Heaven, out of mere pity, if not justice unto those unhappy blacks, be provoked unto a vengeance which may not without honor be thought upon." Similarly, in his treatise *The Negro Christianized,* Cotton Mather argued forcefully that slaves were "men and not beasts" and that "there is a reasonable soul in all of them."

Such proselytizing work reinforced rather than challenged the owners' property rights in slaves. Thus few blacks accepted the earliest Euro-American brand of Christianity. The number of formal converts to Christianity remained minimal, particularly in the Deep South. In 1720, following eleven years of service in St. Thomas Parish, South Carolina, one Anglican minister reported baptizing only eight or nine black converts out of some eight hundred slaves. After five years' service, in 1728 another South Carolina minister baptized none of the fifteen hundred blacks in St. John's Parish. In the Chesapeake region, the Maryland minister Thomas Bacon suggested that most of the baptized African Americans adopted only the outward signs of Christianity, "as if they had remained in the . . . countries from whence their parents had been first imported." In 1724, William Tibbs of St. Paul's Parish, Baltimore County, Maryland, reported that most blacks refused instruction. In 1741, another white minister lamented that blacks rejected Christianity because of "the Fondness they have for their old Heathenish Rites, and the strong prejudice they must have against teachers from among those, whom they serve so unwillingly." In New England, despite substantial proselytizing among blacks, an estimated 50 percent of blacks remained unconverted by the late colonial period. Blacks who did convert to Christianity expected freedom in this world and the next. Thus, masters' fears that Christian teachings might undermine bound labor had a basis in fact.

From the outset of their encounter with Christianity, blacks expressed the view that slavery was incompatible with Christian beliefs. Once enslaved people received baptism, planters regularly complained of "the untoward haughty behavior of those Negroes who have been admitted into the Fellowship of Christ's Religion." In 1723, a New York minister complained that "some [slaves] have under pretense of going to catechizing taken opportunity to absent from their masters service many days." A South Carolina minister reported that some baptized slaves "became lazy and proud, entertaining too high an opinion of themselves, and neglecting their daily labor." In 1731, James Blair, an Anglican church official, reported from Virginia that "when they [slaves] saw that baptism did not change their status they grew angry and saucy, and met in the nighttime in great numbers and talked of rising." Six years earlier, in South Carolina, authorities blamed "secret poisonings and bloody insurrection" on recent converts to Christianity.

Under the impact of the Great Awakening during the 1730s and 1740s, a new brand of white Christianity attracted the attention of blacks. White ministers like Jonathan Edwards and George Whitfield inaugurated a series of revivals. These ministers called the old formalized Anglican and Congregational faiths into question. Emphasizing "regeneration" and "conversion," Edwards and other revivalists believed that stimulating the emotions helped to prepare people to receive God's grace. Such ministers also downplayed theological training and placed primacy on the conversion experience "as evidence of salvation." As a result, more African Americans turned to Christianity than before.

Methodist and Baptist denominations emerged at the forefront of the evangelical movement. These sects stressed piety over theology, emotions over dogma, and the inspired spoken word, or preaching, over learned clerical wisdom. It was this form of religious worship that most appealed to blacks and poor whites and transformed the role of Christianity in the lives of African Americans. Contemporary observers frequently commented on the reception that white evangelical preachers received among the enslaved. In South Carolina, one observer noted how blacks encouraged one Methodist preacher:

> There was a peculiar *unction* that descended upon the preacher in the presence of these sable children of Africa. While they were not good judges of rhetoric, they were excellent judges of good preaching, and by their prayers and that peculiar magnetism which many have felt and none can explain the power of the Holy Ghost seemed often present in the preacher and the hearer.

New England blacks also responded enthusiastically to the new preachings. In November 1741, the Reverend Eleazer Wheelock described reactions to one of his sermons in Taunton, Massachusetts:

> Preached there . . . one or two [blacks] cried out. Appointed another meeting in the evening. . . . I believed 30 cried out; almost all the negroes in town wounded, 3 or 4 converted. A great work in town. . . . Col. Leonard's negro in such distress that it took 3 men to hold him. I was forced to break off my sermon before I had done, the outcry was so great.

Evangelical ministers regularly reported "a great many groaning and crying out."

The evangelical movement had perhaps its greatest impact on African Americans in the Chesapeake. In 1755, two white Baptists initiated the first evangelical mission to blacks on William Byrd's plantation in Mecklenburg County, Virginia. At about the same time, in Hanover County, Virginia, nearly a thousand blacks converted to evangelical Protestantism. According to the Presbyterian minister

Samuel Davies, African Americans understood not only "the important doctrines of the Christian Religion, but also a deep sense of things upon their spirits, and a life of the strictest Morality and Piety." Still, even the Baptists and Methodists would soon accommodate to the system of human bondage and short-circuit the full incorporation of Africans into the "brotherhood of man" and "fatherhood of God."

Whether under the influence of the formal Congregationalist and Anglican churches on the one hand and the new revivalist Methodist and Baptist bodies on the other, African Americans developed their own distinctive beliefs and practices, a blend of their African traditions with New World ideas. White observers often commented on the different forms of worship among blacks as compared with those of whites. In the Chesapeake, one eighteenth-century observer reported that "their religious services are wild, and at times almost raving." Another said that "they commonly are more noisy in time of preaching than the whites, and are more subject to bodily exercise, and if they meet with any encouragement in these things, they grow extravagant." The evangelical use of the psalmody, in which a lead singer read aloud line by line the words of a song, not only enabled blacks to learn new songs but also allowed them to adapt their African singing style of "call and response" to New World Christianity. As one Virginia observer put it:

> I cannot but observe . . . that the Negroes, above all the human species I ever knew, have an ear for music, and a kind of ecstatic delight in Psalmody; and there are no books they learn so soon, or take so much pleasure in, as those used in that part of the divine worship.

Family and Community

African American kinship and family formation also revealed the impact of Old and New World ideas on African American life. Africans from diverse ethnic groups perceived kinship as the principal means of organizing relations between individuals and groups. West African societies incorporated a variety of people from outside the immediate family and developed an elaborate kinship system. Because New World slaveholders denied black families legal recognition and subjected them to breakup by sale and sexual exploitation, African ideas helped enslaved blacks to sustain notions of kinship and to survive labor, social, and sexual tyranny. At the same time, African Americans gradually made the transition to European-type monogamous families.

As the ratio of men to women evened out, growing numbers of black men and women lived in household units with spouses and children. As early as 1733, for example, over 50 percent of the blacks on Robert "King" Carter's Virginia plantation lived as families with husband, wife, and children. And one study shows that on four large Chesapeake plantations between 1759 and 1775, over 53 percent of slave children under ten years of age lived with both parents (see table). This process emerged more slowly in the Deep South colonies of Georgia and South Carolina but surfaced much earlier in the northern colonies. In 1659, New

African American Slave Household Structure on Four Large Plantations of the Chesapeake, 1759–1775					
	Percentage Occupying, by Age				
Household Type	Males, 15+ (*N* = 189)	Females, 15+ (*N* = 158)	Children, 0–9 (*N* = 224)	Children, 10–14 (*N* = 99)	Overall (*N* = 670)
Husband-wife	3	4			2
Husband-wife-children	37	42	53	46	45
Mother-children	2	19	25	10	15
Father-children	7	0	7	6	5
Siblings	5	3	5	9	5
Mother-children-other kin	3	11	6	10	7
Other extended	3	4	2	5	4
No family in household	40	18	2	15	18
Total	100	101	100	101	100

Source: Adapted from Allan Kulikoff, *Tobacco and Slaves: The Development of Southern Culture in the Chesapeake, 1680–1800* (Chapel Hill: University of North Carolina Press, 1986), p. 370. Copyright © 1986 by The University of North Carolina Press. Used by permission of the publisher.

England court records showed black men and women living as man and wife. By the early 1700s, such instances became even more prominent. New England authorities regularly recorded the marriages of enslaved blacks by both clergymen and magistrates. Moreover, such couples had to publicize their intentions before marriage. In early November 1700, for example, the city of Boston published the banns of "Charles Negro & Peggee Negro." Two weeks later the same city recorded the intentions of "Semit Negro & Jane Negro."

African Americans valued their families and pressured owners to respect the sanctity of their marriages. On some occasions, their protests forced owners to sell families intact or not at all. In April 1751, for example, the slaveholder Isaac Roberts of Philadelphia advertised the sale of a black family but warned prospective buyers that he was "not inclined to sell them separate." Some colonial era blacks made it known that they would "spill" their "last drop of blood" rather than see their families separated.

Although nuclear-type families slowly increased over time, African Americans continued to validate certain African forms of family life. As recent scholars note, although polygyny was not a universal practice in West African societies, it did inform New World black responses to family life. During the eighteenth century, for example, despite the dearth of African women on Maryland's Eastern Shore, some male slaves lived with more than one woman. In 1713, the Reverend John Sharp reported from New York that some male slaves could not cement Christian marriages because of "polygamy contracted before baptism where none or neither of the wives will accept a divorce." In 1738, Boston's Elihu Coleman complained that Yankees allowed blacks "to take husbands and wives at their pleasure, and then leave again when they please, and then take others again as fast and as suddenly as they will and then leave them again." Although white contemporaries and some historians later described such practices as evidence of promiscuity, and even animal-like breeding, such practices also reveal the complicated transformation of African marriage and family patterns under the impact of New World slavery and racial oppression.

Naming practices offer additional evidence of African influences on black families. Africans brought to the New World a tradition of naming male and female children after the day of the week on which they were born: Cudjo (Monday), Quashee (Sunday), Quaco (Wednesday) for males; and, for females, Cuba (Wednesday), Phibbi or Phiba (Friday), and Abba (Thursday). When one South Carolina slaveowner died, his estate listed a variety of African names among the enslaved—Allahay, Assey, Cumbo, Cush, Quash, Quashey, Rinah, and Sambo, to name a few. Moreover, blacks often named their sons after their fathers but seldom named daughters after mothers, as whites frequently did.

African American language, religion, and family formation underlay the gradual rise of New World slave communities and the emergence of new black aesthetics and leisure time activities. The interplay of African ideas and certain European cultural traditions shaped New World slave music, dance, art, and celebrations. Unlike Europeans, however, Africans and their American descendants blurred the distinction between the sacred and the secular. Music and dance marked African American work and play as well as worship. Groups of blacks performed both spiritual and secular songs as they toiled in the fields, rowed boats, loaded goods, and dug ditches. Closely intertwined with music, sometimes described by whites in positive terms as "sweet chants," were rhythms and styles of dance, particularly the African ring dances, which facilitated interaction between the individual and the group. Songs, music, and dance not only lifted the spirits of the enslaved and enabled them to endure bondage but also informed bondsmen and -women of secret meetings, conveyed helpful information to runaways, and served the larger cause of resistance. It was partly the subversive potential of African American culture that led several colonies to outlaw the beating of drums during the colonial era.

Africans also used their own notions of aesthetics and taste to modify Euro-American forms of dress, food, furnishings, and even architecture. Although slaveowners determined the types and quality of fabrics, foods, and building materials that blacks had at their disposal, Africans introduced their own food crops—including yams, okra, sesame seeds, and peanuts—and used their own ideas about beauty and seasoning to change the look of European clothing and the taste of New World dishes. African Americans preferred heavily seasoned foods and clothing of bright colors and contrasting patterns, which European elites considered gaudy and distasteful. Moreover, using African-style mud walls and thatched roofs, blacks often constructed and furnished their own dwellings in Virginia, South Carolina, and Georgia. In some cases, their aesthetic principles and styles influenced the architecture of buildings constructed for planters' use, as suggested by the conical-roofed powder house built in Clarke County, Virginia. Blacks also employed African motifs, designs, and techniques in their basket weavings and pottery. Although African Americans also gradually adopted European dress styles,

A conical-roofed powder house at Greenway Court, Clarke County, Virginia, c. 1750. The roof's style suggests the impact of African culture on southern architecture. *Library of Congress*

planters hampered this process by passing laws restricting the types of clothing that enslaved blacks could wear.

Annual festivals or carnivals provided occasions for the most public display of African American culture. These public expressions of black culture gained perhaps their greatest prominence in the northern colonies. In New York, African Americans celebrated Pinkster Day; in New Jersey, General Training Day; and in New England, Election Day. African Americans used these occasions to display their stylish dress, enjoy music and dance, drink, eat, and play games such as "Paw Paw" or "Props," a West African gambling game that became popular among whites as well as blacks. Although owners permitted slaves to take a holiday for these events, African Americans also used these festive occasions to critique the injustices of white society under the guise of satire. At the same time, they elected their own black "kings," "governors," and other lesser officials and established an internal system of rules and behavior. Although whites ridiculed the notion of black elected officials, blacks crowned such officials with a great deal of influence within the enslaved community. Indeed, influential whites gradually came to rely on such kings and governors to obtain "settlements and adjustments, and arrange many matters in their relations with the negroes."

FROM DAY-TO-DAY RESISTANCE TO OPEN REBELLION

African American culture, family, and community life reinforced and intensified resistance to slave labor. Community and leisure time activities enabled blacks to participate in numerous acts of resistance, ranging from day-to-day skirmishes with slaveowners and overseers to overt rebellion. After completing the dreaded Middle Passage and time on Caribbean plantations, Africans responded to bondage in the households, shops, and fields of British North America.

Workplace and Economic Struggles

As in religion, language, and aesthetics, Africans brought their own notions of work to North America and resisted efforts to exploit their labor and deny their humanity. Although West African ideas about work were not monolithic, most Africans brought to the New World rural work habits and rhythms governed by the seasons rather than the clock. They were accustomed to cycles of intense labor followed by periods of relaxation. As such, like European indentured servants and other white workers, they faced criticism from white elites, who complained that Africans practiced "slovenly" work habits. As blacks became slaves for life, however, such criticisms took on increasingly racial overtones. During the early to mid-eighteenth century, the Virginia planter Landon Carter wrote, "Where the General is absent . . . Idleness is Preferred to all business." On another occasion, he stated, "Negroes tyre with the Continuance of the same work." And at another point, he said, "I can't make my people work or do anything." During the late eighteenth century, George Washington made similar complaints, urging his overseers to guard against permitting blacks to set the work pace. As he put it, some overseers, finding "it a little troublesome to instruct the Negroes" in systematic work habits, adopted the "slovenly" labor practices of the slaves.

Although slaveowner complaints represented rising stereotypes about black people as "lazy" and "unwilling" to work, they also suggest African resistance to forced labor. Africans not only slowed the work pace but also resisted European technology designed to increase productivity. On Maryland's Eastern Shore in 1747, for example, visitor Edward Kinner reported that "you would really be surpriz'd at their Perseverance; let an hundred Men shew him how to hoe, or drive a Wheelbarrow, he'll still take the one by the Bottom, and the other by the Wheel." During the same period, when Dorchester, Massachusetts, imported Africans to work excavating a hill, the Africans transported the dirt away in baskets or trays on their heads. When slaveowners introduced wheelbarrows, seeking to improve efficiency, according to one contemporary source, the laborers at first hampered the effort by placing the "barrows on their heads." Although Europeans and later historians frequently ridiculed Africans as "backward" and "lazy," such criticisms failed to acknowledge the efforts of blacks to shape the work process to their own advantage.

Africans and their descendants were not uniformly hostile to European technology and mechanisms for improving productivity, however. Because Deep South and some Upper South planters adopted the task system, slaves also gradually turned the new technology—especially iron plows and wheeled carts—to their advantage. They used the new implements to hasten the completion of assigned tasks and increase time for work and leisure for themselves. Similarly, some people made themselves even more valuable to their owners by acquiring indispensable skills, which gave them a greater measure of freedom within the context of bondage. In advertisements for the sale of slaves, owners frequently stressed the skills of black artisans. In December 1742, a South Carolina woman offered to sell "A Fine young Negro man, born in this county, . . . brought up to the Ship Carpenter's trade." Two weeks later, another slaveowner presented "A likely Negro Fellow to be sold, . . . a Ship Carpenter and Wheelwright by Trade." Although black women had fewer opportunities for gaining artisan skills, they sometimes expanded their margin of options by mastering a variety of household and field tasks. The *South Carolina Gazette,* on 1 February 1739, advertised the sale of a black woman "fit either for the Field or House, being used to both." More importantly, the ad stated that the woman could "milk very well, wash and iron, dress vituals, and do anything that is necessary to be done in the House."

African Americans who hired out their own time had the greatest opportunities for expanding the margin of freedom. Planters frequently complained that the hired slaves took work "clandestinely about town, and thereby defrauded [their] master of several sums of money." In South Carolina, one master reported that "A Negroman named Lancaster, commonly known about the town for a white washer, and fisherman, has of late imposed upon his employers, and defrauded me of his wages; I do therefore advertise all persons not to employ the said Lancaster, without first agree with me."

Despite prohibitions on their participation in commercial pursuits for profit, African Americans constructed an extensive underground economy. By the 1720s, enslaved people sold a variety of goods and services to Europeans and to each other through an extensive network of informal contacts. Europeans kept this network and practice alive by eagerly capitalizing on the lower costs enslaved people were obliged to offer. In 1721, the governor of South Carolina urged that "a sufficient provision be made against trading with Negroes, or other Servants, & Slaves, and receiving anything from them." By 1734, Charleston officials accused blacks of cornering the market on certain products. When slave crops entered Charleston, South Carolina, black women took charge of the urban marketing operation. These women developed a reputation for their bargaining skills within and outside the slave community. Although Virginia and Maryland planters relied on slaves to take products to market and to shop for plantation wares in nearby towns and cities like Baltimore, Norfolk, and Alexandria, they reported that such trade provided blacks opportunities for "defrauding" them of their money. Blacks gained some commercial opportunities because some whites were ashamed to sell certain products, especially chickens. One Virginia writer asked: "Pray why is a fowl more disgraceful . . . in the sale of it at market, than a pig, lamb, a mutton, a veal, a cow or an ox." Another Virginia observer described blacks as "the general chicken merchants," an occupation based partly on widespread theft. In New York, the Geneva Club, a group of enslaved blacks, transformed theft and the sale of illegal goods into a thriving business.

Closely intertwined with the underground economy and various forms of work slowdowns, running away represented the colonial blacks' most powerful form of resistance to human bondage. From the vantage point of slaveowners, fugitives also represented the most damaging theft of the master's property. Following the decline of white indentured servitude, the number of black runaways increased dramatically. Colonial officials and slaveowners regularly reported the names, ages, and sexes of runaways and advertised for their return. From the founding of the *South Carolina Gazette* in 1732, owners advertised for the recovery of fugitives. Although the proportion of runaways as a percentage of imports seldom exceeded 5 percent,

Runaways as Proportion of Imports to Colonial South Carolina			
Date	Imports	Runaways	Percentage
1735–39	11,849	512	4.32
1740–49	1,563	619	39.60
1750–59	15,912	847	5.32
1760–69	20,810	1,037	4.98
1770–75	20,808	844	4.05
Total	70,943	3,862	5.43

Source: Daniel C. Littlefield, *Rice and Slaves: Ethnicity and the Slave Trade in Colonial South Carolina* (1981; reprint, Urbana: University of Illinois Press, 1991), p. 162. Copyright © 1991 by Daniel C. Littlefield. Used with the permission of the University of Illinois Press.

the absolute number of runaways steadily increased between 1735 and 1770, rising from 512 at the outset of the period to over 1,000 near the end (see table).

Although American-born men, artisans, and those with a proficiency in English stood the best chance of permanent escape, most escapees were field hands. Between 1736 and roughly the American Revolution, an estimated 1,500 notices of runaways appeared in newspapers published in the Upper South cities of Williamsburg, Richmond, and Fredericksburg. These notices described 1,138 men and 142 women, mostly American-born rather than African-born blacks. On 21 November 1745, the *Virginia Gazette* offered a typical example of such runaway ads:

RUN AWAY about the First Day of *June* last from the Subscriber, living on *Chickahominy* River, *James City* County. A Negro Man, short and well-set, aged between 30 and 40 Years, but looks younger, having no Beard, is smooth-fac'd, and has some Scars on his Temples, being the Marks of his Country; talks pretty good *English*; is a cunning, subtile Fellow, and pretends to be a Doctor. It is likely, as he has a great Acquaintance, he may have procur'd a false Pass. Whoever brings him to me at my House aforesaid, shall have two Pistoles Reward, besides what the Law allows.

In the New England and the middle colonies, too, slaveowners regularly advertised for the recovery of runaways. In 1718, a Rhode Islander advertised in the *Boston News Letter:*

Ran away from his master Charles Dickinson of Boston-neck in Kingstown, in Narragansett in Rhode Island Colony, a Negro man aged about 25 years. . . . Who shall take up said Negro and convey him to his Master above said, or advise him so that he may have him again shall be fully paid for the same.

In 1738, a New Hampshire minister offered three pounds sterling for the recovery of a fugitive. Similarly, in 1749, a Massachusetts owner promised "a reasonable reward and all necessary charges" for the return of a runaway. Although some runaways eluded capture and others were returned to owners and punished for their infraction, others chose death over return. In Coventry, Rhode Island, for example, one fugitive "cut his own throat and soon after expired" rather than return to bondage. Suicide, however, was rarely employed as a mode of resistance.

Poison, Arson, and Revolt

Blacks not only resisted by running away, participating in the underground economy, and slowing down the work pace. They also employed poisoning, arson, and revolts or conspiracies to revolt against owners and overseers. As discussed earlier, African Americans had extensive knowledge of plants and their medicinal properties. Indeed, some blacks gained freedom or other rewards for introducing whites to various cures and antidotes for poisoning. The *South Carolina Gazette* reprinted one bondsman's poisoning antidotes for more than thirty years. As the system of bondage tightened, however, blacks also turned such knowledge on their masters. By the early 1770s, for example, the Virginia court convicted and executed growing numbers of enslaved people for poisoning whites. Similarly, although South Carolina made poisoning a felony offense in the Negro Act of 1740, such occurrences persisted. In 1761, the *Gazette* reported that "the Negroes have again began the hellish practice of poisoning."

Along with reports of poisoning, enslaved blacks burned naval stores, houses, grain storage facilities, and especially barns. Colonial newspapers regularly reported barns burning "down to the Ground, and all that was in [them]." Barn burning increased markedly during the harvesting and marketing seasons between October and January. In 1732, the *South Carolina Gazette* exclaimed:

> I Have taken Notice for Several years past, that there has not one Winter elapsed, without one or more Barns being burnt, and two Winters since, there was no less than five. Whether it is owning to Accident, Carelessness or Severity, I will not pretend to determine; but am afraid, chiefly to the two latter.

Arson was particularly destructive in the towns, with their densely settled populations, frame buildings, and poor water supplies and provisions for fighting fires. In November 1740, a fire broke out in Charleston and raged out of control for six hours, destroying an estimated three hundred houses and new town fortifications. Property losses reached an estimated 250,000 pounds sterling.

Whether the fires were set by blacks or not, they were repeatedly blamed for arson. During the early 1720s, a Boston official accused blacks of setting a rash of fires. As he put it, such fires were "designedly and industriously kindled by some villainous and desperate Negroes." Indeed, some of the most serious cases of arson as a form of revolt broke out in New York. In 1712, New York blacks and some Native Americans responded to "some hard dosage . . . received from their masters" and vowed "to destroy all the whites in the town." The conspirators set fire to an outhouse, and when whites responded to the blaze, they killed nine persons before soldiers put down the revolt. In the revolt's aftermath, colonial authorities burned several members of the group alive at the stake while breaking another on the wheel.

In 1741, when several fires erupted on the night of 28 February, white elites concluded that a slave plot was underway. Authorities soon arrested some 150 persons, including 25 poor whites. Penalties fell most heavily on the 134 blacks brought to trial. Authorities burned 13 of these blacks alive, hanged another 18, and deported 70 to the West Indies. Only about 33 blacks were discharged and cleared of charges.

Colonial era responses to bondage gained their most violent expression in the Stono Rebellion in South Carolina. In 1733, Spanish officials at St. Augustine, Florida, encouraged the revolt when they offered freedom to any slaves who deserted the British rice plantations. Encouraged by these actions as well as their own expanding numbers, on 9 September 1739, about twenty blacks gathered at the Stono River, twenty miles from Charleston, and launched a full-scale rebellion. Under the leadership of an Angolan slave named Jimmy, they raided a store for weapons and ammunition and turned southward toward Georgia and St. Augustine. They not only burned several houses and killed some twenty white occupants but also secured more guns, supplies, and slave recruits, which swelled their numbers to over fifty people. After marching over ten miles from their point of departure, they stopped on a field to regroup. As they relaxed, danced, and beat drums to attract additional recruits, armed whites mounted a counterattack and overwhelmed the group. In addition to killing as many of the rebels as possible, they cut off the heads of the dead men and mounted them on posts along the road. Some rebels nonetheless escaped and remained at large for several weeks. Only a month later would colonists report that "the rebellious Negros are quite stopt from doing any further Mischief, many of them [an estimated forty to fifty] having been put to the most cruel Death."

Although some blacks rebelled against the authority of the state, others used the state as an instrument of their liberation. As early as 1661, Emanuel Pieterson, a free black man, and his wife, Reytory, petitioned the New Netherlands court for the freedom of a young black man named Anthony. The petitioners explained that Anthony, whom they had adopted and reared at their own expense, was the orphaned child of free black parents and prayed that "he may be declared by your noble honors to be a free person." The court granted their request and saved Anthony from enslavement. In 1675, Phillip Corven petitioned the Virginia court for his freedom. According to Corven, his emancipation had been guaranteed in the will of his deceased mistress. The will specified that Corven would serve the woman's cousin for eight years after her death; at that time, he would gain his freedom, along with "three barrels of corne and a sute of clothes." Corven's petition stated that he had been sold to another master, "contrary to all honesty and good conscience with threats and a high hand," and twenty years added to his service. In 1726, Peter Vantrump sought his freedom before the General Court of North Carolina, describing himself as "a Free Negro" who "at his own voluntary disposal . . . hired himself" to employers," but on the latest occasion a North Carolina employer held him in bondage against his will: "Your complainant often told the Sayd porter that he was not a Slave but a free man yet nevertheless the Sayd porter now against all right now pretends your complainant to be his Slave and hath held and used him as Such." Despite the desperate pleas of Vantrump and Corven, the state denied their requests for freedom. Yet their petitions demonstrated how some blacks sought to use the law as a tool in their own struggle for freedom.

In their petitions for freedom, African American bondsmen and -women gradually gained moral support from a few whites. In 1688, the Mennonites of Germantown, Pennsylvania, issued the earliest protest against slavery in the English-speaking colonies of North America. The Germantown meeting condemned the "traffic" in human bodies and urged members to stop "robbing and stealing" other people for profit. The statement also concluded that blacks had "as much right to fight for their freedom as you have to keep them slaves," but few Quakers followed the lead of the Germantown meeting during the late seventeenth and early eighteenth centuries. By the 1750s, however, such antislavery sentiment had slowly expanded, as evidenced in New Jersey Quaker John Woolman's famous pamphlet "Some Considerations on the Keeping of Negroes: Recommended to the professors of Christianity of every Denomination." Woolman urged Quakers to bring their antislavery practices in line with their antislavery beliefs. In 1758, the yearly meeting voted to exclude Quaker slaveholders and slave merchants from a voice in the business of the church. The order also rejected slaveholders' financial contributions to the congregation's upkeep. In 1766, the Philadelphia school teacher and abolitionist Anthony Benezet also published an influential antislavery tract, "A Caution and Warning to Great Britain and Her Colonies, in a Short Representation of the Calamitous State of the Enslaved Negroes in the British Dominions." Although such pronouncements did little to diminish the spread of slavery, they did form an important ideological support for the African American struggle against bondage. They also suggested that the struggle against slavery would proceed with a few white allies.

INTER- AND INTRAETHNIC RELATIONS

African American culture and forms of resistance not only were influenced by their confrontation and interactions with Europeans but also were shaped by the widespread interaction of African Americans and Native Americans. From the outset of the colonial era through the eve of the Revolution, blacks and indigenous people developed oscillating relationships characterized by both hostility and friendliness. In Bacon's Rebellion of 1676, African Americans not only helped lower- and middle-class whites challenge the unjust authority of colonial elites but also joined rabidly anti-Indian whites in raids on Indians in Virginia and Maryland. After the rebellion collapsed, eighty enslaved blacks and thirty white indentured servants refused to surrender but were later captured and returned to bondage and servitude. The rebellion also resulted in an act in 1676 that empowered soldiers who had captured Indians to "reteyne and keepe all such Indian slaves or other Indian goods as they either have or hereafter shall take." In 1682, the Virginia assembly provided for the enslavement of Amerindians for life. Indeed, for a while the numbers of Indian slaves expanded along with those of African slaves.

During the eighteenth century, most Africans and their descendants continued to fight alongside whites in European-Indian conflicts. On the one hand—for example, in South Carolina's Yamasee War (c. 1715)—colonial officials enlisted large numbers of blacks to fight against indigenous Americans. On the other hand, some

Amerindians, notably members of the Creek and Cherokee nations, became "slave catchers." They regularly rounded up runaway slaves for profit and returned them to owners. On some occasions, planters charged the indigenous groups like the Creeks with "robbing and plundering us of our Slaves and Goods" in order to return them later for rewards. In 1728, an English agent reported that Indians "have now a Negro belonging to a Man at Pan Pan who has run away from his master and has been catch'd several times and still gets away."

Although most blacks fought alongside whites, they sometimes fought on both sides of Indian-European wars. As early as 1690, New Jersey officials uncovered an African-Indian plot to "cut off" the English and "save none but the Indians and Negroes." In the Tuscarora War of 1711–1712, Native Americans not only captured and tortured some blacks along with whites but also harbored runaways, who eventually intermarried with members of the group and later took part in wars against its enemies. In 1735, the South Carolina assembly reported that "Several Slaves have made their Escape from these Province and very probably are sheltered and protected by the Tuskerora Indians." Blacks also played a major role in Native American trade networks, which officials discouraged and drove deeper underground. In addition to disrupting black-indigenous trade networks, colonial authorities also moved to disrupt social relations between African Americans and Indians by passing legislation to "prevent any Negroe from taking a Wife among the Free Indians, or Free Indians from taking a Slave a Wife."

The emergence of African American culture and responses to bondage were complicated by interactions with Europeans and Amerindians and by the interplay of blacks from different cultural, gender, and class backgrounds as well (see box). The development of the African American slave community was by no means monolithic, smooth, or unproblematic. Blacks from different strata of West African society experienced varied adjustments and responses to New World bondage. Slaveowners often identified enslaved upper-class Africans as the major source of their problems with African labor. European colonial officials frequently complained that such people were "nursed up in luxury and ease, and wholly unaccustomed to work." Since many slaves arrived in North America via the West Indies, slaveowners paid particular attention to the assessments of Caribbean slaveowners like Captain John Stedman of the Dutch colony of Surinam. During the eighteenth century, Stedman reported:

> I have seen some instances of newly imported Negroes refusing to work, nor could promises, threats, rewards nor even blows, prevail; but these had been princes or people of the first rank in their native country . . . whose heroic sentiments still preferred instant death to the baseness and miseries of servitude.

In Virginia one slaveowner, Hugh Jones, agreed that enslaved members of the African aristocracy made the worst slaves:

> Those Negroes make the best slaves that have been slaves in their own country; for they that have been kings and great men are generally lazy, haughty, and obstinate; whereas the others are sharper, better humored, and more laborious.

CHANGING HISTORICAL INTERPRETATIONS

The Slave Culture Debate

Closely interrelated with the controversy over the origins of slavery, discussed in Chapter 3, is the dispute over the fate of African culture under the impact of widespread human bondage in North America. Pro-slavery, segregationist, and racist interpretations of African American history emphasized the inferiority of African culture. According to leading white scholars, slavery served a positive function. It introduced an "inferior people" to the "civilizing processes" of western culture. In this view, the persistence of African culture in the New World, not slavery or racial subordination, restricted black participation in the fruits of European civilization and democratic institutions.

Conversely, antislavery, integrationist, and liberal writers condemned slavery as an inhumane institution that sought to transform human beings into "things." However, although antiracist scholars agreed on the destructive nature of slavery for African people, they offered contrasting interpretations of black culture.

During the inter–World War years, W. E. B. Du Bois and the anthropologist Melville Herskovits argued that important facets of African culture survived the transatlantic crossing. According to these analysts, African culture had a positive impact on the creation of a unique African American culture in the New World. This culture enabled blacks to preserve their humanity under the trying circumstances of bondage, and later Jim Crow, as free but unequal citizens.

On the other hand, E. Franklin Frazier, one of the most influential black sociologists of the period, accented the destruction of African cultural norms in the vortex of the international slave trade and the rapid spread of the plantation system through the American South. In 1939, Frazier published his classic *The Negro Family in the United States*. He argued that the institution of slavery not only destroyed the African language, ideas, beliefs, and social practices but also hampered enslaved blacks' acquisition of the rudiments of western culture, including viable forms of family and kinship relations.

In the aftermath of World War II, a growing number of scholars and public policy experts adopted Frazier's interpretation of African American culture and family life. This scholarship peaked with the publication of Daniel Patrick Moynihan's *The Negro Family: The Case for National Action* (1965). Moynihan and others argued that "the slave was totally removed from the protection of organized society," was "totally ignorant of and completely cut off" from the past, and possessed "absolutely no hope for the future."

To be sure, Frazier, Moynihan, and others counteracted prevailing racist interpretations of slave culture. They accented the ways that color- or race-based slavery undercut the humanity of African people and forged a brutal context for the development of African American life. Yet, by overlooking the precise ways that African Americans survived the horrors of human bondage, such scholars and public policy experts reinforced certain stereotypes about black responses to slavery and racial subordination.

CONTINUED

Beginning with John Blassingame's groundbreaking study *The Slave Community* (1972), growing numbers of scholars (most notably Herbert Gutman in *The Black Family in Slavery and Freedom* [1976]) resuscitated the ideas of Herskovits and Du Bois. They stressed the ways that blacks built on their African experiences to create a new African American culture and forged a variety of subtle and not so subtle forms of resistance to enslavement.

Similar to recent scholarship on the origins of slavery controversy, contemporary research underscores African American culture creation as a dynamic historical process. The development of New World black culture entailed the autonomous activities of Africans themselves as well as their ongoing socioeconomic, demographic, cultural, and political interactions with Europeans and Amerindians. In recent years, however, scholars like Deborah Gray White, Jacqueline Jones, and Brenda Stevenson have emphasized the role that women as well as men played in developing African American culture and families and against what odds.

Perhaps even more so than the origins debate, the culture contest carries huge import for contemporary forms of inequality and efforts to redress racial injustice. Contemporary historical scholarship underscores the ongoing intersections and separations of African American ideas, beliefs, and social practices on the one hand and those of Euro-Americans on the other. Current social movement activists, leaders, teachers, and public policy makers might well learn from these insights.

The Muslim captive Job Ben Solomon, discussed earlier, had not only participated in the sale of Africans before his capture but also agreed to continue the practice in exchange for his freedom.

Like other aspects of black life, the African background also conditioned gender differences within the African American community. In societies like eighteenth-century Gambia, women carried out the consistent, heavy, and laborious farming and household chores. In some cases, "the men were occupied for only about two months of the year, at seed time and harvest . . . but for the rest of the year they hardly seemed even to bother to hunt or fish." As noted in Chapter 1, women were highly valued as childbearers and agriculturists in African societies. Thus, the preponderance of men over women was a consequence not merely of European demand for males, but of African societies' restrictions on who could be enslaved. In the New World, black women continued to combine field and household labor, whereas few enslaved men performed domestic chores. Moreover, as planters adopted new technology, moved from hoe to plow, and diversified the production of farm crops, men dominated work with the new tools and learned a wider variety of skills and jobs beyond field labor. For their part, women continued to hoe by hand, often concentrating on areas that the plows missed. Only domestic service in the planters' households relieved women of field work. Even here, planters preferred to use young girls and elderly women for such household duties.

The division between African-born and American-born blacks also represented an important source of difference within the slave community. The American-born, or "seasoned," Africans instructed the "new Negroes," took the lion's share of skilled jobs, and gained opportunities for mobility beyond the master's household and plantation. Before sex ratios evened out, American-born black men also took a disproportionate share of available black women as spouses. As the African population increased, planters elevated the American-born blacks of earlier years to favored status. In the Chesapeake, the American-born concentrated in the established Tidewater region, whereas the new Africans occupied the harsh and quite isolated Piedmont frontier, where they had relatively fewer contacts with whites or with the most highly Americanized portions of the black population. Similarly, South Carolina's plantation majority developed in substantial isolation from whites and the highly assimilated African American population in and around Charlestown. Here, efforts to create a new African American language and culture entailed substantial internal conflict and turmoil. Africans who turned to European forms of reading sometimes faced ridicule from others, for example. When one European minister trained a few baptized blacks for missionary work among the slaves, he soon reported "some Profane men who laught at their Devotions." Another minister reported simply that "all other slaves do laugh at them."

Unlike in the Chesapeake and early Deep South colonies, the line between the American- and African-born was less sharply drawn in the northern colonies. Seasoned Africans from the West Indies and American-born blacks dominated the northern black population. During the 1740s and 1750s, however, the rapid upsurge of new imports revitalized African elements of northern black culture and modified the previous salience of European forms. By the eve of the American Revolution, a new and more Africanized black culture had emerged in the North.

∼

FROM THEIR SETTLEMENT AT JAMESTOWN through the late seventeenth century, blacks in North America responded to bondage within the context of indentured servitude. During the late seventeenth and early eighteenth centuries, however, the transformation of Africans into "slaves for life" undermined the multiracial nature of the labor force while introducing new cultural tensions and social conflicts among Africans and their American-born descendants. Despite such difficulties, as the African slave trade declined and blacks made the transition to a self-reproducing population, the gap between African- and American-born blacks closed considerably. By the eve of the American Revolution, African American culture and slave communities gradually took shape in British North America. These processes gained potent expression in African American language, family life, religion, leisure time activities, and diverse modes of resistance, ranging from subtle day-to-day conflicts with overseers and plantation owners to open protests and rebellion against the system of bondage itself. In the meantime, as the ideas of the American Revolution—liberty, equality, and citizenship—gained momentum among white colonists, African Americans prepared to launch a more overt, articulate, and concerted effort to win their own freedom. This story is told in Chapter 5.

CHAPTER 5

~

African Americans and the American Revolution

Following the conclusion of the French and Indian War in 1763, the relations between the colonies and Great Britain deteriorated. The British imperial government imposed new taxes and tightened control over colonial commerce. As the new restrictions took effect, the colonies increasingly resorted to revolutionary ideology to justify their resistance. White colonists protested against what they called the British Parliament's effort to "enslave" them. Their ideas of revolution rested on the premise that human beings had certain "natural" and "inalienable rights" to freedom that were given to them at birth. As the colonists filled the air with cries of "liberty" against "tyranny," enslaved and free blacks, particularly in the northern colonies, not only joined street demonstrations but also participated in the first military engagements between the colonial forces and the imperial army. Their efforts played an important role in the American Declaration of Independence in 1776.

Although African Americans supported the independence movement, the colonists soon defined the revolutionary struggle in racist terms and barred blacks from the Continental army. Blacks clearly understood this contradiction between the colonists' insistence on freedom for themselves and their enslavement of Africans and African Americans. As whites excluded blacks from the struggle for national liberation, African Americans employed the rhetoric of the Revolution to buttress their own fight for freedom. For blacks, bond and free, however, the road to liberation was not necessarily synonymous with support for the American revolutionaries. Following rejection by the American forces, large numbers of enslaved people escaped from the plantations and took refuge behind British lines. Only then, as the British welcomed blacks into their ranks, did the colonists drop the racial bar and enlist blacks in the revolutionary struggle.

BLACK RESISTANCE, ANTISLAVERY SENTIMENT, AND THE BEGINNINGS OF THE REVOLUTION

From the Stamp Act crisis of the 1760s through the mid-1770s, African Americans took advantage of the revolutionary struggle and raised their own chants for "Liberty." Although contemporary whites like Henry Laurens of South Carolina interpreted the words of African Americans as "thoughtless imitation," blacks soon demonstrated the deep meaning that freedom held for them. In November 1773, a group of enslaved Virginians held a "secret meeting" to select a leader to guide their participation in the war. When the Virginian James Madison heard of their efforts, he exclaimed that the "revolutionary rhetoric" and growing resistance of slaves "should be concealed as well as suppressed." At about the same time, a South Carolina legislator complained that "it was already known, [the slaves] entertained ideas that the present contest was for obliging us to give them their liberty."

Freedom Petitions and Resistance Activities

African American use of republican ideology emerged most forcefully in the northern colonies, where blacks lodged a rising number of freedom petitions with colonial officials. In 1773, enslaved Bostonians delivered emancipation petitions to General Thomas Gage, commander in chief of the British forces in North America; to the governor of the Massachusetts Bay Colony; and to the Massachusetts General Court. In one case, a group of blacks petitioned for freedom, exclaiming that "a Grate Number of Blacks" were "held in a state of slavery within the bowels of a free and christian country." Another group petitioned the governor for permission to work for themselves one day a week and to use their earnings to purchase themselves. The petitioners expected "great things from men who have made such a noble stand against the designs of their *fellow men* to enslave them." Such petitions not only invoked the principles of "liberty" but also underscored the point with references to the Bible: "We desire to bless GOD, who loves Mankind, who sent his Son to die for their Salvation, and who is no Respecter of Persons (see box)."

During the war years, black men and women escalated their petition drive for freedom. The language of such petitions became even more forceful. In Pennsylvania, when conservatives sought to limit their freedom, blacks petitioned the legislature in no uncertain terms: "We fear we are too bold, but our all is at stake. The grand question of slavery or liberty is too important for us to be silent—it is the momentous passion of our lives; if we are silent this day, we may be silent forever." In January 1777, Massachusetts blacks based their demand for freedom on the same principles that led to the break with England, pleading that the principle of liberty "pleads stronger than a thousand arguments." Two years later, in Portsmouth, New Hampshire, some nineteen blacks asked that "the name of slave may not more be heard in a land gloriously contending for the sweets of freedom." Portsmouth blacks also proclaimed that "the God of nature gave them life and freedom, upon

1773

Africans in Boston Petition the Governor for Relief

PROVINCE OF THE MASSACHUSETTS-BAY.

To his Excellancy THOMAS HUTCHINSON, Esq; Governor;

To the Honorable His Majesty's Council, and

To the Honorable House of REPRESENTATIVES in General Court assembled at BOSTON, the 6th Day of January, 1773.

The humble PETITION of many SLAVES, living in the Town of BOSTON, and other Towns in the Province, is this, namely,

That your Excellency and Honors, and the Honorable the Representatives would be pleased to take their unhappy State and Condition under your wise and just Consideration.

We desire to bless GOD, who loves Mankind, who sent his Son to die for their Salvation, and who is no Respector of Persons; that he hath lately put it into the Hearts of Multitudes on both Sides of the Water, to bear our Burthens, some of whom are Men of great Note and Influence; who have pleaded our Cause with Arguments which we hope will have their weight with this Honorable Court.

We presume not to dictate to your EXCELLENCY and Honors, being willing to rest our Cause on your Humanity and Justice; yet would beg leave to say a Word or two on the Subject.

Although some of the Negroes are vicious, (who doubtless may be punished and restrained by the same Laws which are in Force against other of the King's Subjects) there are many others of a quite different Character, and who if made free, would soon be able as well as willing to bear a Part in the Public Charges; many of them good natural Parts, are discreet, sober, honest, and industrious; and may it not be said of many, that they are virtuous and religious, although their Condition is in itself so unfriendly to Religion, and every moral Virtue except *Patience.* How many of that Number have there been, and now are in this Province, who have had every Day of their Lives imbittered with this most intolerable Reflection, That, let their Behaviour be what it will, neither they, nor their Children to all Generations, shall ever be able to do, or to possess and enjoy any Thing, no, not even *Life itself,* but in a Manner as the *Beasts that perish.*

We have no Property! We have no Wives! No Children! We have no City! No Country! But we have a Father in Heaven, and we are determined as far as his Grace shall enable us, and as far as our degraded contemptuous Life will admit, to keep all his Commandments: Especially will we be obedient to our Masters, so long as GOD in his sovereign Providence shall *suffer* us to be holden in Bondage. . . .

We humbly beg leave to add but this one Thing more: We pray for such Relief only, which by no Possibility can ever be productive of the least Wrong or Injury to our Masters; but to us will be as Life from the dead.

Signed, FELIX
1773

Source: Deirdre Mullane, ed., *Crossing the Danger Water: Three Hundred Years of African-American Writing* (New York: Doubleday, 1993), pp. 32–33.

the terms of most perfect equality with other men. That freedom is an inherent right of the human species."

Blacks also hoped to alleviate the poverty of their children and ensure their freedom. A Connecticut petition referred to "the miserable conditions" of children "who are training up, and kept in preparation, for a like State of Bondage and Servitude as their parents." In Boston, Belinda petitioned for the freedom of her daughter as well as her own. Belinda decried the injustice of slavery and the exploitation of her labor:

> The face of your petitioner is now marked with the furrows of time, and her frame feebly bending under the oppression of years, while she, by the laws of the land, is denied the enjoyment of one morsel of that immense wealth, a part whereof hath been accumulated by her own industry, and the whole augmented by her servitude.

The petitioner urged the general court to provide a living allowance "out of the estate of Colonel Royall [her owner], as will prevent her, and her more infirm daughter, from misery in the greatest extreme." Another black woman suggested that she would continue to work "most agreeable" for herself and her family if placed "on terms of freedom."

African Americans not only petitioned governmental bodies but also participated in street demonstrations and overt encounters with imperial authorities. In 1770, they took part in the street fighting that became known as the Boston Massacre. In the violent encounter between British soldiers and colonists, the black sailor Crispus Attucks lost his life. Part African and part Nantucket Indian, Attucks was a runaway slave who worked on ships and in a local rope factory. When the English government increased the number of troops stationed in Boston, soldiers sometimes supplemented their pay by taking civilian jobs. This practice undercut the livelihood of black and white workers like Attucks, who blamed British officials for widespread suffering among his fellow workers. In a letter to the governor, Attucks also warned, "You will hear further from us hereafter."

Under the leadership of Crispus Attucks, a multiracial group of working people marched against the British military guard at the Custom House on King Street. Attucks urged the group to "attack the main-guard," or as he exclaimed, "strike at the root." Ignoring the fact that Attucks was over forty years old at the time, one contemporary observer described the group as "saucy boys, negroes and mulattoes, Irish Teagues and outlandish jacktarrs." When British soldiers finally fired into the crowd, Attucks was the first of four colonials to die in the revolution that transformed the thirteen colonies into an independent nation. At the funeral services for fallen victims of English tyranny, white Bostonians honored the dead without regard to the color line. As the *Massachusetts Gazette* reported, "all the Bells tolled a solemn Peal," and the townsmen laid Attucks to rest with his white compatriots "in one vault in the middle burying ground."

In the throes of social conflict, black women also found a militant voice. When the earl of Dartmouth, the king's representative in North America, arrived in

British troops fire on Crispus Attucks and other demonstrators in the confrontation that became known as the Boston Massacre. *Bettmann/Corbis*

Boston in August 1772, the black poet Phillis Wheatley expressed hope that he would fight tyranny:

No more *America*, in mournnful strain
Of wrongs, and grievances unredress'd complain,
No longer shall thou dread the iron chain,
Which wanton *Tyranny* with lawless hand
Has made, and with it meant t' en-slave the land.
Should you, my lord, while you peruse my song,
Wonder from whence my love for *Freedom* sprung,
Whence flow these wishes for the common good,
By feeling hearts alone best understood,
I, young in life, by seeming cruel fate,
Was snatch'd from *Afric's* fancy'd happy seat:
What pangs excruciating must molest,
What sorrows labour in my parent's breast?
Steel'd was that soul and by no misery mov'd

That from a father seiz'd his babe belov'd
Such, such my case. And can I then but pray
Others may never feel tyrannic sway?

Whereas during the 1760s, Wheatley had written, "Twas mercy brought me from my Pagan Land," she now concluded: "Such, such my case. And can I then but pray / Others may never feel tyrannic sway?"

Three years later, black women supported colonial military encounters with British forces. In early 1775, when British commander General Thomas Gage sent officers from Boston to explore the roads of Suffolk and Worcester, they encountered a black woman cook in a local tavern. The woman understood and discouraged their plans, as suggested by the report of a British officer:

At first she was very civil, but afterwards began to eye us very attentively . . . when we observed to her that it was a very fine country, upon which she answered so it is, and we have brave fellows to defend it, and if you go up any higher you will find it is so.

Fearing for their lives, the British officers "resolved not to sleep there that night."

Black men fought in the first battles of war. They served in early regiments from Connecticut, Rhode Island, New Hampshire, New York, Virginia, and especially

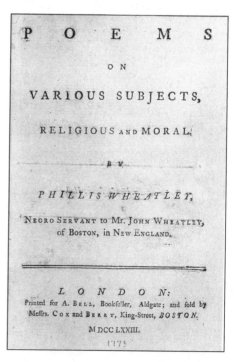

A London publisher released Phillis Wheatley's collection of poems, with this portrait, in 1773.
Left: Boston Athenaeum; Right: American Antiquarian Society

Massachusetts, which early on accepted black volunteers for its "minutemen" and militia units. Some historians describe the slave Prince Easterbrook as "the first to get into the fight" at the Battles of Lexington and Concord on 19 April 1775. At the Battle of Bunker Hill in Boston, according to contemporary sources, the black soldier Cuff Whittemore "fought to the last, and when compelled to retreat, though wounded . . . he seized the sword [of a British officer] slain in the redoubt. . . . He served faithfully throughout the war, with many hair-breadth scrapes from sword and pestilence." Also, at the Battle of Bunker Hill, another black man, Peter Salem, received credit for killing a British officer, one Major Pitcairn: "A negro man belonging to Grotan, took aim at Major Pitcairn, as he was rallying the dispersed British troops, & shot him thro' the head. . . ."

Following the Battle of Bunker Hill, fourteen white Massachusetts officers petitioned the legislature to recognize the valor of another black rebel, Salem Poor. "In the person of this said Negro," the petition stated, "centers a brave and gallant soldier." General John Thomas, commander of a brigade in Boston, later described black soldiers as "in General, Equally serviceable with other men, for Fatigue & in action; many of them have proved themselves brave." In Virginia, a free black, William Flora, and an anonymous bondsman participated in the Battle of Great Bridge. The bondsman rendered invaluable service as a spy, while Flora "was the last sentinel that came into the breast work" and "did not leave his post until he had fired several times . . . amidst a shower of musket balls [from the British]."

The homefront activities of black men and women reinforced the exploits of black soldiers. As the Virginian Edmund Randolph noted, black women "could handle deadly weapons" and joined their men in Maroon settlements in the swamps of South Carolina, Georgia, and parts of North Carolina. In December 1774, in St. Andrew Parish, Georgia, six black men and four women owned by Captain Morris made a desperate bid for freedom. They not only killed the overseer and his wife but also murdered or wounded neighboring plantation owners and members of their families. Similarly, in the summer of 1775, in St. Bartholomew Parish, South Carolina, several preachers, including two black women, confessed that they planned "to take" their freedom by "killing the whites." In Wilmington, North Carolina, authorities uncovered a conspiracy to emancipate slaves from Beaufort, Pitt, and Craven Counties. According to reports, under the leadership of a bondsman named Merrick, blacks planned to "fall on and destroy the family where they lived, then to proceed, from House to House (burning as they went) until they arrived in the Back Country."

In the North and South, enslaved blacks often defied the law and met in secret religious meetings before sunrise and after sunset. In these secret gatherings, black ministers sometimes preached to "Great crowds of Negroes" in their own language and style, telling them that "Our Lord . . . was about to alter the World & set the Negroes Free." In Savannah, the black preacher named David spoke for many when he declared that he "did not doubt, but God would send Deliverance to the Negroes, from the power of their Masters as he freed the Children of Israel from Egyptian Bondage." In 1782, the New York minister and writer Jupiter Hammon published a sermon entitled "A Winter Piece." In this sermon, Hammon supported the quest for freedom in this world:

> My Brothers, many of us are seeking temporal freedom, and I wish you may obtain it; remember that all power in heaven and on earth belongs to God. . . . But how art we to forget that God spoke these words, saying, I am the Lord thy God, which brought thee out of the house of bondage.

At another point, Hammon echoed the rights-of-man movement:

> That liberty is a great thing we may know from our feelings, and we may likewise judge from the conduct of the white people in this war. . . . I must say that I have hoped that God would open up their eyes, when they were so much engaged for liberty, to think of the state of the poor blacks.

Antislavery Sentiment

As African Americans deepened their resistance activities, the contradiction between their enslavement and the struggle for national liberation loomed large. Some white revolutionary leaders gradually recognized the contradiction and spoke out against human bondage. As early as the 1760s, James Otis of Boston had expressed the belief that blacks and whites, born in America, "are free born by the law of nature." In August 1772, Benjamin Franklin wrote from England to the Quaker Anthony Benezet: "I am glad to hear that the disposition against keeping Negroes grows more general in North America. Several pieces had been lately printed here against the practice, and I hope in time it will be taken into consideration and suppressed by the legislature." In October 1773, the *Pennsylvania Chronicle* was even more direct. "While we persist in the practice of enslaving Africans," the editor exclaimed, "our mouths ought to be shut entirely as to any duties or taxes which Great Britain may see cause to lay upon us."

In 1774, the Continental Congress voted to outlaw the continuation of the slave trade and sanctioned a boycott against those who continued the practice. Although some states, such as Pennsylvania, imposed prohibitively high tariffs on the traffic, Connecticut and Rhode Island outlawed it altogether. According to the Rhode Island law, "Those who are desirous of enjoying all the advantages of liberty themselves should be willing to extend personal liberty to others." In a similar vein, the *New Jersey Gazette* proclaimed that "the man who only abhors tyranny when it points to himself . . . is altogether unworthy of the esteem of the virtuous, and can never . . . merit the confidence of a free people." Likewise, in the *Massachusetts Spy,* the Worcester County committee of correspondence denounced the institution of slavery and resolved to use its influence toward "emancipating the NEGROES." In New York, the young attorney John Jay warned that if the new nation failed to free blacks, then "her own prayers to Heaven for liberty will be impious."

WHEREAS the NEGROES in the counties of Briftol and Worcefter, the 24th of March laft, petitioned the Committees of Correfpondence for the county of Worcefter (then convened in Worcefter) to affift them in obtaining their freedom. THEREFORE,
In County Convention, June 14th, 1775.
RESOLVED, That we abhor the enflaving of any of the human race, and particularly of the NEGROES in this country. And that whenever there fhall be a door opened, or opportunity prefent, for any thing to be done toward the emancipating the NEGROES; we will ufe our influence and endeavour that fuch a thing may be effected.
Atteft. WILLIAM HENSHAW, Clerk.

Antislavery resolution of the Worcester County Committee of Correspondence. *American Antiquarian Society*

After putting down the slave revolt of 1774, slaveholders of St. Andrew Parish, Georgia, adopted an antislavery resolution. The signatories declared their intention "to show the world that we are not influenced by any contracted or interested motives, but a general philanthropy for all mankind." The resolution condemned slavery as an unnatural practice and then promised "to use our utmost endeavors for the manumission of our Slaves in this Colony." In his "A Summary View of the Rights of British America" (1774), the Virginian Thomas Jefferson condemned Britain for perpetuating the slave trade and slavery. In his early draft of the Declaration of Independence, Jefferson elaborated upon this antislavery theme. According to Jefferson, the King had waged "cruel war against human nature itself, violating its most sacred rights of life and liberty in the person of a distant people, who never offended him, captivating and carrying them into slavery in another hemisphere, or to incur miserable death in their transportation thither." (See the Documents section.) Although slaveholders rejected this passage and Jefferson deleted it from the final draft of the Declaration of Independence, it demonstrated how some whites moved toward antislavery ideas during the struggle with England. In April 1775, the abolitionist movement gained even greater articulation when Anthony Benezet, Thomas Paine, and several Quakers met at a tavern in Philadelphia and formed the Society for the Relief of Free Negroes Unlawfully Held in Bondage. Nearly a decade later, the society became the Society for Promoting the Abolition of Slavery, Relief of Free Negroes Unlawfully Held in Bondage and for Improving the Condition of the African Race.

Some white women also spoke out against slavery. The countess of Huntingdon in England and Sarah Osborne of Newport, Rhode Island, played crucial roles in the spread of abolitionist ideas. As promoters of the evangelical faith and religious and educational activities, these women influenced blacks like Bristol Yamma, John Quamine, Newport Gardner, and Osborn Tanner as well as white ministers like Ezra Stiles and Samuel Hopkins of Newport. These women had a lot to do with the forthright words of men like Reverend Hopkins, who warned that "if we continue in this evil practice . . . have we any reason to expect deliverance from the calamities we are under?" Abigail Adams of Boston expressed best the revolutionary sentiment of white women when she wrote to her husband, John: "It always appeared a most iniquitous scheme to me to fight ourselves for what we are daily robbing and plundering from those who have as good a right to freedom as we have." As such sentiments took hold, some slaveholders freed enslaved blacks before joining the Continental army. One Connecticut slaveowner freed his slaves, declaring, "I will not fight for liberty and leave a slave at home."

Exclusion from the Military

Despite the spread of antislavery sentiment and the participation of blacks in the early skirmishes of the war, colonists soon rejected the participation of blacks as soldiers. In May 1775, the Massachusetts Committee on Public Safety prohibited the enlistment of "any deserter from the ministerial army" as well as "any stroller, negro, or vagabond." Another enunciation of the decree barred "Negroes, Boys unable to bear Arms nor Old men unfit to endure the Fatigues of the Campaign." The commonwealth's new militia act excluded "Negroes, Indians and Mulattoes." Washington, the Continental army, and other New England and mid-Atlantic states followed suit: Rhode Island, Connecticut, Pennsylvania, Delaware, New Jersey, and New York. The language of such statutes varied, but the end result was the same. As the New York statute put it, "All bought servants during their Servitude shall be free from being listed in any Troop or Company within this Colony." After a brief period of debate, the colonies decided to bar all blacks, enslaved and free, from armed service. The order also called for the expulsion of blacks already under arms. Only the vigorous protests of black soldiers allowed them to serve out their terms.

As white authorities would do later during the Civil War, colonial officials offered conflicting reasons for excluding blacks. Some argued that white soldiers would resist serving alongside blacks, whom they considered "inferior." Others argued that blacks were "cowardly" and would not fight. Still others maintained that armed blacks would take revenge against whites. In Maryland, by the fall of 1775, authorities reported that "the insolence of the Negroes in this country is come to such a height, that we are under a necessity of disarming them which we affected [sic] on Saturday last. We took about eighty guns, some bayonets, swords, etc." For their part, the antislavery friends of blacks argued that it was improper or wrong to ask blacks to spill blood for a cause that would not result in their own freedom. The Massachusetts Committee on Public Safety argued that the use of bondsmen was "inconsistent with the principles that are to be supported, and reflect dishonor on this colony." Above all, however, slaveowners perceived the enlistment of blacks as a threat to their property investment.

As the struggle for liberty intensified, slaveholders increased rather than lessened their vigilance and repression of African Americans. Southern colonists set up special committees to investigate rumors of slave insurrections, formed new militia companies, and increased their efforts to apprehend suspects in revolts or plots to revolt. Throughout the war, planters continued to execute enslaved blacks for insurrectionary activities, both real and imagined. In Virginia, in April 1781, authorities tried and convicted Jack, a bondsman, for robberies, attempted poisoning, and "Engaging and Enlisting several Negroes to raise in Arms and Join the British, the said Jack to be their Captain." Before his execution, Jack managed to escape, freeing a number of other "slaves, deserters, and Tories" in the process. He remained at large for several weeks before being captured and apparently put to death. In the same year, the Virginia court found another slave, John Taylor's Billy, guilty of waging war against the state. The court sentenced Billy "to be hanged by the neck until dead and his head to be severed from his body and stuck up at some public cross road on a pole." Although Billy received a reprieve from the governor, others were not so lucky.

Not all enslaved blacks took advantage of the opportunity to desert their owners. One slaveowner reported that "not one of them left me during the war . . . although they had had great offers." Even when captured by the British, according to the same slaveholder, "they always contrived to make their escapes and return home." The British offered "clothes," "money," and "freedom" to a Virginia bondsman, William Hooper, who pretended to accept the offer but later deserted and rejoined his owner some seventy miles away. Other blacks stayed put and became virtually free people on their owners' land. In South Carolina, blacks often produced and sold crops for their own benefit. In some cases, when an overseer sought to exert his authority, blacks paid no attention to his orders, or as some owners reported, they showed "no subjection" to the overseer's commands.

SHIFTING MILITARY POLICIES AND THE RECRUITMENT OF BLACK TROOPS

Although African American resistance was by no means limited to the conditions ushered in by the revolutionary struggle, the growing conflict between England and the colonists opened up new possibilities for freedom. British officials took advantage of the colonists' efforts to protect their property rights in slaves. On one occasion, General Gage warned South Carolina planters that their opposition to the Crown might mean "that your rice and indigo will be brought to market by Negroes instead of white people." After seizing the city of Williamsburg for the English Crown in the spring of 1775, Lord Dunmore threatened to emancipate the enslaved people and "reduce the City of Williamsburg to ashes." On 7 November 1775, he dropped the threat and issued a proclamation promising slaves of rebels freedom in exchange for service in the British army. Dunmore's proclamation stated in part:

> I do hereby further declare all indented servants, negroes, or others, (appertaining to rebels,) free, that are able to bear arms, they adjoining His Majesty's Troops, as soon as may be, for the more speedily reducing the Colony to a proper sense of their duty, to His Majesty's Crown and dignity.

Similarly, as the war unfolded and spread from the North and Upper South into the Deep South, British officials expanded on Dunmore's strategy. On 30 June 1779, the commander in chief of the British army, Henry Clinton, issued the Philipsburg Proclamation, which extended freedom to blacks in exchange for participation in the military forces.

British Recruitment

The Philipsburg and Dunmore Proclamations were by no means humanitarian or emancipationist policies. They were military measures designed to bring the recalcitrant colonies into line. Before Lord Dunmore issued his famous edict, for example, African Americans had offered "to join him and take up arms." Dunmore not only dismissed their overture but also threatened "severe" reprisals against them should they "renew their application." Dunmore's proclamation applied to able-bodied slaves of "rebels" only, leaving slaves of loyalists in chains. In addition, the Philipsburg Proclamation stipulated that blacks captured behind enemy lines would be sold for the profit of their captors.

Despite limitations, British military policies increased opportunities for blacks to escape from rebel plantations. African Americans had already increased their perception of England as an ally when the English court delivered its ruling in the famous Somerset case of 1772. James Somerset had been purchased in Virginia, but his master later took him abroad, where Somerset escaped after two years on English soil. Through the intervention of the English abolitionist Granville Sharp, Somerset gained his freedom on English soil, where, the chief justice argued, the free "law of England" overruled the institution of slavery. This ruling encouraged many North American blacks, and some took dramatic and direct steps to test its promise. Described as a "cunning, artful, sensible Fellow," a Georgia house servant named Bacchus forged a pass, assumed the name John Christian, and headed for a "Vessel bound for Great Britain, from knowledge he has determined of Somerset's case." As early as June 1775, when Dunmore abandoned Williamsburg and took refuge aboard the ship *Fowey* at Yorktown, he added black runaways to his fleeing contingent of three hundred white soldiers. Following his proclamation, however, some sources suggest that some two hundred runaways joined Dunmore "immediately" and that another hundred followed within a week.

By early December 1775, the British had armed three hundred blacks. They outfitted them in military uniforms with the words "Liberty to Slaves" inscribed across the breast. The governor dubbed these soldiers Lord Dunmore's Ethiopian Regiment. Before the New Year, black soldiers fought at the Battle of Kemp's Landing, where they pushed the revolutionaries back and captured two of their commanding officers. In the Battle of Great Bridge, however, the revolutionary forces, which also included enslaved and free blacks, forced the governor's troops to retreat. Although Dunmore would abandon his Chesapeake landbase by August 1776, he retained naval operations along the coast. Chesapeake planters soon transported blacks, their families, and other valuables inland away from the coast, where English ships offered asylum to runaways and launched raids on nearby plantations. Chesapeake authorities also increased the number of militia companies charged with stopping "the Negros flocking down from the interior parts of the country" to British lines. Despite such precautions, blacks continued to desert the plantations of Virginia and Maryland. In February 1777, British ships reported receiving an estimated 3,000 runaways from the tobacco counties of Virginia. After the Philipsburg decree and the opening of the Deep South campaign, South Carolina and Georgia also reported growing numbers of fugitives. By war's end, some 15,000 to 20,000 blacks had deserted to British lines. Some 800 to 1,000 of these blacks served as soldiers in the British army. As one report stated, they were not "enticed" but "came as freemen and demanded protection." They often presented themselves, saying that "they came for the King." Some expressed the belief that "the War was come to help the poor Negroes."

Some northern blacks also joined loyalists and resisted the patriots. The black contingents, however, generally disappeared with the retreat of the British. In late 1775, a small number of loyalist blacks supplemented the 561 blacks in Boston. By early 1776, when the British departed, they took their "company of Negroes" with them. In New York, however, the British occupied the state for most of the war and recruited blacks as teamsters and members of the "Light Dragoons." In New Jersey, a black man named Tye led a group of loyalists in attacks on plantations and liberated enslaved blacks and white indentured servants.

Revolutionary Enlistment of Black Troops

As enslaved and free blacks defected to British lines in rising numbers, the revolutionaries dropped racial barriers and enlisted blacks into the military. Washington became convinced that the outcome of the war hinged on "which side can arm the Negroes the faster." Moreover, white draftees remained low, and desertion among whites had become a major problem. An estimated one-third of white American troops deserted during the course of their service. In the Deep South, turnover among the troops was especially large, requiring about four hundred thousand enlisted men to maintain only thirty-five thousand men in active duty. Furthermore, the Continental army faced increasing reverses on the battlefield. Key military defeats at Forts Washington and Lee forced the Continental army to retreat across the state of New Jersey. Under the impact of these military setbacks, one historian concludes that "the Continental Army dissolved like a morning fog."

As early as 1777, when the Continental Congress set troop quotas for the various states, the racial bar started to fall. Military officials in the northern, mid-Atlantic, and Upper South states ignored state laws and informally admitted blacks to the military. At the same time, states gradually modified their legal ban on blacks. By October 1777, the Connecticut legislature had exempted from military service any two white men who secured one able-bodied substitute, without regard to "color or status." Another Connecticut statute exonerated from financial responsibility any slaveholder who manumitted his or her slaves. This law not only encouraged masters to free blacks but also encouraged bondsmen to enlist in military service in exchange for freedom.

By 1781, most northern states had passed laws permitting whites to send enslaved men to fight on their behalf. Rhode Island declared "free" any slave who enlisted and passed muster. The state compensated slaveowners and then requested reimbursement from the Continental Congress. Most northern states compensated masters about $400 and promised the bondsmen freedom and a bounty of $50 upon discharge from military service. In lieu of cash, however, New York provided a sizable land grant to any master who enrolled an able-bodied slave into the armed forces for a period of three years. A white officer applauded the change, writing in his journal that "the Negro can take the field instead of his master, and therefore no regiment is to be seen in which there are not Negroes in abundance, and . . . among them are able-bodied and strong fellows." Some states used historical precedent to justify their decision. As Rhode Island officials put it: "History affords us frequent precedents of the wisest, freest and bravest nations having liberated their slaves, and enlist them as soldiers to fight in defence of their country." In a letter to Washington, one northern governor exclaimed that it was "impossible" to "recruit our battalions in any other way."

Upper South states also enlisted black troops. Between the summer of 1780 and the spring of 1781, Maryland authorized the enlistment of enslaved and free blacks. One officer urged the governor to reconsider the execution of a young black convicted of crime, because "he is young healthy and would make a fine soldier." Some Virginians also contemplated, then dropped, plans to raise a regiment of 750 slaves. One advocate declared: "I am of the opinion that the Blacks will make excellent soldiers—indeed experience proves it." Another attacked the opposition: "As to the danger of training them to Arms—tis the child of distempered imagination. There are some people who are forever frightening themselves with Bugbears of their own Creation." But planters feared an economic loss and refused to put the patriot cause above their material interests. As one planter put it, "The price if paid . . . is not equal to the value of a healthy, strong young negro man." Many Virginia slaveholders, as one observer stated, "considered it unjust, sacrificing the property of a part of the community to the exoneration of the rest." Although Virginia banned the enlistment of slaves, it opened its ranks to free blacks.

As northern and Upper South states enabled slaveowners to escape military service by enlisting slaves and free blacks, Deep South states used slaves as an incentive to attract whites to the revolutionary army. South Carolina and Georgia offered slaves as gifts to reward high-ranking officers, pay expenses, and entice poor whites into the military. In April 1781, some South Carolina military officials offered slave bounties by rank: private (one adult slave servant), a colonel (three adult slaves and a child servant). Since these bounties were usually predicated on raiding loyalist property and taking of slaves, they often fell short of their promise and left many white enlisted men and officers disgruntled. Consequently, some slave raids included the property of patriots as well as loyalists.

Although Deep South states rejected the direct use of black troops, the Continental Congress eventually approved the use of black troops, enslaved and free. Like state governments, the central government promised bondsmen freedom and a cash bounty following the war. By 24 August 1778, the Continental army listed some 755 blacks distributed among fourteen brigades. By war's end, an estimated 5,000 blacks had served in the revolutionary army. Contemporary observers soon reported growing numbers of blacks among the white troops. African American soldiers had adopted such surnames as Freeman, Freedom, Liberty, and Free. Many of these blacks represented direct substitutes for whites seeking to elude military service. In New Fairfield, Connecticut, a black man substituted for Jonathan Giddings. In Newark, New Jersey, a slave named Cudjoe served for his master. In Anne Arundel County, Maryland, a slave named Anthony substituted for a Thomas Johnson Jr. In North Carolina, when military officials caught the white deserter William Kitchen, he produced a slave to serve out his time. In another case, a New Jersey man purchased Samuel Suffin for the express purpose of fulfilling his military obligation.

AFRICAN AMERICANS IN THE REVOLUTIONARY FORCES

Black soldiers performed the hard labor and drudgery tasks for fellow white troops as well as officers. Military records are replete with references to blacks as laborers, orderlies, or semidomestic servants. They transported supplies, repaired roads, erected fortifications, dug graves, cooked, washed, and cleaned encampments. White soldiers detested such duties and insisted that blacks perform them wherever and whenever possible. In June 1777, the quartermaster general at Ticonderoga formed a black regiment of "constant fatigue men." In addition to fatigue duty, African Americans became personal servants of white officers. William Lee, Washington's assistant, was perhaps the most renowned. In addition to seven years before the war, Lee served Washington through the entire war years and for twenty years thereafter. Lee is pictured in the background of Washington's famous portrait at West Point in 1780. Similarly, the free black Agrippa Hull, formerly a servant of the evangelist Jonathan Edwards, enlisted in the Massachusetts brigade of General John Paterson, whom he served as an orderly for two years of the war. After leaving the service of Paterson, Hull performed similar duties for the Polish commander Kosciuszko. Another black soldier, Prince Whipple, served as a bodyguard to General Whipple, an aide to George Washington.

George Washington and his assistant, William Lee. This 1780 portrait is by John Trumbull. *Canvas 91.4 × 71.1 cm. Metropolitan Museum of Art. Bequest of Charles Allen Munn, 1924. Accession #24.109.88*

Labor Battalions and Hired Bondsmen

Although Virginia, South Carolina, and Georgia barred the use of slaves as soldiers, slaveowners nonetheless hired or leased blacks to the military. Hired bondsmen worked at the garrisons, in military hospitals and munitions plants, and on the construction of roads and forts. In Virginia, hired blacks performed a variety of duties with the Lancaster District Minutemen and the Second Regiment. In South Carolina, hired slaves erected the double-walled fort at Sullivan's Island and prepared the outworks for the mounting of thirty cannon. Enslaved men erected these structures with such skill that the British assault on the fortress failed. Hired bondsmen also added to the munitions supply when they removed lead ornaments from public buildings, melted them down, and manufactured bullets.

In the North and South, military officials compelled some African Americans to work on defense projects against their will. In March 1776, New York empowered military officials to command the labor of all slaves and free blacks. The law required blacks to appear at a central locale, with all the shovels, axes, hoes, picks, and other tools that they could muster. The city and county of New York compelled blacks to work around the clock on fortifications. Whereas one-half of white male inhabitants were required to work on the Long Island defense project, all blacks were so ordered.

When southerners failed to cooperate in providing hired slave hands, volunteers, or draftees to the military, legislators authorized the impressment of slave laborers against their owners' will. As early as November 1775, Georgia impressed one hundred blacks to erect barriers around the arsenal in Savannah. Two years later, the state passed a comprehensive law requiring slaves to work building forts and other public works to defend the state. Almost from the outset of hostilities, South Carolina also empowered military authorities to take able-bodied black men as pioneers and laborers. When Charleston faced the threat of a British invasion in 1780, military officials forced black men into work on building fortifications. Only a note from the governor excused any slave from duty. If masters failed to comply, their slaves were taken by force.

Infantry, Cavalry, and Artillerymen

Although most blacks served in labor battalions, the intensification of hostilities pressed them into a variety of military occupations, including duty as drummers, infantry, cavalry, and artillerymen. Jabez Jolly, William Nickens, and "Negro Bob" were drummers in the Massachusetts, Virginia, and South Carolina regiments, respectively. In Goochland County, Virginia, the free black John Banks served for two years in the cavalry. This branch of the service involved extraordinary expenses in the maintenance of horses and equipment. The cavalry recruited few poor whites or blacks. As part of the Third Pennsylvania Artillery Regiment, another African American, Edward Hector, distinguished himself as one of a few black artillerymen. The Pennsylvania legislature later rewarded Hector for protecting his horses and ammunition wagon from capture by the enemy. The Georgia legislature rewarded the former slave Austin Dabney for similar artillery service.

Black soldiers helped to purchase American freedom with their lives and limbs in numerous battles and encampments. In addition to the early battles of Lexington, Concord, and Bunker Hill, their service included engagements at Saratoga, Ticonderoga, and Valley Forge. In 1776, Prince Whipple and Oliver Cromwell were at the oars of the boat that transported Washington across the Delaware River to attack the British forces in New Jersey on Christmas Eve. Black soldiers were also present at the final great battle of the war at Yorktown. Although most blacks fought alongside whites, there were three black units: the First Rhode Island Regiment, a Massachusetts company dubbed the Bucks of America, and the Black Brigade of Saint-Domingue. A white army surgeon later remarked that the black soldiers "discharged their duties with zeal and fidelity."

Under the command of Colonel Christopher Greene, the First Rhode Island Regiment engaged the enemy at the Battle of Rhode Island. Composed of a core of ninety-five ex-slaves and thirty-five freedmen, the Rhode Island unit drove the British and their mercenary Hessian troops back in three separate attacks upon their encampment. According to one observer, the Hessian colonel asked permission to change command and go to New York, because he "dared not lead his regiment again to battle, lest his men shoot him for having caused so much loss." The French general Lafayette later described the battle as "the best fought action of the war."

The Rhode Island regiment also fought at Red Bank, Points Bridge, and Yorktown. One contemporary traveler reported that the Rhode Island regiment "is the most neatly dressed, the best under arms, and the most precise in its maneuvers." Indeed, throughout the war, the Rhode Island unit received credit for serving with "efficiency and gallantry." For its part, the Black Brigade, called the Frontages Legion after its French commander, was made up of some 545 black volunteers. Described by the *Paris Gazette* as "colored: volunteer Chasseurs, Mulattoes, and Negroes," the Saint-Domingue blacks helped to save American forces from annihilation in the siege of Georgia during the fall of 1779. Two of these soldiers, Henri Christophe and Martial Besse, received wounds but returned to Saint-Domingue and later became leaders in the Haitian Revolution. Although there is little direct evidence on Boston's black unit, the Bucks of America, John Hancock presented the regiment a banner "bearing his initials" as a "tribute to their courage and devotion throughout the struggle."

In addition to the regular rigors of war, black troops fought under special burdens. They faced antiblack attitudes and social practices within and outside the armed forces. Although some whites, such as Alexander Hamilton, argued that the "natural faculties" of blacks were equal to whites, others, such as Thomas Jefferson, continued to question their valor and intelligence. As Hamilton put it, whites insisted on believing things about blacks that were "founded neither on reason nor in experience." White officers sometimes expressed the greatest disdain for the black troops under their charge. One captain in the Continental army wrote home to his wife that the "nasty lousy appearance" of his black troops was enough "to make one sick of the service." In contrast to its policy with white soldiers, the government denied black soldiers regular pay during the duration of the war. Moreover, most whites served in special volunteer units and state militia, which offered short terms of three, six, nine, or twelve months of service, close to home. Conversely, blacks served mainly in the Continental army, with tours of three years or more. Although a few blacks, such as Thomas Hall of Philadelphia, served close to home during their enlistment, most African Americans traveled long distances from their families and communities of origin.

Compared with their attempts to join the army, blacks faced less resistance to enlistment in the navy. When war broke out, African Americans had already established a long tradition as seamen in colonial navies. In the major port cities of Boston, Baltimore, Philadelphia, New York, and Charleston, among others, black sailors were a vital part of the various state navies as well as the Continental navy. Like their army counterparts, they served primarily in the labor and service departments as "cabin boys," "powder boys," body servants, cooks, general laborers, and stevedores. In addition, the navy employed large numbers of black pilots, particularly on small crafts designed to navigate the inland rivers. In January 1777, for example, one slaveowner sent two of his enslaved pilots to the Maryland Council to be used to transport goods and men along the Chesapeake Bay. The man described his "two sailor negroes" as "fine fellows as ever crost the sea" and urged the council to take good care of them. In Virginia, the black pilot Caesar of Hampton later received his freedom for piloting the "armed vessels of this state during the . . . war years." His exploits included steering the schooner *Patriot* and capturing the British supply vessel *Fanny*. Following the war, Captain James Barron of the navy of Virginia recalled the contributions of black sailors Harry, Cupid, and Aberdeen. Barron believed that these "coloured men, in justice to their merits should not be forgotten."

In South Carolina, as in Virginia, the state authorized the hiring of enslaved blacks on boats at Charleston, Stono Inlet, Georgetown, and Beaufort. The state compensated owners for work performed as well as for any injury or death. The South Carolina navy also purchased its own blacks for labor on the docks and in shipyards. In May 1777, the South Carolina navy purchased a man named Titus for 700 pounds sterling, and at about the same time, it bought two other black men for work in the rope walk. The navy also advertised for such bondsmen in newspapers. One advertisement in the *South Carolina Gazette* announced: "The Commissioners of the Navy are in want of a Number of Negro ship carpenters or caulkers; any person having such to hire by the year are desired to apply."

James Forten would become one of the most renowned black veterans of the revolutionary navy. A free black of Philadelphia, Forten was the son of an African captive. He received some education at the school of the antislavery Quaker Anthony Benezet. At age fifteen, he became a powder boy on a privateer vessel named *Royal Louis.* Under the command of Stephen Decatur Sr., the ship faced defeat at the hands of the English frigate *Amphyon.* Forten and other black and white sailors were taken prisoner. Although most blacks were sold into the West Indies, Forten escaped that fate when the son of a British sea captain took an interest in his welfare. After serving seven months aboard a British prison ship, preferable to being sold in the West Indies, Forten escaped and returned to Philadelphia.

African Americans also served the revolutionary forces as spies, messengers, and guides. When the French major general Lafayette arrived in Williamsburg, Virginia, in March 1781, he received invaluable assistance from James, a bondsman belonging to William Armstead of Kent County. James spied on the movement of the British units under the command of Benedict Arnold and used his knowledge of the Portsmouth region to deliver clandestine letters to other spies operating in or near the British lines. Lafayette later wrote that James "properly acquitted himself with some important communication I g[a]ve him . . . his intelligence from the enemy's camp were industriously collected and more faithfully delivered." For his service, the Virginia assembly granted James his freedom and a pension.

If James was the most well known of the black spies in the service of the revolutionary army, he was not alone. The bondsman Saul Matthews also worked as a spy in the Portsmouth area. He entered the British lines on several different occasions and provided useful information on British troop movements up and down the James River. In March 1783, the South Carolina legislature freed a man named Antiqua, as well as his wife and child, for securing information on "the enemy's movements and designs." Supplementing the formal efforts of spies like James, Saul Matthews, and others was an informal network of enslaved blacks who delivered important information to military officials on a regular basis. Since the British also sent black spies into rebel territory, these networks could be used to deceive as well as to inform.

Blacks in the British Forces

The British army, like the revolutionary forces, employed blacks mainly in labor battalions. More so than the revolutionary forces, however, the British gained their greatest productivity from southern blacks. In Savannah and Charleston, blacks worked on British fortifications, transported supplies, and labored as skilled carpenters, coopers, wheelwrights, and blacksmiths. African Americans also served as foragers, spies, guides, messengers, and soldiers for the British army. In defense of Savannah against the French and Saint-Domingue forces, a black guide steered a much-needed contingent of British reinforcement troops around enemy lines. According to one source, the black guide eluded the revolutionary forces by taking the British troops over land previously covered only "by bears, wolves and runaway Negroes." When General Cornwallis moved north from Charleston across North Carolina into Yorktown, Virginia, during the last days of the war, blacks raided plantations and confiscated food and supplies for the imperial army. In the Savannah area, the British armed an estimated two hundred blacks in 1779; by June 1781, another two hundred blacks served at the fort in Augusta. In the defense of Savannah against rebel American and French troops, Georgia governor James Wright credited blacks with saving the city: "They contributed greatly to our defense and safety." The *Virginia Gazette* also wrote that "a greater number of sailors, marines, militia and armed blacks accounted for the rebels' retreat."

Blacks were even more prominent in the British navy. They represented a mixture of fugitives, forced laborers, and hired "property" of loyalist slaveowners. Like their revolutionary counterparts, these men were considered invaluable. When Dunmore abandoned his landbase and took refuge aboard ship, blacks deserted to his ranks via water. The British incorporated these ex-slaves into its navy as pilots and crewmen. When Virginia rebels captured the pilot boat *Hawk Tender,* its crew included two blacks. The British praised black pilots like Joseph Harris, a runaway. "I think him too useful to His Majesty's service to take away," a naval officer wrote. "He is well acquainted with many creeks in the Eastern Shore, at York, James River, and Nansemand, and many others." In July 1775, Governor Lord William Campbell of South Carolina hoped to outmaneuver the rebels by taking on black pilots. Officials described one black pilot as "by far the best Pilot in this Harbour, and has marks of his own by which he will carry any vessel in spite of what they [patriots] can do." When the British launched its attack on Charleston, enslaved black men piloted three frigates—the *Byron,* the *Sphinx,* and the *Acteon*—up the channel.

Although blacks used the rift between the colonies and England to fight for their own liberation, it was an exceedingly difficult task. If the war offered new opportunities for enslaved and free blacks to fight for their own freedom, it also presented new perils and disruptions in their lives. Indeed, as one historian notes, African Americans stood between "two fires," and many were victimized by both sides of the war. In 1776, for example, after the British launched a series of raids on revolutionary forces in Georgia, the colonists retaliated by attacking loyalist forces and confiscating large numbers of enslaved people, whether they desired to leave or not. In a counterattack, the loyalists organized small guerrilla raids on rebel property and duplicated the process. The British, no less than American forces, asserted their right to sell, hire out, or employ blacks for their own profit. Commanders frequently instructed their subordinates to "sell a Negro to help provide for yourself," "to sell them, and buy shoes for your corps." In short, the imperial army and navy were not only havens for black fugitives but also instruments in the extension of African bondage as well.

When Cornwallis entered Yorktown, where the war officially ended, some four to five thousand blacks accompanied him. They served in capacities similar to those they had known on the plantations, mainly as cooks and laborers for white soldiers, officers, and their women. One officer recalled that "every officer had four to six horses and three or four Negroes, as well as one or two Negresses for cook and maid. Every soldier's woman was mounted and also had a Negro and Negress on horseback for her servants." In the last days of the war, to conserve on food and supplies, Cornwallis expelled large numbers of black refugees from the camp. As the Hessian officer Johann Ewald reported: "We had used them to good advantage . . . and set them free, and now, with fear and trembling, they had to face the reward of their cruel masters." Although Cornwallis surrendered on 19 October 1781, the fighting continued intermittently until the Treaty of Paris was signed in 1783.

An estimated one hundred thousand people left North America in the wake of the American Revolution. Most of these exiles were blacks—loyalist free blacks or slaves of loyalist slaveowners. The majority of these immigrants departed from three American ports—Savannah, Charleston, and New York—and the Spanish port of St. Augustine. Some moved to England; others to Canada, especially Nova Scotia; and others to the West Indies. Still others returned to West Africa. The war itself had witnessed the use of black soldiers from the French colony of Saint-Domingue, which for years had maintained a black militia. As these African Americans established black communities in other parts of the world, they would not only expand the scope of the African diaspora but also spread revolutionary ideas about liberty, equality, and social justice.

THE REVOLUTIONARY WAR SET THE STAGE for the transformation of African American life. Although enslaved and free blacks fought and served on a discriminatory and unequal basis, they adopted the language of "liberty" and sought to transform the Revolution into a struggle for their own liberation. They decried racial limitations on their rights and pushed for a more inclusive, nonracist definition of the independence movement. As their freedom struggle intersected with the rising labor and military demands of war, they achieved partial victory when first the British and then the revolutionary government dropped racial barriers and enlisted blacks into the armed forces. As a result of their part on the fields of battle, some five thousand black soldiers would gain their freedom. Yet, even as the new nation made good on its promise to some blacks, it failed to live up to its revolutionary creed and abolish the institution of slavery. Both the promise and limits of the revolution would become apparent during the early postwar years. African American life in the early republic is the subject of Chapter 6.

~

Race, Republicanism, and the Limits of Democracy

In the wake of the American Revolution, African Americans gained new hope for the future. The Revolution not only stimulated the manumission movement and growth of the free black population but also modified some of the harshest features of slave codes and unleashed a powerful ideology of freedom, rights, and equality. Enslaved and free blacks would use the new ideas to reinforce their efforts to end the system of human bondage. Before African Americans could make good on the promise of the Revolution, however, they faced the intensification of racist ideology, extension of the international slave trade, and new restrictions on the small free black population.

Limitations on the rights-of-man movement for African Americans were inextricably interwoven with growing class conflicts among whites. Middle- and working-class whites exhibited dissatisfaction with elite domination of the new nation's economy and polity. In their view, the Revolution enriched large landowners and merchants at the expense of the small yeoman farmers. Their discontent gained violent expression in Shays's Rebellion of 1786. Commercial elites rallied their forces, put down the revolt, and called for a new constitutional convention in 1787. The new federal constitution that they adopted not only represented the triumph of a class-biased republic but also strengthened the institution of slavery as a race-based system of labor exploitation and social relations. Still, enslaved and free blacks would repeatedly invoke revolutionary ideas to buttress their efforts to end slavery and gain their own independence.

~

FREE BLACKS AND THE PROMISE OF THE REVOLUTION

The Revolutionary War represented the beginning of a new era in African American history. As the revolutionary states established independent constitutions, they adopted the rhetoric of the "rights of man," encouraged freedom suits, and passed gradual manumission statutes (see box). In 1780, Pennsylvania initiated the process of gradual manumission when it outlawed the perpetual enslavement of black people. Specifically, the law stipulated that any person born to slave parents after 1780 would be free on their twenty-eighth birthday. Between the early 1780s and 1804, Connecticut, Rhode Island, New York, and New Jersey enacted similar statutes. In 1783, for its part, the Massachusetts Supreme Court concluded that slavery was "inconsistent with our own conduct and constitution [adopted in 1778]" and set the slave Quok Walker free. Two years after the famous Quok Walker case, the court outlawed slavery by judicial decree.

Antislavery Sentiment and the Second Great Awakening

Although southern states rejected gradual emancipation legislation, they did entertain freedom suits, eased the process of individual manumission, and allowed slaveowners to free blacks by will or by deed. Except for North Carolina, which limited emancipation to persons performing "meritorious service" for the state, southern states revoked their bans on private acts of manumission. The new state constitutions of Delaware, Maryland, Kentucky, North Carolina, and Tennessee went a step further and enfranchised free blacks on the basis of the same property qualifications that governed the voting of free white men. As such laws took effect, some slaveholders emancipated captives and sought to reconcile their practice with their belief in "liberty for all." A Virginian reported: "I cannot satisfy my conscience . . . to have my negro slaves separated from each other, from their husbands and wives." A Maryland slaveowner freed her slaves because human bondage contradicted "the inalienable rights of Mankind." In Kentucky, an emancipator said simply that slavery "was inconsistent with republican principles . . . which declare that all men are by nature equally free." Although most manumissions took place in the Upper South, Deep South planters also freed some of their slaves. Unlike their Upper South counterparts, however, Deep South planters usually freed the products of their own interracial sexual relations with black women.

The manumission movement was reinforced by the Northwest Ordinance of 1787, the expansion of antislavery societies, and the evangelical sentiment unleashed by the Second Great Awakening. The Northwest Ordinance prohibited slavery north of the Ohio River, in what was known as the Northwest Territory— the states of Ohio, Indiana, Illinois, Wisconsin, and Michigan. Although such states would develop antiblack policies that limited the in-migration of free blacks, they also became important sources of antislavery sentiment and support for the underground railroad, which aided fugitives fleeing southern bondage for the North. In varying forms, antislavery societies in New York, Massachusetts, and Virginia envisioned the complete abolition of slavery. Ministers and teachers like Samuel Hopkins of Rhode Island and St. George Tucker of Virginia advocated individual manumission of blacks as "a matter of Christian conscience."

In 1785, the Second Great Awakening emerged in the James River, Virginia, area. Similar to the Great Awakening of the 1730s and 1740s, this religious movement reinforced the emancipation process. Evangelicals merged antislavery

SOURCES FROM THE PAST

1783

Virginia Emancipates Slaves for Military Service During the American Revolution

An act directing the emancipation of certain slaves who have served as Soldiers in this State, and for the Emancipation of the Slave Aberdeen.

I. Whereas it hath been represented to the present General Assembly, that during the course of the war, many persons in this State had caused their slaves to enlist in certain regiments or corps raised within the same, having tendered such slaves to the officers appointed to recruit forces within the States, as substitutes for free persons whose lot or duty it was to serve in such regiments or corps, at the same time representing to such recruiting officers that the slaves, so enlisted by their direction and concurrence, were freemen; and it appearing further to this Assembly, that on the expiration of the term of enlistment of such slaves, that the former owners have attempted again to force them to return to a state of servitude, contrary to the principles of justice, and to their own solemn promise;

II. And whereas it appears just and reasonable, that all persons enlisted as aforesaid, who have faithfully served agreeable to the terms of their enlistment, and have thereby of course contributed towards the establishment of American liberty and independence, should enjoy the blessings of freedom as a reward for their toils and labors;

Be it therefore enacted, That each and every slave who, by the appointment and direction of his owner, hath enlisted in any regiment or corps raised within this State, either on Continental or State establishment, and hath been received as a substitute for any free person whose duty or lot it was to serve in such regiment or corps, and hath served faithfully during the terms of such enlistment, or hath been discharged from such service by some officer duly authorized to grant such discharge, shall, from and after the passing of this act, be fully and completely emancipated, and shall be held and deemed free, in as full and ample a manner as if each and every [one] of them were specially named in this act. . . .

III. And whereas it has been represented to this General Assembly, that Aberdeen, a negro man slave, hath labored a number of years in the public service at the lead mines, and for his meritorious services is entitled to freedom; *Be it therefore enacted,* That the said slave Aberdeen shall be, and he is hereby, emancipated and declared free in as full and ample a manner as if he had been born free.

Source: Hening's Statutes at Large of Virginia, 1783, in Deirdre Mullane, ed., Crossing the Danger Water: Three Hundred Years of African-American Writing (New York: Doubleday, 1993), pp. 37–38.

---

religious traditions with the new revolutionary ideology and used it to promote the abolitionist movement. With the arrival of the English minister Thomas Coke in 1784, English and northern white religious leaders entered the Chesapeake region with their "revitalized notions of the brotherhood of man." Coke strongly urged Methodists to "emancipate their Slaves." Although Coke would soon modify his position on emancipation under pressure from influential slaveholders, the Methodist church adopted antislavery principles, declaring slavery "contrary to the laws of God, of men, and of nature, and that it was hurtful to society and contrary to the dictates of conscience and pure religion." In 1785, Baptists pursued a similar course when representatives from various churches condemned hereditary slavery as "contrary to the word of God." By 1790, the Virginia Baptists also endorsed the use of the state "to extirpate the horrid evil [slavery] from the land and pray Almighty god, that our Honorable Legislature may have it in their power, to proclaim the general jubilee, consistent with the principles of good policy." Although North Carolina limited manumission to those showing evidence of "meritorious service" to the state, Quakers regularly violated the law and became trustees of slaves liberated by non-Quaker masters.

The belief that all people were equal in the sight of God struck a deep chord in the hearts and

In 1787, the English abolitionist and potter Josiah Wedgwood carved this cameo for the London Society for the Abolition of Slavery. This symbol of bondage would become widely known in America, with both male and female versions in use by the eve of the Civil War. *Library of Congress*

minds of African Americans. Between the end of the American Revolution and the early nineteenth century, thousands of Methodist and Baptist churches admitted blacks. By 1800, black Methodists sometimes outnumbered white parishioners in the churches of Maryland and South Carolina. When the revival movement erupted, one master lamented that his bondsman Sam

> was raised in a family of religious persons, commonly called Methodists, and has lived with some of them for years past, on terms of perfect equality. . . . The refusal to continue him on these terms . . . has given him offense, and is the sole cause of his absconding.

During the 1780s and 1790s, the black Methodist minister Harry Hosier, usually called "Black Harry," traveled with white itinerant ministers Coke, Asbury, Garrettson, and Whatcoat. In Maryland and Virginia, "Black Harry" preached to both enslaved and white audiences.

African Americans made up an even greater proportion of Baptist congregations than of Methodist ones. Until the early 1800s, black and white worshippers also shared the same buildings and frequently seated themselves as they pleased. As late as 1792, in Charles City, Virginia, free black men voted on church affairs along with other "free male members" of the congregation. In some cases, enslaved preachers were so effective among white as well as black congregations that whites helped them gain their freedom. In North Hampton, Virginia, white Baptists raised money and purchased the freedom of Jacob Bishop. In Roanoke, Virginia, a white congregation bought the freedom of a man named Simon, stating that "we think him ordained of God to preach the gospel."

In Charleston, South Carolina, blacks not only outnumbered whites but also controlled the finances, discipline, and roster of delegates to quarterly conferences. In Tennessee, as late as 1806, the Baptist church permitted "Black Brethren . . . [to] enjoy the same liberty . . . as white members have and do enjoy." Moreover, black and white preachers headed interracial churches and often shared the same pulpit. In Gloucester County, Virginia, the black minister William Lemon pastored the predominantly white Petsworth Baptist Church. He also served as a delegate to the local Baptist Association meetings between 1797 and 1801. In Fayetteville, North Carolina, the black Methodist minister Henry Evans, a shoemaker by trade, organized the city's first Methodist church and preached to a mixed congregation of blacks and whites until his death in 1810. In the Deep South, black ministers also preached to white congregations, especially in Georgia, where Andrew Bryan, Jesse Peters, and David George addressed white as well as black audiences.

Growth of the Free Black Population

As the manumission movement gained momentum, the promise of the Revolution found its greatest expression in the rise of the free black population. Most of the 5,000 blacks who served in the Continental army soon gained their freedom. Through natural increase and immigration, among other sources, the free black population increased from negligible numbers at the onset of the American Revolution to 60,000 in 1790 and to nearly 234,000 in 1820. Most of this increase occurred during the first two decades after the war, when the free black population rose by an estimated 70 to 80 percent. By the early 1800s, free blacks made up nearly 10 percent of the black population and about 5 percent of all free people in the South, particularly the Chesapeake region, which claimed over 134,200 free blacks, compared with about 20,150 in the Deep South. Free people of color made up a faster-growing component of the southern population than enslaved and free whites. Although most free blacks lived in the rural South, the free black population was disproportionately northern. By 1820, nearly 42 percent (about 99,280) of all free blacks lived in the North.

The rapid growth of the free black population reinforced the flight from bondage in the postwar years. Fugitives now included blacks who had military experience on the side of both British and American forces. In Massachusetts, for example, along with Felix Cuff, a Revolutionary War veteran, a group of blacks ran away from their owners and took refuge in a cave called Devil's Den, in a snake-infested area in the town of Waltham called "Snake Hill." These Maroons defended themselves from outside attack and eventually gained their freedom. Virginia and North Carolina slaves escaped into the Dismal Swamp, where they erected a Maroon community, replete with agriculture, livestock, and a system of governance and physical defense. The group remained intact through the early 1790s. In Georgia and South Carolina, bands of blacks retained their arms from the war years and used them to establish new runaway camps in the swamps of the lower Savannah River. Fugitives cleared swampland, erected houses, planted rice fields, and set up elaborate fortifications to protect the settlement from invasion. After securing their location in the spring of 1787, some one hundred armed men not only attacked plantations on both sides of the Savannah River but also assaulted two militia companies of Georgia state troops. Under the leadership of "Captain Cudjoe" and "Captain Lewis," these men called themselves "the King of England's Soldiers." Only the combined forces of Georgia state troops and Indians destroyed the settlement. According to the commanding officer of the Georgia militia, the leaders of these Lower South fugitives "are the very fellows that fought, and maintained their ground against the brave lancers at the siege of Savannah."

In the wake of the Haitian Revolution in 1792, free black émigrés moved into South Carolina and Georgia in rising numbers. Since these free black immigrants had opposed the slave revolt and sided with the French, they were forced to flee for their lives when enslaved blacks rose up and drove slaveowners off the island. The Haitian revolt also played a key role in the U.S. acquisition of the Louisiana Territory in 1803. As blacks broke the French grip on their key Caribbean stronghold, Napoleon found it difficult to hold on to the vast North American territory and sold it to the United States for a pittance, and without regard for the indigenous peoples in the region. The Louisiana Purchase brought nearly 10,500 free blacks into the union. As with the Haitian refugees, the French- and Spanish-speaking free blacks of Louisiana had sided with slaveowners in the area and occupied a privileged position. In the Upper South, too, the number of Haitian immigrants increased. "Within a few weeks" of Haitian immigration, a Virginia resident wrote to the governor that several blacks had "eloped from their master's plantations."

Cities offered the greatest opportunities for runaways to make good their escape. In 1795, a Virginia owner reported that his bondsman had "inquired very particularly" about the way to Philadelphia because "he heard Negroes were free there." The growth of free black urban communities enabled rising numbers of enslaved blacks to forge certificates and "pass for free men." Planters frequently advertised that fugitives were probably bound for places where they had friends and relatives who would "conceal and assist them." Bordered by three slave states, Pennsylvania attracted large numbers of free blacks and fugitives from the Upper South. Philadelphia's free black population increased by nearly 210 percent between 1790 and 1800 and by another 50.4 percent the following decade. New York experienced 83.5- and 54.3-percent increases during the same periods. Though less dramatically, Boston's black population rose by 53.3 and 26.4 percent in these decades. The percentage of northeastern blacks living in cities increased from roughly 12 to 17 percent in 1790 to nearly 30 percent by 1820 (see tables).

Blacks as Percentage of Total Population, 1790			
New England		**Upper South**	
Maine	0.6%	Delaware	21.6
New Hampshire	0.6	Maryland	34.7
Vermont	0.3	Virginia	40.9
Massachusetts	1.4	North Carolina	26.8
Rhode Island	6.3	Kentucky	17.0
Connecticut	2.3	Tennessee	10.6
Middle States		**Lower South**	
New York	7.6	South Carolina	43.7
New Jersey	7.7	Georgia	35.9
Pennsylvania	2.4		

Source: Ira Berlin, *Slaves Without Masters: The Free Negro in the Antebellum South* (New York: The New Press, 1974), p. 23. Data from U.S. Bureau of the Census.

Growth of Enslaved and Free Black Population, 1790–1820				
	1790	**1800**	**1810**	**1820**
Slave	697,624	893,602	1,191,362	1,538,022
Free	59,557	108,435	186,446	233,634
Total	**757,181**	**1,002,037**	**1,377,808**	**1,771,656**

Source: *Negro Population, 1790–1915* (1918; reprint, New York: Arno Press, 1968), p. 53. Data from U.S. Bureau of the Census.

Although cities like New York, Boston, and Philadelphia claimed the largest concentration of free northern blacks, Baltimore, Alexandria, Richmond, Petersburg, and Norfolk accounted for the bulk of free blacks in the Upper South states of Maryland and Virginia. In the Deep South, Savannah, Charleston, and New Orleans registered the largest numbers of free people of color in Georgia, South Carolina, and Louisiana. Urban officials often complained that "large numbers of free blacks flock from the country to the towns." As whites moved to the rural western frontier as the site of new opportunities, African Americans moved to the urban frontier in rising numbers.

The expansion of black families and kin networks underlay and reinforced urban population growth. A growing proportion of runaway advertisements listed blacks as belonging to family units that linked them to urban and rural places. In 1803, one newspaper advertisement sought to recover a forty-five-year-old runaway. According to the ad, the woman had a husband at the plantation of Hugh Wilson, esq., James Island, has relatives at the plantation of the Rev. Dr. Frost, Goosecreek and has a son at the plantation of Doctor Jones, in the same parish; she is well known in the city, probably she may make for Georgetown, being well acquainted there.

When one enslaved mechanic continued to run away to visit the plantation where his wife resided, a Maryland master promised to "purchase his wife if her master will sell her at a reasonable price." Planters regularly reported blacks absconding through a complicated network of families and friends, as indicated by the following phrases: "related to a family of negroes, who lately obtained their freedom"; "went off in company with a mulatto, free fellow named Tom Turner, who follows the water for a living"; "several relations will conceal and assist him to make his escape." For their part, new African runaways also utilized communal and kin networks forged in Africa and on slaveships. Newspapers frequently listed new arrivals as members of the same runaway parties. Unlike blacks in the prewar period, who came from a variety of West African sources, most of the new Africans came from the Angolan region and facilitated the process of African American culture and community formation. Advertisements seeking their recovery reiterated the point: last observed with "fellow of the same country"; "supposed to be secreted by some of his country people"; were "purchased out of same ship."

Black Family Life

Although slavery subordinated black family life to the imperatives of profits, such calculations sometimes encouraged slave families as a means of promoting the natural increase of the black work force. Thomas Jefferson and other planters encouraged their overseers to maintain sexually balanced work forces—"half men & half women." Jefferson stated that he regarded "a woman who brings a child every two years as more valuable than the best man on the farm. What she produces is an addition to capital, while his labor disappears in mere consumption." Jefferson also approved slave marriages but sought to limit them to his own plantation: "There is nothing I desire so much as that all the young people on the estate should intermarry with one another and stay home. . . . They are worth a great deal more in that case than when they have husbands and wives abroad." On Charles Carroll's large estate in Annapolis, Maryland, an estimated two-thirds of enslaved blacks under fifteen years old lived with both parents.

Chesapeake black families also extended outward from "intimate ties of blood" to encompass aunts and uncles, nephews and nieces, cousins, and grandparents. Of 128 blacks on Carroll's home plantation, all but 30 belonged to such extended kin groupings. A similar pattern characterized Thomas Jefferson's Bear Creek Quarter in Bedford County, Virginia. Low-country planters also expressed an increasing preference for American-born blacks "in large families" rather than "gangs" of African-born blacks separated from their families. The proportion of African-born blacks in South Carolina's population had dropped from 45 percent on the eve of the war to between 10 and 20 percent by 1820. While only about one-third of a sample of low-country estates listed blacks living in family units on the eve of the Revolution, the proportion had increased to four-fifths by the early 1800s.

Although the system of bondage subordinated black families to the imperatives of profit, African Americans imbued such units with their own familiar and communal meanings. Bondsmen and -women worked to vouchsafe the family from sale and arbitrary breakup. Enslaved blacks repeatedly petitioned planters for permission to move to another plantation to be with a spouse and their children. Conversely, they also asked planters to purchase family members from other places and reunite broken families. Although it often took them five to ten years to purchase a single slave, free blacks dedicated their lives to purchasing the freedom of others. Between 1792 and 1805, the freeman Graham Bell of Petersburg, Virginia, bought and liberated nine people. Another free black, the barber John C. Stanly of North Carolina, not only purchased his wife and children in 1805 but also, over the next thirteen years, liberated nineteen slaves, one of them a brother-in-law. The free black woman of Washington, D.C., Althea Tanner, bought her own freedom as well as that of twenty-two relatives and friends.

African American naming practices also underscored the significance of extended kinship networks. Enslaved children often received the names of deceased relatives. On the Charles Carroll plantation, the majority of blacks received the names of blood relatives. Such naming practices reinforced ties between the past and present, which enabled slaves to transmit cultural values and establish the groundwork for building the larger African American community. Slaves used their families not only to transmit cultural values about kinship and community but also to pass on what historians have referred to as slaves' "most valuable property: their skill." In both the Upper and Lower South, slave parents, men and women, invariably taught their children the same skills that they had acquired. In the Chesapeake, Sam, a slave of C. C. Pinckney, passed his skills as carpenter to his oldest son, Anthony. On the Carroll estate, the cooper Joe trained both of his sons in the trade of barrel making. Similarly, black women taught their female children specialized skills, such as midwifery, as well as knowledge of a variety of household tasks. Such work experiences not only enabled some blacks to purchase their freedom but also in turn enabled free people of color to earn a living, gain access to resources, and purchase loved ones out of bondage.

In contrast to the prerevolutionary period, when few northern blacks lived in two-parent households, they now moved toward the establishment of separate independent households free of interference from their masters. As late as 1790, only one of every three Boston blacks lived in their own independent households. By 1820, an estimated 84 percent of Boston blacks lived in autonomous households. Similarly, in Philadelphia, 50 percent of blacks lived in white households in 1790, but by 1820 some 75 percent were living in their own households. This process was much slower in New York, where emancipation came late and most free blacks continued to live in white households. In New York, consequently, the independent households of single male or female adults were almost nil, whereas they made up 7 to 8 percent of such households in Philadelphia and Boston. By 1820, most northern black households had at least one adult male and one adult female. The ratio of black households with adult men and women ranged from 76 percent in Boston, to 79 percent in Philadelphia, to 81 percent in New York. Since black mortality rates were usually two to three times those of whites, northern black families also had a lower ratio of children per adult than whites. In 1820, children made up about 35 percent of Philadelphia's white population, compared with under 30 percent of the blacks. The ratios were even lower in Boston and New York.

As in the South, the meaning of family for northern blacks also emerged clearly in naming practices. The prerevolutionary generation had African, Anglicized African, classical, and even place names: Cuffee, Quash, and Cudjoe; Caesar, Pompey, and Cato; York, London, and Jamaica. The new generation shed the old names and donned new ones, many with biblical, mainstream English, and artisan derivations: forenames such as Elizabeth, Sarah, Abraham, Isaac, Jacob, Daniel, David, and Joseph, and surnames such as Mason, Cooper, Carpenter, Johnson, Brown, Smith, Williams, and Thomas. However, northern blacks assiduously avoided taking the names of the most prominent slave-owning white families, such as Wharton, Shippen, and Dickinson.

Occupational Opportunities in the Early Republic

Freedom opened up new occupational opportunities for African Americans, and by the early 1800s, some had secured jobs as painters, poets, authors, astronomers, entertainers, and merchants. The Bostonian Paul Cuffee and the Philadelphian James Forten Sr. emerged as the most prominent of the early American black merchants. Born on the Massachusetts island of Cuttyhunk, Cuffee was the seventh of the ten children of a formerly enslaved father and a Native American mother. During the Revolutionary War, Cuffee established a successful whaling and coastal fishing business. Cuffee's business activities expanded during the early years of the republic, his fleet of ships sailing not only to the Caribbean but also to such European countries as Sweden, France, and Russia. Cuffee's fortune enabled him to buy land and to play a major role in the early establishment of black institutions. He also became an early pioneer in the efforts to resettle African Americans in Africa when he gained approval from the British government to trade with Sierra Leone, established on the west coast of Africa as a haven for emancipated blacks from the English-speaking parts of the New World. For his part, James Forten developed a successful sail-manufacturing business. Following his escape from a British ship during the Revolutionary War, he returned to Philadelphia and took a job in a sail-making firm owned by a free black named Robert Bridges. Following Bridges's retirement in 1798, Forten purchased the business. Over the next three decades, he hired both black and white workers and amassed a fortune of $100,000. Like Cuffee, Forten also used his resources to support community-building and antislavery activities.

Although some blacks like Cuffee and Forten developed successful business enterprises, the skilled trades represented the most significant opportunities for free blacks in early America. Such opportunities were most pronounced in the Deep South, where planters manumitted only a few bondsmen and -women, usually

Paul Cuffee became not only a renowned entrepreneur but also a pioneer in the resettlement of African Americans in Africa.
Library of Congress

with kinship ties, and helped them to establish a foothold in the economy. In cities like Charleston, Savannah, and New Orleans, free blacks gained access to jobs as masons, carpenters, cartwrights, shoemakers, tailors, and butchers, among others. In the Upper South, too, a few white planters assisted free blacks to gain a footing in the economy as skilled craftsmen or landowners. The Virginia planters George Washington and Robert Carter provided some blacks small plots of land, access to firewood, opportunities to hire their wives and children for pay, apprenticeship training, and aid for the aged and infirm. Carter, and to some extent Washington, also enabled some blacks to become tenant farmers, with agreements to give them a specified amount of the produce or profits, along with opportunities to hire their own workers to produce crops. Such free black tenant farmers invariably hired free blacks. One planter reported good results with black tenantry, or sharecropping, as it would later be called: "I am the gainer . . . and they seem to be happy and cheerful and do more than twice the labour than when they were in a state of bondage, and make themselves a comfortable livelihood."

AFRICAN AMERICANS AND THE LIMITS OF DEMOCRACY

Despite substantial progress, African Americans faced a tough battle turning the Revolution to their benefit. Although freedom provided new economic opportunities, most free blacks and fugitives gained jobs at the bottom of the postrevolutionary economy. They worked mainly as general laborers, domestics, and personal service workers. A 1795 Philadelphia census listed 41 percent of free black men as "unskilled" laborers, sawyers, and whitewashers. Another 12 percent worked as domestic or personal servants or waitingmen and coachmen. Others worked as mariners (10 percent), artisans (12 percent), professionals (5 percent), and proprietors, hucksters, craters, bakers, and grocers (21 percent). About one-third of free black women worked as retailers and boardinghouse keepers, and 50 percent labored as laundry- or washerwomen.

For some free blacks, emancipation ushered in not upward but downward occupational mobility. In 1816, another Philadelphia census revealed a decline in professional positions and a rise in domestic and personal service. As long as blacks with skills remained enslaved, masters had a stake in their profitable employment, either in their own households or shops or as hirees elsewhere. When these skilled blacks gained their freedom, however, they faced stiff competition from enslaved artisans as well as free whites. As a result, they were often forced out of their trades or made to work at much lower wages than their enslaved and free white counterparts. Consequently, whites from diverse class backgrounds, including merchants, landowners, and artisans, exploited free black labor.

Restrictions and Racial Hostility

From the outset, despite the manumission movement, southern states established stiff restrictions on free blacks. Virginia law stipulated that free blacks could be sold into slavery for failing to pay their taxes. Maryland decreed that such people would have property rights, but not all "the rights of free men." Moreover, when the Haitian revolt sent thousands of West Indians into the South, whites welcomed white French émigrés but resisted the in-migration of blacks. All along the southeastern seaboard except Virginia, southern states erected barriers against the black émigrés. When black immigrants continued their trek into ports like Charleston and Savannah, whites held mass meetings and sent angry petitions to legislatures demanding an end to the influx. For its part, the city of Savannah barred any ship that had docked in Saint-Domingue from its harbor.

African Americans not only faced restrictions in the South but also confronted barriers in the North. Although abolitionism gained support among influential whites, the gradual emancipation movement was insufficient to guarantee the full citizenship rights of ex-slaves. Moreover, New York (1799) and New Jersey (1804) enacted gradual emancipation laws later than elsewhere. In New Jersey, the number of enslaved actually increased between 1790 and 1800. More importantly, northern states imposed racial restrictions on the "right to vote and hold office," on marriage, and on in-migration from other states. In 1800, Boston invoked a state law against the settlement of free blacks from other countries and ordered the deportation of 240 free blacks from the city. Most of these blacks were from Rhode Island, New York, Philadelphia, and the Caribbean. Despite the decline of slavery in the North, one contemporary traveler remarked that "chains of a stronger kind still manacled their [free blacks'] limbs, from which no legislative act could free them; a mental and moral subordination and inferiority, to which tyrant custom has here subjected all the sons and daughters of Africa."

Although the Northwest Ordinance prohibited slavery north of the Ohio River, blacks also confronted racial hostility in the old northwest (Ohio, Indiana, Illinois, Wisconsin, and Michigan). Northern journalists and political leaders referred to free and enslaved blacks alike "as depraved and ignorant a set of people as any of their kind." On one occasion, for example, the Ohio legislature reported free blacks as "more idle and vicious than slaves" and urged strong measures to prevent their migration into the state. Similarly, an Indiana Supreme Court judge opposed the migration of what he called "a low ignorant, degraded multitude of free blacks." Free blacks, the Indiana Colonization Society argued, "add nothing to the strength, and little to the wealth" of the state and nation. As nonslaveholding whites moved into the territories in rising numbers, they were exceedingly hostile to slavery. They believed that the use of enslaved blacks would spawn a large free black population, which would in turn compete with whites for land and other resources. Moreover, according to northern whites, southerners released their most troublesome and unproductive blacks onto the Northwest Territory. Thus, antislavery sentiment, intertwined with antiblack beliefs, hampered the in-migration of free blacks.

The state constitutions and laws of the Northwest Territory contained discriminatory provisions against free blacks. In 1804, the Ohio legislature passed a law requiring free blacks and mulattoes to provide proof of their freedom on entering the state. In 1807, Ohio intensified such restrictions by prohibiting free blacks and mulattoes from settling in the state unless they posted a $500 bond to guarantee their ability to support themselves. In 1815, Indiana passed a law imposing a $300 annual poll tax on all adult black and mulatto men. For its part, the federal government reinforced state and local restrictions against free blacks. Congress regularly admitted new states into the union—both north and south of the border—with explicit restrictions against free blacks in their constitutions. The federal government also limited naturalization and the acquisition of citizenship to "foreign whites" (1790), restricted enlistment into the federal militia to white men (1792), eliminated blacks from service as U.S. mail carriers (1810), and disfranchised free blacks in the nation's capital (1820).

By the War of 1812 and its aftermath, most whites perceived free blacks as a problem. Southern slaveholders viewed free blacks as a threat to the institution of slavery, while northerners viewed them as economic competitors and a threat to their Euro-American cultural way of life. Thus, popular opinion in both the North and South coalesced around efforts to transport free blacks out of the country. In 1817, this new viewpoint gained organized expression when a group of influential whites—including John Randolph, Francis Scott Key, and Richard Rush—founded the American Colonization Society and sought ways to resettle free blacks on African soil.

The racial limitations of the Revolution were intertwined with class conflicts among whites. Highlighting the conservative character of the new polity was Shays's Rebellion, which broke out among farmers in western Massachusetts in 1786. Under the leadership of the Revolutionary War veteran Daniel Shays, these farmers rebelled against eastern bankers and merchants who passed the high cost of living in the new nation on to the medium-sized and small landowners and the poor. Although some blacks like Prince Hall of Boston volunteered to help put down the rebellion, other blacks like Tobias Green of Plainfield, Aaron Carter of Colrain, and Moses Sash of Worthington joined white farmers in their resistance movement. According to contemporary court records, Moses Sash, described as a farmer and laborer, was not only a participant in the uprising but also "a Captain & one of Shaises [Shays's] Council." In contrast to the single indictment handed down on the white participants in the rebellion, the court returned two indictments against Sash. Whereas both Sash and the whites were indicted for "disorderly, riotous & seditious" behavior "by force of arms," Sash was additionally indicted for "fraudulently, unlawfully & feloniously" stealing two guns. Although Governor John Hancock eventually pardoned most of the participants, Shays's Rebellion precipitated growing fear among the nation's small elite that lower-class whites might undermine the independence and sovereignty of the new nation. It was partly this fear, as well as the persistence of slavery as a labor system, that led to the creation of a new federal constitution.

The New Constitution and Defense of Slavery

In 1787, representatives of the thirteen states met in Philadelphia and drafted a new, more centralized constitution. The new document made substantial concessions to slaveowners and reinforced African and African American bondage. In his *Notes on the State of Virginia*, published in the same year, Thomas Jefferson articulated the racial ideology of the new nation that justified the perpetual enslavement of blacks on American soil. According to Jefferson, not slavery but blacks degraded whites and undermined the strength of the nation. In his view, African Americans were an inferior people—in color, culture, physique, intelligence, and morality. More specifically, Jefferson concluded that blacks were "in memory . . . equal to the white; in reason much inferior; . . . and in imagination . . . dull, tasteless, and anomalous . . . never yet could I find that a black had uttered a thought above the level of plain narration."

The new constitution underscored the triumph of racialist thought in the nation-building process. Specifically, the founding document expanded southern representation in Congress by counting slaves as three-fifths of a person; guaranteed the extension of the international slave trade for twenty years, or until 1808; and mandated the return of fugitive slaves who escaped across state lines. In 1793, Congress also passed the Fugitive Slave Act, which authorized slaveowners to enter free territory and seize runaway slaves. Since the law denied alleged fugitives an opportunity to prove their status, it made free blacks no less vulnerable to enslavement than escaped bondsmen and -women. (See the Documents section.) In short, the new republic justified the perpetual enslavement of Africans on American soil.

The international slave trade played a pivotal role in limiting the promise of the Revolution. As the prospective deadline for the termination of the international slave trade drew near, southern planters augmented their enslaved work forces with fresh "imports from Africa and the Caribbean." Between the end of the Revolution and the end of the slave trade, an estimated 100,000 Africans entered the human flesh markets of the United States; most of these arrived after 1790. In 1807, Congress banned the international slave trade; violators of the ban could be fined $800 and given various prison terms. Any person convicted of outfitting slave-ships was subject to even stiffer penalties, including a $2,000 fine. In the early aftermath of the law, however, most states did little to enforce the ban on slave imports. As historian John Hope Franklin has noted, "The first underground railroad was not that carried on by the abolitionists to get the Negro slaves to freedom but the one carried on by merchants, and others to introduce more Negroes into slavery."

Until the early 1800s, the western lands of Kentucky and Tennessee received most of their slave labor from the Chesapeake, while the international slave trade supplied the Deep South states of South Carolina and Georgia. Thereafter, the Chesapeake supplied the slave labor demands of the Upper and Lower South. In the decade between 1810 and 1820, an estimated 137,000 blacks left the Chesapeake for the frontier south, most moving into the southwestern states of Mississippi and Alabama. In rapid succession, cotton lands opened in western, central, and southern Georgia, Alabama, Mississippi, and Louisiana. Before the United States could take the western lands and initiate cotton production, however, it had to confront Amerindians, defeat them, and push them farther west. In 1814, Andrew Jackson's frontier army attacked the Creek nation and forced concessions from the Chickasaw, Choctaw, and Cherokee nations. These concessions enabled white settlers to spread across the "rich virgin soil" known as the "black belt." By the 1810s, southerners moved toward a vigorous defense of slavery as a "positive good" in the enrichment of the white commonwealth.

Other southerners defended slavery as "a necessary evil" in the social control of what they called "an inferior people." Accordingly, as the demand for slave labor increased, southern states established new restrictions against free blacks. New state constitutions or amendments disfranchised blacks except in Tennessee and North Carolina; at the same time, Virginia, Georgia, Kentucky, Maryland, North Carolina, and South Carolina barred free black migrants or made their entrance difficult by bond and other requirements. In 1806, Virginia went a step further and required any newly manumitted blacks to leave the state. To enforce these provisions of the law and control the interstate movement of free blacks, southern states also initiated a complicated system of registration and passes. These laws not only allowed authorities to imprison indigent or vagrant free blacks but also prohibited their participation in commercial activities. By the early 1800s, Georgia and Mississippi reinstituted bans against freeing slaves and made emancipation a prerogative of the state legislature rather than of individual masters. According to one angry Virginia planter, "A man has almost as much right to set fire to his own building though his neighbor['s] is to be destroyed by it, as to free his slaves." Whites regularly harassed free blacks and deprived them of their freedom, including permitting enslaved blacks to testify against free people of color (but not against whites). Moreover, although officials of slaveholding states publicly condemned the kidnapping of free blacks for sale and reenslavement, hundreds of blacks lost their freedom through the operation of kidnapping rings, particularly in the Delaware-Virginia area.

As southerners moved increasingly toward a defense of slavery as either a "necessary evil" or a "positive good," the nascent southern antislavery movement declined. By 1820, it had failed to penetrate the Deep South and held only a tenuous grip on Virginia and Maryland. In the new western states of Kentucky and Tennessee, slaveholders also successfully resisted the establishment of abolitionist societies. As early as the 1790s, southern legislators in Virginia and Maryland had passed new laws restricting the ability of abolitionists and blacks to lodge freedom suits, mainly by instituting new prohibitively high court costs. The Virginia assembly even barred abolitionists from service on freedom suit juries while permitting hostile slaveowners to serve. Similarly, as early as 1793, southern Baptists and Methodists had revoked their antislavery decrees and reconciled their brand of evangelicalism with the system of bondage. In 1797, the Roanoke Baptist Association barred free blacks from the church's business meetings. Most churches now practiced some form of racial discrimination, including separate seats for blacks (enslaved and free) and whites. In an extreme case, a Virginia church painted its benches for African Americans black. Others relegated blacks to back rows, corners, or galleries.

The new racial order did not entirely preclude interracial cooperation. In early 1791, Secretary of State Thomas Jefferson approved Benjamin Banneker's appointment as "scientific assistant" to Major Andrew Ellicott, the presidential appointee to survey the District of Columbia as the location of the nation's capital. Banneker played a key role in the location of the White House, Treasury, and other public buildings. In March 1791, the *Georgetown Weekly Ledger* reported that Ellicott was "attended by *Benjamin Banneker*, an Ethiopian, whose abilities, as a surveyor, and

Benjamin Bannaker's
PENNSYLVANIA, DELAWARE, MARYLAND, AND VIRGINIA
ALMANAC,
FOR THE
YEAR of our LORD 1795;
Being the Third after Leap-Year.

BANNAKER.

PHILADELPHIA:
Printed for WILLIAM GIBBONS, Cherry Street

The black astronomer, mathematician, and farmer Benjamin Banneker produced a widely acclaimed almanac and also served on the commission that planned the nation's capital in Washington, D.C. Benjamin Banneker was the grandson of an enslaved African named Banna Ka, who later became known as Bannaky, a name passed on to Banneker's father, Robert Bannaky. No doubt the spelling *Bannaker*, which appears on the almanac above, represents another change in the family's surname before it became Banneker. *American Antiquarian Society* an astronomer, clearly prove Mr. Jefferson's concluding that race of men were void of mental endowments, was without foundation." A certain level of cooperation also persisted among blacks and working-class whites. Some planters continued to report blacks running away with white servants, while others complained that runaway slaves and poor whites collaborated in defrauding masters of their property: "It is suspected those two fellows have joined themselves together again, and . . . that it is their design for Peter to be sold as often as they find it convenient if either of them is in need of money." Sometimes white women joined runaway slaves, including men who were the fathers of their children. One enslaved man, Jacob, escaped with an Irish woman, Betty Larkey, and their mulatto son.

THE RISE OF BLACK INSTITUTIONS: CIVIL AND HUMAN RIGHTS STRUGGLES

Despite evidence of collaboration across racial lines, such efforts were insufficient to offset the increasing coalescence of whites around notions of black inferiority. Consequently, African Americans heightened their own independent struggle for freedom. Their efforts gained sharp expression in the growth of protest movements, community-building activities, and plots against the institution of bondage itself. From the outset of the postrevolutionary era, African Americans rejected notions of racial inferiority by founding their own institutions and launching their own struggles for equal rights. In the summer of 1791, Benjamin Banneker, astronomer, mathematician, and creator of almanacs, countered Thomas Jefferson's racist assessment of African American abilities on two levels. On the one hand, Banneker based his case on the brotherhood of man and the fatherhood of God:

One universal Father hath . . . not only made us all of one flesh, but . . . without partiality afforded us all the Same Sensations, and endued us all with the same faculties . . . however diversified in Situation or colour, we are all of the Same Family, and Stand in the Same relation to him.

On the other hand, he based his arguments on the rhetoric of the Revolution:

Sir, Suffer me to recall to your mind that time . . . in which you clearly saw into the injustice of a State of Slavery.

On 17 October 1787, Boston blacks petitioned the state legislature for equal access to education. Under the leadership of Prince Hall—the Barbados-born black Revolutionary War veteran, minister, and fraternal order leader—the petition stated that blacks shouldered their share of the taxes and should

have the right to enjoy privileges of free men. . . . But [we] . . . now receive no benefit from the free schools in the town of Boston, which we think is a great

grievance, as by woful experience we now feel the want of a common education. . . . We therefore pray . . . same provision may be made for the education of
our children. And in duty bound we pray.

In December 1793, the South Carolina legislature received a petition that stated
that the excessive taxes levied on the state's free blacks made their lives "but a small
remove from Slavery. . . . In confidence therefore . . . We do most humbly pray,
That your Honours would condescend to take the distressed Case of your Petitioners into your wise consideration, and Vouchsafe to Grant them such relief." Another petition decried the extraordinary hardship imposed on free black "widows
with large families, & women scarcely able to support themselves, being frequently
followed & payment extorted by your tax gatherers."

In 1797, free blacks moved their protests from the local to the national level.
Precipitating the increasing nationalization of the freedom struggle was a North
Carolina law providing for the reenslavement of any free black manumitted without approval of the state. Four North Carolina free blacks—Jacob Nicholson,
Jupiter Nicholson, Joe Albert, and Thomas Pritchett—migrated to Philadelphia
and soon filed a petition with the president, Senate, and House of Representatives.
Their petition, widely regarded as the first presented by blacks to the Congress of
the United States, not only appealed for help against North Carolina but also
protested the federal Fugitive Slave Act. Rather than ruling on the petition, however, the U.S. Congress voted fifty to thirty-three to reject the petition without consideration of its merits.

African American Churches, Schools, and Fraternal Orders

As whites ignored the appeals of free blacks for citizenship rights and social justice,
African Americans embarked on their own community-building activities. African
American churches, schools, fraternal orders, and mutual benefit societies gradually
increased (see box). Against the determined opposition of whites, free and enslaved
blacks gradually broke ranks with white bodies and established their own churches.
Independent black churches first emerged in the cities of Charleston, Augusta, and
Savannah. Urban blacks took advantage of their greater geographical, economic,
and social mobility and founded separate black churches between 1773 and 1775.
On the eve of the Revolution, a white Baptist minister named Palmer preached
among the enslaved people of Silver Bluff, near Savannah. Under the impact of
Palmer's preaching, eight slaves, including David George and his wife and Jesse
Galphin (or Jesse Peter), converted to the Baptist faith. Shortly thereafter, David
George, George Liele, Jesse Galphin, and Andrew Bryan emerged as gifted exhort-
ers of the early black Baptist faith.

When George Liele and David George left the country during the British evacu-
ation, it was men like Galphin and Bryan who shouldered the burden of building
the black Baptist church in the war's aftermath. In 1793, Galphin spearheaded the
formation of the First African Church of Augusta, Georgia. One white contemporary
described Galphin's countenance as "grave, his voice charming, his delivery good."

SOURCES FROM THE PAST

— 1802

John Marrant Reports His Conversion to Evangelical Christianity

I, JOHN MARRANT, born June 15th, 1755, in New York, in North America wish these gracious dealings of the Lord with me to be published, in hopes they may be useful to others, to encourage the fearful, to confirm the wavering, and to refresh the hearts of true believers. My father died when I was little more than four years of age, and before I was five my mother removed from New York. . . . Some time after I had been in Charlestown, as I was walking one day, I passed by a school, and heard music and dancing, which took my fancy very much, and I felt a strong inclination to learn the music. . . . I became master both of the violin and of the French horn, and was much respected by the gentlemen and ladies whose children attended the school, as also by my master. This opened to me a large door of vanity and vice, for I was invited to all the balls and assemblies that were held in the town, and met with the general applause of the inhabitants. I was a stranger to want, being supplied with as much money as I had any occasion for; which my sister observing, said, "You have now no need of a trade." I was now in my thirteenth year, devoted to pleasure, and drinking in iniquity like water; a slave to every vice suited to my nature and to my years. The time I had engaged to serve my master being expired, he persuaded me to stay with him, and offered me anything, or any money, not to leave him. His entreaties proving ineffectual, I quitted his service, and visited my mother in the country; with her I staid two months, living without God or hope in the world, fishing and hunting on the Sabbath-day. Unstable as water I returned to town, and wished to go to some trade. . . . One evening I was sent for in a very particular manner to go and play for some gentlemen, which I agreed to do, and was on my way to fulfill my promise; and passing by a large meetinghouse I saw many lights in it, and crowds of people going in. I enquired what it meant, and was answered by my companion, that a crazy man was hallooing there; this raised my curiosity to go in, that I might hear what he was hallooing about. He persuaded me not to go in, but in vain. He then said, "If you will do one thing I will go in with you." I asked him what that was? He replied, "Blow the French horn among them." I liked the proposal well enough, but expressed my fears of being beaten for disturbing them; but upon his promising to stand by and defend me, I agreed. So we went, and with much difficulty got within the doors. I was pushing the people to make room, to get the horn off my shoulder to blow it, just as Mr. Whitefield was naming his text, and looking round, and, as I thought, directly upon me, and pointing with his finger, he uttered these words, "Prepare to meet thy God, O Israel." The Lord accompanied the word with such power that I was struck to the ground, and lay both speechless and senseless near half an hour. When I was come a little too, I found two men attending me, and a woman throwing water in my face, and holding a smelling-bottle to my nose; and when something more recovered, every word I heard from the minister was like a parcel of swords thrust into me, and what added to my distress, I thought I saw the devil on every side of me. I was constrained in the bitterness of my spirit to halloo out in the midst of the congregation, which disturbing them, they took me away; but finding

CONTINUED

I could neither walk or stand, they carried me as far as the vestry, and there I remained till the service was over. When the people were dismissed Mr. Whitefield came into the vestry, and being told of my condition he came immediately and the first word he said to me was, "Jesus Christ has got thee at last."

Source: John Marrant, *Narrative* (London: Plummer, 1802). This document is also available in Dorothy Porter, ed., *Early Negro Writing, 1760–1837* (Boston: Beacon Press, 1971), pp. 429–432.

Moreover, the minister said, Galphin understood "the mysteries of the kingdom." For his part, Bryan preached to both blacks and whites in Savannah and its surrounding area. Before Bryan could secure the independence of Savannah's First African Baptist Church, however, he and his congregation faced violent opposition from local whites. Bryan himself suffered whippings and imprisonment on two different occasions, but he and his congregation stood firm. On one occasion, according to one report, Bryan "told his persecutors that he rejoiced not only to be whipped, but *would freely suffer death for the cause of Jesus Christ.*" By 1812, Bryan's Savannah African Baptist Church had splintered twice, giving rise to the Second and Third African Baptist Churches in the city. Independent black Baptist churches spread even more rapidly through the Upper South and the new western states of Kentucky and Missouri.

Although the decentralized structure of the Baptist denomination enabled black churches to expand rapidly, independent black Methodist churches also increased. The black Methodist movement was especially strong in the North. Under the leadership of Richard Allen and Absalom Jones, African Americans formed independent African Episcopal churches in Philadelphia. Born a slave in Philadelphia in 1760, Allen converted to Methodism at age seventeen. For several years he traveled through parts of Delaware, Pennsylvania, and New Jersey, working as a general laborer and preaching the gospel before returning to Philadelphia in 1786. When members of the white St. George's Church forced blacks from their seats to make room for whites, Richard Allen and the slave-born Absalom Jones spearheaded the formation of black Episcopal churches. By 1794, under the leadership of Allen, Philadelphia blacks had built and dedicated Bethel African Methodist Episcopal Church. At the same time, under the leadership of Jones, Philadelphia blacks formed St. Thomas Episcopal Church. Within one year after opening its doors, St. Thomas claimed a membership of over 400. By the onset of the War of 1812, St. Thomas had 560 members, and Bethel had soared to over 1,270. In 1816, free black African Methodist Episcopal church leaders from Maryland, Pennsylvania, Delaware, and New Jersey convened in Philadelphia and formed the independent African Methodist Episcopal (AME) church.

If southern whites resisted independent black churches, they were even more hostile to independent black schools and fraternal orders. In Richmond, Virginia,

Richard Allen, a founding leader of the African Methodist Episcopal church. *Bettmann/Corbis*

when Christopher McPherson sought to establish a black school, authorities jailed him and then committed him to the Williamsburg Lunatic Asylum. When blacks sought a charter for a Masonic order, they were repeatedly denied by the American order. Still, African Americans soon established their own Masonic orders and schools. In Baltimore, for example, the Sharp Street AME church soon doubled as "a school for the education of black children of every persuasion." Similarly, as early as 1787, when white citizens rejected their application for a charter, black masons turned to England and gained approval to set up an African Masonic lodge. They gained authority to administer mutual benefit funds, conduct processions, and perform burial rites.

Under the leadership of Prince Hall of Boston, the new Masonic order not only formed the foundation for mutual support and fellowship but also established, along with the church, a training ground for black leadership. By 1791, Prince Hall became the "Provincial Grand Master of North America and Dominions and Territories there unto belonging." The movement spread rapidly to other northern cities. Since the white Masonic orders of Europe and America turned to ancient Egypt as well as the Greeks and Romans for guidance, African Americans found the order's rituals and beliefs especially appealing. In 1787, at the same time that Boston blacks formed the Masonic order, Philadelphia blacks gained the cooperation of Quakers and formed the Free African Society, designed to offer mutual aid, leadership training, and charity work to "the free *Africans* and their descendants." Members of the Free African Society later formed Philadelphia's first independent black churches. Blacks repeatedly expressed their kinship with Africa in their institution-building activities: benefit societies, such as the Angolan Society, the Angola Beneficial Association, the Sons of Africa, the African Female Benevolent Society, and the Male African Benevolent Society; and schools and businesses, such as the African School, the Friends African School, and the African Insurance Company, to name a few.

Urbanization and Resistance Movements

The emergence of black institutions was the consequence not merely of racial discrimination in white institutions but also of the increasing spatial concentration of blacks in the urban environment. By 1820, Charleston and New Orleans had black majorities, and blacks made up a disproportionately large percentage of other southern cities like Savannah, Louisville, Mobile, and Norfolk. In the North, predominantly black clusters gradually emerged in cities like Philadelphia, Boston, and New York. From the early postrevolutionary years, for example, blacks in Philadelphia gradually increased their numbers in two separate parts of the city. The oldest cluster formed in the northern part of the city, in the North and South Mulberry wards, a poor district that also housed Irish and German working-class families. A new area also opened in the southern part of the city, encompassing the Cedar and Locust wards and the western section of the South ward. As realtors erected low-rent tenements in this area, it also attracted grow-

Andrew Bryan, a pioneer Baptist minister and founder of the First African Baptist Church of Savannah. *The Granger Collection, New York*

ing numbers of free blacks and fugitive slaves. The black population in this area rose from 265 free blacks in 1790 to nearly 4,200 in 1820. Blacks also moved into West Southwark and Moyamensing, an area south of the Cedar ward community. Although some blacks continued to live in the old northern location, by 1820 over three-fifths of all blacks in the city lived in the southern part of the city, in the Locust and Cedar wards, West Southwark, and Moyamensing. Blacks also gradually concentrated in certain sections of other cities.

Increasing urbanization also fueled Gabriel Prosser's plot to rebel, the most prominent manifestation of black resistance in the aftermath of the American Revolution. In the summer of 1800, enslaved blacks planned an assault on the city of Richmond. Beginning around April, several bondsmen—mainly urban artisans, blacksmiths, coopers, weavers, carpenters, and shoemakers—took advantage of their ability to travel to and from the various plantations to plan the rebellion. Over a period of several months, enslaved blacks participated in a mass organizing campaign. Although it is not clear who originated the idea, the blacksmith Gabriel Prosser, or Prosser's Gabriel, as he was called, soon emerged as the principal leader. According to recent scholarship, Gabriel headed the plot because of his extraordinary skill at making decisions, delegating tasks, and attending to details "to avert the strong possibility of disaster." Gabriel also exhibited a keen awareness of the growing class conflict among whites, which, like the Revolution itself, suggested

As the free black population expanded in the wake of the American Revolution, it faced exclusion and discrimination in virtually every aspect of American life. Free blacks especially resented the participation of Christian churches in this system of racial inequality and responded by setting up their own independent churches in the urban centers of both the North and South. This lithograph shows the edifice and parishioners of the African Episcopal Church of St. Thomas, Philadelphia, 1829. *The Historical Society of Pennsylvania,* A Sunday Morning View of the African Episcopal Church of St. Thomas in Philadelphia. *Lithograph by William L. Breton, 1829 (Accession #Bb862 B756)*

new possibilities for blacks to obtain their freedom. As plans for the revolt took shape, Gabriel and his two brothers locked hands and affirmed that "here are our hands and hearts. We will Wade to our Knees in blood sooner than fail in the attempt." The revolt failed when a heavy storm washed out roads, bridges, and access routes to the city. In the meantime, someone had leaked word about the conspiracy. Officials soon arrested several bondsmen, and within one month, authorities completed trials and hanged twenty-seven African Americans, including Gabriel Prosser. Twenty conspirators were acquitted and another seven pardoned.

Before authorities discovered the plan, enslaved blacks had organized their numbers over six counties and several cities. Gabriel claimed a force of 10,000 men ready to join the revolt, but other contemporary estimates put the number at 1,000 to 3,000. Under Gabriel's leadership, recruiters had fanned out over the area, asking prospective participants if they wished to join "a society to fight the white people for [their] freedom." One recruit later recalled his endorsement of the plan. When asked if he was a recruit, he replied: "By God I am. . . . I will fight for my freedom as long as I have breath and that is as much as any man can do." Under a banner reading "Death or Liberty," the men planned to arm themselves with guns, knives, and clubs; meet at a bridge on the outskirts of Richmond; kill all whites except Quakers, Methodists, and others associated with the abolitionist movement; and force slaveowners to liberate their slaves. If the owners resisted, the armed band would move into the countryside, organizing blacks for a general revolt against the entire system. Thus, despite its failure, the Virginia plot demonstrated the new role that the Revolution, work skills, and increasing urbanization would play in African American political struggles during the late eighteenth and nineteenth centuries.

Although enslaved and free blacks devised a variety of strategies for combating the institution of slavery and racial oppression, their efforts would remain insufficient. As the demand for slave labor escalated alongside a more intense and hostile racial climate, it not only reinforced and extended the institution of slavery and undercut the growth of the free black population but also aggravated internal conflicts within the free black population and between bond and free blacks. Color divisions emerged as one of the most potent conflicts within the free black community. The free black population had been disproportionately light-skinned but was now increasingly black. In the North and Upper South, slaveowners manumitted blacks with little regard to color differences and blood ties. The arrival of large numbers of Haitian refugees and the acquisition of Louisiana, however, reinforced the number of light-skinned blacks, particularly in Charleston, Savannah, and New Orleans. In Charleston, South Carolina, color conflict gained institutional expression in the creation of the Brown Fellowship Society during the 1790s. The society limited "its membership to free brown men only" and barred dark-skinned blacks, who later established their own society of dark men.

The West Indians were also people of considerable skills and wealth. As artisans, landowners, and slaveowners, their presence helped to instill class consciousness as well as color consciousness into social relations. In the West Indies, these people often held the balance of power between the enslaved and planters and frequently sided with planters in squashing slave revolts. A similar pattern prevailed in Louisiana, where free people of color secured the right to bear arms and participated in the wars of the region against Native Americans, other European powers, and even enslaved blacks. As such, European policymakers sought their help not only as allies in intercolonial and Indian wars but also as potential allies in their struggle to put down slave rebellions.

When the United States took control of Louisiana, officials at first sought to weaken the black militia. In the wake of the huge slave rebellion in St. John the Baptist Parish in 1811 and the War of 1812, however, Louisiana approved and strengthened the free black militia. Drawing on their earlier history in the colony, free blacks volunteered to help put down the rebellion of 1811. The state governor,

William C. C. Claiborne, accepted the offer, placed free blacks under white officers, and armed them against the bondsmen. After two weeks of warfare, the governor reported that the free blacks had "performed with great exactitude and propriety." A year later, the legislature approved and recognized the free black militia of Louisiana. These free blacks would play a key role in Andrew Jackson's defense of the city of New Orleans during the British invasion. Their service enabled free people of color to resist the further erosion of their status by white American officials. A similar experience greeted free blacks in Mobile and Natchez. In these areas, whites would sometimes say that "there is . . . all the difference between a free man of color and a slave, that there is between a white man and a slave."

∾

AFTER A VERY HOPEFUL BEGINNING during the early years of the republic, African Americans faced increasing limitations on their lives. Despite the growth of the free black population as the most visible symbol of the fruits of the Revolution for African Americans, the architects of the new nation elaborated on its racist design. African Americans faced the extension of the international slave trade through 1808, the expansion of bondage into the new western territories, and the intensification of racist ideology, which justified the institution of slavery and the denial of full citizenship to free blacks. Although free and enslaved blacks experienced substantial internal conflicts, they acknowledged their common interests and participated in individual and collective struggles for full citizenship rights for themselves, their families, and their communities. They appealed not only to the Declaration of Independence but also to the principles of evangelical religion. They repeatedly urged authorities to remove a variety of disabilities confronting enslaved and free blacks alike. Although blacks gained significant white support during the postwar years, white assistance had dissipated by the early 1800s. Only during the acceleration of the cotton kingdom during the 1820s and 1830s would blacks gain a growing number of white supporters. These efforts would culminate in the rise of a militant abolitionist movement, the Civil War, and the emancipation of some 4 million people during the 1860s. Part III examines these developments.

The Antebellum Era, Expansion of Cotton Culture, and Civil War

1820–1865

B y the early nineteenth century, technological changes and the opening of new agricultural land in the Deep South had intensified the demand for slave labor. By effectively and cheaply separating cotton fiber from its seed, the cotton gin enabled cotton to become the United States's leading industry. Cotton dominated the nation's foreign exports and fueled the early industrialization of Great Britain and the northern United States, including the early industrial towns of Lowell and Waltham, Massachusetts. As huge profits from the production of cotton rolled into the South and the nation, it became apparent that African American labor stood at the center of the nation's wealth and economic well-being. Accordingly, a vigorous internal slave trade developed. Nearly a million blacks experienced forced migration from the Upper South states of Virginia and Maryland to the booming cotton states of Georgia, South Carolina, Alabama, Mississippi, and Louisiana.

Seeking to stabilize the enslaved African American labor force, large landowners increasingly combined what some analysts have called the "hard" and "soft" sides of labor discipline—that is, stiff restrictions on African American movement, cultural expression, and manumission, coupled with improvements in material conditions, including food, clothing, and shelter. Although such antebellum labor practices introduced a certain ambiguity into the lives of some blacks, the measures failed to create the desired pliant black work force. On the contrary, enslaved people used their improved material conditions to strengthen their families and forge new communal links, with each other on the one hand and with the free black population on the other. Their efforts involved not only greater communication from plantation to plantation but also closer relations between town and country as well as between regions.

The African American struggle against slavery gradually gained the support of influential white abolitionists and culminated in the coming of the Civil War. Enslaved and free blacks joined the Union forces and helped to transform the war between the states into a war for their own liberation. Part III focuses on the rapid spread of cotton production; the internal slave trade and the forced migration of blacks from the Upper to the Lower South; and the role of enslaved and free blacks in the advent and outcome of the Civil War.

CHAPTER 7

~

Under the Lash: Migration, Work, and Social Conditions

The late antebellum years witnessed the triumph of cotton as the South's and the nation's dominant growth industry. Like sugar, tobacco, and rice farming, cotton agriculture imposed its own technological, locational, and skill requirements and helped to transform African American life and labor. More specifically, large-scale cotton production stimulated the geographical reorientation of the black population from the Upper to the Lower South, the growth of a vigorous domestic slave trade, and the urban and industrial use of bondsmen and -women. As planters increased their dependence on black labor, however, they instituted new slave codes and social policies designed to stabilize black work forces. The new policies reflected what some historians call the "hard" and "soft" sides of human bondage.

On the one hand, planters took steps to improve the physical well-being of enslaved people. New laws not only redefined "the willful, malicious, and deliberate killing of slaves" as murder but also required slaveowners to provide "necessary" food, clothing, housing, and medical care for their bondsmen and -women. On the other hand, planters strengthened laws regulating slave movement, assembly, and self-expression, including new restrictions on reading, writing, and preaching. The coupling of material improvements and harsh disciplinary procedures established a new and more complicated context for the growth of African American culture and communities. Still, African American bondsmen and -women were by no means deceived by the growing complexities of the plantation system. They would use their access to improved material conditions to wage an ongoing battle against disciplinary measures, making it impossible for planters to fully stabilize the work force.

COTTON AND THE JOURNEY TO THE DEEP SOUTH

The confluence of a number of national and international changes established cotton as a new foundation for the nation's wealth. In England, revolutionary changes

in the textile industry—that is, new spinning and weaving machines—cheapened
the production of cotton fabrics and created huge demands for raw cotton. At the
same time, northern states rapidly set up
their own textile mills and created their
own demand for cotton. Manufacturers
had long recognized the value of cotton,
but technological obstacles precluded use
of the fiber on a massive scale. The difficulty of separating the cotton fiber from its
seed represented a major barrier that made
the production of cotton an extremely
slow, labor-intensive, and costly enterprise.
The fibers clung to the seed so firmly that
they had to be cut or torn away by hand.
This was particularly true for short-staple
cotton, which grew in the interior, as compared with long-staple sea island cotton,
which grew in the low-lying coastal areas
of Georgia and South Carolina.

During the 1790s, when inventors like
Eli Whitney perfected the cotton gin,
which effectively separated fiber from seed,
growing numbers of planters shifted out of
rice, indigo, and tobacco into cotton production. The cotton gin enabled planters
to expand the production of cotton beyond the coastal areas of Georgia and the
Carolinas into the interior, where short-

At the gin house: blacks feed raw cotton into a
ginning machine. Eli Whitney's technological inno-
vation effectively separated cotton fiber from its
seed and stimulated huge demands for slave labor.
*Schomburg Center for Research in Black Culture/The
New York Public Library*

staple cotton predominated. Cotton soon emerged at the center of southern and
U.S. economic growth. Production rose from less than 300,000 bales in 1820, to
over 700,000 bales in 1830, to over 2 million in 1850, to nearly 4.5 million in
1860. Cotton not only dominated the nation's foreign exports but also fueled the
early industrialization of the North as textile mills opened in New England cities
like Lowell and Waltham, Massachusetts.

The rapid rise of the "cotton kingdom" involved the painful relocation of blacks
from the older Chesapeake and southeast coastal regions to the southwest. In the
aftermath of the American Revolution through the early nineteenth century, Upper
South tobacco planters and Deep South rice growers faced soil exhaustion, declining productivity, and a shrinking demand for slave labor. In Virginia, the price for
an able-bodied male field hand increased from $350 during the early nineteenth
century to $1,000 in 1860. By contrast, in New Orleans, the price of the same
hand rose from $1,000 to $1,500. Although black women and children sold for
much less than men, their value on the market also increased.

As the demand for slave labor escalated, nearly 1 million blacks migrated under the lash from the Upper to the Lower South. The Deep South states of Georgia, South Carolina, Alabama, Mississippi, and Louisiana absorbed the bulk of this black population movement. Between 1820 and 1860, although enslaved blacks continued to make up about one-third of the total southern population, they now lived mainly in the Deep South. In Georgia, Louisiana, and Alabama, African Americans made up over 40 percent of the total population, ranging from about 330,000 to 460,000 people in each state. In South Carolina and Mississippi, they were a majority. By 1860, nearly 60 percent of the estimated 4 million blacks lived in the Deep South (see map).

The Increasing Demand for Slave Labor

Under the impact of growing demands for slave labor, many planters adopted a "breeding" mentality. According to the writer and observer Frederick Law Olmsted, planters "commonly esteemed" black women less for their "laboring qualities" than for their procreative potential. One Virginia planter stated that his women were "uncommonly good breeders" and that he "never heard of babies coming so fast as they did on his plantation." Most importantly, he said, "every one of them . . . was worth two hundred dollars . . . the moment it drew breath." As an added incentive to childbearing black women, some planters freed them after they had given birth to ten to fifteen children. On one occasion, in an estate settlement case, a Tennessee court prohibited the sale of an enslaved woman because she was "so peculiarly valuable for her physical capacity of childbearing." It would be unjust, the court ruled, to deprive the heirs of her "service."

Some men were also valued for their sexual prowess. Ex-slave Elige Davison of Virginia recalled: "I been marry once 'fore freedom with home weddin', Massa, he bring some more women to see me. He wouldn't let me have jus' one woman. I have 'bout fifteen and I don't know how many children. Some over a hundred, I's sho'." Texas-born ex-slave Jeptha Choice recalled: "When I was young they took care not to strain me. . . . [I] was in demand for breedin'." According to Choice, his master "used strong healthy" men "to stand the healthy" black girls. A few traders specialized in the so-called fancy girl market—that is, mulatto women who served as house servants and prostitutes.

Traders frequently expressed an interest in buying "all likely and handsome fancy girls." Often described as "bright" or "brown skinned," such females sold for as much as 30 percent more than field women. Despite emphasis on the "fancy girl" market, breeding, and procreative potential, black women and men were highly valued for both their productive and reproductive capabilities. Moreover, as we will see, having children was part of the familial, cultural, and value systems of enslaved blacks themselves.

The rising demand for black labor stimulated a thriving domestic trade in human beings. Numerous small traders entered the field and worked aggressively to build up "their stock." According to a recent study, rural "grassroots" traders dominated the domestic slave trade. During the 1850s, over ninety-seven "documented" slave-trading firms operated in South Carolina alone. Interchangeably

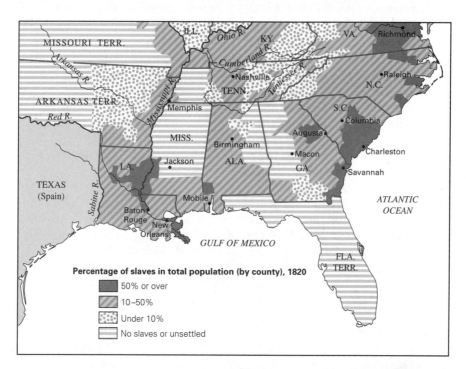

Percentage of slaves in total population (by county), 1820

- ■ 50% or over
- ▨ 10–50%
- ⠶ Under 10%
- □ No slaves or unsettled

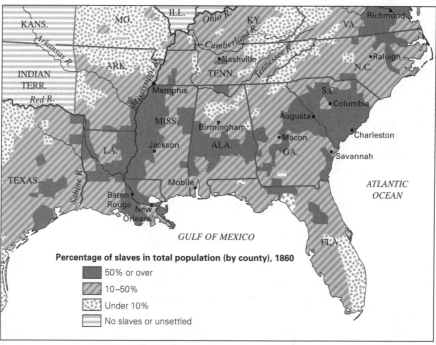

Percentage of slaves in total population (by county), 1860

- ■ 50% or over
- ▨ 10–50%
- ⠶ Under 10%
- □ No slaves or unsettled

Distribution of the U.S. Slave Population, 1820 and 1860. Under the impact of cotton production, the center of African American population shifted from the Upper South states of Maryland and Virginia to Deep South states like Georgia, Alabama, and Mississippi. By the beginning of the Civil War, the Deep South states claimed over 60 percent of all blacks in the United States.

referred to as "Negro traders," "slave traders," or "Negro speculators," such firms spread deep into the countryside, where owners and agents attended estate and execution sales and worked hard to locate private owners who desired to sell "a few Negro slaves." An advertisement of the firm of Clinkscales and Boozer on the North Carolina–Virginia border urged planters "having such property to sell . . . to bring them to us, or drop a line to us and we will come and see them." In a letter to a fellow trader, a South Carolinian wrote, "I have just met Mr. Barr from Alabama. He tells me prime fellows are worth [$]1050."

In addition to small traders, the domestic trade gave rise to huge urban-based slave-trading firms. Upper South and border cities like Richmond, Baltimore, Washington, and Norfolk became the key export centers, while Deep South cities like Charleston, New Orleans, Memphis, and Montgomery became the principal importers. Large traders included Austin Woolfolk of Baltimore; Seth Woodruff of Lynchburg; Hart and Davis, also of Lynchburg; and Franklin and Armfield of Alexandria, Virginia. Large firms deployed substantial capital and transformed the internal slave trade into an elaborate business with specialized functions. They employed their own sales and marketing forces, built their own holding facilities, and launched intense advertising campaigns. Franklin and Armfield, one of the earliest, largest, and most elaborately developed slave-trading firms, also maintained its own fleet of slavers.

Slave traders invariably advertised for large numbers of young blacks. Their business correspondence repeatedly emphasized that "persons having young slaves for sale will find this a favorable opportunity to sell." Although traders made some purchases "upon a short credit," they usually emphasized "cash" payments. On one occasion, the firm of Austin Woolfolk advertised for three hundred blacks ages thirteen to twenty-five: "Persons having such to sell shall have cash, and the highest prices. . . . Liberal commissions will be paid to those who will aid in purchasing for the subscriber." Such cash transactions sometimes included the sale of people by the pound, especially children. One trader wrote to his brother that he "would be willing and glad to [pay] for plough boys 5 or 6 dollars per pound. If the boy is very likely and weys 60 to 90 or 100—may be gone. If you can get Ned's boy at 7 per pound take him." The trader also instructed his brother to buy "likely girls" for slightly less per pound.

Migration Southward

African Americans entered the Deep South by water, land, and rail. Water transport included coastwise vessels down the Atlantic or "flatboats and steamers" on inland river systems. The journey from the Chesapeake to New Orleans was the principal component of the coastwise trade (see map). Many of these blacks left from Alexandria, Virginia, home of Franklin and Armfield, whose advertisements announced the array of ships available for carrying people to the Crescent City. On one occasion, the company announced the availability of the brigs *Tribune, Uncas,* and *Franklin.* In a visit to the firm in 1835, Ethan Allen Andrews, a Latin teacher from New Haven, Connecticut, reported that

Principal Routes of the Internal Slave Trade, 1810–1860. Key to the redistribution of the black population from the Upper South to Lower South was the emergence of an extensive internal slave-trade network. Enslaved African Americans from the declining tobacco-growing areas of the Chesapeake entered the cotton-producing region by rail, water, and overland transportation, often on foot.

the number of slaves, now in the establishment, is about one hundred. They are commonly sent by water from this city to New Orleans. Brigs of the first class, built expressly for this trade, are employed to transport them. The average number, sent at each shipment, does not much exceed one hundred and fifty, and they ship a cargo once in two months.

Some observers described the coastal trade as an extension of the Middle Passage. In 1834, following a tour of one slaver, a visitor reported that

the hold was appropriated to the slaves, and is divided into two apartments. The after-hold will carry about eighty women, and the other about one hundred men.

> On either side [of the hold] were two platforms running the whole length; one raised a few inches, and the other half way up the deck. They were about five or six feet deep. On these the slaves lie, as close as they can be stowed.

Partly because of fear of revolt, some blacks entered the Deep South under even tighter controls. In January 1830, for example, one group of Norfolk blacks arrived in New Orleans "bolted down to the deck." Nonetheless, for most African Americans the relatively short journey along the eastern seaboard was less harrowing than the long Middle Passage from West Africa.

The Mississippi, Ohio, Missouri, and Alabama Rivers figured prominently in the inland transport and sale of people. Inland rivers produced their own tales of suffering and pain. According to William Wells Brown, an ex-slave, traders on the Mississippi, from St. Louis to New Orleans, confined bondsmen and -women to a "large room on the lower deck . . . men and women promiscuously—all chained two by two." During the 1840s, the traders Hughes and Downing transported people from Kentucky down the Ohio and Mississippi Rivers to Natchez. The partners placed their human cargo "on deck of the steamboat . . . chained two by two." In his recollection of sale down the Alabama River, the educated ex-slave Sella Martin later wrote: "In our journey of five months down the banks of the Alabama river, from Montgomery to Mobile in that state, I saw sights of suffering and wrong-doing, the remembrance of which makes me shudder as I write."

"Sale down river" entered the consciousness of blacks as an awful prospect. As a disciplinary measure to control slaves who remained behind, Upper South planters routinely threatened bondsmen and -women with sale to the cotton plantations in the southwest, the Georgia rice swamps, or the Louisiana sugar district. One bondsman later recalled that

> the traders was all around, the slave-pen at hand, and we did not know what time any of us might be in it. Then there were the rice-swamps, and the sugar and cotton plantations; we had had them held before us as terrors, by our masters and mistresses, all our lives. We knew about them all; and when a friend was carried off, why, it was the same as death, for we could not write or hear, never expected to see them again.

In his autobiography, Frederick Douglass later recalled the painful sale of a Maryland man to a Georgia trader. After the man offended his master with remarks about "mistreatment" and "hard work," "he was immediately chained and handcuffed. Without a moment's warning," according to Douglass, "he was snatched away, and forever sundered, from his family and friends, by a hand more unrelenting than death."

Although many blacks reached the Deep South cotton region by water, most traveled overland. Ex-slaves frequently recalled their sale and transport in caravans numbering more than fifty enslaved people (see box). Traders harnessed the women together with halters, similar to the ones used to restrain horses, and linked the men together with long chains and iron neck collars, which were padlocked. According to a former Maryland bondsman, the men were also "handcuffed in pairs,

SOURCES FROM THE PAST

1847

Fugitive William Wells Brown Describes the Domestic Slave Trade

On our arrival at St. Louis I went to Dr. Young [Brown's owner], and told him that I did not wish to live with Mr. Walker any longer. I was heart-sick at seeing my fellow-creatures bought and sold. But the Dr. had hired me for the year, and stay I must. Mr. Walker again commenced purchasing another gang of slaves. He bought a man of Colonel John O'Fallon, who resided in the suburbs of the city. This man had a wife and three children. As soon as the purchase was made, he was put in jail for safe keeping, until we should be ready to start for New Orleans. His wife visited him while there, several times, and several times when she went for that purpose was refused admittance.

In the course of eight or nine weeks Mr. Walker had his cargo of human flesh made up. There was in this lot a number of old men and women, some of them with gray locks. We left St. Louis in the steamboat Carlton, Captain Swan, bound for New Orleans. On our way down, and before we reached Rodney [Mississippi], the place where we made our first stop, I had to prepare the old slaves for market. I was ordered to have the old men's whiskers shaved off, and the gray hairs plucked out where they were not too numerous, in which case we had a preparation of blacking to color it, and with a blacking brush we would put it on. This was new business to me, and was performed in a room where the passengers could not see us. These slaves were also taught how old they were by Mr. Walker, and after going through the blacking process they looked ten or fifteen years younger; and I am sure that some of those who purchased slaves of Mr. Walker were dreadfully cheated, especially in the ages of the slaves which they bought.

We landed at Rodney, and the slaves were driven to the pen in the back part of the village. Several were sold at this place, during our stay of four or five days, when we proceeded to Natchez. There we landed at night, and the gang were put in the warehouse until morning, when they were driven to the pen. As soon as the slaves are put in these pens, swarms of planters may be seen in and about them. They knew when Walker was expected, as he always had the time advertised beforehand when he would be in Rodney, Natchez, and New Orleans. These were the principal places where he offered his slaves for sale.

Source: The Narrative of William Wells Brown: A Fugitive Slave (Boston, 1847), pp. 41–45.

with iron staples and bolts, with a short chain about a foot long uniting the hand-cuffs and their wearers." According to Charles Ball, who later experienced bondage in both the Upper and Lower South, "The poor man to whom I was ironed, wept like an infant when the blacksmith, with his heavy hammer, fastened the ends of the bolts that kept the staples from slipping from our arms." As for Ball himself, he added, "I felt indifferent to my fate. It appeared to me that the worst that could come had come and that no change of fortune could harm me."

Yoked together, men, women, and children often walked for miles, and for several weeks, before reaching their destination. Such caravans averaged on foot between twenty and twenty-five miles per day. One coffle traveling from Richmond to Natchez took forty-four days. Another traveling from Pittsylvania County, Virginia, took seven weeks. Still another from Yancyville, North Carolina, to Hinds County, Mississippi, took about thirty days. Catherine Beal, a former slave, recalled parts of her trip from Richmond to Macon, Georgia. "Late in the even's we stretched the tents and cooked and spread out blankets an' slept. Then after breakfas', bout sunup we start travelin' again." In 1834, the British author and geographer George W. Featherstonhaugh offered a similar but more detailed description of another overland coffle in western Virginia:

> Just as we reached New River . . . we came up with a singular spectacle. . . . It was a camp of . . . about three hundred slaves . . . who had bivouacked the preceding night *in chains* in the woods. . . . The female slaves were, some of them, sitting on logs of wood, whilst others were standing, and a great many little black children were warming themselves at the fires of the bivouac. In front of them all, and prepared for the march, stood, in double files, about two hundred male slaves, *manacled and chained to each other.*

Although most blacks entered the Deep South by land or water, some came by rail "on the cars," as the journey was called. In 1856, according to a northern visitor to the South, "every train going south has slaves on board . . . twenty or more, and [has] a 'nigger car,' which is generally also the smokers' car, and sometimes the luggage car." In February 1859, the *Petersburg Express* reported on the "SLAVE EXODUS"—"the car allotted to servants [slaves] on the Richmond and Petersburg

Overland coffles usually harnessed women together with halters, similar to ones used to restrain horses, and linked the men together with long chains and iron neck collars, which were padlocked. In this illustration, the carpenter and artist Lewis Miller depicts a less-regimented scene of slaves bound from Virginia to Tennessee. *Abby Aldrich Rockefeller Folk Art Center, Williamsburg, Virginia, Accession #1978.301.1*

Railroad was filled to such an extent that one of the spring bars over the track broke down, without, however, producing any harm." In 1848, a Boston newspaper described preparations for the transport of enslaved people from a Washington, D.C., railroad depot: "Quite a large number of colored people gathered round one of the cars. . . . I found in the car towards which they were so eagerly gazing fifty colored people some of whom were nearly as white as myself." In some cases, the railroads transported blacks to waterfronts, where they were then transferred to boats or ships.

Most African Americans entered the Deep South via the domestic slave trade, but some came via the underground international slave trade. Southwestern states regularly violated the ban on African imports until the eve of the Civil War. An estimated 54,000 Africans entered the country after 1808. In 1839, rather than insisting on enforcement of the ban, President Van Buren proposed an amendment to reopen the slave trade. Such a change, he said, would help to preserve the "integrity and honor of our flag." Other American statesmen and lawmakers were less easily persuaded. In the same year, for example, the Cuban slaver *Amistad* sailed into Long Island Sound near Culloden Point, carrying fifty-three Africans and two Spaniards. Under the leadership of Joseph Cinque, a member of the Mende ethnic group in the region of Sierra Leone, the Africans had overpowered the vessel's crew near Havana, Cuba. Although the rebels had killed the captain and another white man, they had also released all but two members of the crew and allowed them to go ashore. The African rebels had ordered the Spanish navigators to set sail for Africa, but the ship sailed into U.S. waters. The U.S. Supreme Court heard the case and set the men free. According to Justice Storey, "Upon the whole, our opinion is . . . that the said negroes be declared free, and be dismissed from the custody of the court."

Although the U.S. Supreme Court set the *Amistad* Africans free, by the 1850s, the movement for legalization of the international slave trade escalated. As late as 1859, the *Texas State Gazette* attacked the ban on the overseas trade as a violation of "every principle of justice" and "free trade." "The same reason which would induce us to approve a high protective tariff," the editor concluded, "leads us to protest against the fanatical laws passed to prohibit the African slave trade." Deep South planters feared that the increasing sale of blacks into the Lower South would transform the Upper South into hostile antislavery territory. In the *Montgomery Advertiser*, one pro-slave advocate declared that "free labor will necessarily take the place of slave labor, and when [it] preponderates . . . they will become antislavery states."

Although Upper South and northern states defeated such proposals, the underground trade remained a significant part of the slave labor system until the Civil War. Baltimore shipbuilders played a major role in building slavers for the international trade. The city became famous for its "fast, seaworthy clippers." The clippers sailed to ports around the world but were perhaps best known in the slave ports of Africa. The *Amistad*, for example, was a speedy Baltimore-built schooner. New York, Boston, and New Orleans merchants were also involved in the people trade. In June 1858, these cities accounted for all but one of twenty-two vessels captured and detained by the British navy for participation in the illegal slave trade, which some captains took few precautions to conceal. In 1859, the *Clothilde*, the last known slave ship to dock in a U.S. port, entered Mobile, Alabama. The ship carried nearly 130 West African men, women, and children.

Whether blacks arrived in the Deep South via the domestic or international trade, they usually arrived exhausted, ragged, hungry, and often sick. Nonetheless, the traders enthusiastically announced:

> Just arrived, with a choice lot of VIRGINIA and CAROLINA NEGROES, consisting of plantation hands, blacksmiths, carpenters, cooks, washers, ironers, and seamstresses, and will be receiving fresh supplies during the season.

Traders also used the language of advertising to describe their holding pens. In New Orleans, one trader described his facility as a "large and commodious showroom." Ex-slaves often recalled how the traders "instructed" the bondsmen and -women "how to show ourselves off." Traders ordered people to "talk up," "look spry," and even "sing." On such occasions, the food improved, the overt discipline eased, and the hard task of enlisting bondspeople in the business of selling themselves commenced. As one ex-slave put it, "When he go to sell a slave, he feed that one good for a few days, then . . . makes 'em look like they been eating plenty meat and such like and was good and strong and able to work."

Stories of the auction block were integral to the narratives of ex-slaves and the travelers' accounts of whites who visited the region. James Martin, an ex-Virginia slave, later recalled the details of the auction block for black men, women, and children. According to Martin, the traders put people "in stalls like the pens they use for cattle." Referring to black men as "Bucks" and women as "Wenches," the auctioneer supervised the bidding with "a big black snake whip and pepperbox pistol in his belt."

> The overseer yells, say, you bucks and wenches, get in your hole. Come out here. Then, he make 'em hop, he makes 'em trot, he makes 'em jump. How much, he yells, for this buck? A thousand? Eleven hundred? Twelve hundred dollars? Then the bidders makes offers accordin' to size and build.

In 1853, William Chambers, a Scotsman, reported an auction in Richmond, Virginia:

> "Sale is going to commence—this way gentlemen" . . . with her infant at the breast, and one of her girls at each side . . . "Well, gentlemen . . . here is a capital woman and her three children, all in good health—What do you say for them? Give me an offer?"

As with the early development of tobacco, rice, and sugar plantations, the first wave of Deep South enslaved migrants prepared the cotton plantations for cultivation and human habitation. They cut down trees, removed stumps, and burned brush. They constructed "big houses," slave quarters, barns, stables, and gin houses. During this phase of settlement and work, planters preferred a preponderance of able-bodied single young men and women. When newly arrived émigrés entered the expanding southwest, the "old planters" advised them "to buy none in families, but to select only choice, first rate, young hands from 14 to 25 years of age (buying no children or aged negroes)." After completion of this pioneering phase, the sex ratio evened out, and African Americans embarked on the actual work of cultivating the new crop.

PLANTATION, INDUSTRIAL, AND URBAN WORK

Cotton cultivation required extensive plowing, hoeing, and picking. In the spring, blacks plowed the ground, sometimes with double mule teams; opened "drills," or light furrows, in the cotton beds; and sowed the seed. During the hot and humid summer months, they repeatedly "chopped" cotton with heavy hoes to remove weeds and grass until the plants were large enough and secure enough to stand on their own and be "laid by"—that is, until the plant could grow and flower into ripened bolls. From September through December, bondsmen and -women moved the cotton crop from field to gin house to buyers. In this phase of the work process, African Americans picked, ginned, pressed, and loaded cotton onto wagons for shipment. Enslaved cartmen, horsemen, and boatmen transported the product over land and water to market. Beyond the fields, blacks repaired fences, houses, and barns; cut, gathered, and stored firewood; raised hogs; canned vegetables; and cured meat.

As cotton cultivation expanded, rice, sugar, and, to some extent, tobacco growers added cotton to their repertoire of crops. On his travels through the Deep South, Captain Basil Hall of the British navy noted the frequent combination of rice and cotton cultivation in the coastal areas of South Carolina and Georgia. On one South Carolina rice plantation, he observed that "this plantation, at the time [of] our visit [during the 1820s], consisted of 270 acres of rice, 50 of cotton, 80 of Indian corn, and 12 of potatoes. . . ."

In Louisiana, the sugar district competed quite closely with cotton for black labor. Firms frequently advertised explicitly for "NEGROES suited to the New Orleans market." During the late 1850s, for example, one trader advertised in the Charleston area: "500 NEGROES WANTED, WILL PAY MORE THAN ANY OTHER PERSON, FOR NO. 1 NEGROES suited for the New Orleans market." In the 1830s, another advertisement stated: "Fellows will be preferred with proper certificate for the New Orleans market." When the New Orleans sugar district advertised for women, it specified young "girls 16–20 heavy set and very smart, suitable for shipping purposes." Another trader lamented: "I am sorry that I have not got any good negroes on hand that will suit the New Orleans market. . . . Likely young men such as I think would suit the New Orleans market are very hard to find and also stout young women." In Louisiana's sugar district, some 68 percent of the blacks were males, compared with about equal percentages of men and women in the cotton district. In his enslavement on a Louisiana cotton plantation, Solomon Northrup later reported that his master hired him out on sugar plantations in the area "during the season of cane cutting and sugar-making" because of his "inability in cotton-picking."

Division of Labor on Plantations

Most antebellum blacks lived and labored on large plantations with twenty or more enslaved blacks. Whether they specialized in rice, tobacco, sugar, or cotton, large slaveowners concentrated on marketing, finance, and general management and hired overseers to supervise the day-to-day details of the plantation labor force. Overseers, usually poor whites, worked on annual contracts, with an annual income that ranged from as low as $100 to a high of $1,200 plus a house, food, and a slave as a personal servant. According to the instructions of one Mississippi planter:

> The overseer will never be expected to work in the field, but he must always be with the hands. When not otherwise engaged in the employers business and must do everything that is required of him, provided it is directly or indirectly connected with the planting or other pecuniary interests of the employer.

In other words, owners charged overseers with keeping daily records of plantation activities, making oral and/or written reports, and serving as guardian of the employer's property.

Although some overseers received good reports, most did not. Both employers and bondspeople regularly lodged complaints against overseers. A Virginia planter declared that the overseers were "the curse of [the] country, sir, the worst men in the community." A Mississippi planter described the majority of overseers as "passionate, careless, inefficient men, generally intemperate, and totally unfitted for the duties of the position." An ex-slave from Ashland, Kentucky, recalled "floggings and abuse" by "cruel overseers." A Missouri ex-slave referred to the various overseers on his plantation as "hard men, real devils."

The management hierarchy not only separated enslaved people from owners and overseers but also instituted divisions among the enslaved. Owners appointed drivers to conduct the direct supervision of other blacks. As a designated "head driver," some blacks were sometimes exempt from direct labor in the field, equipped with a horse and whip, and required to set the work pace for others. One South Carolina planter defined the duties of the drivers:

> . . . under the Overseer, to maintain discipline and order on the places . . . to be responsible for the quiet of the negrohouses, for proper performance of tasks, for bringing out the people early in the morning, and generally for immediate inspection of such things as the Overseer only generally superintends.

African American drivers occupied a precarious place in the plantation command system. If they pushed the enslaved people too hard, they invited the wrath of their fellow bondsmen and -women. If production lagged, they confronted the prospect of getting a flogging themselves and falling back into the ranks of field hands. In a letter to John H. Cocke, the owner of plantations in Virginia and Alabama, one driver, George Skipwith, described how difficult it was to discipline the black labor force. After he whipped one field hand for slowing down the work pace, the man then rallied other blacks against the driver. As the driver related, "He came up to the house to our preacher and his family because he knoed they would protect him in his rascality."

Despite such difficulties, some drivers developed effective managerial skills. A South Carolina planter, William Elliott, entrusted his plantations to two black "servants," who gained his approval to borrow and loan money in his name. Such practices breached the law; and, on one occasion, authorities fined Elliott for failing to retain a white overseer on his place. According to Olmsted, some planters employed white overseers "as a matter of form." Some female household workers and field hands also obtained supervisory positions. One ex-slave, Louis Hughes, recalled that each plantation had a slave "fore-woman who . . . had charge of the female slaves and also the boys and girls from twelve to sixteen years of age, and all the old people that were feeble." In Mississippi, another enslaved black later recalled a "colored woman as foreman."

As suggested by the use of drivers and forewomen, African Americans experienced substantial occupational differentiation and hierarchy. Beneath drivers was a broad range of craftsmen—carpenters, blacksmiths, weavers, and coopers, among others. Artisans occupied an even more pivotal role in the labor force than supervisors. Planters frequently valued skilled men more highly than drivers: Perry-Driver, $900; Jack Cooper, "good hand," $1,000; Pleasant Carpenter, "fine Negro," $1,000; and Moses Engineer, "good Negro," $1,000. Below these skilled craftsmen was a tier of field and household specialists—male plowmen, butlers, valets, and coachmen on the one hand, and female cooks, nurses, midwives, laundresses, seamstresses, and manufacturers of household items like soap and candles on the other. Finally, at the bottom were the general field hands, household laborers, and personal servants. As individuals, they were the least valued of all workers. Yet, as a group, the antebellum plantation economy turned on their labor. By 1860, an estimated 60 to 75 percent of enslaved men and women worked as field hands. In the field itself, planters often divided their work force into "full hands," able-bodied males in their prime working ages; "three-quarter hands," women, older children, and some older male workers; and "half hands," younger children, partially disabled men, and pregnant women. Owners subdivided field labor into "plow gangs," mainly men, and "hoe" gangs, which included the majority of men and women.

The gender division of labor was less sharply drawn among enslaved men and women than it was among plantation owners, their families, and white employees. With the exception of skilled craftsmen, large numbers of black women performed the same range of jobs as black men. They plowed fields, worked in hoe gangs, dug ditches, and picked cotton. Planters frequently remarked that black women could "do plowing very well & full well with the hoes" and were "equal to men at picking." Hoeing was backbreaking labor in the antebellum South, partly because the hoes were made out of heavy pig iron and were "broad like a shovel." One ex-slave recalled that manufacturers made the hoes heavy so that they fell hard, but the biggest problem "was lifin 'em up."

Although most women were classified as three-quarter hands, a substantial number ranked as full hands. In some cases, they were among the leading pickers on their place. On a Virginia plantation, Susan Mabry picked 400 to 500 pounds of cotton a day. An average worker picked 150 to 200 pounds per day. In eastern Georgia, Emily Burke observed men and women plowing "side by side and day after day." According to her observations, "the part the women sustained in this [otherwise] masculine employment, was quite as efficient as that of the more athletic sex." Another observer said that he saw no "indication that their sex unfitted them for the occupation." Although men usually did the heaviest lifting, hauling, and digging, some women routinely participated in these tasks as well. Ex-slave women from Mississippi and Georgia recalled that women "split rails . . . just like a man . . . split wood jus' like a man." The child of one black woman recalled that her mother was "strong an could roll and cut logs like a man, and was much of a woman."

Work Experiences on Plantations

Whether enslaved blacks worked on tobacco, rice, sugar, or cotton farms, their experiences varied somewhat by the size of units, the labor and skill requirements of different crops, and the principal mode of organizing work assignments. Although most blacks cultivated large plantations with twenty bondspeople or more, most slaveowners held fewer than ten blacks. Indeed, many slave-owning families owned fewer than five. On these small units, enslaved people worked under the direct supervision of their owners, who often drove plows and wielded hoes, while the owners' wives performed a variety of household tasks. According to one white South Carolina youth who grew up in a small slaveholding family, his mother "ran a spinning wheel, wove cloth, did her own cooking and milked cows," while his father "plowed, drove the wagon, and made shoes." Even when they could afford to delegate tasks to blacks and withdraw from the field, small owners often found it necessary to enter the field to work alongside bondspeople to save the crop. Observers often noted how such planters would "temporarily forget their pride" when illness or weather conditions created a shortage of hands.

The work experiences of black bondsmen and -women also varied by the skill requirements of different staples. In their autobiographical writings, ex-slaves regularly reported variations in the labor demands of the different crops. According to Charles Ball, who worked on plantations in both the Chesapeake and the Deep South, "the tasks" in the tobacco fields of Maryland and Virginia were not as excessive as those in the cotton region, nor was "the press of labour so incessant throughout the year." In his view, "the utmost rigor of the system" of bondage greeted slaves "on the cotton plantations of Carolina and Georgia, or the rice fields which skirt the deep swamps and morasses of the southern rivers." Rice production involved an intricate system of banks, ditches, flooding, and drainage, all highly labor intensive and hazardous to the health of workers. Similarly, as suggested in Chapter 2, sugar production involved not only its own seasonal agricultural cycle of plowing, planting, and harvesting but also the extensive heat, ditch digging, and drainage of water from the sugar houses. Tobacco was somewhat less labor intensive than rice, sugar, and cotton, but it still required sustained and strenuous manual labor. Tobacco workers not only had to plow and plant but also had to carefully transplant small budding plants from one cultivated field to another.

If the labor requirements of rice and sugar produced greater physical hardships for workers than tobacco or cotton production, the mode of organizing work assignments evened the score considerably. Although planters frequently used a mixture of "gang" and "task" systems, rice and sugar planters employed the task system more widely than their tobacco or cotton counterparts. The task system assigned enslaved workers a specific number of "daily tasks" and required their satisfactory completion. As Olmsted observed in eastern Georgia and South Carolina:

> Nearly all ordinary and regular work is performed *by tasks*. . . . For instance, in making drains in . . . clean meadow land, each man or woman of the full hands is required to dig one thousand cubic feet; in swampland . . . the task for ditches is five hundred feet [200 feet in a strong cypress swamp] . . . in hoeing rice, a certain number of rows, equal to one-half or two thirds of an acre.

At the end of a task, overseers and drivers inspected and approved the work before releasing bondsmen and -women from their day's labor. Partly because planters allotted small garden plots to blacks for their own use during "off time," enslaved people preferred the task system. After completing assigned tasks, they used their remaining time as they saw fit, including working their own fields, hunting, fishing, or enjoying a measure of leisure. One ex-slave woman recalled the possibilities of greater autonomy under the task system: "Oh, no, we was nebber hurried. . . . Master nebber once said, 'Get up an' go to wok', an' no oberseer effer said it, neither. . . . Oh, no we was nebber hurried."

In contrast, the "gang" system placed large numbers of workers in one group under close supervision of an overseer or driver. In a contemporary description of the gang system, the Englishman James Silk Buckingham underscored what enslaved people called work from "can see 'til can't." According to Buckingham:

> The slaves are all up by daylight; and every one who is able to work, from eight or nine years old and upwards, repair to their several departments of field labor. They do not return to the houses either to breakfast or dinner; but have their food cooked for them in the field. . . . They continue that at work til dark. . . . Absence from work, or neglect of duty, was punished with stinted allowance, imprisonment, and flogging.

The ex-slave Solomon Northrup, who was kidnapped in New York and sold into slavery in the Deep South, reinforced the same point. For him, there was "no such thing as rest." On the Louisiana plantation where he lived and worked,

> the hands are required to be in the cotton field as soon as it is light in the morning, and, with the exception of ten or fifteen minutes, which is given them at noon to swallow their allowance of cold bacon, they are not permitted to be a moment idle until it is too dark to see, and when the moon is full, they often times labor till the middle of the night.

Under the lash of the whip, "gang" laborers had few incentives to work harder or faster. The harder they worked, the more planters and overseers expected. At each phase of the agricultural cycle, especially during the harvest season, blacks faced a vigorous work regimen. After a day's work, according to Northrup, cotton hands faced a fearful moment at the gin house, where planters and overseers weighed the cotton and punished those considered unproductive. Whether they produced too little or a lot, he said, they approached the gin house in fear. As Northrup put it, "If it falls short in weight, . . . he knows that he must suffer. And if [he] has exceeded it by ten or twenty pounds, in all probability his master will measure the next day's task accordingly." Although blacks preferred the task system, the heavy labor demands of planters made both the task system and the "gang" system unpleasant. They were both slave labor systems that enabled masters to appropriate the fruits of black labor.

Urban and Industrial Slavery

Although slavery was fundamentally an agricultural labor system, it was not limited to the countryside or to farming. Alongside the expansion of southern plantations was the growing use of slave labor in rural industries and cities. Urban and industrial slavery was more flexible and diverse in its labor requirements than plantation slavery. Industrial bondspeople gained opportunities to arrange contracts with employers, compete with white workers, and move from one industrial site to another. Consequently, some contemporary observers (and later scholars as well) suggested that slavery could not survive in the urban environment. In 1848, a Kentucky observer reported that "slavery exists in Louisville and St. Louis only in name." In New Orleans, at about the same time, a visitor remarked that slavery is by "nature eminently patriarchal and altogether agricultural . . . it does not thrive . . . when transplanted to cities." Frederick Douglass later remarked that "slavery dislikes a dense population."

By the late antebellum years, enslaved blacks had declined as a percentage of the urban population in most cities. By 1860, with nearly 28,000 blacks, Baltimore had the largest concentration of blacks of any southern city, but most of them were free people of color. Between 1820 and 1860, except for Richmond—and for some decades, Mobile—women also outnumbered urban bondsmen, partly because of the high demand for female domestic servants, and partly because plantation-based buyers outbid their urban counterparts for the higher-priced male slaves.

Although enslaved people declined as a percentage of the population in antebellum cities, their absolute numbers actually increased. Between 1820 and 1860, Richmond's bound population experienced the most dramatic growth, rising from under 4,400 in 1820 to about 11,700 in 1860. Savannah's enslaved population rose less rapidly, from nearly 3,100 in 1820 to over 7,700 in 1860. In New Orleans, Charleston, Louisville, and Mobile, the population of bondsmen experienced substantial growth during the first half of the period but declined thereafter. Despite the decline, however, by 1860, Charleston and New Orleans had the first (13,900) and second (13,400) highest number of urban enslaved blacks, respectively.

Urban slavery suggests that human bondage was quite adaptable to a variety of settings. During slack periods in the agricultural cycle, planters hired or leased their slaves to a variety of employers. The system of "hiring out" augmented the ranks of urban and industrial bondsmen. Most cities designated a "hiring day" when planters came to town to rent or hire bondspeople to employers seeking to increase their own free white, black, or mixed labor forces. Although the hiring-out system existed throughout the South, it was most prominent in the Upper South, where

Virginia planters alone hired out some 15,000 enslaved people per year during the 1850s. Planters and prospective employers not only came together in town on hiring days but also placed advertisements in local newspapers, participated in public auctions, arranged private deals, and even used specialized hiring and rental agencies like Richmond's P. M. Tabb and Son.

Southern elites regularly touted the virtues of industrial slavery. In 1859, the New Orleans *Daily Picayune* predicted global success for the industrial South, based on its low transportation costs, abundant raw materials, and slave labor: "With raw material growing within sight of the factory; with slave labor that, under all circumstances and at all times is absolutely reliable . . . manufactured fabrics can be produced so as to compete successfully with the world." In Richmond, a tavern advertised for "fifteen men" and "three or four boys." A coach repair shop advertised for "six strong, active, intelligent, coloured boys, for a term of not less than five years." Another firm assured owners that their hired bondsmen would be "well fed, well clothed and well treated."

Bondsmen and -women frequently expressed a preference for the hiring-out system. It provided substantial latitude in negotiating working and living conditions, movement across the urban landscape, and opportunities to accumulate cash. In some cases, labor agreements involved negotiations around marriage and family. In a letter to a man who owned the husband of his hired woman, the owner of Virginia's Cloverdale Iron Furnace wrote, "We have hired the wife of your boy Nathan, and he is anxious that we should hire him—we are willing to take him at the rate of $125 per year." The owner approved the deal, but the employer made it clear that the details should be discussed with Nathan: "Talk with him about it and if you conclude to let him [come], . . . send him on as soon as possible."

Enslaved urban blacks also insisted on contracts that protected them from some of the most dangerous jobs, especially in the coal and iron industry. In 1825, one owner told an ironmaster that "his bondsman says that working in the furnace is ruinous to his eyes therefore I do not wish him to work there against his will." Similarly, another owner informed an employer about his "man Will"—emphasizing that he did not want Will "to work in the ore or blowing rock as he has been so much injured by it and he is very dissatisfied at it—but he is willing to work at anything that thear is not so much danger." Still another employer consented to let "my boy George . . . work at the blacksmith trade" but added emphatically, "I want you to understand me fully, I do not want him to work at the ore bank."

As the system of hiring out became more lucrative, planters permitted growing numbers of enslaved blacks to hire themselves. Artisans were the most numerous of these self-hirees. These included carpenters, coopers, blacksmiths, masons, shoemakers, cabinet makers, painters, tailors, seamstresses, and mechanics, particularly in cities of the Deep South. Contemporary descriptions of these artisans frequently employed terms like "first rate" and "excellent." Although many of these enslaved men negotiated year-long contracts, others arranged short seasonal or even shorter-term agreements. Such people gained access to resources and economic opportunities that sometimes allowed them to purchase their own freedom. Since southern states placed stiff constraints on manumission, some of the hirees became "free slaves" who worked unsupervised by owners that still retained legal title to their person. Accordingly, many whites abhorred the hiring-out system. Some newspaper editors complained that such practices "weakened the close connection of master and servant" and undercut "the respect which the servant should entertain for the master." One South Carolina committee investigated the issue and concluded that "the evil is he buys the control of his own time from his owner. . . . He avoids the discipline and surveillance of his master and is separated from his observation and superintendance."

Despite such protests, the hiring-out system was a lucrative arrangement. It served the needs of diverse parties and persisted through the antebellum era. As hired, leased, or corporately owned blacks, African Americans worked in a broad range of jobs in southern industries. Slave labor fueled the rise of southern lumber, naval stores, coal, railroad, textile, tobacco, and iron companies. By 1860, hundreds of enslaved blacks cut, loaded, and transported hardwood, cypress, oak, and pine to sawmills, where they not only hauled, stacked, and loaded finished slabs for transport to market but also fired and operated the steam engines. Forestry workers learned and executed the techniques of "girdling" trees, collecting resin, and manufacturing tar and turpentine products. At the same time, some 2,000 enslaved men entered "the darkest abode of man" to load and transport coal to manufacturing sites. As owners instituted boilers, steam-powered elevators, and water pumps, enslaved miners also operated the new equipment. Bondsmen also mined gold in Georgia, North Carolina, and Virginia—before the Comstock lode opened in California—and salt in the Kanawha Valley of western Virginia and eastern Kentucky.

In addition to rural-based industries like coal, lumber, and salt, African American bondsmen and -women worked in a plethora of jobs in the manufacturing, commercial, and transportation sectors of the urban economy. Slave labor fueled the construction of southern railroads like the Richmond and Fredericksburg, the Richmond and Petersburg, the New Orleans Pontchartrain Railroad Company, and the South Carolina Railway, among others. In a letter to one large slaveowner, an official of the Virginia and Tennessee Railroad hoped "to hire a lot of hands for the ensueing year to work upon the Rail road." The company also promised to "feed and clothe [slaves] well and treat hands with the utmost degree of humanity in every respect." In this case, the company's agent expressed desperation: "Give me a trial and I will warrant satisfaction." Railroad workers represented an important bridge between blacks in the rural-industrial, urban, and plantation sectors of the economy. Enslaved blacks served not only as general laborers, porters, and baggage and freight handlers but also as repairmen, firemen, and mechanics.

Antebellum industrialists also employed slave labor in textile mills, tobacco factories, and iron mills. By 1860, southern cotton and woolen industries employed some 5,000 slaves. Although some textile manufacturers started to replace blacks with free white labor during the 1850s, the southern textile industry had its origins in slave labor. After visiting one of the most well known of these establishments, the Saluda mill in South Carolina, a visitor reported:

We had the gratification recently of visiting this factory situated on the Saluda River, near Columbia [S.C.], and of inspecting its operations. It is on the slave-labor, or anti-free soil system; no operators in the establishment but blacks. The superintendent and overseers are white, and . . . principally from the manufacturing districts of the North, and although strongly prejudiced on their first arrival at the establishment against African labor, from observation and more experience they all testify to their equal efficiency, and great superiority in many respects.

Enslaved blacks also made up the work force of textile mills in Georgia, Florida, Mississippi, and Alabama. In some of these factories, bondsmen, -women, and children worked alongside white operatives.

The most prominent case of urban-industrial slavery emerged in the antebellum Chesapeake. By 1850, Richmond, Petersburg, and Lynchburg tobacco manufacturers owned, hired, or leased over 6,000 captive people. At the same time, an estimated 7,000 enslaved men labored in the ironworks of Maryland and Virginia. In the tobacco mills, different groups of workers carried out a series of interlocking assignments. One group separated the product leaf by leaf; another group arranged the leaves in layers and applied an "extract of licorice"; another group "rolled the [leaves] into long, even rolls, and then cut them into [tobacco] plugs of about four inches in length"; and, finally, another group packaged, loaded, and shipped the finished product.

Formed in 1836, Richmond's Tredegar Iron Works emerged as the South's leading manufacturing firm. Initially the company employed a mixed labor force of enslaved blacks and free whites. In 1847, however, when white workers walked out to protest the training and hiring of skilled blacks, the company dismissed the whites and turned to a slave labor force, except for "Boss men." In the iron plants, enslaved men not only did the hot, heavy, and dirty tasks of cleaning the plant and lifting and hauling the ore, but also performed the skilled jobs of puddling, heating, and rolling the iron ore into bars for market. As recent historians of the Tredegar Iron Works note, the proprietor selected a small core of bondsmen for skilled training. He depended on these men to train others, often their sons and/or other relatives and friends, for specific jobs in the ironworks. Moreover, the owner instituted an overwork system that allowed bondsmen to work beyond the specified ten-hour day to earn money for their own personal use.

Urban industries did not exhaust the use of slave labor. A variety of private and public sector agencies purchased, rented, or hired slave labor. These included churches, hospitals, social welfare institutions, and municipal governments. Southern municipalities employed enslaved blacks not only to clean streets and collect garbage but also to build and repair bridges, roads, waterlines, and other aspects of the city's physical infrastructure. Under close supervision and often in chains, blacks worked on these projects as hired slaves and also as convicts punished for infraction of slave codes. Deep South cities—Savannah, New Orleans, and Charleston—depended more heavily on slave labor for public works than their Upper South counterparts. In Savannah and Charleston, for example, enslaved firemen headed engine teams as well as serving as bucket and axe men. Municipal officials often praised these slave fire units as "efficient" and "well-managed" fire companies. In New Orleans, the city paid an estimated $30,000 per year to cover the costs of hired slaves. Such costs suggest that owners managed to profit from hiring out their bondsmen to public as well as private employers.

Although urban bondsmen and -women worked in a variety of jobs, most worked as general laborers and as household and personal servants. Men worked mainly as carriage drivers, draymen, wagoners, roadmen, refuse collectors, gardeners, messengers, and couriers of packages and letters. For their part, women cooked food, washed clothing, cleaned houses, and performed countless chores within and outside the home, including nursing children, caring for the sick and aged, and going to market. Such household workers were constantly on call. Whether performed by black men or women, general labor and household work was designated by elites as "menial service." A New Orleans doctor stated: "They are ever at the elbow . . . behind a table, in hotels and steamboats, ever ready, brush in hand, to brush the coat or black the shoes, or to perform any *menial service* which may be required." Yet, even here, the language of "menial service" camouflaged the enslaved black's mastery of a certain set of skills and know-how. Only indirectly, when they complained about the "difficulty" of "getting good service," did elites acknowledge the skills of general laborers.

Slavery in the West

Slavery not only characterized African American life in the antebellum South but also marked the experiences of blacks in the westward movement. In varying degrees, slavery extended into the states and territories of Texas, Kansas, Oregon, Utah, California, and the land of diverse Indian nations. The state of Texas had few blacks in 1840, but an estimated 200,000 by 1860. Although blacks cultivated the state's cotton crop, they also played a pivotal role in the state's expanding cattle industry. By 1860, some scholars suggest that African Americans made up the majority of the state's cowboys. The Mormon territory of Utah also legalized the institution of slavery but counted less than 30 slaves among its 59 black residents in 1860.

Some Native Americans also sanctioned the institution of human bondage. When the Indian removal treaties pushed Native Americans west during the 1830s, the Cherokee, Choctaw, Chickasaw, Creek, and Seminole held African Americans in bondage. Slave labor helped to alleviate the suffering of some Native American elites on their infamous Trail of Tears, which symbolized the "white man's" destruction of the "red man's" way of life. An estimated 175 slaves died on the journey west with the Cherokee. On the trail itself, African Americans served some Native Americans as cooks, nurses, and even night watchmen during encampments. On reaching their destination, Native American elites employed slave labor to reestablish themselves on the new western land.

Under the protection of federal law, the five Indian nations established their own plantation economy. In 1838, for example, George Lawer left northwest Georgia with 30 enslaved blacks. Within half a year, he had resettled in the Western Cherokee Nation and soon reported several hundred acres of farmland under cultivation with slave labor. By 1860, the five Indian nations held an estimated 7,000 African Americans in bondage, making up about 14 percent of the total population. As in the South, these blacks carried out a broad range of tasks, including the cultivation of corn, rice, and cotton crops.

Although other western states and territories outlawed human bondage, white settlers from Washington to New Mexico routinely violated the law. In 1852, for example, a Kentuckian in California wrote home to his father that "although the law made it impossible to hold a slave . . . longer than the present year . . . no one, will put themselves to the trouble of investigating the matter." Consequently, some 300 enslaved blacks worked in the goldfields of the state, and others worked in household service and general labor. After the Oregon Territory banned slavery, one territorial representative reported bondsmen in Benton, Lane, Polk, and Yamhill Counties. Still, compared with the antebellum South, slavery failed to gain a firm foothold in the West, partly because elites had access to abundant sources of coerced Mexican and Indian labor.

BONDAGE, LAW, HEALTH, AND LIVING CONDITIONS

As the demand for slave labor diversified as well as increased in the antebellum South, planters took steps to stabilize their work forces. Slave states instituted new laws and social policies designed to improve the physical treatment of bondsmen and -women while tightening restrictions on African American access to freedom of movement, culture, and political expression. By the late antebellum period, most southern states prohibited "the willful, malicious, and deliberate killing of slaves," as well as "branding," "mutilation," and "starvation." The codes redefined the "malicious killing" of slaves as murder and prescribed the same penalty as murder of a free white person. Although the codes varied somewhat from state to state, they resembled the Alabama Code of 1852, which stated:

> The master must treat his slave with humanity, and must not inflict upon him any cruel punishment. Any person who with malice aforethought causes the death of a slave, by cruel whipping or beating, or by any inhumane treatment or by the use of any weapon in its nature calculated to produce death, is guilty of murder in the first degree.

The Alabama Code further mandated that owners provide a slave "with a sufficiency of healthy food and necessary clothing; cause him to be properly attended during sickness, and provide for his necessary wants in old age."

Antebellum southern courts sometimes found owners and overseers guilty of brutality or murder of blacks. During the late 1840s, a South Carolina court convicted an owner of starving his slaves. When the defendant appealed the ruling, the state Supreme Court upheld the conviction. At about the same time, a North Carolina court sentenced an owner to death for the murder of his female slave. The man had repeatedly beat the woman "with clubs, iron chains, and other deadly weapons, time after time; burnt her; [and] inflicted stripes . . . which literally excoriated her whole body."

Beyond changes in the law, some planters took practical steps to improve the physical well-being of enslaved people. Slave management literature proliferated. In magazines, newspapers, and journals, slaveowners regularly exhorted each other to provide clean, sanitary, dry, and warm slave quarters; hire physicians; and vary the diet of the enslaved. In 1836, in a letter to the *Southern Agriculturist*, one planter wrote: "*Cleanliness* is a matter which cannot be too closely attended to. Every owner should make it a rule to appoint a certain day in the week; for reviewing his negroes and their habitations, to see that both are clean and in good order." In 1856, a Virginia planter recommended that slave quarters "be built of plank, have large glass windows, and good chimneys, and should be elevated at least two feet above ground." Since most owners provided slave homes beyond sight of the "big house," one planter recommended "a coat of paint" and "some cheap ornamental cornice," which "makes a very pretty house and obviates the necessity for sticking the negro cabin out [of] sight of the mansion."

Not all slave housing was miserable. Some enslaved blacks lived in relatively good quarters. By the late antebellum years, on some of the largest and most productive plantations, owners replaced barns, sheds, and lofts with somewhat better wooden cabins. In Work Projects Administration (WPA) interviews, ex-slaves later recalled a mixture of one-, two-, three-, and even four-room houses. Olmsted described a Georgia village of some thirty tenement houses representing the upper end of slave quarters:

> Each cabin was a framed building, the walls, boarded and white-washed on the outside, lathed and plastered within, the roof shingled; forty-two feet long, twenty-one feet wide, divided into two family tenements, each tenement divided into three rooms—one, the common household apartment . . . each of the other [bedrooms].

Bondsmen and -women also gained access to small garden plots, which they used to raise corn, peas, squash, and sometimes sweet potatoes. Such garden vegetables supplemented their regular diet of corn and pork. One ex-slave wrote that "every plantation" had gardens, "patches, as they are called . . . in which they plant corn, potatoes, pumpkins, melons, etc. for themselves." As suggested by their diary entries, large planters and mistresses also exhibited a growing interest in the health of blacks: "I walked over to the quarters this morning before breakfast, to see a sick woman, found her quite sick." "Aunt Olivia went . . . to the quarters, found one of [the] negroes very sick." "On yesterday we [had] 16 grown negroes lying up—today 14." Partly through such housing, health, and nutritional improvements, the enslaved population increased by 23 to 30 percent each decade from 1820 through 1860.

Despite changes in the material conditions of enslaved blacks and their increasing life expectancy, their housing, health, clothing, and living conditions remained inadequate. Since most worked on plantations with large numbers of other blacks, their living quarters were more densely populated than the housing of rural whites. Whereas planters, small farmers, and poor whites lived in widely scattered rural households, blacks often occupied three-, ten-, or thirty-family communities. Josiah Henson, an ex-slave from Maryland, reported:

Most slaves lived in inadequate quarters, but their housing did vary from place to place. At the "model" Oak Lawn, Louisiana, plantation, the "Negro Quarters" included forty-two units. *From* Frank Leslie's Illustrated Newspaper, *6 February 1864. General Research Division, New York Public Library*

We [were] lodged in log huts, and on the bare ground. Wooden floors were an unknown luxury. In a single room were huddled, like cattle, ten or a dozen persons, men, women, and children. . . . The wind whistled and the rain and snow blew in through the cracks. . . . Here were the children born and the sick neglected.

In Georgia, according to Fanny (Frances Anne) Kemble, the well-known British actress and wife of a southern plantation owner, overseers also made it difficult for enslaved women to maintain clean quarters:

This morning I paid my second visit to the infirmary. . . . The poor woman Harriet . . . was crying bitterly. . . . She and old Rose informed me that Mr. O___ [the overseer] had flogged her that morning for having told me that the women had not time to keep their children [and quarters] clean.

Ella Johnson, an ex-slave from the South Carolina Piedmont, recalled that enslaved people lived in "just little old one-room log cabins," usually with two windows and wooden floors, but other "poor old slaves had just the bare ground for a floor." The ex-slave Bill Homer of Louisiana recalled that the slave quarters comprised "fifty one-room cabins and dey was ten in a row and dere was five rows. De cabins was built of logs and had dirt floors and a hole where a window should be and a stone fireplace for de cookin' and de heat." An ex-slave from Georgia recalled "chimblies made of sticks and red mud. Dem chimblies was all de time catchin' fire." In Alabama, another ex-slave reported, "Us have cabins of logs . . . with one room and one door and one window hole." J. L. Tims of Mississippi remembered, "We lived in an old log house. It had one window, one door, and one room."

Although planters clothed their personal servants and household workers in the best garments, they usually cut costs in dressing the field hands and industrial bondsmen. Many planters relied on enslaved women to produce "homespun" garments for blacks, whereas others allotted small amounts for cheap northern fabrics called "negro cloth."

Enslaved blacks often suffered from acute respiratory and intestinal diseases. Respiratory diseases ranged from bad colds and sore throats to influenza, pneumonia, tuberculosis, and diphtheria. These diseases were especially widespread during the winter months when blacks inhabited poorly ventilated and unhealthy quarters. Planters frequently complained that "myself & several of the colored people have bad colds," or "hands & children have suffered very much from colds—in fact cold has been quite an epidemic."

Intestinal diseases increased during the summer months, when people spent more time outdoors in direct contact with the earth. Inadequate disposal of human waste and contaminated water led to epidemics of cholera, dysentery, diarrhea, typhoid, and hepatitis. According to one South Carolina physician, blacks usually entered "the open air for the calls of nature, in all kinds of weather." A Richmond physician later recalled how the accumulated piles of human waste were "regularly [but not often enough] scraped up, and hauled off to enrich the land" as "night soil."

Winter and summer, enslaved people faced the ravages of intestinal parasites. These worms affected the lungs, liver, blood vessels, gallbladder, vagina, anus, and skin. A recent study estimates that 30 percent of Virginia slaves "harbored worms during their lifetimes." These included tapeworms, associated with eating poorly cooked meat; roundworms, related to poor sanitation; and hookworms, which entered the body through contact with the ground. Barefoot, field workers and ditch diggers were especially vulnerable to the hookworm.

African Americans also suffered from sexually transmitted diseases, mainly syphilis and gonorrhea; various types of tumors, especially those afflicting the skin and bones; and mental disorders. Slaves with the latter were described in historical accounts as "deranged," "slightly deranged," or "lunatic" or as having "fits of insanity." Moreover, plantation blacks endured countless everyday mishaps that injured and sometimes even killed them: runaway mule teams and overturned carts, kicks from mules, and cuts and bruises from axes, scythes, and pitchforks. On one occasion, a 260-pound field hand jumped eight feet from a hay loft onto a sharpened pitchfork concealed under the hay below. Only miraculously did he survive the wound to his stomach.

Urban and industrial bondsmen and -women faced special health hazards, as they lived and labored under even more congested and unsanitary conditions than their rural brothers and sisters. When one Virginia slaveowner moved his family and enslaved blacks from the farm to a house in town, over twenty blacks died, as well as a few of his own family members. According to a report of the man's friend, crowded and unsanitary conditions precipitated the epidemic: "The lot was small, and back yard so much crowded with out houses, and trees, as to exclude the sun almost entirely. The cellars of course must have been exceedingly damp, and in them the Negroes lodged." Epidemics of cholera hit the city of Richmond in 1832, 1834, 1849, and 1854. Poor whites and especially blacks suffered disproportionately from such outbreaks. In the Norfolk, Virginia, cholera epidemic of 1832, an estimated 75 percent of the victims were blacks, who "lived in *low* damp places, in the basements of houses, in cellars and in kitchens without floors."

Among various ailments, specific occupational hazards compounded the medical difficulties of industrial bondsmen: lung disease afflicted tobacco workers; rock falls, deadly gases, and explosions injured and killed miners; and hot molten metal burned and damaged the skin and eyes of iron workers. Only in yellow fever epidemics, as a result of immunity provided by their sickle cell trait, did blacks have lower death rates than whites. In 1821, Norfolk whites made up 81 percent of yellow fever deaths. In Portsmouth, Virginia, in 1855, whites made up over 90 percent of such deaths.

Enslaved women and children experienced unique health problems. Females suffered recurring menstrual pain, discomfort, and often severe damage to their reproductive system. They regularly complained of amenorrhea, or "lack of menstrual flow"; excessive bleeding between menstrual cycles; and complications from both benign and malignant tumors. The plight of these women was often noted by visitors to southern plantations. "The first morning I was on the estate," wrote one visitor to a Mississippi plantation, "an old negro woman came into the room and said to him [the owner], 'Dat gal's bin bleedin' agin dis mornin'; 'How much did she bleed?' 'About a pint, sir.'" Moreover, childbearing women faced more life-threatening cases of puerperal (childbed) fever and prolapsed uterus than their

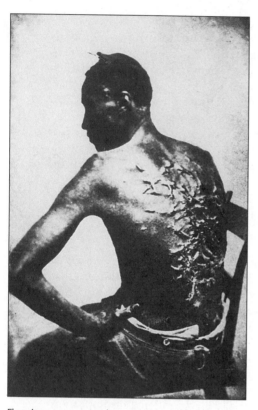

Floggings represented an ongoing source of pain for bondsmen and -women. Such whippings not only broke the flesh but also damaged internal organs.
Corbis

white counterparts. For their part, children not only faced the full range of childhood diseases—including mumps, measles, and chickenpox, among others—but also suffered sickness or death more often than white children from neonatal tetanus (caused by improper umbilical cord procedures at birth); worms (partly from eating dirt); and "smothering," "overlaying," or "suffocation" (now referred to as sudden infant death syndrome), which afflicted babies between two weeks and four months old. Although antebellum physicians frequently referred to the death of black children who were "overlaid by the wearied [slave] mother, who sleeps so dead a sleep as not to be aware of the injury to her infant," most enslaved children died from serious medical complications during early infancy.

Although women and children faced special health conditions, their well-being was inextricably interwoven with that of black men. Floggings represented both a symbolic and concrete link in the living conditions of all bondspeople. Whippings not only constituted an ongoing source of pain and discomfort but also undermined the physical well-being of enslaved people. Floggings broke the flesh, weakened the physical constitution, and made the recipients vulnerable to disease. Overseers and drivers used a variety of whips: a narrow strip of tough cowhide, a whipcord, or a cat-o'-nine-tails, all of which left deep gashes in the skin. Others employed paddles or broad leather straps, which did not remove the skin with each lash but nonetheless caused blisters and often damaged internal organs. Plantation records, advertisements, and medical reports noted the impact of repeated whippings on the bodies of enslaved people. One male had "numerous scars and extensive callous ridges on his back, constituting permanent injury." Another man had "numerous scars, from severe whipping, over almost every part of his body." Still another was described as "very feeble, badly used, and much whipped."

In an unusual case, the governor of Virginia commuted the sentence of five hundred lashes on the back of a bondsman. A physician persuaded him that repeated floggings, even when punctuated by periods of cessation, left the "skin more sensitive to pain" and subjected the slave to intense "constitutional suffering" and damage to the entire body. As one ex-slave recalled after a whipping, "You be jes' as raw as a piece of beef an' hit eats you up. He loose yore [labor] an' you go to house no work done dat day." One female ex-slave recalled the beating of her brothers: "I can' never forgit how my massa beat my brothers cause dey didn' wuk. He beat 'em so bad dey was sick a long time." Following a brutal whipping, one hundred lashes on his bare back, Josiah Henson's father was a changed man:

> . . . previous to this affair my father . . . had been a good-humoured and light-hearted man, the ringleader in all fun at corn-huskings and Christmas buffoonery. His banjo was the life of the farm . . . but from this hour he became utterly changed. Sullen, morose, and dogged . . . no fear or threats of being sold to the far south— the greatest of all terrors to the Maryland slave—would render him tractable.

White mistresses also wielded the whip, especially against women. According to the recollections of one ex-slave, when one mistress got sick after drinking water and eating food served by an enslaved woman named Alice, she accused the woman of trying to poison her:

> She sez dat Alice done try ter pizen her. Ter sho yo' how sick she wuz, she gits out of de bed, strips dat gal ter de waist an' whip her wid a cowhide till de blood runs down her back. Dat gal's back wuz cut in gashes an' de blood run down ter 'er heels.

The injured woman was chained down until she recovered from the whipping and then sold to slave traders in Richmond. Harriet Jacobs later described her day-to-day fear of a jealous mistress (see box). As Frederick Douglass recalled: "A mere look, word, or motion—a mistake, accident, or want of power—are all matters for which a slave may be whipped at any time."

Planters and overseers supplemented whippings with a range of inhuman devices for inflicting punishment. While some planters built penitentiaries on the plantations to confine people for certain offenses, others continued to force enslaved people to wear eleven- to fourteen-pound iron bells and horns fastened and padlocked around their heads. One Kentuckian punished blacks by floggings, after which he placed them in the smokehouse. William Wells Brown recalled, "He made a fire of tobacco stems, which soon set me to coughing and sneezing." Moses Roper, who was enslaved in the Carolinas and Georgia, described how his owner, his son, and his brother each gave him 150 lashes which "ploughed up" his back. With his "back ploughed up by lashes," Roper recalled that his owner then poured tar on his head "and set it on fire . . . the pain which I endured was the most excruciating, nearly all my hair having been burnt off." Mistresses also supplemented the rawhide with other instruments of corporal punishment. As Lewis Clarke, a Kentucky bondsman, recalled, his mistress

> could relish a beating with a chair, the broom, tongs, shovel, shears, knife-handle, the heavy heel of her slipper, or a bunch of keys; her zeal was so active in these

SOURCES FROM THE PAST

1861

Harriet Jacobs Describes Life with an "Unprincipled Master and a Jealous Mistress"

I would ten thousand times rather that my children should be the half-starved paupers of Ireland than to be the most pampered among the slaves of America. I would rather drudge out my life on a cotton plantation, till the grave opened to give me rest, than to live with an unprincipled master and a jealous mistress. The felon's home in a penitentiary is preferable. He may repent, and turn from the error of his ways, and so find peace; but it is not so with a favorite slave. She is not allowed to have any pride of character. It is deemed a crime in her to wish to be virtuous.

Mrs. Flint possessed the key to her husband's character before I was born. She might have used this knowledge to counsel and to screen the young and the innocent among her slaves; but for them she had no sympathy. They were the objects of her constant suspicion and malevolence. She watched her husband with unceasing vigilance; but he was well practised in means to evade it. . . .

I had entered my sixteenth year, and every day it became more apparent that my presence was intolerable to Mrs. Flint. Angry words frequently passed between her and her husband. He had never punished me himself, and he would not allow any body else to punish me. In that respect, she was never satisfied; but, in her angry moods, no terms were too vile for her to bestow upon me. Yet I, whom she detested so bitterly, had far more pity for her than he had, whose duty it was to make her life happy. I never wronged her, or wished to wrong her; and one word of kindness from her would have brought me to her feet.

After repeated quarrels between the doctor and his wife, he announced his intention to take his youngest daughter, then four years old, to sleep in his apartment. It was necessary that a servant should sleep in the same room, to be on hand if the child stirred. I was selected for that office, and informed for what purpose that arrangement had been made. . . . During the day Mrs. Flint heard of his new arrangement and a storm followed. I rejoiced to hear it rage. . . .

. . . The fire of her temper kindled from small sparks, and now the flame became so intense that the doctor was obliged to give up his intended arrangement.

I knew I had ignited the torch, and I expected to suffer for it afterwards; but I felt too thankful to my mistress for the timely aid she rendered me to care much about that. She now took me to sleep in a room adjoining her own. There I was an object of her especial care, though not of her especial comfort, for she spent many a sleepless night to watch over me. . . . At last, I began to be fearful for my life. It had been often threatened; and you can imagine, better than I can describe, what an unpleasant sensation it must produce to wake up in the dead of the night and find a jealous woman bending over you. Terrible as this experience was, I had fears that it would give place to one more terrible.

Source: Harriet Jacobs, *Incidents in the Life of a Slave Girl* (1861), ed. Jean Fagan/Yellin (Cambridge, Mass.: Harvard University Press, 1987).

barbarous inflictions, that her invention was wonderfully quick, and some way of inflicting the requisite torture was soon found.

Despite the enactment of new laws prohibiting brutality to slaves, southern courts rarely convicted whites, particularly owners, of brutality against blacks. Bondsmen and -women could not initiate legal proceedings on their own behalf or testify against whites. As the Louisiana Code of 1824 put it, "The [slave] . . . cannot be a party in any civil action, either as plaintiff or defendant, except he has to claim or prove his freedom." Even when planters were brought up on charges of brutality or neglect of enslaved people, they dominated local juries and exonerated each other. In some of the most brutal cases, judges often took the position that "the power of the master must be absolute to render the submission of the slave perfect." Moreover, when the state put an enslaved person to death for committing a capital crime, it compensated the owner for loss of property. In Alabama, for example, the law stated:

> Whenever on the trial of any slave for a capital offense, the jury returns a verdict of guilty, the presiding judge must cause the same or another jury to be impaneled, and sworn to assess the value of such slave. . . . The owner of such slave . . . is entitled to receive . . . one-half the amount assessed by the jury, to be paid out of the fund assessed for that purpose.

In effect, the law defined most crimes against blacks as property crimes against whites. Slaveowners usually initiated such cases against an employee, lessee, or overseer of enslaved blacks. These men sought compensation for monetary damages to "their property." The enslaved person's "right" to live in a humane and safe environment played little role in such proceedings.

Although planters now provided blacks more medical treatment than before, such medical care left much to be desired. Preferred remedies for all kinds of ailments included "bleeding" and/or "vomiting," dangerous practices that undermined the body's constitution and damaged the health of the enslaved. Moreover, southern medical schools waged concerted campaigns to attract bondspeople and poor whites to their clinics. Under the guise of providing free or low-priced medical treatment, medical school clinics attracted enslaved blacks, compiled extensive records, and conducted outright experiments. Enslaved women served as subjects of early cesarean operations, and men and women were subjects of experimental vaccines and numerous operations designed to demonstrate certain procedures to young medical students. Abuse was widespread. On one occasion, when a master sent his slave to a local medical school for treatment of a leg ulcer caused by a burn, the surgeon amputated the man's leg, "just to let students see the operation, and bring the doctor, as well as the medical college . . . into notice." The editor of a leading medical journal denounced the procedure as unnecessary and the doctor as "heartless." Black cadavers represented a big business in cities like Richmond, which supplied the University of Virginia Medical School with "specimens" for "teaching purposes."

Slaves became the subject of ruthless medical experiments in antebellum hospitals. In some cases, they apparently benefited from "professional" medical care, but in too many cases they suffered more from their ailments. This sketch shows a man who apparently benefited from the treatment, but many others died. *Special Collections and Archives, Tompkins-McCaw Library, Virginia Commonwealth University*

Policies designed to discipline and control the slave work force took precedence over those aimed at improving the enslaved people's physical well-being. Accordingly, planters intensified their call for the vigorous enforcement of laws "on the books," including prohibitions on bondsmen and -women possessing guns, walking with canes, beating drums, blowing horns, and possessing liquor. The definition of crimes as well as prescribed punishments continued to differ radically for enslaved blacks and free whites. For the enslaved, capital crimes included murder, manslaughter, rape, and even attempted rape of a white woman; rebellion and attempted rebellion; and arson, robbery, and poisoning. Blacks could also suffer death for "striking" a white person. Since the demand for slave labor was so great, few enslaved people faced imprisonment or the death penalty, however. Whippings continued to be the most common form of punishment for blacks.

As antebellum southern states reinforced former restrictions, they also added new ones. They not only prohibited teaching enslaved people to read, write, or preach but also outlawed the practice of employing bondspeople in printing offices and giving them access to books and pamphlets. Planters, public officials, and religious leaders increasingly argued that it was not necessary for blacks to read the Bible to find salvation. One religious publication said, "Millions of those now in heaven never owned a bible." The prohibitions on black preachers and literacy were closely related to tightening definitions of "unlawful assembly" among bondsmen, which now included as few as five people. Other aspects of the codes prohibited slaves from administering drugs to whites or practicing medicine among blacks other than on the home plantation. A Tennessee judge declared: "A slave under pretense of practicing medicine . . . might convey intelligence from one plantation to another, of a contemplated insurrectionary movement; and thus enable the slaves to act in concert." In addition to the old laws requiring "submission" to the master's will, the new regulations and judicial interpretations aimed to control every "gesture, facial expression, or tone" of the bondsperson's interaction with whites. A North Carolina judge said, "insolence" could be construed as "a look, the pointing of a finger, a refusal or neglect to step out of the way, when a white person is seen to approach." The judge believed such acts performed by enslaved people violated "the rules of propriety, and if tolerated, would destroy that subordination, upon which our social system rests."

Southern cities and towns elaborated on the state codes and added their own regulations. They enacted strict curfew laws; required enslaved people to live in with their masters or employers; and took even greater steps to regulate their deportment and interactions with whites in public places. When blacks and whites met on the streets of Richmond, both law and custom required blacks to "step aside." Charleston prohibited enslaved people from swearing, smoking, or making "joyful demonstrations." Southern cities defined black communal activities as "disorderly" and prohibited the "shouting and dancing . . . and assemblies . . . of slaves and free Negroes in the streets and other [public] places."

Compared with the antebellum South, slave codes and social practices varied more widely in the antebellum West. Texas developed both law and customs that paralleled other parts of the antebellum South. Austin, Galveston, and Houston developed elaborate legal and extralegal restrictions on bondspeople. In 1855, an Austin ordinance outlawed the association of "any white man or Mexican" with enslaved blacks and empowered the city authorities to "control" and supervise the conduct, carriage, "demeanor and deportment of any and all slaves" within the city limits. For their part, although the Mormons approved the institution of slavery and blocked blacks from full fellowship in the church, the Utah "slave code" and church officials accented the responsibilities and duties of the slaveholders to enslaved people's material well-being. As such, they limited the ability of slaveowners to bring blacks into the territory. Among the Native Americans, the Cherokee instituted stiff slave codes that barred black-Indian marriages and expressed the "strongest color prejudice," while the Seminoles provided substantial opportunities for enslaved blacks to own livestock, bear arms, and pursue greater autonomy in day-to-day living.

The federal government reinforced the enslavement of antebellum blacks. In 1820, northern and southern states approved the Missouri Compromise, which admitted Missouri into the union as a slave state in exchange for the admission of Maine as a free state. The Missouri question had sparked some of the most acrimonious sectional debate since the nation's formation. It was the crisis over Missouri and slavery that prompted the aging Thomas Jefferson to write, "This momentous question . . . like a fire bell in the night, awakened and filled me with terror." The Missouri Compromise violated the Northwest Ordinance of 1787, which banned slavery northwest of the Ohio River. As a slave state, Missouri drove a wedge between the "free states" of Illinois, Indiana, and Ohio on the one hand and the far western states and territories on the other. Still, the Missouri Compromise established a firm ban on slavery north of 36°30' north latitude.

In 1846, as the nation waged war with Mexico, the U.S. Senate rejected the Wilmot Proviso, which called for a ban on "involuntary servitude" or "slavery" in any territory gained as a result of military conquest. Four years later, Congress strengthened the Fugitive Slave Act. Although the new law called for the suppression of the slave trade in Washington, D.C., it actually strengthened the hand of slaveholders, allowing them and their representatives to enter northern states and apprehend fugitives. Since alleged fugitives had no recourse to due process of law, the law encouraged the capture of free blacks as well as runaways.

Despite the ban on slavery north of 36°30' in the Missouri Compromise, the Kansas-Nebraska Act of 1854 disrupted that arrangement. The new law permitted slavery to spread well above the restricted boundary. As pro- and antislavery whites rushed into the territory to determine the outcome of its status as a state, violence erupted and helped to set the stage for the growing sectional conflict that would lead to the Civil War. In 1857, when the Missouri black Dred Scott sued for his freedom, the U.S. Supreme Court ruled that blacks "were not intended to be included, under the word citizens in the Constitution, and can therefore claim none of the rights and privileges which that instrument provides for and secures to citizens of the United States." As Chief Justice Roger B. Taney put it, blacks had "no rights that whites were bound to respect." Two years later, the U.S. attorney general also ruled that enslaved people were not citizens and therefore could not receive patents for their inventions. Until then, some enslaved blacks had gained official recognition of their inventions, notably Norbert Rillieux of Louisiana and Henry Blair of Maryland, who had received patents for sugar refining equipment and mechanical corn harvesters, respectively. The Dred Scott case, the fugitive slave law, recurring political compromises, and prohibitions on slave inventions all revealed how the federal government no less than southern state and local governments reinforced the institution of human bondage.

~

BY THE LATE ANTEBELLUM YEARS, the profits, power, and prestige associated with the plantation system underlay the transformation of African American life and labor. The growth of the antebellum economy entailed the spatial relocation of the black population from the Chesapeake to the Deep South, expansion of the internal slave trade, and the diversification of black labor. African Americans not only continued to cultivate sugar, tobacco, and rice but also added cotton cultivation and a variety of urban-industrial pursuits to their repertoire of skills. In other words, black bondsmen and -women not only helped to build the plantation system but also fueled the growth of southern cities and industrialization. Although planters introduced new policies designed to stabilize their enslaved work forces, stabilization was an incomplete process. As we will see in Chapter 8, black bondsmen and -women would use their improved physical conditions to build families, strengthen the bonds of community, and counteract the debilitating impact of bondage on their lives.

≈

Community, Culture, and Resistance

The antebellum era ushered in more complex conditions for the development of African American life. Enslaved families and communities fragmented under the impact of the domestic slave trade, the difficult journey to the Deep South, and the double crush of old and new restrictions on their geographical mobility, literacy, speech, and assembly. To some extent, however, these forces were counteracted by the end of the international slave trade and the expansion of a self-reproducing black population. African Americans used the gradual improvements in their living conditions, diet, and health care to deepen their efforts to build families, cement bonds of community, and resist the impact of bondage on their lives. Bondsmen and -women carefully evaluated the benefits of material improvements against the pain of social injustice and rejected the notion of paternal kindness. One ex-slave spoke for many when he exclaimed:

> Kind! I was dat man's slave; and he sold my wife, and he sold my two chill'en. . . . Kind!, yes, he gib me corn enough, and he gib me pork enough, and he neber gib me one lick wid de whip, but whar's my wife?—Whar's my chill'en? Take away de pork, I say; take away de corn, I can work and raise dese for myself; but gib me back de wife of my bossom, and gib me back my poor chill'en as was sold away.

Bondsmen and -women defied both formal and informal restrictions on their lives and pushed for the liberation of themselves, their families, and the enslaved community. Rooted deeply in African American ideas about work, family, God, and social justice, antebellum resistance included a broad range of day-to-day confrontations with masters, mistresses, and overseers, as well as outright rebellion and plots to rebel. Although the struggle for freedom entailed significant internal conflicts along cultural, status, and gender lines, black bondsmen and -women not only made common cause with each other on plantations, farms, and industrial sites of the Upper and Lower South but also joined free and unfree urban blacks to fight for the abolition of slavery and the freedom of all African Americans.

JUDEO-CHRISTIAN/AFRICAN IDEAS AND THE BLACK FAMILY

During the antebellum years, Judeo-Christian ideas of monogamy and the nuclear family gained increasing ground among African Americans. Couples announced "marriage plans" with masters' consent and scheduled "weddings" where planters or enslaved or white preachers officiated. Plantation ministers stressed biblical prohibitions against "pre-marital sexual intercourse, adultery, fornication, and the separation of mates." Southern Protestants encouraged enslaved blacks to memorize such passages as

> Thou shalt not commit adultery. . . . He who looketh on a woman, to lust after her, hath committed adultery with her already in his heart. . . . St. Paul saith, fornication and all uncleanness, let it not be once among you. . . . Let every man have his own wife, and every woman her own husband.

Despite such pronouncements, over and over again former bondsmen and -women recalled how their marriage ceremonies stopped short of the important Christian phrase "What God has joined together let no man put asunder." By 1860, according to recent scholarship, a majority of antebellum blacks lived in double-headed households composed of husband, wife, and children. Enslaved men and women also had most of their children by the same mate. On the Good Hope Plantation of South Carolina, seventy-three of ninety enslaved men and women had all of their children by a single partner. Only four women out of this sample had children by more than two men, and in each case they settled into a permanent union with the third. On the eve of the Civil War, a study of Nelson County, Virginia, revealed that 31 percent of African American marriages had lasted more than twenty years. On sample plantations in Tennessee, Mississippi, and Louisiana, planters broke up an estimated 32 percent of marriages by the callous sale of mates, but the remaining 68 percent were considered "unbroken" over a long period of time.

Although enslaved families gravitated toward the Euro-American model, it was an incomplete process. Partly because the institution of human bondage often ignored gender differences, black men and women developed more cooperative and reciprocal relations than white planters, their families, and employees. In the master's household, for example, childrearing responsibilities seldom fell on the shoulders of white men, and white women usually escaped hard field labor or outside work. Conversely, black men and women often subverted these roles. When the owner sold Charles Ball's mother from her Maryland home to a Georgia trader, his father and grandfather stepped in and raised him. When enslaved women and mothers ran away, men often filled their shoes. When one slave woman, Betty Guwn, accompanied her mistress away from the plantation for long seasonal vacations, her husband took care of the family, including taking the children "to the field" and watching over them during working hours.

Unlike free white families, black married men and women often lived apart. As one ex-slave put it, there were two types of slave marriages: those on the "home" plantation and those "abroad," where men and women lived on separate units. Oscar Rogers recalled how his father used to visit the family only one day a week, but "he came early and stay till bedtime." When men with abroad marriages visited their wives without passes, they risked severe whippings. Millie Barber recalled how patrollers caught her father on her mother's place without a pass. "They stripped him right befo' mammy and give him thirty-nine lashes." Since married women remained subject to the unwanted advances of white men, some men preferred abroad marriages to avoid witnessing the sexual abuse of their wives and children. When federal officials interviewed black women after the Civil War, they frequently recalled unwanted sexual relations and rape by white men, using such phrases as "he made me mean" and "he took away my shame."

Although a plethora of circumstances could break up marriages and families, African Americans devised their own sanctions for families and defined appropriate roles for men, women, and children. "You see," a Virginia ex-slave said, "God made marriage" but "white men" made the law. In their familial relations with wives and children, black men sought to "provide and protect." During their off-time, men hunted, built furniture, and worked small garden plots to enhance the diet and comfort of their families. Men who performed these tasks, the former bondsman William Green recalled, became "great men in the family and the quarters." When black women faced punishment from overseers or masters, enslaved men frequently interceded with masters and overseers to "put de whippin'" on them instead of their wives. Despite risk of life or limb, some black men took extraordinary steps to protect their wives from abusive masters and overseers. One ex-slave, Josiah Henson, recalled:

> I can remember the appearance of my father one day with his head, bloody and his back lacerated . . . his right ear had been cut off close to his head. He received a hundred lashes on his back. He had beaten the overseer for a brutal assault on my mother, and this was his punishment.

When another man sought to untie his wife from a whipping post, the overseer shot and killed him.

Enslaved women also worked for the well-being of their families. They made, mended, and washed clothing; manufactured candles, soap, and dye; and raised, prepared, preserved, and cooked food. One ex-slave remembered: "My mother . . . could do everything. She cooked, washed, ironed, spun, nursed and labored in the field. She made as good a field hand as she did a cook." Some women also hunted and fished. Frederick Douglass recalled that his grandmother was not only a good nurse but also "a capital hand at making nets for catching shad and herring." Betty Brown of Arkansas testified: "My mamma could hunt good as any man. . . . She'd have 'coon hides n' deer n' mink, n' beavers, lawd." Women also improved the taste of food through creative cooking. African Americans regularly recalled their mother's or grandmother's "hoe" or "ashcakes," which required considerable skill. According to one ex-slave:

> She'd take a poker before she put the bread in and rake the ashes off the hearth down to the solid stone or earth bottom, and the ashes would be banked in two hills to one side and the other. Then she would put the batter down on it; the

batter would be about an inch thick and about nine inches across. She'd put down three cakes at a time and let 'em stay there till the ashes were firm—about five minutes on the bare hot hearth. They would almost bake before she covered them up. Sometimes she would lay down as many as four at a time. The cakes had to dry before they were covered up, because if they were wet, there would be ashes in them when you would take them out to eat. She'd take her poker then and rake the ashes back on top of the cakes and let 'em stay there till the cakes were done. . . . Then she'd rake down the hearth gently, backward and forward, with the poker till she got down to them and then she'd put the poker under them and lift them out. That poker was a kind of flat iron. It wasn't a round one. Then we'd wash' em off like I told you and they be ready to eat. . . . Two-thirds of the water used in the ash cake was hot water, and that made the batter stick together like it was a biscuit dough. She could put it together and take it in her hand and pat it out flat and lay it on the hearth. It would be just as round! That was the art of it!

Enslaved families enabled black men and women to demonstrate their love for each other, offer each other and their children a modicum of protection, and initiate the young into the intricacies of human bondage and resistance. It was in the black family and community that children first learned how to express their humanity, while training the tongue "to remain silent" and "mask" innermost thoughts in the larger world of plantation masters, overseers, and slave patrols. In the quarters, according to William Wells Brown: "The slave . . . is brought up to look upon every white man as an enemy to him and his race." Such discipline was necessary for both their own and their parents' protection. The ex-slave Elijah P. Marrs stated: "Mothers were necessarily compelled to be severe on their children to keep them from talking too much." Since black children played with white children until they reached nine or ten years of age, they sometimes said things to white children that got their parents into trouble. As Marrs further noted, "Many a poor mother has been whipped nearly to death on account of their children telling white children things." At the same time, enslaved parents instructed their children on modes of direct resistance. W. H. Robinson's father instructed him "to die in defense" of his mother. According to the testimony of a Tennessee woman, her mother instilled into her a sense of resistance to abuse. "Ma fussed, fought, and kicked all the time. I tell you, she was a demon. She said that she wouldn't be whipped, and when she fussed, all Eden must have known it." She instilled the same fighting spirit into her daughter; "I'll kill you, gal, if you don't stand up for yourself. . . . Fight, and if you can't fight, kick; if you can't kick, then bite."

Although enslaved children expressed the greatest admiration and respect for the authority of their parents, they soon learned the limits of their parents' power to protect them from mistreatment by overseers, planters, and members of plantation households. Jacob Stroyer recalled the first time that he was whipped by a white person:

This was the first time I had been whipped by anyone except father or mother, so I cried out in a tone as if I would say, this is the first and last whipping you will give me when father gets hold of you . . . but soon found my expectation blasted, as father very coolly said to me "Go back to your work and be a good boy, for I cannot do anything for you."

Moses Grandy described how his mother resisted the sale of her children:

I remember well my mother often hid us all in the woods to prevent masters selling us. . . . After a time the master would send word to her to come in, promising he would not sell us. But at length persons came who agreed to give the right price. . . . My mother frantic with grief resisted their taking her child away; she was beaten and held down; she fainted.

When she regained consciousness, her children were gone.

Enslaved families not only initiated the young into an oppressive slave society but also worked to provide a protective fold for their growth and development. As Grandy's story demonstrates, however, their best efforts often failed. Thus, black

South Carolina, 1862. This photo reflects the value of family in the lives of slaves, despite much abuse and the absence of legal protection. *Bettmann/Corbis*

families continued to rely on certain African notions of kinship. Black men, like their white counterparts, initiated courtship and searched for wives on and off the plantation, but they drew on African aspects of their American culture and transformed European courting, marriage, and childbearing patterns. In Maryland and Virginia, as in some West African societies, some black men formally presented the woman with a brass ring as a sign of a proposal for marriage. If she accepted the ring, the woman became his wife. In like manner, in Georgia, after a period of courtship, the man visited a woman's cabin, roasted peanuts in the ashes, and, while eating, proposed marriage. If the woman agreed, they went to his cabin and became man and wife.

"Jumping the broom" was perhaps the most widespread African marriage ritual practiced by African Americans. Customarily, a relative or close friend from both the man's and the woman's side of the family held opposite ends of the broom, placing it about a foot off the ground. After the couple jumped together across the broom, they became husband and wife. Georgian Sheldrick Waltour recalled that he and his wife "jumped the broom" after the preacher "say de blessin' on us" but "befo' de feastin' begin." Josephine Anderson of Florida stated that the broom ritual "seals de marriage, and at de same time brings . . . good luck. Brooms keep hants away."

African culture influenced not only marriage rituals but also the actual types of families that blacks built on antebellum plantations. Rather than being simple units of husband, wife, and children, enslaved families embraced extended kin. These networks involved uncles, aunts, grandparents, and even nonrelatives—that is, "fictive kin"—in childrearing responsibilities. Numerous blacks later remembered the role of grandparents in their lives. Georgia Baker recalled that her grandfather took care of her and her siblings while their parents worked in the fields. Perry Jemison related that her grandmother was named "Snooky" and her grandfather "Anthony," and they both played an important role in her life as a child. In his recollections of slavery days, Austin Grant reported that his grandfather used "to tell us things, to keep the whip off our backs." When Ellen Thompson's father was sold and her mother later died, her grandmother took care of her with the aid of her uncles. When Mingo White of Alabama was sold away from his family, his father's friend stepped in and took care of him: "The only carin' that I had or ever known anything about was given me by a frien' of my pappy. His name was John White. My pappy tol' him to take care of me for him."

Under the impact of antebellum bondage, certain African ideas about sex and sexual relations also persisted. As recent scholars note, enslaved women adhered to notions of motherhood that were deeply rooted in the African past. As in many West African societies, bondswomen considered motherhood a nearly "sacred" act. Thus, for many, "a marriage was not considered consummated until after the birth of the first child." Consequently, enslaved blacks rejected white society's notion of prenuptial intercourse and out-of-wedlock motherhood as "evil." In so doing, they modified "guilt-laden" Euro-American sexual mores, yet at the same time enslaved mothers worked diligently to protect their young daughters from premature maternal responsibility.

RELIGION, MUSIC, AND LEISURE TIME ACTIVITIES

The transformation of the black family was closely intertwined with changes in African American religious beliefs and practices. During the 1820s and 1830s, planters placed growing restrictions on African American organized religious activities. As discussed in Chapter 7, blacks found it exceedingly difficult to pursue their own modes of worship, particularly following Nat Turner's rebellion in 1831 (see page 203). After Turner's insurrection, for example, a new Mississippi statute stated: "It is unlawful for any slave, free Negro, or mulatto to preach the gospel upon pain of receiving thirty-nine lashes upon the naked back of the . . . preacher." When blacks defied the law, ex-slave West Turner of Virginia said, "Den dey would rush in an' start whippin' and beatin' de slaves unmerciful, saying that 'You ain't got no time to serve God. We bought you to serve us.'"

During the early 1840s, southern Methodists and Baptists split from their northern counterparts over the issue of slavery. After parting ways with northern abolitionist congregations, rising numbers of planters now believed that it was "safe" to proselytize the enslaved. Some planters built "small chapels" or "praise houses" for slaves and hired white ministers to supervise their services, whereas others gradually incorporated blacks into segregated sections of white congregations. Black membership in the Methodist denomination rose from 94,000 in 1840 to 207,000 in 1860. When we add the number of blacks served by missionaries and Sunday schools, the number of black Methodists reached over 453,300. Although the Baptists expended fewer resources proselytizing among enslaved people and kept less systematic statistics, the number of black Baptists also dramatically expanded. In 1846, the Southern Baptist Association reported 150,000 black members. By 1860, an estimated 400,000 blacks belonged to southern Baptist churches. The number reached 600,000 with the addition of blacks attending Baptist Sunday schools. Other denominations—Presbyterian, Episcopalian, Church of Christ, Lutheran, and Quaker—also swelled the ranks of black Protestants by several thousands. In some Baptist and Methodist churches, blacks made up 20 to 40 percent of the total and were often the majority.

In these biracial churches, enslaved blacks received heavy doses of the "Pauline" scriptures. First Corinthians 7:21 represented the key message for slaves: "Let every man abide in the same calling wherein he was called. Art thou called servant? Care not for it. . . ." Ex-slave Henry Bibb recalled the same passages. "Servants be obedient to your masters,—and he that knoweth his master's will and doeth it not shall be beatin' with many stripes;—means that God will send them to hell, if they disobey their masters." Plantation ministers also prohibited the use of musical instruments and what they called "secular dancing" in religious services.

African American Religious Beliefs and Practices

Bondsmen and -women detested the self-serving sermons and restrictions on the physical expression of their beliefs in plantation churches. In his comments on the

Pauline scriptures, one ex-slave remarked that "this kind of preaching has driven thousands into infidelity . . . they cannot believe or trust in such a religion." Thus, blacks pushed for their own independent forms of worship. Since white ministers often appointed enslaved preachers, gave them special passes, and permitted them to travel widely from plantation to plantation, carrying the message to the black community, blacks gained an extraordinary opportunity to worship in their own way. The Baptist minister Reverend John Jasper of Virginia emerged as one of the most renowned of the enslaved antebellum preachers. In the Richmond-Petersburg area of Virginia, whites and blacks acknowledged the fame of Reverend Jasper from about 1830 through the antebellum years. The son of an enslaved field hand father and household servant, Jasper migrated to Richmond from rural Virginia, where he had also worked as a field hand. According to Jasper's biographer, "He marshalled the Scriptures with consummate skill, and built an argument easily understood" by his illiterate hearers, and "yet so compact and tactful was he, that his most cultured hearers bent beneath his force." By the eve of the Civil War, as whites turned toward seminary-trained ministers and curtailed the emotional style of the Great Awakening, African Americans retained the earlier forms and in some ways elaborated on them. Blacks continued to punctuate sermons with verbal responses: "Yes, glory! That's it, hit him again! . . . Yes, sweet Lord! Yes, sir!" Under the influence of enslaved ministers like Jasper, one observer reported, blacks worked "themselves up to a great pitch of excitement, in which they yell and cry along, and finally shriek and leap up, clapping their hands and dancing."

As the Methodist denominations penetrated southern plantations, they silenced slave instruments of music, such as the banjo and the fiddle, and prohibited "secular dancing." In place of previous musical and dance forms, blacks built on their African heritage and created the "ring shout." Charles Lyell, a visitor to the South Carolina and Georgia sea islands offered one of the earliest descriptions of the ring shout:

> At the Methodist prayer meetings, they are permitted to move round rapidly in a ring, joining hands in token brotherly love, presenting the right hand and then the left, in which manner, I am told, they sometimes contrive to take enough exercise to serve as a substitute for the dance.

Among the Gullah, such shouts took place after the regular service and benediction. Moreover, although they sang Baptist and Methodist hymns during regular service, blacks sang only their spirituals during the ring shout.

Even as enslaved blacks worshipped under white supervision or with planters' permission, they also carved out underground churches called "brush arbors" or "hush harbors." According to ex-slave Amanda McCray, "The grass never had a chance ter grow for the troubled knees that kept it crushed down." In these settings, away from the watchful eye of masters, African Americans introduced their own interpretation of evangelical Protestantism and transformed it to meet their own needs. Whereas slaveowners exhorted blacks to obey their masters, blacks emphasized the scriptures that proclaimed all people "equal in the eyes of God." As a result of their deep belief that the Bible held the key to their own liberation, some enslaved people defied the ban on learning to read so that they could read the Bible.

Even as enslaved blacks worshipped under white supervision, they also carved out underground churches called "brush arbors" or "hush harbors," where they worshiped as they pleased, conducting their own baptismal, marriage, and burial rites. Here they conduct a funeral. *The Historic New Orleans Collection, accession no. 1960.46*

One ex-slave, William McWhorter, recalled: "Dey jus' beat 'em up bad when dey catched 'em studin', readin', and writin'." Still, McWhorter continued, "some dat wanted larnin' so bad dey would slip out at night and meet in a deep gully whar dey would study by de light'ood torchers . . . and if dey was lucky enough 'til dey larned to read de Bible, dey kept it a close secret."

Although some planters gradually permitted the distribution of Bibles to enslaved blacks, most continued to withhold the written word. Even so, blacks who could not read gained access to the Bible through the oral transmission of memorized biblical stories. As one Beaufort, South Carolina, ex-slave woman exclaimed:

Oh! I don't know nothing! I can't read a word. But, oh! I read Jesus in my heart, just as you read him in de book. . . . I read him here in my heart just as you read him in de Bible. O, . . . my God! I got Him! I hold him here all de time! He stay with me!

Another ex-slave stated simply: "I reckin somethin' inside just told us about God and that there was a better place hereafter."

"Brush arbors" underscored not only the restrictions on bondspeople in biracial Christian churches but also the persistence of unique African religious expression among African Americans. In these unsupervised settings, blacks replenished the African aspects of their culture and reinforced the growth of distinct African American religious beliefs and practices. Underground black preachers also conducted baptisms, weddings, and funerals. In his narrative, Charles Ball of Maryland recalled the influence of African practices on funeral rites in the Upper South. Ball described in substantial detail the funeral of an enslaved child whom he helped to inter:

> Its father buried with it, a small bow and several arrows; a little bag of parched meal; a miniature canoe, about a foot long, and a little paddle, (with which he said it would cross the ocean to his own country), [a] small stick, with an iron nail, sharpened and fastened into one end of it; and a piece of white muslin, with several curious and strange figures painted on it in blue and red, by which he said, his relatives and countrymen would know the infant to be his son, and would receive it accordingly, on its arrival amongst them. . . . [He] cut a lock of hair from his head, threw it upon the dead infant, and closed the grave with his own hands. He then told us the God of his country was looking at him, and was pleased with what he had done.

Ideas and practices described as "voodoo-like" also persisted. Afro-Christians believed in herbalism, ghost lore, witchcraft, fortune telling, and especially conjuring, the belief that one person could cause harm to another through supernatural practices. A Virginian, Duncan Gaines, recalled the practice in antebellum Virginia: "There was much talk of voodism and anyone ill for a long time without getting relief from herb medicine was thought to be 'fixed' or suffering from some sin that his father had committed." Thus, the conjurers, root doctors, or voodoo doctors competed with slave preachers and retained substantial influence in the enslaved community. Their influence rested on their ability to "fix" and undo "fixes." According to Henry Bibb, "The remedy is most generally some kind of bitter root; they are directed to chew it and spit towards their masters when they are angry with slaves. At other times they prepare certain kinds of powders, to sprinkle about their master's dwellings." Although such practices gained expression in the Upper South, they were most prominent in the Deep South states of South Carolina, Georgia, and Louisiana.

Some conjurers developed the admiration, fear, and respect of all on the place. William Wells Brown recalled how the conjurer Dinkie lived independent of blacks and whites. Fellow blacks, overseers, and masters alike left Dinkie alone. "No one interfered with him. . . . Dinkie hunted, slept, was at the table at meal time, roamed the woods, went to the city, and returned when he pleased." Since so many conjurers endured the whip like other slaves, some argued that only blacks could be conjured. When their medicine failed, however, conjurers sometimes blamed the victim for failing to follow instructions. When one man complained after receiving a whipping despite following the conjurer's advice, the conjurer told him: "I gi' you a runin' han' [a charm that would give the possessor swiftness]! Why didn't yer

1. Slave Drum, Virginia (c. 1645).
From the outset of their enslavement, Africans used their Old World experience to fashion a new culture in the Americas. Modeled after similar drums in West African society, this drum suggests the impact of African culture on black life in colonial America. Because Africans used drums for both leisure and resistance activities, colonial assemblies came to outlaw their use.

2. *The Old Plantation* (c. 1800). Although this watercolor by an unknown artist was found in South Carolina, its precise origins and meaning are uncertain. The most recent interpretation is that the scene represents a double-wedding ceremony with participants playing instruments and wearing clothes that suggest a mixture of West African and European styles.

3. Pieced Quilt, Beaver Dam Plantation, Hanover County, Virginia (late 18th century).
This is the earliest known slave-made quilt in the United States. On southern planta-tions, black women became skilled quilters, and they perfected designs and juxta-posed colors that reflected their own aesthetic values and tastes.

4. Shotgun House, New Orleans (mid-19th century).
The shotgun house (so called from the saying that a bullet fired at the entrance would travel uninterrupted out the back door) represents the chief African American contribution to American vernacular archi-tecture. Black migrants from the Caribbean islands of Haiti and Cuba brought the design to New Orleans and Charleston during the early 1800s.

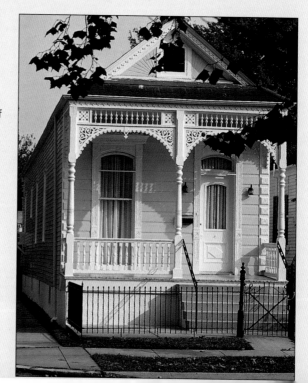

5–6. Dutreuil Barjon, Sleigh Bed (c. 1835), and Peter Bentzon, Footed Cup (c. 1820). African Americans not only worked as general laborers in the fields and factories of the antebellum South but also practiced a number of skilled crafts that offered them greater prospects for purchasing their freedom. Barjon, a free black who made this French-style bed, was trained by the New Orleans free black Jean Rousseau. Similarly, as early as the 1790s, the free black Peter Bentzon opened his own silversmith shop in Philadelphia. In addition to the unadorned vase-like cup shown here, art historians have identified at least eight other pieces produced by Bentzon.

7. Joshua Johnson, *Portrait of a Gentleman* (1805–1810). Joshua Johnson, a resident of Baltimore, is the earliest known professional painter of African descent in the United States. Although Johnson's principal clientele consisted of white elites, he also painted black subjects. The African Methodist Episcopal minister Daniel Coker is the subject of this portrait.

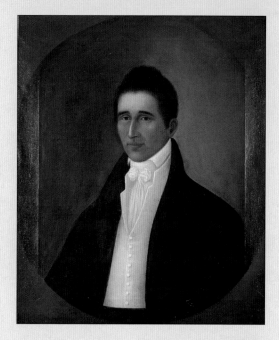

8. Robert S. Duncanson, *The Land of the Lotus Eaters* (1861). A self-taught landscape artist, Duncanson became the first black to gain international recognition for his paintings. After receiving a commission from a wealthy Cincinnati entrepreneur, his reputation soared. Although Duncanson's best-known work is *Blue Hole, Flood Waters, Little Miami River* (1851), his international stature was most closely identified with *Lotus Eaters*.

Photo 1: © The British Museum; **Photo 2:** Abby Aldrich Rockefeller Folk Art Center, Williamsburg, Virginia, Acc. #1935.301.3; **Photo 3:** Valentine Museum, Richmond, Virginia; **Photo 4:** Mitchel Osborne Photography; **Photo 5:** Center for African American Decorative Arts; **Photo 6:** Philadelphia Museum of Art. Purchased with the Thomas Skelton Harrison Fund and partial gift of Wynard Wilkinson; **Photo 7:** Reproduced by permission of the American Museum in Britain, Bath; **Photo 8:** Oil on Canvas. The Royal Collections, Sweden. Photo by Alexis Daflos.

run?" For his part, Bibb gave up the practice when it failed to protect him from a whipping and, most importantly, when it failed to win him the love of his favorite girl:

> One of these conjurers, for a small sum, agreed to teach me to make any girl love me that I wished. After I paid him, he told me to get a bull frog, and take a certain bone out of the frog, dry it, and when I get a chance I must step up to any girl whom I wished to make love me, and scratch her somewhere on her naked skin with this bone, and she would be certain to love me, and follow me in spite of herself; no matter who she might be engaged with, nor who she might be walking with . . . so when I got a chance, I fetched her a tremendous rasp across her neck with this bone, which made her jump. But in place of making her love me, it only made her angry with me. She felt more like running after me for thus abusing her, than she felt like loving me.

Spirituals and Slave Songs

The growth of African American spirituals reinforced the unique features of black religious culture. Central to this process was the "Chosen People" idea. Some ex-slaves recalled songs involving the refrain "Heaven will be my home," partly because they were convinced that their masters would not be there. As one ex-slave recalled, "This is one reason I believe in a hell. I don't believe a just God is going to take no such man as that [her master] into his kingdom." Over and over again, enslaved blacks sprinkled the lyrics of their songs, as later collected by white witnesses, with phrases affirming their belief that they were "children of God," "born of God," "the people of God," or "the people of the Lord." Spirituals left no doubt that blacks believed in a life after death: "to the promised land I'm bound to go"; "I walk the heavenly road"; and "Heaven shall be my home." Blacks also developed their share of sad songs: "rollin'" through "an unfriendly world"; "trouble" in mind; this world is "a hell to me"; and "feeling like a motherless child." Such songs demonstrated that slavery was indeed an incredibly cruel experience, but bondsmen and -women repeatedly bounced back from such sentiments with words of triumph and optimism. Numerous lyrics expressed feeling like "an eagle" and the ability to bear on wings and "fly, fly, fly." Although white Christians held similar beliefs, such ideas took on a different and more profound meaning when uttered by enslaved African Americans.

The creation of slave songs was a dynamic social and cultural process. African Americans adopted white hymns and folk songs but changed the words, musical structure, and mode of performance to fit their own vision—for example, by using African call-and-response patterns, which linked the individual to the larger collectivity or community. Songs also represented what some analysts call "communal recreation," which meant that enslaved people constantly reworked old songs into new versions. In 1845, a white traveler through the South remarked that blacks "leave out old stanzas, and introduce new ones at pleasure. You may, in passing from Virginia to Louisiana, hear the same tune a hundred times, but seldom the same words accompanying it." When later asked where they got their songs, ex-slaves emphasized the spontaneous and communal nature of the process. One collector of such songs later recorded the response of one black woman:

> We'd all be at the "prayer house" [on] de Lord's day, and de white preacher he'd splain de word and rid whar Exekiel done say—Dry bones gwiner lib ergin. . . . I'd jump up dar and den hollar and shout and sing and pat, and dey would all catch de words and I'd sing it to some ole shout song I'd heard 'em sing from Africa, and dey'd all take it up and keep at it, and, keep addin to it, and den it would be a spiritual.

Religion not only offered blacks hope for life beyond the suffering of this world but also instilled confidence that power relations could change in their lifetime. Some songs went straight to the heart of physical suffering on this earth: "No more rain, no more snow, No more cowskin on my back!" Their songs also indicated a fervent wish to change power relations: "Glory be to God that rules on high." Accordingly, African American songs and oral traditions accented Old Testament stories of the weak overcoming the strong: Pharaoh and the Israelites—"did not old Pharaoh get lost . . . get lost . . . get lost in the Red Sea?"; Daniel and the lion's den—"O' my Lord, delivered Daniel. . . . Why not deliver me too?"; and many others —"did not" the Lord deliver "Jonah from de belly of de whale" and "de Hebrew children from de fiery furnace?" Although the New Testament's "Prince of Peace" appealed to African Americans, they sometimes portrayed Jesus as an Old Testament warrior. Mounted on a horse with sword in hand, Jesus engaged in combat with Satan as a champion of the weak. "Ride on, King Jesus," one song stated, "No man can hinder thee."

African American cultural creations revealed the blurring of lines between the spiritual and the secular, between work, worship, and play. In addition to the "praise houses" and "brush arbors," slaves created, recreated, and sang their songs on boats, in the fields, and in the quarters. "Michael Row the Boat Ashore," "Lay This Body Down," and "Brudder, Don' Git Weary" all were quite explicitly work songs with strong spiritual content:

> Brudder, don' git weary,
> Brudder, don' git weary,
> Brudder, don' git weary,
> Fo' de work is most done.
> De ship is in de harbor, harbor, harbor
> De ship is in de harbor, To wait upon de Lord . . .
> 'E got 'e ca' go raidy, raidy, raidy
> 'E got 'e ca' go raidy, Fo' to wait upon de Lord.

Leisure Time Activities

Although African American cultural activities blurred the distinction between work and leisure, by the late antebellum years enslaved blacks claimed a slightly wider margin of off-time activities than before. In addition to Saturday and Sunday, leisure time included Easter, the Fourth of July, Whitsuntide, New Year's Day, and especially Christmas. Lasting from no less than three up to twelve days, Christmas represented the chief seasonal celebration, with gift giving, merriment, and inter-plantation visitations. Off-time activities blended songs, music, dance, food, beverages, and storytelling. One slaveowner reported: "I have a fiddle in my quarters and though some of my good brethren in the church would think hard of me, yet I allow dancing; ay I buy the fiddle and encourage it." A Mississippi planter related:

> I have a good fiddler, and keep him well supplied with catgut.* . . . [He] plays for the negroes every Saturday night until 12 o'clock. They are exceedingly punctual in their attendance at the hall, while Charley's fiddle is always accompanied with Ihurod on the triangle, and Sam to "pat."

According to one historian of African American dance, Africans used the "motor-muscle memory of the various West African ethnic groups," to create new African American dances: the buzzard lope, breakdown, pigeon wing, cakewalk, Charleston, "set de flo," and snake hips. Dance routines also reinforced African culture by use of the "fiddler-caller," who instructed the dancers to execute steps, which varied in complexity and separated the best from the average. The ex-slave Mark Chaney, from Mississippi, related how his father, an African-born slave, taught him how "to dance like dey did in Africa." In 1838, William B. Smith described a "beer dance" on one Prince Edward, Virginia, plantation:

> The banjo man, was seated on the beer barrel, in an old chair. *Tumming* his banjo. . . . Before him stood two athletic blacks, clapping [juba]† to the notes of the Banjor. . . . The rest of the company, male and female were dancers. The clappers rested the right foot on the heel, and its clap on the floor was in perfect unison with the notes of the Banjor and palms of the hands on the corresponding extremities. The dancers having the most . . . flexible contortions of the body and limbs, that human imagination can devise.

African Americans continued to improvise the making as well as the playing of musical instruments. Mark Chaney recalled how his father made his own "fiddle outa pine bark." Wash Wilson, who experienced slavery in Texas and Louisiana, recalled:

> Dere wasn't no music instruments. Us take pieces of a sheep's rib or cow's jaw or a piece of iron, with a old kettle, or a hollow gourd and some horse-hair to make de drum. Sometimes dey'd git a piece of tree trunk and hollow it out and stretch a goat's or sheep's skin over it for de drum. Dey'd take de buffalo horn and scrape it out to make de flute. Den dey'd take a mule's jawbone and rattle de stick 'cross its teeth.

---

* Catgut: a tough cord usually made from sheep intestines, used for instrument strings.
† Juba: an African-inspired dance characterized by handclapping, foot stomping, and slapping of hands against the body.

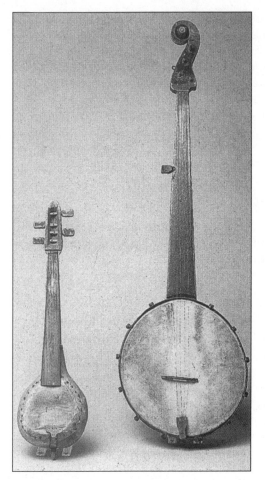

Although African Americans gradually adapted their Old World culture to New World conditions, at the same time they continued to build on their African heritage, such as by using gourds and animal hides to craft banjos. *The Blue Ridge Institute & Museum/Blue Ridge Heritage Archives of Ferrum College, Ferrum, Virginia*

Despite such improvisation, the repertoire of instruments played by enslaved people spanned a broad spectrum, including fifes, flutes, mouth bows, quills (a flutelike instrument usually made from a reed), accordions, French horns, and pianos, as well as the more widespread banjo, of African origins, and fiddle, acquired from poor whites.

Although consumption of alcoholic beverages required the approval of owners, African American dances included plenty of food and alcoholic drinks. The "beer dance" earlier described by Smith included one man holding "in his right hand a jug gourd of persimmon beer, and in his left, a dipper or water gourd, to serve the company while two black women were employed in filling the fireplace, six feet square, with larded persimmon dough." John Crawford of Mississippi later recalled how his grandfather manufactured alcoholic beverages for enslaved blacks: "Grandpappy used to own a still which was ran by grandpappy's friend Billy Bush. . . . They made whiskey out of corn and made whiskey out of peaches. They made apple cider and grape wine and dandelion wine and alder (elderberry) wine." "At the parties and at Christmas," Crawford said, blacks "got plenty of whiskey."

African Americans not only used their off-time to sing, dance, eat, play music, and drink but also used these occasions to tell stories and extend their oral traditions. According to Chaney, his father often placed him on his knee and told him "all 'bout when he lived in Africa . . . Dat Good Ole Land." The trickster figure—involving the ordeal of the smaller and weaker Brer Rabbit outsmarting the larger and stronger Brer Fox or Brer Wolf—occupied a key position in black folk tales. The Rabbit tales were especially prominent in the low country of Georgia and South Carolina, where Brer Rabbit repeatedly outsmarts his foes in stories like the famous "tarbaby" tale. In these tales, enslaved African Americans approved such practices as theft from the master's cupboard as a means of redressing economic exploitation and inequality. As such, these tales also helped to set the stage for more overt forms of resistance to bondage.

DAY-TO-DAY RESISTANCE, REBELLION, AND ATTEMPTS TO REBEL

Antebellum black families, religion, and leisure time activities established the cultural foundations for slave resistance. Even more so than in the early years of the nineteenth century, black resistance spanned the spectrum from day-to-day encounters in the fields, households, and shops of slaveowners to overt revolts and plots to revolt. The historical record is replete with examples of enslaved men and women who took courageous stances against abuse. Early in life, Frederick Douglass, the son of an enslaved woman and a white father, determined to be a free man. Born around 1818 in Talbot County, Maryland, Douglass resisted the routine and discipline of slave labor by age sixteen. When his owner sent him to a professional "Negro Breaker," a person specializing in whipping and subduing slaves for a fee, Douglass not only resisted the "Negro Breaker" but also won the fight. He later wrote: "I was a changed being after that fight. I was nothing before, I was a man now." When an overseer tried to whip Lucy Perry, she said: "De minute he grabs me I seize on ter his thumb an' I bites hit ter de bone." Another ex-slave, Martha Brady, "knocked" an overseer "plum down," when he said something that "he had no bizness to say." One woman shamed an overseer when she fought him "for a whole day and stripped him naked as the day he was born." On one occasion, according to the testimony of another woman, her mother's temper "ran wild."

> For some reason Mistress Jennings struck her with a stick. Ma struck back and a fight followed. Mr. Jennings was not at home and the children became frightened and ran upstairs. For half hour they wrestled in the kitchen. Mistress, seeing that she could not get the better of ma, ran out in the road, with ma on her heels. In the road my mother flew into her again. The thought seemed to race across mother's mind to tear mistress clothing off her body. She suddenly began to tear Mistress Jennings' clothing off. She caught hold, pulled, ripped and tore. Poor mistress was nearly naked when the storekeeper got to them and pulled ma off.

Still, "Ma" refused to accept a whipping for her actions when the mistress's husband returned home. She was then permanently hired out to work away from her home plantation.

Resistance in the Fields and Factories

Antebellum slave resistance gained its most powerful manifestations in the fields. Planters repeatedly complained about field hands breaking farm tools, injuring work animals, and sabotaging crops. According to Olmsted, planters increased the weight and durability of tools like hoes, and substituted mules for horses, because enslaved blacks frequently destroyed tools, injured draft animals, and ruined crops to slow the work pace.

Such tools as we [northerners] constantly give our [free white] laborers, and find our profit in giving them, would not last a day in [the South]. . . . So, too, mules are . . . substituted for horses [because] . . . horses cannot bear the treatment that they *must* get from negroes.

One planter, John Hammond, suspected outright sabotage: "I find [hoe-hands] chopping up cotton dreadfully and begin to think that my stand has every year been ruined in this way."

Blacks frustrated the efforts of overseers and planters to keep them at work non-stop. A Virginia planter angrily recorded in his diary that "hands wont work unless I am in sight." On one plantation, a contemporary observer noted:

The overseer rode among them, on a horse carrying in his hand a raw hide whip, constantly directing and encouraging them; but . . . as often as he visited one line of the operations the hands at the other end would discontinue their labor, until he returned to ride toward them again.

More so than men, women of childbearing age had great latitude in feigning illness as a means of slowing down the work pace. Since planters highly valued black children, they were somewhat more solicitous of black women's complaints of illness. One planter complained that such women

don't come to the field and you go to the quarters and ask the old nurse what's the matter and she says, "Oh, she's not fit to work sir"; and . . . you have to take her word for it . . . and you dare not set her [to] work; and so she will lay up till she feels like taking the air again, and plays the lady at your expense.

When field hands gained the cooperation of drivers, their resistance was most effective. Solomon Northrup, a driver on a Louisiana plantation, developed a technique for feigning the whipping of bondsmen:

Practice makes perfect, truly; and during my eight years' experience as a driver, I learned to handle the whip with marvelous dexterity and precision, throwing the lash within a hair's breadth of the back, the ear, the nose, without, however, touching either of them . . . they would squirm and screech as if in agony, although not one of them had in fact been even grazed.

Black bondsmen and -women also undermined the system through theft and the sale of stolen property. In addition to planters and farmers, who reported theft of garden crops, poultry, and pork, urban and industrial slaveowners recorded the loss of a broad range of products. One rice miller reported that his product "had been much exposed to plunder." In Virginia, the manager of William Weaver's ironworks informed the owner: "I had a notion of comeing down tomorrow evening . . . but I am afraid if I leave here they will steal the place. They come very near it while I am here." At the Tredegar Iron Works, slaves sometimes stole bar iron, which they exchanged for consumer goods. In 1830, in the goldfields, the *Niles Register* reported that blacks stole valuable amounts of gold dust by concealing it "in their hair." According to one contemporary "anonymous" informer, at night African Americans watched for slow-moving trains, boarded them, and threw off what they could." In the train yards, the informer also stated, while railroad agents slept, bondsmen would "take off what they wanted . . . and I have no doubt but hundreds of dollars worth of lost goods go in this way." When a fire destroyed the facilities of one railroad company, blacks saved "nearly all of their plunder" but allowed the "company's tools, supplies, and property to burn!"

Enslaved people not only took goods, slowed down the work pace, destroyed property, injured livestock, and feigned sickness but also sometimes inflicted injuries on themselves and committed suicide and infanticide. Ex-slaves recalled how some women took their own lives as well as the lives of their children. An ex-Kentucky slave, Lewis Clarke, remembered how one "slave mother took her three children and threw them into a well, and then jumped in with them, and they were all drowned." A mother of thirteen children reportedly killed each one of her offspring in infancy rather than have them grow up in bondage. According to reports, the woman belonged to an extraordinarily cruel and brutal master who had, among other atrocities, cut off six of the woman's toes for various offenses. In 1837, in Columbia, South Carolina, when the owner severely whipped one man for an offense that he did not commit:

> As soon as the flogging was over, the slave went into the back yard, where there was an axe and a block, and struck off the upper half of his right hand. He went and held up the bleeding hand before his master, saying, "You have mortified me, so I have made myself useless."

On a Georgia rice plantation, an enslaved man named London drowned himself when the overseer threatened him with a whipping.

Runaways and Fugitives

Rather than taking such desperate measures as self-inflicted injuries, suicide, and infanticide, a growing number of enslaved men and women resisted by running away. Recent scholarship offers a careful profile of the fugitives, derived mainly from newspaper advertisements for the capture and return of such runaways. First, although fugitives were disproportionately young, skilled men, the advertisements show people of all ages, sexes, and skill levels. Second, most runaways traveled short distances and returned after a few days, but permanent fugitives had the greatest impact on the plantation regime. Third, fugitives usually left alone, in twos, or in small groups of three or four. Fourth, whereas most Upper South runaways headed north, Deep South fugitives continued to escape, as earlier, into the nearby swamps, seeking to establish themselves in Maroon communities on land away from owners' control. Fifth, whatever their destination, fugitives depended on the confidential support of family and friends, at the home plantation and throughout their route. Finally, although precipitating incidents included whippings, denial of marriage requests, sale of family members, and intensification of the work regimen, running away was deeply rooted in the accumulated abuses of the slave system.

Fugitives devised a variety of creative ways of escaping bondage. The legendary Henry "Box" Brown had himself crated and shipped from Richmond, Virginia, to freedom in Philadelphia. Similarly, the enslaved woman Lear Green had herself packed into a sailor's chest and transported from slavery in Maryland to freedom in Pennsylvania. Some blacks also subverted gender and racial conventions to gain their freedom. In 1848, the woman Ellen Craft, a seamstress, disguised herself as a man and escaped with her husband, William, a cabinetmaker, from Macon, Georgia, to Philadelphia:

> "Now William," said Ellen, "listen to me and take my advice, and we shall be free in less than a month." "Let me hear your plans, then," said William. "Take part of your money and purchase me a good suit of gentlemen's apparel, and when the white people give us a holiday, let us go to the North. I am white enough to [pass] as the master, and you can pass as my servant."

When William replied, "But you are too short," Ellen requested a pair of high-heeled boots and a "very high hat." When William said, "But your face is smooth, you do not have a beard," Ellen said, "I could bind up my face in a handkerchief . . . as if I was suffering dreadfully from the toothache, and then no one would discover

Slaves devised a variety of techniques for escaping bondage. Henry "Box" Brown, shown here, and Lear Green literally crated and "shipped" themselves to freedom. *Library of Congress*

the want of beard." When William asked, "But how will you sign your name, they will surely detect you then," Ellen replied that she would bind her right hand, place it in a sling, and pretend that she could not write. After such persuasive responses, William conceded that the plan could work and the couple agreed to take the perilous journey to freedom. They arrived in Philadelphia on Christmas morning.

Frederick Douglass and Harriet Tubman became the most well known of the antebellum runaways. At age nineteen, Douglass escaped from a Baltimore shipyard and made his way to New Bedford, Massachusetts. For her part, Harriet Tubman, a field hand, escaped from the Eastern Shore of Maryland. As a child, she recalled that she "prayed to God to make me strong and able to fight." In 1849, a few years after her marriage to John Tubman, a free man, Harriet and her brothers faced the prospect of sale away from their home plantation. After she failed to convince her husband and brothers to join her, Harriet escaped without them. By walking at night and hiding out by day, she finally

Harriet Tubman, the famous conductor on the underground railroad, as a relatively young woman. *Library of Congress*

reached Pennsylvania. When she touched free soil, she later recalled, "I looked at my hands to see if I was the same person. Dere was such a glory ober everything, de sun came like gold throu de trees, and ober de fields, and I felt like I was in heaven." After a period of euphoria, loneliness set in. As Tubman recalled, the most painful part of freedom was the absence of her family:

> I had crossed de line of which I had long been dreaming. I was free; but dere was no one to welcome me to de land of freedom, I was a stranger in a strange land, and my home after all was down [in] de old cabin quarter, wid de ole folks and my brudders and sisters.

At this point, Harriet made a "solemn resolution": "I was free, and dey should be free also; I would make a home for dem in de North, and de Lord helping me, I would bring dem all here." True to her resolution, Harriet made nearly twenty trips into slave territory and led out six of her brothers, their wives, fiancés, nieces, nephews, and finally her elderly parents. For her daring exploits on behalf of her people, Tubman became known by many as "the Moses," or "deliverer," of her people.

Although most fugitives left their owners individually or in small groups, some escaped in large contingents. In July 1845, some seventy-five enslaved blacks from three Maryland counties organized a mass movement toward the Pennsylvania line. Near Rockville, Maryland, whites caught and surrounded the blacks, killing several and recapturing about thirty-one. Three years later, authorities fought another party of seventy-five fugitives near the Ohio River in Kentucky. Although the fugitives fought back, nearly all were killed or recaptured. In Mississippi, a similar effort failed in 1850 when heavily armed whites forced the group to surrender. Large group escapes posed extraordinary risks, but African Americans continued to establish Maroon communities in the swamps and mountains of the antebellum South. In 1827, a group of whites reported a substantial community of runaways at the fork of the Alabama and Tombigbee Rivers. The group had two cabins and were about to build a fort when the settlement was "attacked" and, after a "severe" show of resistance, "conquered." As late as 1856, when whites attacked a Maroon camp in North Carolina, blacks fought back, killing one of their attackers and urging the whites "to come on, they were ready for them again." The most prominent case of black resistance occurred in the Seminole wars of 1835 to 1842, when enslaved people played an important role in the military conflict between U.S. authorities, planters, and the Seminole nation. A black named Abraham served as an effective interpreter and comrade to the Indians. One General Jesup overstated the case: "The negroes rule the Indians and it is important that they should feel themselves secure: if they should become alarmed and hold out, the war will be renewed." The war ended only when federal authorities guaranteed blacks land in the southwest.

Revolts and Rebellions

Individual and collective armed struggle constituted recurring themes in the antebellum blacks' quest for freedom. Southern planters exhibited growing fear of being "murdered" by enslaved people. In 1853, a Texan reported that such murders were "painfully frequent." At about the same time, a Louisiana newspaper reported that "the growing frequency of many murders have taken place, by negroes upon their owners." A Florida editor also recorded "another instance of the destruction of the life of a white man by a slave." In 1852, after the governor commuted the death sentence of an enslaved man convicted and sentenced to hang for the murder of an overseer, the *Richmond Dispatch* editorialized: "We think that full protection should be guaranteed to the overseers in the tobacco factories, by law, against the attacks of turbulent hands." One rice miller feared an enslaved carpenter, Jack Savage. He described Savage as "always giving trouble . . . [and] was the only Negro ever in our possession who I considered capable of murdering me, or burning my dwelling at night."

The most significant antebellum revolts and plots to revolt broke out in Charleston, South Carolina, in 1822 and in Southampton, Virginia, in 1831. In 1822, Denmark Vesey, a free black carpenter, preached against the slaveholders. Inspired by the example of Haiti as a black republic, Vesey and his compatriots made plans to capture the city of Charleston, confiscate its shipping, burn the city to the ground, and set sail for the West Indies. Before Vesey and other black bondsmen could make good on their plans, another slave revealed their intent to authorities. In the wake of the plot's discovery, some thirty-five blacks were executed and another thirty-seven sold out of the state.

In 1831, Nat Turner's rebellion broke out in rural Virginia. An enslaved preacher, carpenter, and trusted carriage driver on the plantation of Joseph Travis, Nat had also learned to read and write. During his childhood, he had received encouragement from his parents and the slave community, who considered him a gifted child who would someday become a prophet (see box). Turner later recalled his growing sense of mission:

> In my childhood a circumstance occurred which made an indelible impression on my mind. . . . Being at play with other children, when three or four years old, I was telling them something, which my mother overhearing, said it happened before I was born. . . . Others being called on, were greatly astonished, knowing that these things had happened, and caused them to say, in my hearing I surely would be a prophet, as the Lord had shown me things that had happened before my birth. And my father and mother strengthened me in this my first impression, saying in [my] presence, I was intended for some great purpose.

At one point, Turner escaped from his master's plantation and remained at large for nearly two months before he voluntarily returned. Before leading the slave revolt, he asked the Lord for a sign. When an eclipse of the sun took place, Turner took that as his cue to rebel.

On 21 August 1831, Turner and a small group of enslaved blacks broke into his master's house and killed the entire family. The group then marched toward the county seat. Their numbers increased to nearly seventy as they marched. Within twenty-four hours, Nat Turner's rebellion had claimed the lives of fifty-nine whites: ten men, fourteen women, and thirty-five children. In their effort to put down the revolt and in the brutal reprisals afterward, whites killed some one hundred black men, but Turner eluded authorities for nearly two months before he was captured and put to death. Turner's rebellion reflected the ways that the abuses of slavery came together in the Upper South and gained expression in a violent revolt under the leadership of a Christian, literate, and skilled bondsman.

Following Vesey's conspiracy and Nat Turner's revolt, southern states increased their surveillance and repression of African American activities. The number of whites serving in slave patrols and state and local militia increased. Because such revolts coincided with the expansion of the abolitionist movement, as we will see later, southern states made it a felony "to say or do anything" that might foment rebellion. Such laws prohibited "the publication, circulation, and promulgation of abolition doctrines," revealing the deep-seated fears that whites had of slave rebellion. When asked if white masters feared insurrections, one ex-slave replied: "They live in constant fear upon [this] subject. . . . The least unusual noise at night alarms them greatly. They cry out 'What is that?' Are the boys all in?"

Despite the resistance activities of Turner, Vesey, fugitives, and countless black men and women, stereotypes of the "docile slave" endured. Southern novelists, journalists, ministers, planters, and later racist historians diligently crafted the antebellum male as "Sambo" and the black woman as "Jezebel" or "Mammy." In planters' eyes, black men were faithful, humorous, musical, and docile, whereas women were deeply religious, asexual, and loyal beings who placed the affective and

SOURCES FROM THE PAST

1831

Nat Turner Discusses His Motives for Leading a Revolt of Enslaved Blacks

Sir,—you have asked me to give a history of the motives which induced me to undertake the late insurrection, as you call it—To do so I must go back to the days of my infancy, and even before I was born. I was thirty-one years of age the second of October last, and born the property of Benjamin Turner, of this county. In my childhood a circumstance occurred which made an indelible impression on my mind, and laid the groundwork of that enthusiasm which has terminated so fatally to many, both white and black, and for which I am about to atone at the gallows. It is here necessary to relate this circumstance. Trifling as it may seem, it was the commencement of that belief which has grown with time, and even now, sir, in this dungeon, helpless and forsaken as I am, I cannot divest myself of. Being at play with other children, when three or four years old, I was telling them something, which my mother, overhearing, said it had happened before I was born. I stuck to my story, however, and related some things which went, in her opinion, to confirm it. Others being called on, were greatly astonished, knowing that these things had happened, and caused them to say, in my hearing, I surely would be a prophet, as the Lord had shown me things that had happened before my birth. And my mother and grandmother strengthened me in this my first impression, saying, in my presence, I was intended for some great purpose, which they had always thought from certain marks on my head and breast. . . .

I was not addicted to stealing in my youth, nor have ever been; yet such was the confidence of the Negroes in the neighborhood, even at this early period of my life, in my superior judgment, that they would often carry me with them when they were going on any roguery, to plan for them. Growing up among them with this confidence in my superior judgment, and when this, in their opinions, was perfected by Divine inspiration, from the circumstances already alluded to in my infancy, and which belief was ever afterwards zealously inculcated by the austerity of my life and manners, which became the subject of remark by white and black; having soon discovered to be great, I must appear so, and therefore studiously avoided mixing in society, and wrapped myself in mystery, devoting my time to fasting and prayer.

By this time, having arrived to man's estate, and hearing the Scriptures commented on at meetings, I was struck with that particular passage which says, "Seek ye the kingdom of heaven, and all things shall be added unto you." I reflected much on this passage, and prayed daily for light on this subject. As I was praying one day at my plough, the Spirit spoke to me, saying, "Seek ye the kingdom of heaven, and all things shall be added unto you.". . .

. . . Knowing the influence I had obtained over the minds of my fellow-servants—(not by the means of conjuring and such-like tricks—for to them I always spoke of such things with contempt), but by the communion of the Spirit, whose revelations I often communicated to them, and they believed and said my wisdom came from God,—I now began to prepare them for my purpose, by telling them something was about to happen that would terminate in fulfilling the great promise that had been made to me. . . .

Source: From "The Confessions of Nat Turner," as recorded by Thomas R. Gray, in Deirdre Mullane, ed., *Crossing the Danger Water: Three Hundred Years of African-American Writing* (New York: Doubleday, 1993), pp. 88–96.

This sketch from an anti-abolitionist publication offers graphic details of Turner's rebellion: (1) Turner attacking a white mother and her children; (2) Turner's master, Mr. Travis, being attacked; (3) Captain John T. Barrow defending himself while his wife escapes; and (4) the militia pursuing Turner and the other rebels. *Library of Congress*

material needs of the plantation household above their own. Such stereotypes ignored the complex personalities, strategies, and ideas that shaped black responses to bondage. Indeed, as the foregoing evidence and recent scholarship suggest, planters invented "Sambo" and "Mammy" to counteract slave resistance and wipe out models of male and female strength and sexuality.

Planters expressed an ongoing fear of "rebellious slaves" who secured firearms, raided plantations, burned buildings, and killed white men, women, and children. Thus, as historian John Bassingame notes, they had a deep-seated need to believe in Sambo to reassure themselves that their fragile system of bondage was secure. Similarly, in the case of black women, some planters worried about the implications of the expanding mulatto population, which reflected the frequency of interracial sex and the often turbulent relationships between white men and women in their own households. Accordingly, planters invented Mammy to counteract their own self-serving stereotype of the black woman as Jezebel—that is, a woman driven by her "libido" or sex, who presumably threatened the "purity" of the white race. At the same time, planters' notions of Mammy and Jezebel enabled them to continue to deny black women the "benefit" of femininity as defined for white women under the rubric of the "cult of true womanhood" or the "Victorian lady." Moreover, contemporary white images of black women provided little room, positive or negative, for resisters like Harriet Tubman and countless others (see box).

Although late antebellum black culture nourished a powerful resistance movement, enslaved blacks nonetheless experienced significant social cleavages. As the number of African-born blacks decreased, other divisions became more prominent within the enslaved community. Occupational, cultural, color, and gender differences undercut black unity. Economic and status tensions were most acute between drivers and general field hands. Because drivers carried the whip and used it to increase production, ex-slaves regularly recalled the driver as "mean as the devil." Henry Cheatam of Mississippi recalled how the driver brutally beat his mama and his pregnant aunt. Consequently, Cheatam vowed "to kill" the driver "if it was de last thing I ever done." Although black culture blurred the line, enslaved people experienced growing tensions between spiritual and secular cultural orientations. In his narrative, the ex-slave Henry Bibb, who lived and labored in Kentucky and Louisiana, complained that many blacks violated the Sabbath. As he put it, "Those who make no profession of religion resort to the woods in large numbers on that day to gamble, fight, get drunk, and break the Sabbath."

Gender conflicts were even more problematic than cultural ones. Although enslaved men and women took risks to protect each other and their children, they also had disagreements and fights. In 1838, for example, on one plantation, a man beat his wife, locked her up, and prevented her from attending New Year's festivities. When her husband, Jim, hit her in the head with an iron poker, one Louisiana woman refused to tell her master how she received "the knot on her forehead." Other enslaved women, however, resisted such abuse. An ex-slave, Anna Baker, later learned why her mother had run away and left her children: "It was 'count o' de slave drivers. Dey kep' a-tryin' to mess 'roun wid her an' she wouln' have nothin' to do wid 'em." In 1859, a Mississippi slave was convicted and sentenced to death for raping a ten-year-old female slave, but the judge reversed the decision and released the man, claiming that "there is no act which embraces either the attempted or actual commission of a rape by a slave on a female slave." A year later, the Mississippi legislature made it a crime punishable by death or whipping for a black man to rape or attempt to rape a black female under age twelve. This law underscored the precarious position of black women and girls within the African American community as well as within southern society. Finally, color consciousness also increased among antebellum blacks. As we will see in Chapter 9, such consciousness favored mulattoes over blacks for the most skilled and supervisory jobs, which offered greater opportunities for self-purchase and freedom.

~

DESPITE THE DESTRUCTIVE IMPACT OF SLAVERY on their lives, antebellum blacks took advantage of improved physical conditions to strengthen their families, extend

SOURCES FROM THE PAST

1849

Harriet Tubman Walks to Freedom

What was to become of the slaves on this plantation now that the master was dead? Were they all to be scattered and sent to different parts of the country? Harriet had many brothers and sisters, all of whom with the exception of the two, who had gone South with the chain-gang, were living on this plantation, or were hired out to planters not far away. The word passed through the cabins that another owner was coming in, and that none of the slaves were to be sold out of the State. This assurance satisfied the others, but it did not satisfy Harriet. Already the inward monitor was whispering to her, "Arise, flee for your life!" and in the visions of the night she saw the horsemen coming, and heard the shrieks of women and children, as they were being torn from each other, and hurried off no one knew whither. . . .

And so without money, and without friends, she started on through unknown regions; walking by night, hiding by day, but always conscious of an invisible pillar of cloud by day, and of fire by night, under the guidance of which she journeyed or rested. Without knowing whom to trust, or how near the pursuers might be, she carefully felt her way, and by her native cunning, or by God given wisdom, she managed to apply to the right people for food, and sometimes for shelter; though often her bed was only the cold ground, and her watchers the stars of night.

After many long and weary days of travel, she found that she had passed the magic line, which then divided the land of bondage from the land of freedom. But where were the lovely white ladies whom in her visions she had seen, who, with arms outstretched, welcomed her to their hearts and homes. All these visions proved deceitful: she was more alone than ever; but she had crossed the line; no one could take her now, and she would never call any man "Master" more.

Source: Sarah H. Bradford, *Harriet Tubman: The Moses of Her People* (1869, 1886; reprint, New York: Citadel Press, 1991).

the boundaries of community, and resist the most debilitating influences of human bondage. From the foundation of evolving African American culture and social practices, antebellum black men and women mounted a broad range of individual and collective protests against the institution of slavery. African American family, culture, and forms of resistance not only demonstrated the creative blending of African and Euro-American ideas but also challenged and exploded certain erroneous stereotypes about the character of black people. Despite its severity, the institution of human bondage destroyed neither the slaves' "creative instincts" nor their "thirst" for freedom and independence. Indeed, despite their own internal social conflicts and cleavages, enslaved and free blacks would play key roles in the growth of the abolitionist movement, the coming of the Civil War, and emancipation.

~

CHAPTER 9

Free Blacks, Abolitionists, and the Antislavery Movement

By 1860, the African American population included a half million free blacks. Although free people of color made up only a tiny fraction of the total, they had a disproportionately large impact on the development of antebellum African American culture, communities, and politics. According to some scholars, the socioeconomic and political experiences of free blacks foreshadowed the future of all blacks in the wake of the Civil War and emancipation. In both the North and South, antebellum free people of color could legally marry, own property, and establish their own institutions. As America moved toward the enfranchisement of working-class and poor white men, however, free black men and women faced economic exploitation, disfranchisement, segregation, and the intensification of the colonization movement, which aimed to transport free people of color to Africa and secure the United States as a republic of slaves and free whites. Although free blacks lived and labored on the precarious borders of antebellum slave society, they were by no means quiescent. They deepened their own institution-building and political activities; strengthened their ties with their enslaved kinfolk and sympathetic white allies; and pushed for the abolition of slavery and the acquisition of full citizenship.

URBANIZATION, WORK, AND THE ECONOMY

As the cotton kingdom expanded and the enslaved population increased, free blacks found it exceedingly difficult to hold their own. Northern and southern journalists and political leaders repeatedly described free blacks as "lazy," "ignorant," and more "depraved" than slaves. Their very presence challenged slavery and notions of white superiority in the North and South. Consequently, both white elites and working-class whites devised a variety of mechanisms for limiting the growth of the free black population. By the 1850s, most southern states had either prohibited manumission altogether or required blacks to leave the state on receiving their freedom. Only the states of Delaware, Missouri, and Arkansas permitted newly emancipated blacks to remain in the state. For their part, the new midwestern states also limited the settlement of free blacks within their borders. An Ohio legislator exclaimed that "the United States were designed by the God in Heaven to be governed and inhabited by the Anglo-Saxon race alone[!]" Accordingly, the states of the old northwest—Ohio, Indiana, Illinois, Michigan, and Iowa—all established laws requiring free blacks to post bonds (as much as $500) before they could legally take up residence. In 1851, such antiblack sentiment culminated in the adoption of a new Indiana state constitution that barred blacks from settlement altogether. According to Article 13, "No negro or mulatto shall come into, or settle in the State, after the adoption of this constitution."

Growth of the Free Black Population

Hostile public opinion and legal constraints undercut the growth of the free black population. Until the 1820s, the number of free blacks had increased at a faster rate than that of enslaved blacks or whites. By 1840, however, the free black population was growing more slowly than both other groups. During the two decades before the Civil War, it increased by 12 percent, as compared with an increase of over 23 percent for bondspeople and whites. The impact of legal and extralegal restrictions on the growth of the free black population was most prominent in the Deep South states of Mississippi, Georgia, South Carolina, and Louisiana. Although these states accounted for well over 50 percent of the total black population, only about 13 percent of the total free black population lived there.

Despite its declining growth rate, the free black population nonetheless continued to increase. Between 1820 and 1860, the number of free blacks rose from about 233,500 to more than 488,000 (see table). Although these numbers were almost equally divided between North and South, most free blacks lived in the southern slave states. The natural increase of the free black population was added to by blacks who continued to gain freedom through manumission, running away, and self-purchase. In 1845, a Baltimore official exclaimed: "With all the restrictions which legislation has imposed on manumission, they still go on. . . . It may be taken for certain that they will go on; that nothing can stop them." Similarly, a Louisiana slaveholder complained that the manumission of enslaved blacks had "become notorious." According to this commentator, "The policy jury invariably yields to the wishes of the master, and enables him . . . to grant the emancipation." Public officials and opinion leaders also regularly complained that fugitives swelled the numbers of free blacks. In Richmond, one journalist noted the many "runaways in this neighborhood who have escaped detection by misrepresenting their condition." In 1834, the mayor of New Orleans said that slaves "crowd in the city, hide, and make our city a den" of free blacks and "mulattoes."

Self-purchase was an exceedingly difficult route to freedom. By the late antebellum years, the high price of slaves made it almost prohibitive for blacks to purchase themselves or for free blacks to purchase loved ones. When a Tennessee free black sought to purchase his wife, the owner responded: "No sum of money would induce me to part with Sarah. . . . The price is so enormously high in the country

U.S. Free Black Population, 1820–1860					
	1820	1830	1840	1850	1860
United States	233,504	319,599	386,303	434,449	488,070
North	99,281	137,529	170,728	196,262	226,152
South	134,223	182,070	215,575	238,187	261,918
Upper South	114,070	151,877	174,357	203,702	224,963
Lower South	20,153	30,193	41,218	34,485	36,955

Percent Increase, 1810–1860					
	1810–1820	1820–1830	1830–1840	1840–1850	1850–1860
United States	25.2%	36.9%	20.9%	12.5%	12.3%
North	27.0	38.5	24.1	15.0	15.2
South	24.0	35.6	18.4	10.5	10.0
Upper South	21.2	33.1	14.8	16.8	10.4
Lower South	42.1	49.8	36.5	−16.3	7.2

Proportion of Blacks Who Were Free, 1820–1860			
	1820	1840	1860
United States	13.2%	13.4%	11.0%
North	83.9	99.3	100.0
South	8.1	8.0	6.2
Upper South	10.6	12.5	12.8
Lower South	3.5	3.1	1.5

Source: Ira Berlin, *Slaves Without Masters: The Free Negro in the Antebellum South* (New York: Oxford University Press, 1974), pp. 136–137. Reprinted by permission of the author.

that I could not replace such a one as her." Still, the process of self-purchase added to the roster of free blacks. In New Orleans, for example, free blacks filed over 30 percent of the formal petitions for manumission between 1827 and 1852. In 1834, an estimated 1,129 of Cincinnati's nearly 1,500 blacks had known slavery. Well over a third had purchased their own freedom, at a cost of $215,522, or about $450 per person. In Kentucky, the experiences of the ex-slave Free Frank reveal the long arduous process of self-purchase in the lives of one family. The process started in 1817, with Frank's purchase of his wife at $800, and continued through 1857, with the purchase of Frank's sons, daughters, and finally grandchildren (see table).

Migration to Urban Centers

Difficult conditions in the rural South stimulated the increasing urban migration of free blacks. In the plantation and rural-industrial areas of the South, the lives of free blacks were tightly interwoven with the experiences of their enslaved counter-

Free Frank Family Members Purchased, 1817–1857			
Date of Purchase	Name	Relationship to Free Frank	Price
1817	Lucy	Wife	$800[1]
1819	Free Frank		800[2]
1829	Frank Jr.	Son	2,500 (est.)[3]
1835	Solomon	Son	500[4]
1843	Sally [Sarah]	Daughter	950[5]
By 1850	Juda [Judah, Julia]	Daughter	4,380 (est.)[6]
	Commodore	Grandson	
	Permilia	Granddaughter	
	Louisa	Daughter-in-law	
By 1856	Calvin	Grandson	3,030[7]
	Calvin	Grandson	
	Robert	Grandson	
	Lucy Ann	Granddaughter	
By 1857	Charlotte	Granddaughter	993.61[8]
	Child of Charlotte	Great Grandchild	
	Child of Charlotte	Great Grandchild	

1. Pulaski County Real Estate Conveyances, Book 3: 228; Certificate of Good Character for Free Frank, Sept. 7, 1830, Free Frank [McWorter] Papers; *Atlas Map of Pike County,* p. 54.
2. Pulaski County Real Estate Conveyances, Book 4: 138; Certificate of Good Character for Free Frank, Sept. 7, 1830, Free Frank [McWorter] Papers; *Atlas Map of Pike County,* p. 54.
3. Pulaski County Real Estate Conveyances, Book 7:55–56.
4. Ibid., Book 8: 199–200.
5. Ibid., Book 12: 379–80.
6. *Pike County Atlas,* p. 54; John E. McWorter to Rev. P. B. West, Aug. 31, 1919, mimeographed; Arthur McWorter to Thelma McWorter Kirkpatrick [Wheaton], Jan. 1937; and Thelma Elise McWorter, "Free Frank of Pike County, Ill." (Chicago, *ca.* 1937, mimeographed), all in Free Frank [McWorter] Papers.
7. Pike County Circuit Court Records, *Solomon, Exr. of Frank McWorter* v. *Lucy McWorter widow et al.* (1857), case no. 8850.
8. Pike County Inventories, Appraisements, Bills, etc., 1866–1869, pp. 28–29, Pike County Courthouse, Pittsfield, Ill.
Source: Juliet E. K. Walker, *Free Frank: A Black Pioneer on the Antebellum Frontier* (Lexington, Ky.: University of Kentucky Press, 1983) p. 162. Copyright © 1983 University of Kentucky Press. Reprinted by permission of the publisher.

parts. They worked alongside enslaved blacks as boatmen, fishermen, farm hands, and wage laborers in a variety of rural industries, including turpentine, lumber, coal, and ironworks. Although some rural free blacks practiced skilled crafts, most found jobs as general laborers. As in the postwar years, some worked the land in exchange for a share of the crop. Free black tenants often found themselves indebted to the landlords at the end of each season and day of reckoning. As with the crop-lien system of the early emancipation years, many of these rural free blacks pledged ungrown crops to secure credit for living expenses, supplies, and equipment for raising the next crop. As a result of these oppressive conditions, rural free blacks moved into cities in rising numbers. Moreover, rural employers often housed free blacks with slaves that they owned, hired, or leased. Thus, the health and living conditions of many rural free blacks were indistinguishable from those of bondsmen and -women. According to available statistics, an estimated 25 percent of rural free blacks resided in housing provided by employers, whereas others took up residence on marginal land, in housing of poor construction and few amenities. According to one contemporary source, most of their houses were "small" and "very tattered." In 1836, one observer reported that "the emancipated negroes generally leave the country, and congregate in the cities and larger towns." By the eve of the Civil War, over 33 percent of southern free blacks and virtually all of their northern kinsmen lived in cities, compared with only 5 percent of slaves, and little more than 15 percent of southern and northern whites. In other words, antebellum free blacks became the most highly urbanized component of the U.S. population. The vast majority of northern free blacks lived in New York, Philadelphia, Boston, Chicago, Cincinnati, Providence, New Haven, and a few smaller urban centers, while southern free blacks concentrated mainly in Baltimore, Richmond, New Orleans, Charleston, Memphis, Mobile, Natchez, and Vicksburg. Free blacks were not only disproportionately urban, as in earlier years, but predominantly light-skinned and female as well. By 1860, women outnumbered men by 100 to 92. Conversely, slaves had a nearly even ratio of men to women.

Manumission and self-purchase favored light-skinned black men and women, frequently the relatives of white landowners. In 1860, the U.S. Census reported an estimated 36 percent of free blacks as "mulattoes," compared to only about 10 percent for slaves. Even when slaveowners refused to emancipate their offspring by black women, they often provided such children with special training, privileges, and contacts that enabled them to purchase their own freedom. Such practices were especially prominent in the Deep South, where persons of mixed racial backgrounds made up about 75 percent of the total free black population. Although some Upper South owners also liberated members of their kin group, declining economic opportunities to use bound labor in the tobacco region of the Upper South opened the door of emancipation to both enslaved dark and light-skinned blacks. Thus, the complexion of the free black population was much darker in the Upper South and northern states than it was in the Deep South.

Free blacks encountered stiff barriers to gaining a foothold in the urban economy. As long as employers could lease, purchase, or hire slaves, they often preferred bondsmen and -women over free blacks. In the Upper South city of Baltimore, for example, the free black population dwarfed its slave counterpart, but employers vigorously advertised for slave labor. In 1840, one employer advertised for servants to wash, iron, and cook but mandated that "they be SLAVES/FOR LIFE." Another employer sought a black porter for his grocery store, emphasizing that a slave was "preferred." Numerous other Baltimore employers appealed for black workers under the rubric "slaves preferred." Compared with free blacks, enslaved people had fewer rights, which permitted employers to exercise greater control over the work force. Indeed, some owners hired out their slaves as a disciplinary measure and urged lessees to apply "the whip" generously. Since, legally, free blacks could walk away from such arrangements, many employers saw them as less desirable workers than slaves.

Free African Americans not only faced competition from their enslaved brothers and sisters but experienced resistance from poor landless white wage earners as well. White workers constantly complained that free people of color depressed their standard of living by working for less. In Petersburg, Virginia, for example, white workers stated: "We consider the Negro mechanic a curse on our working interest in as much as they nearly monopolize work at reduced prices." White artisans and working men detested working alongside blacks. As a white St. Louis dock worker put it, "I despise working by the side of a negro. . . . They are the worst class on the levee . . . a slur on our employment." In the same city, a white artisan exclaimed that "craftsmen and other laborers have an undoubted right to strike for higher wages . . . that is when they are white men. Color of course gives a different complexion to these rights."

In the North, free blacks faced a similar, and in some ways more hostile, environment. As German and Irish immigrants poured into northern cities during the 1830s and 1840s, they took a growing share of artisan and general labor jobs. Before departing his home in Virginia, one free black artisan "expected to find the people of color in free New York far better off than those in Virginia." He was disappointed to find, however, that "many of the skilled tradesmen" that he knew from the South had become "cooks and waiters" in New York. In 1827, a black newcomer to Cincinnati also described his disappointment on arriving in the city:

> I thought upon coming to a free state like Ohio I would find every door thrown open to receive me, but from the treatment I received by the people generally, I found it little better than in Virginia. . . . I found every door was closed against the colored man in a free state, excepting the jails and penitentiaries.

Similarly, when Frederick Douglass, a skilled ship caulker, arrived in New Bedford, Massachusetts, he reported that "every white man would leave the ship . . . if I struck a blow at my trade." Although some northern white abolitionists encouraged the employment of black artisans, blacks repeatedly complained that "we have among us carpenters, plasterers, masons, etc., whose skills as workers is confessed and yet they find no employment not even among [white] friends." European immigrants also barred blacks from the relatively well-paying carting trade. Carters transported a variety of goods, including firewood and manure, which required a "dirt carter's" license.

As competition between free blacks, slaves, and white workers intensified, however, whites defined certain jobs in racial terms and opened the door to the employment of free blacks. In conversations with northern visitors, southern whites repeatedly confirmed that "no white man would ever do certain kinds of work . . . and if you should ask a white man . . . he would get mad and tell you he wasn't a nigger." The South Carolina slaveowner Edward Laurens admitted that whites "degraded" certain occupations by employing blacks and discouraged young white men "whose spirit and highmindedness we endeavor almost daily to incite" from entering "the arena with them." In Cincinnati, a local editor believed that the "evils of slavery . . . infected" the city and relegated blacks to "certain kinds" of labor "despised as being the work of slaves."

Employment Opportunities for Free Blacks

General labor, household, and domestic service occupations emerged at the core of "Negro work." Such jobs required heavy lifting, loading, carrying, and cleaning. In fifteen antebellum northern and southern cities, over 60 percent of free black men worked in jobs defined as unskilled, semiskilled, and personal service. Such jobs tended to become more prominent as one moved from the Deep South to the Upper North. By the 1850s, for example, only 17 percent of free black men in New Orleans and 21 percent in Charleston occupied such jobs, compared with 58 percent in Louisville, 69 percent in St. Louis, 67 percent in Cincinnati, 77 percent in Pittsburgh, 73 percent in New York, and 77 percent in Boston.

Although employers and white workers stereotyped certain jobs as black labor, such jobs varied by region, city, and skill. In New Orleans and Charleston, blacks dominated the barbering, carpentry, masonry, blacksmithing, tailoring, and shoe-making trades. Norfolk, Richmond, and Louisville blacks also gained a substantial footing in the skilled crafts as well as the better-paying laboring jobs like carters or draymen. White workers controlled the drayman job in cities like Baltimore and St. Louis, but blacks dominated the same job in Norfolk, Virginia, and took a large proportion of such jobs in other southern cities. Although blacks in northern cities gained a foothold in the barber trade, few worked in the skilled trades or the more lucrative laboring jobs like draymen. During the late 1830s, for example, the New York *Colored American* urged the mayor to stop discrimination against black carters. According to the editor, city inspectors routinely denied blacks licenses to enter the trade. For their part, white carters reinforced such discrimination by physically assaulting the few black draymen who worked in the city with or without licenses.

In each city and region, free black women gained employment primarily as household or domestic service workers. Whereas free black men often entered freedom as skilled artisans, few black women started their lives with prospects for making a living beyond jobs as "seamstresses," "washers," and "cooks." Young black males, particularly in the South, gained apprenticeships with a variety of skilled craftsmen. A study of Petersburg, Virginia, shows that the city clerk regularly recorded black "boys" as apprentices to carpenters, coopers, bricklayers, painters, blacksmiths, bakers, and barbers, but the options for "girls" were so few that the clerk seldom recorded them. In the urban North and South, available evidence suggests that the majority of free black women worked as domestics in the homes of white employers.

The lowly occupational position of free black women had substantial consequences for the livelihood of free black families. Although the majority of free blacks, like slaves, lived in double-headed households, the number of female-headed families increased over time. In Boston, for example, the percentage of free black families headed by couples decreased from about 66 percent to 60 percent during the 1850s alone. Although only 11 percent of Cincinnati's black households were headed by women in 1830, the figure had doubled by 1860. In the urban South, Petersburg and Charleston, for example, the percentage of families headed by women sometimes exceeded those headed by men. Thus, the poor economic position of free women of color symbolized severe suffering for growing numbers of urban blacks. Yet we must not conclude that such free black families were necessarily "unstable." As one study of Charleston, South Carolina, notes, for example: "The census manuscripts provide data which suggest that the female-headed families were stable."

Restrictions on the entrepreneurial activities of African Americans reinforced their lowly position in the antebellum economy. Southern states undercut the establishment of black taverns by prohibiting free blacks from manufacturing, transporting, and selling alcoholic beverages. In 1833, when the Kentucky legislature set a new minimum of $40 for acquisition of liquor licenses to be issued by the city of Louisville, it excluded free people of color from the privilege. The Louisville city council reinforced the state statute by prohibiting free blacks from opening grocery stores, important outlets for the sale of alcoholic beverages during the period. St. Louis, Charleston, and Washington, D.C., enacted similar restrictions on free black participation in the sale of alcoholic drinks. In 1836, Washington enacted the most comprehensive restrictions. It prohibited free blacks as well as agents of free blacks from keeping "any tavern, ordinary, shop, porter cellar, refectory, or eating house of any kind, for profit or gain." Based on the notion that free blacks represented a channel for the sale of stolen agricultural produce, several southern cities outlawed the licensing of free blacks as "a Hawker, huckster, or peddler." In the North, white competitors accomplished a similar exclusion of blacks by informal means.

Free people of color were not entirely victimized by their position in the economy. They took jobs at the bottom of the labor force and challenged white rhetoric about their "improvidence," "depravity," and "ignorance." As discussed earlier, African Americans used such work not only as a route to their own freedom but also as a vehicle for securing the freedom of loved ones. By the late antebellum years, they also organized their own labor unions and fought to secure their jobs. On the Baltimore docks, for example, free blacks gained a monopoly on work and resisted white efforts to drive them out. Indeed, after white workers moved to exclude blacks, African Americans rallied and excluded the whites, turning the docks into a predominantly black occupational enclave. Similarly, in 1850, New York City blacks formed the American League of Colored Laborers. The ALCL not only aimed to organize skilled black workers but also promoted the training of black youth in mechanical and agricultural pursuits and advocated the establishment of independent black businesses. According to the Reverend Charles B. Ray, a black New York minister and newspaper editor, these black men and women had "the proper materials in their character to become industrious, economical, and reputable citizens."

Black Entrepreneurs and Property Holders

Some free blacks sidestepped constraints and became entrepreneurs and substantial property holders. They parlayed their general labor, household, and craft skills into businesses catering to black and white clients. In Philadelphia, the sailmaker James Forten accumulated more than $100,000 around the docks of the city. The most successful of these black entrepreneurs, however, catered to an elite white clientele, as grocers and proprietors of hotels, restaurants, and especially barbershops. In Boston, Peter Howard became one of the city's most well-known proprietors of a black barbering and hairdressing business. In San Francisco, William Alexander

Elizabeth Hobbs Keckley, ex-Virginia slave and dressmaker who later designed dresses for First Lady Mary Todd Lincoln.
Moorland-Spingarn Research Center, Howard University

Leidesdorff became a prominent merchant and land speculator who bequeathed property worth $1.5 million to his heirs. In 1850, Cincinnati listed the value of black property holdings at $1,317,000. Out of eighty-eight African Americans who held property of $1,000 or more, close to half worked as laborers, stewards, butlers, and cooks. Three of Cincinnati's most renowned residents and property holders were Richard Phillips, a huckster ($13,000); Joseph J. Fowler, another huckster ($18,000); and John G. Gaines, a stevedore ($3,000).

Antebellum free black entrepreneurs also included several women. In New York City, Free Love Slocum, Paul Cuffee's sister, operated an import-export business; in Philadelphia, Grace Bustil Douglass operated a millinery shop; in Washington, D.C., Elizabeth Keckley, a Virginia-born ex-slave, became perhaps the most renowned antebellum black female entrepreneur when she established a successful dressmaking business. Her fame later soared when she designed and made dresses for First Lady Mary Todd Lincoln. Moreover, black property ownership was not exclusively a male affair. In 1850, women made up 31.1, 16.9, and 10.5 percent of black property holders in Louisville, Cincinnati, and Pittsburgh, respectively.

African American property holders offered inspiring stories of individual and group success and entrepreneurship. The barber trade provided black men their most promising opportunities to earn a living, purchase real estate, and increase their standing in antebellum cities. The black editor William Dabney later celebrated the mid-nineteenth-century black barber and barbershop:

> Barber shops were the greatest places for gossip and the white customers were generally well informed as to the doings of Negro society. The Negro barber, as a workman, was an artist. The razor in his hands became an instrument that made sweet melody as it charmed away the grass that grew on facial lawns.

In both northern and southern cities, blacks operated leading downtown barbershops that catered to the city's elite. In Cincinnati, the barber William W. Watson received his freedom in 1832. Within less than a decade he owned his own barbershop and bathhouse that catered to a predominantly white clientele in the Central Business District. He also owned two brick houses and lots within the city and another 560 acres of farmland in nearby Mercer County, bringing his property holdings to an estimated $5,500. In her rationale for *Uncle Tom's Cabin,* Harriet Beecher Stowe, who lived in Cincinnati during her research for the book, named Watson and five other former bondsmen as examples of the race's capacity for "conquering for themselves comparative wealth and social position by their strength of character, energy, patience and honesty."

Black entrepreneurial activities and property ownership were not unmixed blessings. In the Deep South, black wealth included enslaved people as well as land and other material possessions. In Charleston, by 1850, some 371 free people of color paid taxes on real estate valued at more than $1 million. At the same time, New Orleans free blacks owned property estimated at $15 million. This property included bondsmen, -women, and children. In Louisiana, Cyprian Ricard owned 91 slaves, Charles Rogues owned 47, and Marie Metoyer owned 50. As early as 1830, in Louisiana, ten free blacks owned 50 or more enslaved people—that is, enough to qualify as large planters. Although the number of such holdings dropped to six by 1860, free black slaveholders owned 492 people, averaging about 82 persons per unit. Even more so than the free black population itself, all of these large planters were mulattoes. The wealthiest, Auguste Dubuclet of Iberville Parish, owned real property valued at $200,000, including a total of 1,200 acres of land and 94 slaves. In the Sumter District of South Carolina, William Ellison was also a large planter and slaveholder. He received his freedom at age twenty-nine and soon became a gin manufacturer, selling his product to local planters, who sometimes incurred debts with the free black entrepreneur. Ellison later purchased a house from the governor of the state and owned over 60 enslaved people. Until the 1850s, Ellison and his family occupied a privileged position within antebellum South Carolina society.

Although some blacks purchased slaves for profit, others, probably most, purchased people as a means of liberating family members and friends. As suggested above, by the 1830s and 1840s, southern states had largely outlawed the emancipation of slaves by will or deed. Thus, African American slaveholding also included the purchase of friends and kin, especially spouses and children, who, though enslaved, actually lived as free people of color. In other words, although mid-nineteenth-century black elites owed their livelihood to white clients, their lives were closely intertwined with those of black workers and the poor.

As mulatto and dark-skinned blacks alike gained a foothold in the economy, their industriousness did not insulate them from racist attacks. On the contrary, their progress sometimes generated as much resistance and hatred as their alleged intemperance and improvidence. In 1834, an English visitor remarked that whites discussed African American self-help and improvements "with a degree of bitterness that dictated a disposition to be more angry with their virtues than their vices." In 1841, a white working man exclaimed that "white men . . . are naturally indignant . . . when they see a set of idle blacks dressed up like ladies and gentlemen, strutting about our streets and flinging the 'rights of petition' and 'discussion' in our faces." Such attitudes underlay a variety of practices that curtailed the rights of all blacks and helped to forge bonds across intraracial class and color lines. In 1844, for example, one mulatto leader, John Gaines of Cincinnati, rejected the idea of a separate school for mulatto children: "This I anticipate would be fraught with evil consequences. . . . It would not only divide the colored children, but create prejudices too intolerable to be borne."

DISFRANCHISEMENT, SEGREGATION, AND EXCLUSION

Free blacks not only faced restrictions on their role as producers but bore constraints on their access to citizenship as well. White men from diverse ethnic backgrounds—including growing numbers of Irish and German immigrants and their children—gained the franchise and participated in an expanding democratic polity, while federal, state, and local laws and social practices denied free blacks full citizenship rights. Both northern and southern states increasingly blurred the distinction between enslaved and free blacks. Whereas free blacks had retained the vote in North Carolina, Pennsylvania, and New York before 1820, disfranchisement of free blacks became nearly universal during the 1820s and 1830s. In 1837–1838, the Pennsylvania constitutional convention restricted voting to white males twenty-one years of age or older. Until then, African American men had voted in Philadelphia, Pittsburgh, and elsewhere in the state. For its part, New York instituted a high property requirement and blocked most free blacks from the vote. By 1860, only four states—Maine, New Hampshire, Vermont, and Massachusetts—allowed free blacks unrestricted access to the franchise. At the same time that northern states restricted the franchise, they also limited the rights of free blacks to testify in courts against whites, serve in the militia, marry across racial lines, and even petition their government. In 1839, the Ohio legislature redefined the right of petition as a privilege for free blacks, proclaiming that blacks and mulattoes

> who may be residents within the State, have no constitutional right to present their petitions to the General Assembly for any purpose whatsoever, and that any reception of such petitions on the part of the General Assembly is a mere act of privilege or policy and not imposed by any expressed or implied power of the constitution.

The line between slavery and freedom was even less distinct in the South. In 1834, a Tennessee lawyer declared that the "interests and associations" of free blacks "are identified and blended with the slave, and what is for the benefit of one is for the benefit of the other." Although whites paid fines and served prison terms for a variety of offenses, free blacks, like slaves, endured the whip "well laid on" their bare backs. Like bondsmen, free blacks also faced death for crimes like manslaughter, arson, rebellion, and rape of a white woman; searches of their person and homes without warrants; and reenslavement for violation of vagrancy laws. Moreover, southern states jailed free blacks who entered their ports as seamen. Although the U.S. Supreme Court declared such detention laws unconstitutional in 1823, southern states ignored its ruling and continued to incarcerate black sailors. Some northern free blacks like Solomon Northrup were captured and enslaved as a result of such practices.

The fortunes of free blacks ebbed and flowed with the fortunes of the enslaved. In the wake of Nat Turner's rebellion, Virginia prohibited meetings for teaching free blacks to read, North Carolina prohibited free blacks from preaching, and Maryland made it a felony for free blacks to "call for, demand or receive abolition papers." During the 1850s, federal policies also highlighted and reinforced the link between the lives of enslaved and free blacks. The Fugitive Slave Act of 1850 not only undercut the fugitive network but also weakened the free black community by increasing penalties for persons aiding and abetting runaways. On the pretense of apprehending runaways, slave catchers and kidnappers regularly raided free black communities, seeking to entrap free as well as runaway blacks for sale in the domestic slave trade. Similarly, in the Dred Scott case of 1857, the U.S. Supreme Court undermined the liberty of free blacks as well as the enslaved. As Chief Justice Roger B. Taney declared, America was a white republic, with black people having "no rights that whites were bound to respect." (See the Documents section.)

Antebellum America not only weakened the legal status of free blacks but also restricted their access to the housing market. As early as the 1830s, white realtors and homeowners mobilized to prohibit free blacks or mulattoes "from purchasing or holding real estate" within city limits. In Boston, when a free black family made plans to move into a white neighborhood, residents threatened to destroy the structure before allowing blacks to move in. By 1860, the index of segregation showed increasing housing segregation along color lines. Such segregation was much higher in the North than in the South. In order to create an even residential distribution of blacks and whites, a higher percentage of northern blacks would have had to change their current address than would southern blacks: Boston, 61.3; Chicago, 50.0; and Cincinnati, 47.9, compared with Nashville, 43.1; New Orleans, 35.7; and Charleston, 23.2. Southern free blacks continued to live in as domestics, occupied general labor jobs, and, as a population, scattered more widely across the urban landscape than their northern counterparts. Whites often described the growing spatial concentration of northern blacks in such pejorative terms as Bucktown (Cincinnati), Little Africa (New York and Cincinnati), Hayti (Pittsburgh), and Nigger Hill (Boston).

Realtors and landlords regularly charged poor black and white tenants exorbitant rent for dilapidated and unhealthy properties, but blacks faced the brunt of such economic exploitation. One northern journalist stated, "Heaven preserve the shanties . . . and supply proprietors with tenants from whom the rent can be screwed." According to contemporary observers like George C. Foster, free blacks lived in "lofts," "garrets," "cellars," "blind alleys," "narrow courts," and "abandoned land." Such homes were poorly heated during the winter, too hot during the summer, and without proper water and sewer facilities at all times. During periodic outbreaks of diseases like cholera, free blacks suffered disproportionately. In 1832, when an epidemic of cholera hit Baltimore, the first wave of 500 deaths included

104 blacks, some 92 of them free blacks. During the 1850s, in New Haven, Connecticut, a contemporary observer reported that "vice close to their homes was a menace . . . housing was scarce, and colored people were not wanted as tenants." Like their southern urban counterparts, blacks in New Haven also had much higher death rates than whites: between 1830 and 1850, the city's black death rate per 1,000 persons was about 37 to 38, as compared with 15 to 21 for whites.

As free blacks faced difficulties gaining decent housing, they also confronted increasing restrictions on their access to public accommodations. Restaurants, theaters, hotels, and boarding houses routinely barred African Americans or served them on a segregated and unequal basis. By the onset of the Civil War, free blacks were so thoroughly segregated in the institutional life of the nation, including cemeteries, that a northern observer concluded that racial prejudice "haunts its victim wherever he goes, in the hospitals where humanity suffers, in the churches where he kneels to God, in the prisons where he expiates [his] offenses, in the graveyards where [he] sleeps the last sleep."

Discriminatory educational policies proved most damaging to free blacks' attempts to expand opportunities for their children. Antebellum southern states and cities—including Charleston, New Orleans, Baltimore, Louisville, and Washington, D.C.—all excluded free black children from the public schools. In the North, however, following protests from the black community, state legislatures gradually established segregated schools for free blacks and whites. Still, the struggle for education was an uphill battle in the urban North. In 1831, when a committee of white abolitionists proposed to build an interracial manual labor institution of higher education in New Haven, whites used both "lawful" and unlawful means to defeat the proposal. They not only held mass demonstrations against the school but also violently attacked the homes of black and white abolitionists. The most vicious attack on free black education emerged in Canterbury, Connecticut. In 1833, when the black student Sarah Harris requested enrollment in an all-white private girl's school, Prudence Crandall, the Quaker school teacher, admitted her. Parents immediately protested the presence of Harris by removing their children from the institution. Crandall responded by transforming her school into an academy for young women of color. Under pressure from white residents, the state legislature ruled against the establishment of a school for nonresident blacks. When Crandall defied the injunction, she was arrested, convicted, and jailed. After release from jail "on a technicality," Crandall resumed her school, but whites soon closed it down by smashing windows and setting fire to the facility.

Although the American Colonization Society (ACS) declined in the face of widespread free black opposition, it remained the most potent symbol of organized racial hostility against antebellum free people of color. As the nation opened its doors to rising numbers of German and Irish immigrants, the ACS worked hard to rid the country of free blacks. In 1847, it spearheaded the formation of Liberia as an independent nation and urged the federal government to use its surplus revenue to colonize free blacks in Africa. Although the organization's charter called for voluntary emigration of free blacks, such policies increased pressure on free blacks to move. Members regularly expressed their belief that free blacks and whites could not peacefully coexist in the democratic polity.

The antiblack sentiment that fueled ACS efforts to secure a peaceful and lawful removal of free blacks led others to adopt violent methods to secure the same goals. In the South, the patrols regularly conducted midnight raids on the homes of free blacks and threatened inhabitants with bodily harm if they did not leave the region. When free blacks complained of such attacks, authorities advised them to "leave the state." Some of the most destructive attacks on free blacks occurred in northern cities. By 1850, working-class and immigrant whites had launched violent attacks on free black communities in Providence, Boston, Pittsburgh, Washington, D.C., New York City, Cincinnati, and Philadelphia. These riots not only resulted in numerous physical injuries and death but also left black homes, churches, schools, and other institutions in ruins, forcing some free blacks to leave the country for Canada and, to some extent, Africa.

In Cincinnati, the Queen City, African Americans faced riots in 1829, 1836, and 1841. During an economic downturn and the hot summer months of August and September 1841, racial violence erupted when whites attacked black churches and businesses on Sixth and Broadway. Unlike most antebellum riots, African Americans selected Major J. Wilkerson, a twenty-eight-year-old "self-made man of color," to organize an armed defense of the community. For a while, heavily armed black men pushed the white mob out of their community, leading to white as well as black casualties, but whites were able to regroup, move an iron cannon into place, and fire on the black area. When officials finally declared martial law, guardsmen and mobsters herded black people into the square at Sixth and Broadway. Although many had posted bond for their release, they were detained. Authorities arrested some three hundred black men, who were violently attacked by members of the mob en route to jail. Before the mob spent its energy, additional attacks on black homes, churches, and businesses took place. In the wake of the riot, the value of black private property holdings dropped by an estimated $150,000.

INSTITUTIONS, CULTURE, AND POLITICS

As African Americans confronted racial hostility in the antebellum city, they increased their institution-building activities. Black religious, fraternal, and mutual benefit societies dramatically expanded. With only a few churches in 1820, by 1860 northern blacks reported 192 African Methodist Episcopal (AME), 46 AME Zion, 75 Baptist, 21 Presbyterian, and 2 Episcopal churches. Among the AME churches alone, New Orleans, Boston, Cincinnati, Providence, and St. Louis reported 2 to 3; Louisville, Brooklyn, and Pittsburgh, 4 to 6; New York, 7; Philadelphia, 9; and Baltimore, 10, the largest number of any city in the United States. Baltimore's free black Methodist churches included 5 regular Methodist, 3 AME, 1 AME Zion, and 1 Methodist Protestant church. Southern churches claimed the bulk of black church membership among both the Methodists and Baptists. Moreover, in the South, members of regular Methodist churches outnumbered AME members by nearly three to two in such cities as Baltimore. Between 1851 and 1863, membership in the largest black Baptist churches in the North ranged from

The Largest Black Baptist Churches, North and South, 1851–1863		
Church	Year	Membership
North		
African, Boston, Massachusetts	1851	110
Abyssinian, New York City, New York	1860	440
Ebenezer, New York City, New York	1855	108
Zion, New York City, New York	1851	378
First African, Philadelphia, Pennsylvania	1859	268
Shilo, Philadelphia, Pennsylvania	1859	303
Union, Philadelphia, Pennsylvania	1859	359
Chillicothe Baptist, Chillicothe, Ohio	1845	<u>181</u>
Total		**2,144**
South		
First African, Petersburg, Virginia	1851	1,635
Gillfield, Petersburg, Virginia	1851	1,361
First African, Richmond, Virginia	1859	3,160
Second African, Richmond, Virginia	1859	1,029
Springfield, Augusta, Georgia	1863	1,711
First African, Savannah, Georgia	1862	1,815
Second Colored, Savannah, Georgia	1862	1,146
First African, Lexington, Kentucky	1861	<u>2,223</u>
Total		**14,080**

Source: Mechal Sobel, *Trabelin' On: The Slave Journey to an Afro-Baptist Faith.* Copyright © 1988 by Princeton University Press. Reprinted by permission of Princeton University Press.

just over 100 to nearly 450, compared to a southern range of about 1,150 to 3,160 (see table).

At the same time, under the leadership of Richard H. Gleaver, deputy grand master of the African Independent Grand Lodge, the black lodge movement spread from Boston, Philadelphia, and New York into the states of the Midwest, Upper South, and Deep South. By the 1850s, the black lodge movement had reached Cincinnati, Pittsburgh, St. Louis, Washington, D.C., Louisville, Baltimore, and New Orleans. As early as 1838, in Philadelphia alone, free blacks maintained some 100 lodge and benefit societies, with nearly 75,000 members. The lodges had paid out $14,200 in benefits to members and reported $10,000 in their treasuries.

Black newspapers and journals also proliferated. In 1827, African Americans published their first newspaper, *Freedom's Journal,* in New York. Under the editorship of the Presbyterian minister Samuel Cornish and John Russwurm, *Freedom's Journal* placed the struggle against slavery and the fight for full citizenship rights at the top of its agenda. Although it was a short-lived publication, it nonetheless helped spearhead the development of black journalism. Within two months after the paper ceased publication in March 1829, Cornish initiated another short-lived paper, the *Rights of All.* In 1836, however, he teamed with journalist Philip Bell, who would later leave the city for the West, and the minister Charles B. Ray of New York to launch the *Colored American* (originally the *Weekly Advocate*), which became the longest-running antebellum black publication. Like *Freedom's Journal*, it heightened the struggle against slavery in the South and discrimination in the North. Other antebellum black publications followed suit: David Ruggle's *Mirror of Liberty*, the nation's first black magazine, in New York City; Benjamin Robert's *Anti-Slavery Herald* in Boston; Henry Highland Garnet and William H. Allan's *National Watchman Clarion* in Troy, New York; Martin R. Delany's *Mystery* in Pittsburgh; William H. Day's *Aliened American* in Cleveland; and Philip Bell, Mifflin W. Gibbs, and J. H. Townsend's *Pacific Appeal* in San Francisco, to name a few.

Samuel Cornish, New York minister and founder of *Freedom's Journal*, the nation's first black newspaper. In 1836 Cornish also helped to launch the *Colored American. The Granger Collection*

Searching for an "American" Identity

In their community-building activities, free blacks retained a consciousness of their "African" roots, but the colonization movement forced them to reconsider their self-designation. African Americans now scrupulously avoided the term *African* while searching for a way to claim "America" without denying their "African" origins. As suggested by the new black publications and institutions, free blacks experimented with a variety of alternatives—"oppressed American," "aliened American," "people of color," and "colored American." In 1844, for example, a group of Louisville blacks broke from the white First Baptist Church and founded the Second Colored Baptist Church. The African Baptist Church of Boston became the "First Independent Church of the People of Color." According to the church publication, "The name African is ill applied to a church composed of American citizens." Likewise, according to the editors of the *Colored American*, they adopted this newspaper title because "we are Americans—colored Americans." As Cornish further put it, "Many would rob us of the endeared name 'Americans,' a distinction more emphatically belonging to us than five-sixths of this nation, one that we will never yield."

As free people of color searched for an "American" identity, they also gravitated toward middle-class, Euro-American definitions of gender roles. Over and over again, free black publications promoted the idea that women were "the gentler sex," "naturally" more moral, more loving, and more caring than men. Indeed, some free blacks believed that sharper gender distinctions helped counteract racial stereotypes, justified emancipation, and smoothed the path to full citizenship. In an 1839 article, the *Colored American* drew the gender line starkly:

> Man is strong—Woman is beautiful
> Man is daring and confident—Woman is defferent and unassuming
> Man is great in action—Woman in suffering
> Man shines abroad—Woman at home
> Man talks to convince—Woman to persuade and please
> Man has a rugged heart—-Woman a soft and tender one
> Man prevents misery—Woman relieves it
> Man has science—Woman taste
> Man has judgement—Woman sensibility
> Man is a being of justice—Woman an angel of mercy

For their part, black women reinforced certain aspects of the male-dominant idea of gender roles. In the struggle against racial inequality, they believed that it was their duty to "encourage and support the manhood" of their men as "tough and protective" providers for their families and communities. Mary Shadd Cary, a teacher in various schools in New York and Pennsylvania, offers an extreme example. When she moved to Canada during the turbulent 1850s, she soon became the first black female editor in North America with the formation of the *Provincial Freeman*. In addition to promoting the settlement of U.S. free blacks in Canada, the paper vigorously promoted full citizenship for black Canadians. Yet Shadd initially camouflaged her identity as a woman. As such, she revealed her ambivalence about women transcending "woman's sphere" and entering the man's "public sphere." Still, despite the adherence of free blacks to certain aspects of the prevailing gender paradigm, the dynamics of racial and class inequality undercut such notions in practice. As noted earlier, unlike their white counterparts, free black women worked outside the home in large numbers. And as we will see later, they also played key roles in the abolitionist movement and the struggle for full citizenship rights. They developed these roles at a time when most white women were strictly chastised for public speaking and advocacy work.

Black Writers and Artists

Along with black newspapers and magazines, free black men and some women published their life stories. These included the life histories of William Wells Brown (1847), Henry Bibb (1849), Solomon Northrup (1853), and Harriet Jacobs (*Incidents in the Life of a Slave Girl*, published under the pseudonym Linda Brent in 1861). Slave narratives represented the most distinctive African American contribution to antebellum American literature. They highlighted not only the brutalities of slavery but also the ingenuity and courage of African Americans, who devised a variety of strategies (especially escape) for resisting the rigors of human bondage and affirming their humanity. In her narrative, Harriet Jacobs described the plight of the young slave girl who struggled to retain her sense of womanhood in the face of tyranny:

> I entered upon my fifteenth year—a sad epoch in the life of a slave girl. My master began to whisper foul words in my ear. . . . No matter whether the slave girl

be as black as ebony or as fair as her mistress. In either case, there is no shadow of law to protect her from insult, from violence, or even from death.

Jacobs related how she turned away from her owner "with disgust and hatred," because he "tried his utmost to corrupt the pure principles" of womanhood that her grandmother had instilled. Like other ex-slaves, she also recounted her escape to the North: "I was . . . faint in body, but strong of purpose. I did not look back upon the old place, though I felt that I should never see it again." Jacobs also described the escape of a young male slave, under the rubric "The Slave Who Dared to Feel Like a Man." On the eve of his escape Benjamin explained to her that "he was no longer a boy and everyday made his yoke more galling." The narratives of ex-slave men were even more direct. Henry Bibb, for example, crafted his narrative as a "testimony on record against this man-destroying system."

Free blacks also produced their first dramatic works and plays during the antebellum era. In 1821, the black businessman Allen Royce opened the African Grove, America's first black theater in New York City. Two years later, the Grove staged Henry Brown's "The Drama of King Shotaway," considered the first play presented by a black playwright on the U.S. professional stage. This play, about a slave revolt on the Caribbean island of St. Vincent, helped to launch the career of James Hewlett, a West Indian–born black who played the lead role. Ira Alridge, an African-born ex-slave from Maryland, also received his early stage training at the Grove. Alridge would soon gain international renown for his portrayal of Shakespeare's Othello.

Poems, novels, and historical works rounded out the intellectual accomplishments of antebellum free blacks. The free black woman Frances Ellen Watkins Harper (1854), AME bishop Daniel A. Payne (1850), and the North Carolinian George Moses Horton (1829) all produced their own volumes of poetry during the period. Although Horton remained enslaved, his owners gave him latitude to write and sell his poems, which were widely read by northern free blacks and whites in abolitionist papers like the *Liberator*. In 1853, William Wells Brown followed up the narrative of his life with the first novel by a black American author, *Clotel, or, The President's Daughter* (1853), and a play, *The Escape, or, A Leap for Freedom* (1858). In 1859, Harriet E. Wilson published *Our Nig, or, Sketches from the Life of a Free Black*, the first novel by an African American woman. Historical and social studies included works by Rev. J. W. C. Pennington, *A Text Book of the Origin and History of the Colored People* (1841); Martin R. Delany, *The Condition, Elevation, Emigration and Destiny of the Colored People of the United States* (1852); and William Cooper Nell, *Colored Patriots of the American Revolution* (1855) and *Services of Colored Americans in the Wars of 1776 and 1812* (1855).

Taken together, these antebellum black writers and artists were deeply religious and used their pen as an instrument of liberation. Over and over again, they emphasized the "fatherhood of God" and the "brotherhood of man" and challenged popular beliefs about the white man's "manifest destiny" to subjugate peoples of color. Rev. J. W. C. Pennington condemned slavery and color prejudice as a sickness that abhorred the truth and threatened to carry "the total nation down to a state of refined heathenism." In her poem "Bury Me in a Free Land," the poet

SOURCES FROM THE PAST

1854

Free Black Poet Frances Ellen Watkins Harper Decries Slavery

Bury Me in a Free Land

Make me a grave where'er you will,
In a lowly plain, or a lofty hill;
Make it among earth's humblest graves,
But not in a land where men are slaves.

I could not rest if around my grave
I heard the steps of a trembling slave;
His shadow above my silent tomb
Would make it a place of fearful gloom.

I could not rest if I heard the tread
Of a coffle gang to the shambles led,
And the mother's shriek of wild despair
Rise like a curse on the trembling air.

I could not sleep if I saw the lash
Drinking her blood at each fearful gash,
And I saw her babes torn from her breast,
Like trembling doves from their parent nest.

I'd shudder and start if I heard the bay
Of bloodhounds seizing their human prey,
And I heard the captive plead in vain
As they bound afresh his galling chain.

If I saw young girls from their mothers' arms
Bartered and sold for their youthful charms,
My eye would flash with a mournful flame,
My death-paled cheek grow red with shame.

I would sleep, dear friends, where bloated might
Can rob no man of his dearest right;
My rest shall be calm in any grave
Where none can call his brother a slave.

I ask no monument, proud and high,
To arrest the gaze of the passers-by;
All that my yearning spirit craves,
Is bury me not in a land of slaves.

Source: Patricia L. Hill, ed., *Call and Response: The Riverside Anthology of the African American Literary Tradition* (Boston: Houghton Mifflin Company, 1998), p. 352.

Frances Watkins Harper proclaimed: "I could not rest if I heard the tread / Of a coffle gang. . . . I could not sleep if I saw the lash" (see box). In William Wells Brown's play *The Escape*, Glen and Melinda escaped from the labor and sexual abuse of the plantation regime. On reaching their new home in Canada, Glen recalled how he fought the overseer and made the blood "flow freely. . . . It was a leap for freedom."

The Abolitionist Movement and the Underground Railroad

Using their culture and community institutions as a springboard for organization, planning, and strategy, free blacks fought for full citizenship rights and the abolition of slavery. During the 1830s and 1840s, blacks held a series of national conventions in Philadelphia, Buffalo, and Cleveland. Until the 1850s, each of these conventions condemned the ACS effort to transport free blacks to Africa. Black delegates took their stand on the Declaration of Independence and the Preamble of the Constitution: "The latter guarantees in letter and spirit to every freeman born in this country all the rights and immunities of citizenship."

Frederick Douglass and Sojourner Truth emerged as perhaps the most renowned black spokespersons for the peaceful abolition of slavery and the extension of equal rights to free blacks. Shortly after arriving in New Bedford, Massachusetts, Douglass became a full-time agent of the Massachusetts Anti-Slavery Society and spoke out against slavery throughout New England. He soon became such an articulate speaker and debater that some white abolitionists feared that his credibility as a former slave would be compromised. Consequently, under substantial pressure from his white allies, Douglass wrote the *Narrative of the Life of Frederick Douglass* (1845), which revealed important details of his life as a fugitive. On the book's release, Douglass fled to Europe, where he stayed and lectured for two years. In 1846, with the aid of friends, he purchased his freedom, returned to the United States, and two years later launched the *North Star* as a new organ of abolitionism. The paper advocated greater influence for blacks in the abolitionist movement, waged a stronger fight against slavery in the South, and promoted a more diligent struggle against racial discrimination in the North. In the first issue of the *North Star,* Douglass addressed one editorial to white friends and another to blacks. To white friends, he wrote:

It is neither a reflection on the fidelity, nor a disparagement of . . . our [white] friends . . . to assert what common sense affirms and only folly denies; that the man who has suffered the wrong is the man to demand redress—that the man struck is the man to cry out—and that he [who] has endured the cruel pangs of slavery is the man to advocate liberty.

To enslaved and free blacks, he wrote:

We solemnly dedicate the *North Star* to the cause of our long oppressed and plundered fellow countrymen. . . . Giving no quarter to slavery of the South, it will hold no truce with oppressors at the North. While it shall boldly advocate emancipation for our enslaved brethren, it will omit no opportunity to gain for the nominally free, complete enfranchisement. Every effort to degrade you or your cause . . . shall find in it a constant, unswerving and inflexible foe.

Sojourner Truth and Harriet Tubman were the two most famous black women of the nineteenth century. Whereas Tubman was a southern-born slave who later escaped to freedom in the North (discussed in Chapter 8), Truth was a New York–born slave who gained her freedom under the state's Emancipation Act of 1827. Seeking to draw a line between her slave past and freedom, Isabella Baumfree changed her name to Sojourner Truth in June 1843. In a conversation with the Quakers James and Lucretia Mott, she said:

The Lord gave me Sojourner because I was to travel up an' down the land showin' the people their sins an' bein' a sign unto them. Afterward I told the Lord I wanted another name 'cause everybody else had two names; and the Lord gave me Truth, because I was to declare the truth to the people.

Indeed, Truth became one of the most energetic itinerant ministers of her day. She regularly preached against slavery in the South, social injustice in the North, and women's rights. Historian Nell Painter has recently demonstrated that Sojourner Truth's "And Ar'n't I a Woman?" speech, delivered at the Akron, Ohio, Woman's Rights Convention in 1851, was the invention of her white feminist comrade Frances Dana Gage. Still, as Painter concludes, Gage's Truth "triumphs scholarship" as a symbol of Truth's life and struggle against slavery, racism, and sexism: "Look at me! Look at my arm! I have plowed, and planted, and gathered into barns, and no man could head me! And ar'n't I a woman? . . ." (see box on page 230).

Even as Douglass, Truth, and others vigorously promoted the message of "moral suasion," there were other powerful dissenting voices calling for the forceful and "violent" overthrow of the "pecu-

This engraving shows Frederick Douglass as a young man. Douglass launched the *North Star* on 28 July 1848. The paper sought a stronger role for blacks in their own struggle for freedom. *By permission of the Houghton Library, Harvard University*

liar institution" of slavery. In 1829, two years before Nat Turner's rebellion, David Walker, a free black clothier who had moved from North Carolina to Boston, issued his famous pamphlet *Walker's Appeal*. In this militant abolitionist document, Walker urged slaves to rise up and "throw off the yoke" of bondage. At the same time, he exhorted free blacks to stay put and fight: "Let no man of us budge one step. . . . America is more our country, than it is the whites—we have enriched it with blood and tears."

Following Walker's death in 1830, Maria W. Stewart formulated and directed a similar message to enslaved and free blacks. She also declared her readiness to die in the interest of black liberation. On one occasion she urged blacks to affirm their birthright as "true born" Americans and demand their citizenship. Although she faced constraints and complaints from within the black community, she insisted that neither gender nor color should bar black women from speaking out

Sojourner Truth, c. 1870. In June 1843, Isabella Baumfree changed her name to Sojourner Truth and became one of the most outspoken proponents of abolition and women's rights. She continued to be active during the Civil War and Reconstruction years. *National Portrait Gallery, Smithsonian Institution, Washington, D.C./Art Resource, N.Y.*

on behalf of the race. "What if I am a woman? . . . It is not color of skin that makes the man or the woman, but the principal formed in the soul." In a convention held in Buffalo in August 1843, Garnet, Ray, and other New York and Detroit blacks endorsed the Liberty Party and violent defense of their rights if necessary. As Garnet put it, "You cannot suffer greater cruelties than you have already. Rather die freemen than live to be slaves." A year later, one delegate urged the gathering to "let blood flow without measure—until our rights are acknowledged or we [have] perished from the earth."

The struggle for social justice spread well beyond the doings of the most renowned black spokespersons. The fight for freedom was a grassroots social movement that involved numerous ordinary working-class free and enslaved blacks. By the 1850s, free blacks had organized an elaborate underground escape network designed to free fugitives by aiding their escape farther north or by concealing their residence within local black communities. The "underground railroad" depended on the cooperation of large numbers of free blacks. For example, since slaveowners regularly passed through Ohio Valley cities like Cincinnati, Pittsburgh, and

SOURCES FROM THE PAST

1851

Sojourner Truth Addresses the Ohio Women's Rights Convention

Well, children, where there is so much racket there must be somethin' out o'kilter. I think that 'twixt the Negroes of the North and the South and the women at the North, all talkin' 'bout rights, the white men will be in a fix pretty soon. But what's all this here talkin' 'bout?

That man over there say that women needs to be helped into carriages, and lifted over ditches, and to have the best place everywhere. Nobody ever helps me into carriages, or over mud-puddles, or give me any best place! And ar'n't I a woman? Look at me! Look at my arm! I have ploughed, and planted, and gathered into barns, and no man could head me! And ar'n't I a woman? I could work as much and eat as much as a man—when I could get it—and bear the lash as well! And ar'n't I a woman? I have borne thirteen children, and seen 'em mos' all sold off to slavery, and when I cried out with my mother's grief, none but Jesus heard me! And ar'n't I a woman?

Then they talk about this thing in the head; what's this they call it? ["Intellect," whispered some one near.] That's it honey. What's that got to do with women's rights or Negro's rights? If my cup won't hold but a pint and yours holds a quart, wouldn't you be mean not to let me have my little half measure full?

Then that little man in black there, he says women can't have as much rights as men, 'cause Christ wasn't a woman! Where did your Christ come from? Where did your Christ come from? From God and a woman! Man had nothin' to do with Him.

If the first woman God ever made was strong enough to turn the world upside down all alone, these women together ought to be able to turn it back, and get it right side up again? And now they is asking to do it, they better let 'em. 'Bliged to you for hearin' me, and now ole Sojourner hasn't got nothin' more to say.

Akron, Ohio, May 29, 1851

Source: Address by Sojourner Truth to the Ohio Women's Rights Convention. Adapted from Marius Robinson, Pittsburgh Saturday Visitor, 7 June 1851.

Evansville, black hotel and riverboat employees reported on the arrival of planters and slave catchers, informed slaves of their opportunities for gaining freedom, and facilitated contact with conductors. In June 1848, blacks working at the Pittsburgh Merchants Hotel helped two female slaves escape from a visiting planter. In early August 1841, a letter from a Cincinnati fugitive informed his enslaved wife and her friends that black boatmen would guide them to abolitionists and freedom. For their part, numerous black women joined Anti-Slavery Sewing Society circles, which produced clothing for runaways and aided their escape from bondage. These free African American men and women took great pride in their resistance activities. The free black Cincinnati agent John Hatfield reported, "I never felt better pleased with anything I ever did in my life, than in getting a slave woman clear, when her master was taking her from Virginia."

Whether blacks called for peaceful and voluntary abolition, violence, or the intensification of the underground railroad, the struggle for liberation was by no means an
all-black affair. The most well-known white allies and abolitionists included
William Lloyd Garrison, Harriet Beecher Stowe, and John Brown. In 1831, Garrison issued the opening number of the *Liberator,* declaring: "I will be as harsh as
truth and as uncompromising as justice. . . . I am in earnest—I will not equivo-
cate—I will not excuse—I will not retreat a single inch—and I WILL BE
HEARD." At about the same time, blacks and whites formed new antislavery societies: the New England Anti-Slavery Society (1832), the American Anti-Slavery Society (1833), and the American Moral Reform Society (1835), the latter of which
aimed to link abolitionism with the evangelical reform and temperance movements. These organizations reinforced the struggle against slavery at the state and
local levels. In 1842, for example, when the U.S. Supreme Court's ruling in *Prigg
v. Pennsylvania* weakened the underground railroad, several states passed personal
liberty laws prohibiting state participation in the apprehension of fugitives.

In the wake of the Fugitive Slave Act of 1850, northern whites escalated their efforts on behalf of free blacks and bondspeople. In Boston, the abolitionist minister
Theodore Parker warned blacks against "kidnappers and slave catchers." In the
Christiana Riot of 1851, Pennsylvania's free blacks and their white allies killed one
slave catcher and mortally wounded another. All parties in the incident were later
tried and acquitted. Although opponents destroyed Crandall's school and the New
Haven project for free blacks, discussed earlier, interracial institutes of education
developed and succeeded in other states: the Oneida Institute near Utica, New
York; Lane Seminary and College in Cincinnati; the short-lived Noyer Academy in
Canaan, New Hampshire; New York Central College in McGrawville, New York;
and Oberlin Collegiate Institute in northern Ohio. Black schools like New York's
African Free School provided students to these new interracial abolitionist institutions, which offered advanced training for future black leaders like Henry Highland Garnet, Alexander Crummell, and Charles Reason.

In 1852, Harriet Beecher Stowe published *Uncle Tom's Cabin.* The novel highlighted the evils of slavery and generated widespread white support for the abolitionist cause. This outpouring of white support culminated with John Brown's attack on
the federal arsenal at Harpers Ferry, Virginia. On 16 October 1859, under Brown's
leadership, thirteen whites and five blacks aimed to capture the arsenal, arm slaves,
and lead a war of liberation. The five blacks included Lewis Sheridan Leary and Dan-
gerfield Newby, killed during the attack; John Anthony Copeland and Shields Green,
both captured and hanged along with Brown; and Osborne Perry Anderson, who escaped. Although Brown's effort failed, it confirmed for many African Americans that
a war of liberation was possible and that some whites were prepared to pay the
supreme price for their freedom. John Rock, the free black Bostonian, dentist, and
lawyer, said: "Sooner or later the clashing of arms will be heard in this country. . . .
The black man's service will be needed . . . to strike a genuine blow for freedom . . .
[with a] power which white men will be bound to respect."

Inter- and intraracial solidarity was difficult to achieve. Free blacks repeatedly
complained that white abolitionists viewed them as "exhibits" rather than as "advocates" for their own liberation. They also criticized their white counterparts for

John Brown, a Connecticut minister, and thirteen of the men (including three of his sons) who joined his effort to liberate slaves by armed force. On 16 October 1859, the group attacked the federal arsenal at Harpers Ferry, Virginia. Brown was hanged along with other members of his party, including two blacks. *Division of Political History, Smithsonian Institution*

using blacks as service personnel or "colored mail-wrappers" and denying them leadership positions. Despite intense class and ethnic fragmentation among whites over the slavery issue, they rallied around notions of white superiority, citizenship, and republicanism. Thus, most white abolitionists were willing to go only so far in their defense of black rights. At the same time, African Americans confronted a variety of internal conflicts among themselves.

Differences of Color, Class, Gender, and Ideology

Class, color, gender, cultural, ideological, and political differences threatened racial solidarity. Light-skinned blacks gained economic and political opportunities and privileges denied to their darker-skinned counterparts. During the 1840s, on two occasions, for example, the Ohio State Supreme Court sanctioned the right of mulattoes to vote, arguing that they were not "Negroes." When Democrats gained control of the Ohio legislature and passed a law in 1850 disfranchising anyone with a "distinct and visible admixture of African blood," the Ohio Supreme Court again defended mulatto men, insisting that the law could not disfranchise males with over 50 percent of white ancestry. Family relations reinforced such color divisions. Between 1850 and 1860, in a survey of eight cities, 82 percent of the men listed as "black" were married to women listed as "black," whereas 87 percent of those listed as "mulattoes" had spouses who were also "mulattoes."

Educated, propertied, and skilled black elites also sought to revamp the behavior of their working-class counterparts. As the free black Baptist and Methodist churches expanded, they sought to curb the earlier emotional style of black worship. Bishop Richard Allen and Daniel Coker of the AME church urged free blacks to contain the emotional outcry that characterized tent meetings, where "shouting, ring-dancing, and groaning" gained free expression in Methodist revival services. Even more so than church services, elites condemned working-class black music, dance, drinking, gaming, and leisure time activities. Working-class blacks patronized the illegal "cook-shops" and "groggeries." In Richmond, Virginia, according to a police report of one shop, "The house has four rooms on the first floor . . . the first was used as a grocery, the second as a bar room, the third as a snack room, and the fourth as a kitchen." Black customers visited the shop to drink, dance, play cards, throw dice, and enjoy the company of the opposite sex. Although the police regularly raided such places and middle-class blacks condemned them as detrimental to the health of the community, large numbers of working-class blacks kept them in business.

Paradoxically, at the same time that middle-class and elite blacks sought to suppress certain aspects of black culture, whites developed mechanisms for imbibing those very elements of African American life. Urban whites formed minstrel companies and adapted black songs for white audiences. Performing in "blackface," white performers like Thomas Dartmouth "Daddy" Rice popularized stereotypical black rural images like "Jim Crow" and his urban counterpart, "Zip Coon." By 1850, the most well-known minstrel companies—the Virginia Minstrels and the Christy Minstrels—regularly performed at some of the leading theaters of the nation and Europe. Although some blacks, like the dancer and musician William Henry Love, toured with early minstrel companies, blacks were largely excluded from these jobs, which enabled whites to observe and absorb black culture while defending themselves against its full impact.

African American women played a key role in the community life of free blacks. They made up the bulk of church members and spearheaded the formation of a plethora of antislavery societies, temperance unions, sewing circles, and mutual aid and benefit societies. In Philadelphia, for example, women made up more than three-fifths of the membership of mutual aid societies, although male societies maintained the largest treasuries and paid the highest benefits. Women also swelled the ranks of black political and civil rights conventions. Yet black women were often disfranchised within the black community. During the early 1840s, in Boston, for example, the Reverend Jehial C. Beman, minister of the AME Zion church, dismissed Julia Foote from the congregation when she refused to stop holding services and preaching to women in her home. Foote later joined three other AME women denied the privilege of preaching and protested at the AME's annual Philadelphia conference. Following the negative response to their protests, Foote launched her career as an independent preacher and traveled widely across the northern states of New England and the mid-Atlantic. In Philadelphia, following her husband's death in 1823, the free black woman Zilpha Elaw also became an itinerant Methodist preacher. Over the next fifteen years, she traveled widely through New England and the middle states, made at least two trips to the South, and preached for five years in England.

Free black women were not only denied access to the pulpit as ministers in established black churches but also refused a voice on key political matters. They did not, however, accept these constraints without a fight. At one of the early conventions, black women passed and delivered a resolution to the men: "Where as we the ladies have been invited to attend the Convention and have been deprived of a voice, which we the ladies deem wrong and shameful. Therefore, resolved, That we will attend no more after tonight, unless the privilege is granted." As a result of the women's protest, the men introduced and passed a resolution "inviting the ladies to share in the doings of the Convention." Indeed, unlike most of their white counterparts, leading black spokesmen offered growing support to the women's movement. When the predominantly white advocates of women's rights held their famous Seneca Falls Convention in 1848, Frederick Douglass was the only male to speak out in support of women's suffrage. Similarly, the black nationalist Martin Delany not only encouraged the presence of female delegates at the black conventions but also endorsed the right of women to gain equal access to education. In his view, "The potency and respectability of a nation . . . depends entirely upon the position of their women."

Free blacks also faced important ideological and political differences. They fought slavery and the American Colonization Society in different ways. As noted above, not all free black leaders adhered to Douglass's mode of abolitionism, emphasizing as he did "moral suasion" and close cooperation between black and white abolitionists. In 1840, the abolitionist movement split when William Lloyd Garrison supported full female participation. Many whites withdrew from the American Anti-Slavery Society and formed the American and Foreign Anti-Slavery Society. The new organization opposed Garrison's pro-woman, antichurch, and antigovernment stance. Although Douglass and leading black Boston and Philadelphia abolitionists like Charles Lenox Remond and Robert Purvis remained loyal to Garrison, New Yorkers like Cornish, Garnet, and others gradually rejected Garrison's prohibition on party politics. In New York, some blacks continued to vote and used their leverage to fight remaining restrictions on the franchise. African Americans also increasingly questioned Garrison's pacifist tactics, particularly as black communities faced increasing mob attacks. The New York–based *Colored American* called on blacks to "die virtuous martyrs in a holy cause" of self-defense, emancipation, and enfranchisement.

After fighting against the colonization movement for more than three decades, however, substantial numbers of free blacks moved toward an emigration position during the turbulent 1850s. Martin R. Delany emerged as the most forceful spokesperson for such ideas. Born in Charlestown, Virginia, around 1812, Delany had moved to western Pennsylvania with his family by the 1820s. In Pittsburgh, between 1843 and 1847, Delany published a newspaper, the *Mystery*. He also co-edited the *North Star* with Frederick Douglass. In 1849, Delany and Douglass parted ways as Delany moved increasingly toward a black nationalist stance. Delany advocated pride in blackness, independent action, and gradually emigration to a new homeland. In 1852, he first advocated movement to some part of the Caribbean or South America before targeting the Niger Valley of West Africa as a promising new site of African American return to Africa. Similarly, in 1858, the Reverend Henry Highland Garnet of Troy, New York, formed the African Civilization Society and sought "to establish a grand center of Negro nationality from which shall flow the streams of commercial, intellectual, and political power which shall make colored respected everywhere." Garnet emphasized "giving the Gospel to Africa, and thus render obedience unto the [divine] command of our Lord Jesus Christ to go into all the world and preach the Gospel to every creature." For his part, Delany also said that Africa would be "civilized and enlightened" as a result of the African American search for independence in Africa. As such, these nineteenth-century black nationalists also exhibited certain New World cultural biases toward Africa and its people.

By the late 1850s, even Frederick Douglass despaired of abolitionist protest. As early as 1849, he expressed sympathy for the use of violence. He now asked, "Who dare say that the criminals deserve less than death at the hands of their long-abused chattels?" In 1859, he also supported John Brown's plans to launch a violent attack on slaveholders in the South. When word reached Douglass that Brown's effort had failed and that federal authorities had ordered his arrest, Douglass fled to Canada and then to England. Shortly before the outbreak of the Civil War, Douglass moved toward the emigration idea. He decided to investigate Haiti as a site for black settlement. Although he chartered a boat and wrote an editorial announcing the proposed trip, he postponed his plans in the wake of news that southern whites had fired on the federal forces at Fort Sumter and that civil war seemed imminent. Douglass wrote, "Since this article upon Haiti was put to type . . . we find ourselves in circumstances which induce us to forego a much desired trip to Haiti, for the present." Douglass would soon turn his attention to the recruitment of black soldiers for the Union army. In taking up this work of liberation, he would also conclude that "the World" had not seen "a nobler and grander war than that which the loyal people of this country are now waging."

≈

ANTEBELLUM FREE BLACKS TOOK JOBS at the bottom of the urban economy and transformed them into instruments of freedom for themselves, relatives, and friends. Still, they faced significant internal conflicts and social differences. Free blacks catering to white clients amassed resources, power, and prestige that enabled them to protect themselves better than their working-class, poor, and enslaved counterparts. Such internal differences were not only economic but also social, cultural, and political. Although some free blacks supported spirited worship services; leisure time dancing, gambling, and drinking; and even violence in the fight for their rights, others called for formal modes of worship and leisure; temperance; and "moral suasion" to secure their rights. Despite such differences, however, racist notions of republicanism undercut the opportunities and rights of all blacks—enslaved and free, men and women—and reinforced racial solidarity across status lines. Although African Americans gained the support of white abolitionists, such support was insufficient to overturn the system of slavery and transform free blacks into citizens. Only the events of the Civil War and the rapid expansion of industrial capitalism would bring blacks more fully into the economy and polity as citizens as well as producers. Building on their antebellum communities, ideas, and strategies for social change, African Americans would play a key role in their own emancipation during the Civil War years, the subject of Chapter 10.

CHAPTER 10

◊

The Civil War and the Struggle
for Freedom

Although slavery was a pivotal factor in the coming of the Civil War, African Americans faced an uphill battle transforming the war into a struggle for their own freedom. Like southern slaveholders, northern whites perceived blacks as inferior, socially and biologically. They not only initially rejected blacks for military service but also respected southerners' claims to "property rights" in slaves. Accordingly, when federal forces first arrived in the South, they returned fugitives to their owners and helped to curb black resistance. For their part, the Confederate states used slave labor to supply their armed forces with food, medical supplies, and services, including labor on defense installations and munitions plants, which enabled the Confederacy to achieve victories on the battlefield. Consequently, federal officials gradually dropped restrictions on the employment of black labor and the recruitment of black troops. The shift in federal policy was related not only to reverses on the battlefield but also to the activism of African Americans themselves. Enslaved black men and women deserted the plantations in rising numbers while at the same time their free black counterparts, particularly in the North, waged a militant campaign to end restrictions on the recruitment of black troops. Thus, federal policy changed under the combined impact of defeat on the battlefield and growing black resistance to bondage.

Once recruited, black soldiers fought in nearly five hundred battles, many of them major engagements. The growing political and military participation of blacks hastened the defeat of the Confederacy, the abolition of slavery, and the rise of a free black wage-earning working class. Still, despite their display of valor on the battlefield, African Americans fought under extraordinary hardships and forms of discrimination. They not only served in segregated units under white officers but also faced discrimination in recruitment procedures, assignments, pay, and aid to their families. Black women and children and the aged and infirm endured the brunt of deprivation on the home front and in fugitive or contraband camps organized by the federal government. These forms of inequality transcended the institution of slavery. They were also related to persistent patterns of discrimination against free blacks in the North and South. Consequently, during the war years,

African Americans not only mobilized against the institution of slavery but also waged a consistent struggle against the denial of full citizenship rights to free blacks, including the franchise and equal access to public accommodations.

WHITE ATTITUDES TOWARD BLACKS IN THE NORTH AND THE SOUTH

In November 1860, the election of Abraham Lincoln as president helped to precipitate the Civil War and the emancipation of some 4 million enslaved African Americans. Although the Republican Party disavowed any intention of emancipating slaves, or interfering with the institution where it existed, Lincoln's victory reinforced southern fears that their future and the institution of slavery were imperiled. A month later, South Carolina seceded from the Union. By February 1861, Mississippi, Alabama, Georgia, Texas, Louisiana, and Florida had followed suit. Southern secessionists established the Confederate States of America, selected Jefferson Davis as president, and chose Montgomery and later Richmond as its capital city. Although the slaveholding Upper South and border states of Missouri, Kentucky, Maryland, Delaware, and later the new state of West Virginia remained in the Union, the states of Virginia, Tennessee, and North Carolina joined the Confederacy. Thus, even before Lincoln delivered his inaugural address and took the reins of government in March 1861, the slaveholders had already challenged his authority to run the country. In his inaugural address, Lincoln not only reiterated his aim to "save the Union" but also held the line on the spread of slavery into the new territories west of the Mississippi River. His stand, along with southern obstinacy, set the stage for the bloodiest war in the nation's history. The collision came on 12 April 1861, when the Confederate states launched an attack on Fort Sumter in Charleston Harbor.

Recruitment of Black Troops

Despite Republican victory in the election of 1860 and the swift advent of the Civil War thereafter, northerners initially rejected blacks as soldiers and citizens. Much like southern whites, they defined the war as a white man's war. When Ohio blacks petitioned Governor David Tod for permission to raise a black regiment, he replied: "Do you not know . . . that this is a white man's government; that white men are able to defend and protect it?" At the local level, when Cincinnati blacks planned public demonstrations to support the Union's war effort, municipal officials prohibited such meetings. Even the staunchest northern Unionists believed that the enlistment of black troops would violate the "accepted mode of warfare" and prove "shocking to our sense of humanity." According to one midwestern Republican senator, "Negro warfare" would unleash "all the scenes of desolation attendant upon savage warfare." Similarly, a border state congressman exclaimed that the use of black troops would belittle "the manhood of 20 millions of [white] freemen."

According to public officials, white soldiers would refuse to volunteer if forced to serve with blacks; if drafted, they would desert. A northern white soldier confirmed such beliefs when he exclaimed that the use of black troops "will raise a rebellion in the army that all the abolitionist(s) this Side of hell could not stop." Moreover, the soldier further stated that the "Southern People are rebels to the government but they are White and God never intended a nigger to put white people Down."

At the same time that some whites expressed the belief that blacks would fight "savagely," shock white sensibilities, and undermine the manhood of white soldiers, others argued that blacks were too timid and would not make good soldiers. As late as September 1862, President Lincoln himself declared: "If we arm them . . . I fear that in a few weeks the arms would be in the hands of the rebels." Conversely, some whites feared that blacks would serve honorably and as such make claims for equal treatment. A northern congressman declared: "If you make him the instrument by which your battles are fought, the means by which your victories are won . . . you must treat him as a victor is entitled to be treated, with all decent and becoming respect." Like southern whites, most northerners rejected this prospect. Indeed, by remaining loyal to the Union, northern whites hoped to contain slavery where it existed and to maintain the status quo for free blacks.

At the outset of the war, federal officials not only rejected blacks as soldiers but also repeatedly reassured "loyal southerners" that their "property right" in slaves would be "scrupulously protected." In his 1861 Independence Day speech, Lincoln reiterated the resolve of Union forces to preserve the institution of slavery among loyal pro-Union southerners. At the same time, Congress adopted the so-called Crittenden resolution. Put forward by the Kentucky congressman John J. Crittenden, the resolution reassured southerners that the North only hoped to "preserve the Union." Military officials soon reinforced such pro-slavery pledges of the president and the Congress. When General Benjamin F. Butler took his post in Maryland, he loudly proclaimed the services of the U.S. Army to put down any evidence of slave rebellion and bar fugitives from Union lines. Similar pronouncements were issued by General William S. Harney, Department of the West; General Robert Patterson, at Harpers Ferry; General George B. McClellan, in western Virginia; General Henry W. Haller, in Missouri and western Kentucky; General Don Carlos Buell, in central Kentucky; and General Dix in Maryland.

Accordingly, when federal troops first moved into the South, Union generals returned enslaved blacks to their owners. General Harney stated: "I should as soon expect to hear that the orders of the Government were directed towards the overthrow of any other kind of property as of this [in] negro slaves." When McClellan took command of the Army of the Potomac and fought against slave-built fortifications, he retained his conviction that neither "confiscation of property . . . [n]or forcible abolition of slavery, should be contemplated." As late as February 1862, as Hallers forces entered Tennessee and then the Mississippi area, he reiterated the doctrine of noninterference with the institution of human bondage: "Let us show to our fellow citizens . . . that we come to crush out rebellion . . . [and that] they shall enjoy . . . the same protection of life and property as in former days."

Blacks in the North

Restrictions on black participation in the military were closely intertwined with restrictions on the civil rights of free blacks in the North and South. As discussed in Chapter 9, at the outset of the Civil War, free blacks endured a variety of civil disabilities. Not only did they enjoy few citizenship rights in the South but they also could not testify against whites in the courts of Indiana, Illinois, Iowa, California, and Oregon. With the exception of Massachusetts, northern and western states also barred blacks from jury service. Although most New England and midwestern states accepted blacks into the public schools along with whites, the major cities of Pennsylvania, New Jersey, and southern Ohio established segregated and "unequal" public schools for black and white children. Only five states (Vermont, Massachusetts, Maine, Iowa, and New Hampshire) permitted blacks to vote on an equal footing with whites. Free blacks also faced increasing residential segregation as well as discrimination in hotels and restaurants and on streetcars. In Philadelphia and other northern cities, streetcar companies either excluded blacks altogether or forced them to ride on the outside platform, rain or shine, in heat or cold.

Despite the tight labor market and increasing wartime demand for workers, northern blacks found it exceedingly difficult to enter skilled jobs, expand their entrepreneurial activities, and enter the professions. Even in Boston, where blacks enjoyed a broader range of civil rights than African Americans elsewhere, they were nonetheless circumscribed. As the black Boston attorney John Rock stated:

> We are colonized in Boston. It is five times as difficult to get a home in a good location in Boston as it is in Philadelphia, and it is ten times more difficult for a colored mechanic to get employment than in Charleston. Colored men in business in Massachusetts receive more respect, and less patronage than in any place that I know of. In Boston, we are proscribed in some eating houses, many of the hotels, and all the theatres but one.

For their part, laboring black men could scarcely "keep soul and body together." Moreover, several northern states retained their so-called black laws, which made it illegal for free blacks to settle within their borders without posting a security bond. Periodically, law officers sought to enforce these laws. When they did, some blacks faced reenslavement. In 1863, the state of Illinois convicted eight blacks of entering the state illegally and sold seven into "temporary" enslavement to pay their fines. Northern hostility gained its most violent expression in the New York draft riot of 1863. The Draft Act of 1863 permitted wealthy white men to buy their way out of military service by employing a substitute or by paying a $300 fee. In the summer of 1863, hundreds of working-class New Yorkers took to the streets, attacking African Americans as the most visible and vulnerable symbol of their discontent with the federal government. As we will see, such working-class resistance generated support for the recruitment of blacks to alleviate the demand for white soldiers.

Blacks in the South

In the meantime, the Confederacy not only used enslaved blacks as body servants, cooks, orderlies, and gravediggers but also employed slave labor to build roads, erect fortifications, and transport war supplies. On the home front, black bondsmen and -women continued to cultivate the principal crops of southern agriculture, which supplied their own subsistence needs, white families, and the military. Indeed, some wartime planters encouraged blacks more so than before to grow their own food crops and sell the surplus where possible, while others turned their old and incapacitated blacks out to fend for themselves. At the same time, as the northern states blockaded southern ports and cut off access to northern textile-manufacturing products, planters extended the production of cotton fabrics for military and domestic consumption. Black women often bore the brunt of these new productive activities. According to a formerly enslaved woman on a South Carolina plantation, "My old missus made me weave to make clothes for the soldiers till 12 o'clock at night & I was so tired & my own clothes I had to spin over night." Moreover, industrial bondsmen provided a bulwark in the production of southern weapons of war. In Richmond, Virginia, the Tredegar Iron Works, the Confederate's leading industrial firm, employed nearly six thousand slaves during the Civil War.

To meet the growing manpower needs of the Confederacy, slaveowners increased work loads, floggings, and even death as disciplinary procedures. Even more so than before, runaways became a special target of punishment. Planters en-

This engraving shows the lynching of an African American man, William Jones, at the corner of Clarkson and Hudson Streets during the New York Draft Riot of 1863. *New-York Historical Society*

listed the services of the Confederate troops to execute fugitives recaptured from Union ranks. In one affidavit, collected by the Freedmen's Bureau, a Maryland owner "confessed that in August 1861 he had murdered one of his slaves, Jack Scroggins, by whipping him to death for having escaped to the Federal lines." In South Carolina, a group of Confederate scouts disguised themselves as Union soldiers and approached an enslaved man named Harry and asked him to lead them to Confederate hideouts. When Harry led them to a Confederate encampment, they summarily hanged the man as a "traitor."

Since men outnumbered women and children as runaways, planters leveled brutal reprisals against the families of fugitives. In Kentucky, a black woman recalled how her master's son whipped her "severely" when she refused to do some work that she "was not in a condition to perform." According to her testimony, the man beat her in the presence of his father, who had instructed his son to tie her down and give her "a thousand lashes." On a Georgia plantation, one owner bound the feet of his cook in leg irons: "She had to drag herself around her kitchen all day, and at night she was locked into the corn-house." Faced with the prospects of brutal retaliation, some enslaved people urged white southerners to beat the "Yankees," whereas others volunteered their services as personal servants and even arms bearers for the Confederacy. In New Orleans, for example, some free blacks took up arms as part of the Confederate Louisiana Native Guard. As we will see later, however, as the Union army penetrated the South and defeated Confederates, these units would later join the Union army.

EARLY AFRICAN AMERICAN RESPONSES TO THE WAR

As northern whites excluded blacks from the military and southern whites sought to mobilize them against their own interests, African Americans worked to transform the war into an instrument of their own liberation. In the North, African Americans protested their exclusion from Union forces through letter writing campaigns, newspaper editorials, mass meetings, and resolutions to public officials. Over and over again, they insisted that they were U.S. citizens, that they would fight, and that the war itself was a "divinely inspired" conflict to end human bondage. In a letter to General J. S. Negley, African Americans in Pittsburgh and western Pennsylvania exclaimed:

> We consider ourselves American citizens. . . . [A]lthough deprived of all political rights, we yet wish the government of the United States to be sustained against the tyranny of slavery, and are willing to assist in any honorable way or manner to sustain the present administration.

As citizens, free blacks petitioned legislators to remove the word *white* from militia laws and allow blacks to take up arms against the rebels. As one Massachusetts petition put it, "Such a distinction is anomalous to the spirit of justice and equality pervading all the other laws of the commonwealth. . . . We desire to be recognized by the laws as competent to and worthy of defending our homes and the government that protects these homes." In a letter to the *Daily Atlas and Bee* (19 April 1861), Boston blacks predicted that their services would be needed and that they would fight when the time came: "The colored man will fight,—not as a tool, but as an American patriot. He will fight most desperately, because he will be fighting against his enemy, slavery."

In New York, a convention of blacks exclaimed that "ordinary means, such as Reason, Justice [and] Patriotism" had failed and that "more effective remedies ought now to be thoroughly tried in the shape of warm lead and cold steel, duly administered by two hundred thousand black doctors." Accordingly, blacks organized their own drilling companies, as they often put it, "to the end of becoming better skilled in the use of fire-arms; so that when we shall be called upon by the country, we shall be better prepared to make a ready and fitting response." African Americans also believed that their fight for freedom had the support of "the highest authority" in the "universe." As John Rock, the Boston attorney, put it in a speech:

> I think I see the finger of God in all this. Yes, there is the handwriting on the wall: I came not to bring peace, but the sword. Break every yoke, and let the oppressed go free. I have heard the groans of my people, and am come to deliver them.

Another prospective enlistee, William H. Carney, revealed that he had "a strong inclination" to prepare for the ministry, but when the country called for men, he said that he "could best" serve his God by "serving my country and my oppressed brothers."

Between 1861 and 1862, African Americans offered their services to the War Department in no uncertain terms. In April 1861, Jacob Dodson, a janitor in the U.S. Senate chambers, wrote that "some three hundred" reliable "colored citizens" desire to enter the service for the defense of the [capital] City." Dodson also vouched for his own military qualifications: "I have been three times across the Rocky Mountains with Fremont and others." In Battle Creek, Michigan (October 1861), the black physician G. P. Miller sought permission to raise "five to ten thousand free men to report in sixty days to take any position that may be assigned us." If his men were rejected for regular units, Miller offered them to fight as guerrillas, "if armed and equipped by the government." In Canada, black fugitives offered to return to the United States "as soldiers in the Southern parts during the Summer season, or longer if required." In a letter to the governor of Ohio, Cleveland blacks were even more emphatic:

> We heartily offer you two or more regiments of colored men for that purpose [guarding rebel prisoners] and we will assure you that no one of them shall escape; and we will discharge any duty imposed upon us as soldiers and appertaining to camp duty. And, in our judgment, we could not offer any more severe rebuke to the rebel master.

As northern blacks held mass meetings, passed resolutions, and launched letter writing campaigns, southern blacks "voted for freedom with their feet." In rising numbers, fugitives left the Confederate states and moved into Union territory. As during the revolutionary era, they heightened their resistance to slavery by running away and joining the ranks of the enemy army. When federal forces defeated Confederates in the

SOURCES FROM THE PAST

1863

Testimony on the Number of Fugitives Entering Union Lines After the Emancipation Proclamation

[Fortress Monroe, Va.] May 9, 1863

Question   How many of the people called contrabands, have come under your observation?

Answer   Some 10,000 have come under our control, to be fed in part, and clothed in part, but I cannot speak accurately in regard to the number. This is the rendezvous. They come here from all about, from Richmond and 200 miles off in North Carolina. There was one gang that started from Richmond 23 strong and only 3 got through. . . .

Question   In your opinion, is there any communication between the refugees and the black men still in slavery?

Answer   Yes Sir, we have had men here who have gone back 200 miles.

Question   In your opinion would a change in our policy which would cause them to be treated with fairness, their wages punctually paid and employment furnished them in the army, become known and would it have any effect upon others in slavery?

Answer   Yes—Thousands upon Thousands. I went to Suffolk a short time ago to enquire into the state of things there—for I found I could not get any foot hold to make things work there, through the Commanding General, and I went to the Provost Marshall and all hands— and the colored people actually sent a deputation to me one morning before I was up to know if we put black men in irons and sent them off to Cuba to be sold or set them at work and put balls on their legs and whipped them, just as in slavery; because that was the story up there, and they were frightened and didn't know what to do. When I got at the feelings of these people I found they were not afraid of the slaveholders. They said there was nobody on the plantations but women and they were not afraid of them. One woman came through 200 miles in Men's clothes. The most valuable information we received in regard to the Merrimack and the operations of the rebels came from the colored people and they got no credit for it. I found hundreds who had left their wives and families behind. I asked them "Why did you come away and leave them there?" and I found they had heard these stories, and wanted to come and see how it was. "I am going back again after my wife" some of them have said "When I have earned a little money." "What as far as that?" "Yes" and I have had them come to me to borrow money, or to get their pay, if they had earned a months wages, and to get passes. "I am going for my family" they say. "Are you not afraid to risk it?" "No I know the Way." Colored men will help colored men and they will work along the by paths and get through. . . .

Source: Testimony Before the American Freeman's Inquiry Commission, 9 May 1863. This document appears in Ira Berlin et al., *Free at Last: A Documentary History of Slavery, Freedom, and the Civil War* (New York: The New Press, 1992), pp. 107–110.

Battle of Vicksburg in the summer of 1863, they brought the Mississippi River valley under increasing control, and slaves flocked to Union encampments. By war's end, some five hundred thousand fugitives had moved within Union lines (see box).

The perils of escape fell especially hard on black women. Since they had primary responsibility for large numbers of children, fewer black women escaped than men.

Compared with the prewar years, growing numbers of black women now escaped in family and even community groups. The disruption of war made the prospects of holding on to their children and living among other kin less promising. An enslaved Missouri woman wrote to her husband: "They are treating me worse and worse every day. Our child cries for you." Still, she assured her husband, "Do not fret too much for me for it wont be long before I will be free." Two years into the war, a seventy-year-old Georgia woman led some twenty-two of her children and grandchildren to freedom. The woman and other kin boarded a flatboat and traveled some forty miles down the Savannah River to federal forces. In careful detail, Elizabeth Botume, a northern teacher, described the flight of another woman, who escaped

> with her hominy pot, in which was a live chicken, poised on her head. One child was on her back with its arms tightly clasped around her neck, and its feet about her waist, and under each arm was a smaller child. Her apron was tucked up in front, evidently filled with articles of clothing. Her feet were bare, and in her mouth was a short clay pipe. A poor little yellow dog ran by her side, and a half-grown pig trotted on before.

In another instance, when a Louisiana owner shot and killed the child of one woman as she escaped, she insisted on bringing the dead child into Union lines "to be buried . . . *free.*"

Black runaways took a toll on the southern economy and forced a reorientation of Confederate labor and military policies. Whereas planters largely volunteered the use of slaves during the early war years, they soon resisted the contribution of

The line between fugitives and refugees blurred as the war escalated and thousands of blacks left the plantations. Here a group of fugitives ford the Rappahannock River, Virginia, in July or August 1862, following the Second Battle of Bull Run. *Library of Congress*

bondsmen to the war effort. Southern state militia faced a difficult time recruiting men. As one frustrated official put it, "If there is any more men taken out of this county . . . we may as well give it to the negroes . . . now we have to patrol every night to keep them down." At the same time, as casualties mounted, nonslave-holding whites resented the disproportionate burden of the war effort that fell on them. Consequently, in October 1863, the Confederacy passed a new law that allowed the government to take slaves from their owners for military use. At about the same time, the Confederacy instituted new tax laws that permitted the government to confiscate farm animals and implements in lieu of monetary payments. Such activities angered slaveholders, who increasingly relocated their blacks to the interior, not only to escape the encroachment of Union forces but also to elude the Confederate impressment agents. This process, known as "refugeeing" slaves, further disrupted black families and communities and stimulated even more escapes. When one Georgetown, South Carolina, owner moved enslaved people inland, he soon reported twenty-one of his men leaving "to join the Yankees."

FEDERAL POLICY AND THE ENLISTMENT OF BLACKS

Although black bondsmen and -women increasingly voted for freedom with their feet and undercut the Confederate labor force, only slowly did federal officials turn to the use of blacks as laborers and then soldiers. Before African Americans became combatants on behalf of the Union, they served the war effort in a variety of non-military and semimilitary activities as laborers, spies, scouts, and guides. An estimated two hundred thousand free blacks worked as teamsters, cooks, carpenters, nurses, scouts, and general laborers on a plethora of wartime projects. When federal forces captured and occupied territory along the coast of North Carolina in late 1861 and early 1862, black men built federal forts at New Bern; the upper end of Roanoke Island; and Washington, North Carolina. Vincent Colyer, an agent of the Brooklyn YMCA and superintendent of the organization's poor relief in North Carolina, reported that "these three forts were our chief reliance for defense against the rebels, in case of an attack; and have since been successfully used for that purpose by our forces under Major-Generals Foster and Peck, in the two attempts which have been made by the rebels to retake Newbern." Colyer also described the broad range of other tasks that blacks performed as stevedores, blacksmiths, coopers, wheelwrights, and bridge builders: "The large rail-road bridge across the Trent was built chiefly by them, as were also the bridges across the Batchelor's and other Creeks, and the docks at Roanoke Island and elsewhere."

Behind Union lines, blacks often worked in large gangs under strict supervision of foremen, with insufficient rations, clothing, rest, and medical care. At a post in southern Louisiana, one northern officer stated that his "cattle at home" were "better cared for than these unfortunate persons." Black laborers invariably took jobs that white soldiers detested—that is, "cleaning cesspools, scrubbing privies, and policing grounds." Few black military workers received wages. Instead they received in-kind payments of clothing and food. In loyalist territory, many never received direct compensation at all; instead, military officers issued checks for black labor to slaveowners. One northern employer said that such practices made him "ashamed to look a negro in the face."

The employment of black labor behind Union lines was by no means limited to the South. Some northern municipalities coerced blacks into service on military installations, particularly in southern Ohio. In Cincinnati, according to a governor's report, city officials forced black men to work on fortifications:

> The police acting in concert and in obedience to some common order, in a rude and violent manner arrested the colored men wherever found—in the street, at their places of business, in their homes and hurried them to a mule pen on Plum Street, and thence across the river to the fortifications, giving them no explanation of this conduct and no opportunity to prepare for camp life.

When General Lewis Wallace (later author of *Ben Hur*) received word of these abusive tactics, he demolished the camp and set up headquarters for the voluntary recruitment of the "Black Brigade." On the brigade's discharge after three weeks of intensive labor, Colonel Dickerson praised them for having "labored faithfully, building miles of roads, rifle pits and magazines, and clearing acres of forest land."

The distinction between combat and noncombat laborers blurred considerably in practice. Black men were often asked to pick up arms and defend Union encampments. Captain James B. Tolbert, head of a contraband camp at Pine Bluff, Arkansas, described the "armed services" of black nonmilitary personnel:

> Fifteen of them had arms; and were ordered to hold the point along the river; which they did throughout the action, some of them firing as many as 30 rounds, and one actually ventured out and captured a prisoner. Their total loss is five killed and twelve wounded.

Noncombat laborers not only took up arms behind Union lines but also performed the dangerous tasks of spies, scouts, and guides for federal troops. One observer reported from North Carolina:

> In this work they were invaluable and almost indispensable. They frequently went from thirty to three hundred miles within the enemy's lines; visiting his principal camps and most important posts, and bringing us back important and reliable information. . . . They were pursued on several occasions by bloodhounds, two or three of them were taken prisoners; one of these was known to have been shot, and the fate of the others was not ascertained.

Black men exploited certain stereotypes of their character to become effective spies. In Virginia, Allan Pinkerton, chief of the U.S. Secret Service, reported on the techniques of the spy John Scobell. In addition to being able to read and write, according to Pinkerton, Scobell had "what seemed an inexhaustible stock of negro plantation melodies . . . [and] a charming variety of Scotch ballads, which he sang with a voice of remarkable power and sweetness." More importantly, Pinkerton concluded:

Possessing the talents which he did, I felt sure, that he had only to assume the character of the light-headed, happy darky and no one would suspect the cool-headed, vigilant detective, in the rollicking negro whose aim in life appeared to be to get enough to eat, and a comfortable place to toast his shins.

In successful raids on their camps, Confederate officials frequently complained that "the guides of the enemy are nearly always free negroes and slaves."

As the Union faced difficulties subduing southern rebels on the battlefield, they turned to black soldiers to help prosecute the war and alleviate hardships on whites. Rather than appeal to the justice of black enlistment, northern whites often expressed the desire for black troops in racist terms. Samuel J. Kirkwood, the governor of Iowa, not only urged the use of blacks to fill "menial labor" assignments but also exclaimed: "When this war is over . . . I shall not have any regrets if it is found that a part of the dead are *niggers* and that *all* are not white men." During the war years, a racist poem, presumably by an Irish immigrant, reflected working-class white sentiment. According to the poem, "Sambo's Right to Be Kilt," it was appropriate to allow blacks to die in the place of whites:

Some tell us 'Tis a burnin shame to make the Naygers Fight;
An' That The Thrade [threat] of bein Kilt
Belongs but to the White;
But as For Me, Upon my Soul:
So Liberal are we here,
I'll Let Sambo be murthered instead myself
On every day in the year.

Shortly after General Butler announced his intention to aid slave catchers in Maryland, he reversed himself when he took command of Fortress Monroe in the Virginia Tidewater region in the summer of 1861. As blacks deserted the plantation and moved into his lines, Butler secured permission from the general in chief and the secretary of war to retain such fugitives as "contraband" of war. In August 1861, Congress legalized Butler's policy with passage of the First Confiscation Act, which undercut the Confederate war effort by making "all property" used to support the war "subject of . . . capture wherever found." The law included bondsmen and -women who had been "employed in or upon any fort, navy yard, dock armory, ship, entrenchment, or in any military or naval service." Only in July 1862 did Congress pass the Second Confiscation Act, which proclaimed all slaves owned by southern rebels "forever free of their servitude." At the same time, Congress passed the Militia Act, which allowed federal authorities to use enslaved blacks for "any military or naval service for which they may be found competent." For such service, black men and their families would receive their freedom.

In September 1862, Lincoln issued his preliminary Emancipation Proclamation, which became official on New Year's Day of 1863. Whereas the preliminary edict referred to compensated emancipation and the desirability of exporting free blacks to Africa or some other territory outside the United States, the official order dropped such considerations and affirmed the liberation and recruitment of enslaved blacks into the Union military as key goals. Although the Emancipation Proclamation exempted slaves in the loyal border states and loyalist enclaves of southern territory, it set in motion a set of policies that undermined slavery everywhere. The proclamation specified the use of blacks "to garrison forts, positions, stations, and other places, and to man vessels." (See the Documents section.) In the fall of 1863, the War Department issued General Order #329, which authorized the systematic recruitment of slave men—even in the loyalist border state strongholds of Maryland, Kentucky, Missouri, and Delaware—based on compensated emancipation. Along with the continuing activity of African Americans on their own behalf, federal policy now helped to transform the Civil War into a war of liberation for enslaved and free blacks.

Federal authorities, blacks, and their white abolitionist allies wasted little time pushing the enlistment of black soldiers. As early as January 1863, the secretary of war authorized the state of Massachusetts to raise a black regiment. Massachusetts quickly advertised for black men:

> To Colored Men—Wanted. Good men for the 54th Regiment of Massachusetts Volunteers of African Descent, Col. Robert G. Shaw. $100 bounty at the expiration of term of service. Pay $13.00 a month and State Aid to families. All necessary information can be obtained at the office, corner of Cambridge and North Russell Streets—Lieut. J. W. M. Appleton—Recruiting Officer.

Other northern states—Pennsylvania, Connecticut, and Ohio—soon followed suit. Three months later, the War Department sent General Lorenzo Thomas, adjutant general of the army, to the Mississippi Valley to carry out a full-scale recruitment of black troops in the South. In May 1863, the Union escalated the recruitment of blacks by establishing the Bureau of Negro Troops in the War Department. Although state regiments like the Massachusetts Fifty-Fourth and Fifty-Fifth were quite significant, most black soldiers served as part of the federal U.S. Colored Troops.

Despite the vigorous "fight to fight," recruitment was not easy. Blacks were not eager to give their lives without guarantees that joining the war would indeed purchase the freedom of their people. When recruitment agents first entered black communities, black leaders often complained that not more than ten or twelve men showed an interest. According to one report, as the war dragged on, northern blacks, like northern whites, showed a waning interest in fighting:

> At the beginning of the War . . . every man you met wanted to go to War, but now when they know that hard fighting is to be done, hardships to be suffered and privations endured, it is rather difficult, in fact impossible to get their courage screwed to the fighting pitch.

One Ohio black said simply, "I have no inclination to go to War."

Since the war had absorbed growing numbers of young able-bodied white men, some northern African Americans had gradually improved their economic position by taking jobs that paid much higher wages than before. In addition to expanding employment in established general labor occupations—in hotels, boarding houses, barbershops, restaurants, freight depots, and commercial outlets—the war produced new opportunities in government- and military-related services. Although some free blacks, as noted earlier, faced coercion on these projects, others were able to use them to their advantage. In November 1861, for example, the Washington correspondent of the *Anglo-African* newspaper reported the positive economic impact of the war on blacks in the District of Columbia:

> This being the seat of war all classes here are benefitted by it. Five hundred men find employment each day in the Quartermaster's department. . . . Business of every kind for males has increased fully ten per cent. . . . Three or four thousand men are employed at cutting wood in Virginia around the different fortifications, and on the northern front of Washington. Laundresses are doing a fine business. They have the exclusive wash of entire regiments and the families of U.S. officers; also for the hospital inmates. Many females are securing a comfortable livelihood by peddling little notions around the different camps. In a word, we are all doing well as far as employment is concerned. None need be idle.

Understandably, then, as wartime employment improved for some blacks, they were reluctant to give up their jobs for the uncertainties of military training and warfare. Frustrated with such reluctance on the part of free northern blacks, a white Bostonian declared that "the blacks here are too comfortable to do anything more than talk about freedom." The increasing recruitment activities of black leaders like Martin R. Delany, John Mercer Langston, Henry Highland Garnet, Frederick Douglass, and Mary Ann Shadd Cary helped to change the picture. Frederick Douglass captured the urgent tone of black recruits when he exclaimed:

> There is no time to delay. The tide is at its flood that leads on to fortune. From East to West, from North to South, the sky is written all over Now or Never.

In his recruiting efforts Douglass also appealed to notions of manhood and self-respect:

> Liberty won by white men would lose half its luster. Who would be free themselves must strike the first blow. Better even die free, than to live slaves.

In Nashville, Tennessee, one black leader urged "every able bodied descendent of Africa to rally to arms, for arms alone will achieve our rights." The speaker also identified war with the will of God: "God will rule over our destinies. He will guide us, for he is the friend of the oppressed and downtrodden. The God of battles will watch over us and lead us."

In August 1863, Mary Ann Shadd Cary became the first official woman recruiter for the Union army. Soon thereafter, according to William Still, Cary recruited black men in the West and brought them to Boston: "Her men were always considered the best lot brought to headquarters. Indeed, the examining surgeon never failed to speak of Mrs. Cary's recruits as faultless." In Still's view, Cary's recruitment efforts proved the truth of the old adage, that "it takes a woman to pick out a good man." Other black women—particularly Harriet Jacobs and Josephine

Ruffin—served as unofficial recruiters. By vigorously recruiting black men for military service, these black women demonstrated that they perceived their gender interests in racial terms. Similarly, black men envisioned their fight as a "divinely inspired" way to gain their citizenship, defend their manhood, and retain their integrity. Following a Washington, D.C., meeting where the recruiter stressed the connection between liberty, manhood, honor, and self-respect, 140 black men enlisted in the Union army. As the speaker put it, "When we show that we are men, we can then demand our liberty, as did the revolutionary fathers—peaceably if we can, forcibly if we must."

Under the impact of such vigorous recruitment efforts, growing numbers of black men joined the Union army. After deciding that he could best serve his God by serving his country and liberating slaves, one recruit, William H. Carney, spoke for many when he said, "The sequel is short—*I enlisted for the war.*" In the North, nearly 75 percent of military-age black men soon volunteered for military service, but Union forces recruited their first black regiments in South Carolina, Louisiana, and Kansas. Even before Lincoln's proclamation, the exigencies of war had led to the gradual recruitment of southern blacks. As early as May 1862, General Hunter, commander of the Department of the South, defied War Department orders and recruited the First Regiment of South Carolina Volunteers. Although the War Department forced Hunter to disband most of these units, one company remained active through the entire war. In Kansas (August 1862), General Lane also violated federal guidelines and recruited over five hundred black troops. When the federal government changed its policy toward blacks, the Kansas Colored Volunteers became the first black regiment raised in a free state.

In Louisiana, General Butler pursued a similar policy. He mustered free and enslaved blacks into the First, Second, and Third "Native Guards," with their own black officers. Butler presumably recruited only "free blacks," but he actually ignored the distinctions between slaves, fugitives, and free blacks. In late August 1862, Secretary of War Stanton approved the arming of some five thousand black volunteers in the Department of the South. The order required the emancipation of all male slaves, as well as their wives and their children, who volunteered their service. Accordingly, federal officials initiated the recruitment of the First South Carolina Volunteers at Port Royal. Under the command of the white officer Thomas Wentworth Higginson, an abolitionist and friend of John Brown, the unit received official status as part of the Union army in January 1863. With the exception of the Massachusetts Fifty-Fourth and Fifty-Fifth, all black soldiers entered the federal service as part of the U.S. Colored Troops.

In July 1864, the federal government allowed northern states to meet their draft quotas by recruiting southern slaves and free blacks. The enlistment of black troops soared. By war's end, an estimated 180,000 blacks had served in Union forces. Most of these blacks came from the border and southern states: Kentucky, Delaware, Maryland, and Missouri, 42,000; Tennessee, 20,000; Louisiana, 24,000; Mississippi, 18,000; the remaining Confederate states, 37,000; and all northern states, about 38,000, but this figure represented about three times the proportion of blacks in the total eligible northern population pool. As black men in the Union blue penetrated Confederate territory, they took the initiative, urging blacks to desert the plantations and become part of their liberating forces. Hundreds of enslaved blacks left their owners and marched to Union encampments, where black men were inducted into the military and their families organized into contraband labor camps.

ON THE BATTLEFIELD AND THE FIGHT WITHIN THE FIGHT

Black soldiers fought in an estimated 450 battles. Nearly 40 of these were major engagements, including the Battles of Port Hudson, Milliken's Bend, and Fort Wagner. In these engagements, as in the Revolutionary War, African Americans received praise for valor. In May 1863, two Louisiana regiments of ex-slaves and free blacks attacked Confederate forces at Port Hudson on the lower Mississippi River. Although the assault failed, black soldiers proved their mettle by repeatedly defying enemy artillery fire. According to contemporary historian and ex-slave William Wells Brown:

> Six charges in all were made. . . . Shells from the rebel guns cut down trees three feet in diameter, and they fell, at one time burying a whole company beneath their branches. . . . Seeing it to be a hopeless effort . . . the troops were called off. But had they accomplished anything more than the loss of many of their brave men? yes: they had. . . . [T]he undaunted heroism, and the great endurance of

Although most African American soldiers served in labor battalions, here a group of black Union soldiers, recruited in Tennessee, man an artillery battery. *Chicago Historical Society*

the negro, as exhibited that day, created a new chapter in American history for the colored man.

The white general Nathaniel P. Banks later reported: "The severe test to which they were subjected, and the determined manner in which they encountered the enemy, leaves upon my mind no doubt of their ultimate success." The government, Banks concluded, "will find in this class of troops effective supporters and defenders." Another white officer, in charge of engineers, reported that his "prejudices with regard to negro troops have been dispelled by the battle. . . . The brigade of negroes behaved magnificently and fought splendidly. . . . They are far superior in discipline to the white troops, and just as brave."

Milliken's Bend produced similar results. At this installation on the Mississippi River just above Vicksburg, black soldiers turned back a Confederate assault with furious bayonet charges. In a letter to his aunt, a white captain, M. M. Miller of Galena, Illinois, described the bravery of black soldiers:

> I never more wish to hear the expression, "the niggers won't fight," come with me 100 yards from where I sit, and I can show you the wounds that cover the bodies of 16 as brave, loyal and patriotic soldiers as ever drew bead on a Rebel. The enemy charged us so close that we fought with our bayonets, hand to hand. . . . It was a horrible fight, the worst I was ever engaged in—not even excepting Shiloh. . . . I can say for them that I never saw a braver company of men in my life.

In July 1863, the Massachusetts Fifty-Fourth Colored Troops attacked Fort Wagner in the Charleston, South Carolina, harbor. Under the command of the white colonel Robert G. Shaw, black troops launched charge after charge. Despite heavy artillery fire that cut "wide swaths" out of their ranks, black troops fought their way into the fort, where Shaw was killed. Despite the death of their commander, the Fifty-Fourth continued to overpower their enemy. Only the failure of white troops to come forward forced them to retreat. About 250 of the 600 black men who launched the attack lost their lives (some accounts say 1,500 blacks died). Lewis Douglass, the son of Frederick Douglass, participated in the attack. He later wrote to his future wife:

> Dear Amelia: I have been in two fights, and am unhurt. I am about to go in another I believe to-night. Our men fought well on both occasions. The last was desperate we charged that terrible battery on Morris Island known as Fort Wagener. . . . This regiment has established its reputation as a fighting regiment not a man flinched, though it was a trying time. Men fell all around me. A shell would explode and clear a space of twenty feet, our men would close up again, but it was no use we had to retreat, which was a very hazardous undertaking. How I got out alive I cannot tell, but I am here. . . . Remember if I die I die in a good cause.

An estimated 10,000 blacks served in the U.S. Navy. As early as September 1861, the navy accepted the enlistment of blacks. As in the army, black naval personnel were initially restricted to the bottom ranks as "first class boys." By 1862, however, the navy opened the rank of seaman to blacks and thus provided more mobility for black naval recruits than for their army counterparts. Still, although blacks served in a wide range of naval occupations, they were barred from the rank of petty officer. Nonetheless, blacks made up nearly 25 percent of the country's naval forces. Robert and John Smalls of South Carolina became the most renowned black naval heroes when they delivered the Confederate vessel *Planter* to Union forces in May 1862. As Confederate officers slept ashore, the Smalls and seven other enslaved men, along with their wives and children, steered the craft out of Charleston Harbor into the waters patrolled by the Union navy. It was a daring feat. On the one hand, the crew had to carefully navigate past enemy guns by flying the Confederate flag. On the other, before the Union navy could fire on and sink the craft, the Smalls' party had to lower the Confederate colors and hoist a white flag of surrender. For this accomplishment, Robert Smalls received an appointment in the Union navy.

Both black civilians and black enlisted men aided the operations of the Union navy in southern waters. They served as cooks, stewards, and laborers. They also joined raids on nearby plantations, stole supplies, and liberated slaves. According to an account by George W. Reed, a black sailor aboard the U.S. gunboat *Commodore Reed*:

> Our crew are principally colored; and a braver set of men never trod the deck of an American ship. We have been on several expeditions recently. . . . At first, there was a little prejudice against our colored men going on shore, but it soon died away. We succeeded in capturing 3 fine horses, 6 cows, 5 hogs, 6 sheep, 3 calves, an abundance of chickens, 600 pounds of pork, 300 bushels of corn, and succeeded in liberating from the horrible pit of bondage 10 men, 6 women, and 8 children. The principal part of the men have enlisted on this ship.

Indeed, according to recent historians, black seamen played a "primary" role in the success of the federal navy during the Civil War.

Similar to their part in antebellum resistance movements, black women enhanced the struggle for freedom. In Vienna, Virginia, Lucy Carter served as a spy for the Sixteenth New York Cavalry. In 1862, Susie Baker King Taylor escaped from bondage with her family and joined the Union encampment at St. Catherine's Island in South Carolina. She then moved to Camp Saxton in Beauford, South Carolina, where she became a laundress and nurse for Company E. She later described the suffering that she sought to relieve:

> About fo[u]r o'clock, July 2, the charge was made. . . . When the wounded arrived . . . the first one brought in was Samuel Anderson of our company. He was badly wounded. Then others of our boys, some with legs off, arm gone, foot off, and wounds of all kinds imaginable.

Aided by the white southern abolitionist Elizabeth Van Lew of Richmond, the ex-slave Elizabeth Bowser infiltrated the Confederacy by serving as a domestic in the household of President Jefferson Davis. Pretending illiteracy and partial insanity, Bowser gathered crucial information. She not only read letters and dispatches from the Confederate war front but also absorbed details from conversations during dinner time and conferences.

Sojourner Truth and Harriet Tubman also continued their abolitionist activities during the Civil War years. In her Battle Creek, Michigan, home, Truth went from door to door collecting food for Michigan's First Colored Regiment, stationed at Camp Ward in Detroit. In 1864, Truth moved to Washington, D.C., where she served as a nurse to soldiers and aided refugees and their families. In Washington, Truth also met the seamstress Elizabeth Keckley, who later lost a son in action, and helped to form the Contraband Relief Association (CRA). An organization of black women, the CRA assisted former slaves who flooded into the District of Columbia during the Civil War. Black women spearheaded such relief efforts throughout the urban North and the Union-occupied areas of the South. Their efforts on behalf of black bondsmen and -women were especially important because federal authorities at first avoided responsibility for the families of blacks who deserted plantations and entered Union lines as laborers and later as soldiers. The government initially relied on civilian superintendents of northern black and white churches and benevolent societies to do this work. Contraband relief societies distributed food, clothing, bibles, schoolbooks, and medical supplies to fugitives in Union-occupied territory. Yet, like most northerners and federal officials, these aid societies believed that any aid to freedmen and -women should be temporary, because they feared that "charity" would create a permanently dependent class of black poor. Thus, the activities of black women supplemented and even tempered the often harsh judgments and practices of these white allies.

For her part, Harriet Tubman served as a spy and military scout. Some contemporaries described Tubman as "the head of the intelligence service in the Department of the South." Others described her as "the only American woman to lead troops black and white on the field of battle, as she did in the Department of the South." Tubman traveled widely throughout the war zone, General David Hunter having issued her a pass authorizing her to go "wherever she wishes to go." The pass also allowed her "free passage, at all times, on all government transports." Because she was dark-skinned, wore a bandanna, and seemed to fit the "Mammy" stereotype, her effectiveness as a spy was even greater. In July 1863, the Boston Commonwealth reported her conspicuous role in Colonel James Montgomery's attack on Confederate forces along the Combahee River in South Carolina:

Col. Montgomery and his gallant band of 300 black soldiers, under the guidance of a black woman, dashed into the enemy's country, struck a bold and effective blow, destroying millions of dollars worth of commissary stores, cotton and lordly dwellings, and striking terror into the heart of rebeldom, brought off near 300 slaves and thousands of dollars worth of property, without losing a man or receiving a scratch. It was a glorious consummation.

The Boston paper also reported: "Many and many times she has penetrated the enemy's lines and discovered their situation and condition, and escaped without injury, but not without extreme hazard."

African Americans served the Union cause against great odds. They faced discrimination in modes of recruitment, pay, military occupations, and aid to their wives, widows, and children. Although most blacks volunteered their services, some entered the military against their will. Federal officials and municipal authorities often arrested black men, offering them enlistment in the military as an option to prison. In Helena, Arkansas, one contemporary observer reported that recruiting officers came among blacks and forcibly "carried away . . . the Best men leaving some families without any men to assist them." In Louisville, a black soldier offered a sworn testimony that federal officers coerced him into service:

> When Col. Glenn wanted me to enlist he had me brought up to his office. I told him I did not want to enlist. Lt. Col. Glenn asked me "What in hell was the reason," I did not want to go. He then turned a round to the Sergeant who stood close by and told him to "take this damned nigger to jail," that I was but a "dam[n]ed Secesh [secessionist] nigger anyway." I then replied, "Well rather than go to jail I will join." I was mustered at Louisville by Capt. Womack.

In another case, a Lexington slaveowner requested the arrest and enlistment of a bondsman who had refused to serve him any longer "and affirms that he is as free as I am."

Discrimination in the Military

On entering the Union ranks, African Americans received unequal pay, restrictions on promotions, and maltreatment by white officers in the racially segregated units. Although the Militia Act stipulated the payment of rations and $10 per month (minus $3 for clothing) to black enlistees, white privates received $13 per month plus a $3.50 clothing allowance. Federal authorities also levied a special tax on the pay of black soldiers for the care of their dependents but exempted whites. Moreover, with the exception of the Louisiana "Native Guards," fewer than one hundred African Americans received the rank of commissioned officer. Black men gained such offices mainly as chaplains and surgeons, outside the chain of command. Even so, as commissioned and noncommissioned officers, they received the same pay as privates.

Black men endured not only unequal pay and restrictions on their access to officer slots but excessive fatigue duty as well. On one occasion, Charles P. Bowditch, a captain in the Massachusetts Fifty-Fourth, wrote: "The negroes are kept at work digging trenches, hauling logs and cannon, loading ammunition, etc. . . . They keep us at work pretty steadily. I have been on fatigue duty about thirty hours out of the last seventy." On another occasion, Bowditch wrote that blacks were also ordered "to lay out camps, pitch tents, dig wells, etc. for white regiments who have lain idle until the work was finished for them." In December 1863, General Daniel Ullman, commander of the Louisiana Corps de'Afrique, complained to the Senate

Military Committee that blacks were not only given excessive fatigue duty but also outfitted with inferior equipment as soldiers:

> Since I have been in command such has been the amount of fatigue work thrust upon the organization that it has been the utmost difficulty that any time could be set aside for drill. . . . Then, again I have been forced to put in their hands arms almost entirely unserviceable, and in other respects their equipments have been of the poorest kind. . . . I assure you that these poor fellows are deeply sensible to this gross injustice.

Although the War Department would issue orders barring discrimination in fatigue duty in June 1864, such unequal practices nonetheless continued through the war years.

Black men also faced the greatest risks of injuries and loss of life in combat. A third of black enlisted men, nearly double the rate of whites, were listed as dead or missing by war's end. These figures were not only the product of discrimination behind Union lines but also the result of southern attitudes and policies toward black soldiers. The Confederacy defined blacks as insurrectionists against the state, a capital offense. Although recent scholars argue that the Confederacy failed to implement this policy in practice, Confederate officers and their men nonetheless carried out special punitive measures against blacks, compared with those against white Union soldiers. The Fort Pillow Massacre became the most infamous example of wartime racial injustice. Located on the Mississippi River, Fort Pillow was garrisoned by some 570 Union troops, nearly 50 percent blacks.

Under the command of General Nathan Bedford Forrest, Confederate troops attacked and captured Fort Pillow on 16 April 1864. According to a congressional committee, Confederate soldiers massacred an estimated 300 troops, mainly blacks. When the congressional committee later interrogated twenty-one black survivors of the massacre, they uniformly recalled the shooting and killing of men "in cold blood" after they had surrendered. According to the testimony of one survivor, when one Confederate officer urged the men to stop killing the blacks, another officer rebuked him, saying "Damn it, let them go on; it isn't our law to take any niggers prisoners; kill every one of them." In an editorial of the Fort Pillow tragedy, the *Christian Recorder* partly blamed the federal government for its unequal treatment of black soldiers:

> We say, emphatically, that the massacre, at Fort Pillow, has been invited by the tardiness of the government and the action of Congress. While they have professed to regard every man wearing the U.S. uniform, as being equal in theory, they have acted towards the black soldiers, in such a way, as to convince the confederate government that they, themselves, do not regard the black soldiers as equal to the white. The rebels have taken advantage of this equivocation, to commit just such horrible butchery as that at Fort Pillow.

Following Fort Pillow, however, blacks fought with even greater determination. Some even called for an avengement of Fort Pillow: "Swear anew never to cease fighting. . . . [Make] a rebel bite the dust for every hair of those three hundred of our black brethren massacred at Fort Pillow." Thus, as one white soldier from Pennsylvania put it in a letter back home, "The Johnies [Confederate soldiers] are not as afraid of us as they are of the Mokes [black troops]. When they charge they will not take any prisoners, if they can help it. Their cry is, 'Remember Fort Pillow.'"

Union officials also neglected and even mistreated the families of black soldiers. Although black women served the war effort as laundresses, cooks, seamstresses, and nurses, the wartime demand for able-bodied men far outstripped the demand for women. Thus, black women, children, the elderly, and the infirm swelled the ranks of refugees. Military officers and philanthropic groups alike identified black women with "vice and disease"—"a curse" to the soldier as well as to themselves. Some officers enacted draconian measures. In the fall of 1864, for example, Major General Foster, commander of the Union army in South Carolina, ordered "the arrest and forced labor" of black women without any visible means of support. Foster also barred such women from visiting their kinsmen in army camps. Arguing that their presence slowed troop movements and threatened the outbreak of epidemics, military authorities destroyed the encampments of black women and their families outside Fort Nelson, Kentucky.

Enslaved women also faced rape and sexual abuse at the hands of Union as well as Confederate soldiers. According to one eyewitness account, at Fortress Monroe in Virginia, four Union soldiers

From the early years of the war, black women served Union forces as nurses, cooks, and camp servants. On the far right we see a black woman, identified as Mrs. Fairfax, who served as chief cook in the Union camp of General Fitz John Porter, Army of the Potomac, Harrison's Landing, Virginia, August 1862. *Library of Congress*

went to the house of two colored men (father and son-in-law). Two of them seized a colored woman in the front yard, each in turn gratifying his brutal lusts, while the other stood guard with sword and pistol. The other two went to the house, one stopping at the door to stand guard. The other after a desperate struggle, succeeded in ravishing a young woman in the house in the presence of her father and grandfather.

Following the rape of a nine-year-old black girl by a group of his Union comrades, one white soldier wrote home from South Carolina: "While on picket guard I witnessed misdeeds that made me ashamed of America." In Hanover County, Virginia, another group of Union soldiers stopped five young black women and "cut their arms, legs, and backs with razors." White officers as well as enlisted men showed a disdain for black women and reinforced such sexual assaults. In his testimony before the Freedmen's Inquiry Commission, General Saxton claimed that "the colored women are proud to have illicit intercourse with white men."

The Fight for Equal Pay

African Americans did not accept discriminatory treatment without a fight. They soon protested against "the gross injustice." Black soldiers directed their greatest protests against unequal pay and neglect of their families. In June 1863, a black corporal, James Henry Gooding, wrote to President Lincoln: "Now your excellency, we have done a Soldier's duty. . . . Why can't we have a Soldier's pay?" When federal authorities rejected their claims, the men of the Massachusetts Fifty-Fourth fought without pay to protest the inequity. The state of Massachusetts offered to supplement their federal allowance, placing them on parity with white soldiers, but blacks rejected the offer. "In effect," they said, the offer "advertises us to the world as holding out for money and not from principle, that we sink our manhood in consideration of a few more dollars. . . . What false friend has been misrepresenting us to the Governor, to make him think that our necessities outweigh our self respect." From Jacksonville, Florida, a soldier in the Eighth U.S. Colored Troops wrote to officials for relief for his wife and children: "When we lie down to sleep, the pictures of our families are before us, asking for relief from their sufferings. How can men do their duty, with such agony in their minds?"

As black men faced increasing casualties on the field of battle, their patience wore thin and their demands for equal treatment intensified (see box). In a letter from the war front (around February 1864), Captain Bowditch of the Massachusetts Fifty-Fourth reported the contents of an anonymous letter sent to one of his commanders. The letter stated "that if we are not paid by the 1st of March, the men would stack arms and do no more duty, and that more than half the regiment were of that way of thinking." Later that year, a black soldier of the Fifty-Fifth was court-martialed and executed for his part in a "near mutiny." When they protested against injustice, authorities jailed twenty men of Rhode Island's Fourteenth Colored Heavy Artillery. At about the same time, military officials court-martialed and shot Sergeant William Walker of the Third South Carolina Volunteers. Walker had led his men to the captain's quarters and ordered them to lay down their arms and "re-

SOURCES FROM THE PAST

1863

Corporal James Henry Gooding Writes to President Lincoln Protesting Unequal Pay for Black Soldiers

Morris Island [S.C.] Sept 28th 1863

Your Excelency will pardon the presumtion of an humble individual like myself, in addressing you. but the earnest Solicitation of my Comrades in Arms, besides the genuine interest felt by myself in the matter is my excuse, for placing before the Executive head of the Nation our Common Grievance: On the 6th of the last Month, the Paymaster of the department, informed us, that if we would decide to recieve the sum of $10 (ten dollars) per month, he would come and pay us that sum, but, that, on the sitting of Congress, the Regt would, in his opinion, be *allowed* the other 3 (three). He did not give us any guarantee that this would be, as he hoped, certainly *he* had no authority for making any such guarantee, and we can not supose him acting in any way interested. Now the main question is. Are we *Soldiers*, or are we LABOURERS. We are fully armed, and equipped, have done all the various Duties, pertaining to a Soldiers life, have conducted ourselves, to the complete satisfaction of General Officers, who, were if any, prejudiced *against* us, but who now accord us all the encouragement, and honour due us: have shared the perils, and Labour, of Reducing the first stronghold, that flaunted a Traitor Flag: and more, Mr President. Today, the Anglo Saxon Mother, Wife, or Sister, are not alone, in tears for departed Sons, Husbands, and Brothers. The patient Trusting Decendants of Africs Clime, have dyed the ground with blood, in defense of the Union, and Democracy. Men too your Excellency, who know in a measure, the cruelties of the Iron heel of oppression, which in years gone by, the very Power, their blood is now being spilled to maintain, ever ground them to the dust. But When the war trumpet sounded o'er the land, when men knew not the Friend from the Traitor, the Black man laid his life at the Altar of the Nation,—and he was refused. When the arms of the Union, were beaten, in the first year of the War, And the Executive called more food. for its ravaging maw, again the black man begged, the privelege of Aiding his Country in her need, to be again refused, And now, he is in the War: and how has he conducted himself? Let their dusky forms, rise up, out the mires of James Island, and give the answer. Let the rich mould around Wagners parapets be upturned, and there will be found an Eloquent answer. Obedient and patient, and Solid as a wall are they. all we lack, is a paler hue, and a better acquaintance with the Alphabet. Now Your Excellency, We have done a Soldiers Duty. Why cant we have a Soldiers pay?

Source: Ira Berlin et al., *Free at Last: A Documentary History of Slavery, Freedom, and the Civil War* (New York: New Press, 1992), pp. 461–463.

sign" from an army that failed to uphold its "contract" with the men. In the wake of such punitive decisions by military tribunals, African American soldiers added military justice to their list of grievances. In an anonymous letter to the *Liberator,* one black sergeant appealed for black commissioned officers and representation on military courts: "We want to be represented in court martial, where so many of us are liable to be tried and sentenced. We want to demonstrate our ability to rule, as we have demonstrated our willingness to obey. In short, we want simple justice."

On the home front, black servicemen gained the support of black leaders and their white allies. In Baltimore, the African Methodist Episcopal (AME) churchman Rev. J. P. Campbell supported the movement for equal pay based on the expectation of equal citizenship:

> We ask for equal pay and bounty, not because we set a greater value upon money than we do upon human liberty, . . . but we contend for equal pay and bounty upon the principle, that if we receive equal pay and bounty when we go into the war, we hope to receive equal rights and privileges when we come out of the war.

In April 1864, the AME *Christian Recorder* was even more direct. The paper linked pay equity to success on the battlefield:

> We, in the name of God and humanity . . . call upon Congress to at once pass a law, that these men shall at once be paid the same as all other soldiers are paid. . . . We ask that Congress will remember the words of the Lord God: "Thou shalt not muzzle the ox that treadeth out the corn." Will Congress violate that plain and positive language of the eternal Jehovah? We are frank to say, that God will not let us and our armies have success, until those who have it in their power to do right, do it.

On 15 June 1864, black soldiers finally prevailed. Congress enacted equal pay legislation, retroactive to 1 January 1864, for all black soldiers who had obtained their freedom on or before 19 April 1861. When this distinction between free men and freedmen caused friction over pay, several regiments instituted the "Quaker Oath," which allowed fugitives to claim their freedom by the "law of God" and receive retroactive pay for actual length of their service. Following receipt of this back pay, black soldiers celebrated, and morale soared. After eighteen months, as one officer of the Massachusetts Fifty-Fourth wrote: "Nine hundred men received their money; nine hundred stories rested on the faces of those men . . . now a petty carnival prevails. The fiddle and other music long neglected enlivens the tents day and night. Songs burst out everywhere; dancing is incessant." A sergeant in the Fifty-Fifth wrote simply: "We had a glorious celebration."

The Struggle for Full Citizenship

The "fight to fight" and the struggle for "equal pay" were deeply rooted in the fight for full citizenship for free blacks. Throughout the war years, free blacks intensified their battle against disfranchisement, segregation, and exclusion from the institutional, cultural, and political life of the nation. In February 1865, the *New Orleans Tribune* attacked segregated and unequal institutions: "The strength of the United States will require that the dictates of equity and justice be heeded. A country cannot be powerful unless the people be made one nation. We want to have one country; let us therefore have one law." Free blacks repeatedly assailed racial barriers in jury service, education, public accommodations, and especially voting. The struggle against exclusion from jury service emerged most forcefully in California, where the *Pacific Appeal,* edited by Philip Bell, kept the issue before the public and law makers. In an April 1862 editorial, the editor declared that "such laws are disgraceful to the statutes of our state, are relics of barbarism and slavery, retard the wheels of justice, degrade our manhood, and inflict irreparable damage on our rights and liberties." The editor also attacked the exclusion of blacks from testifying against whites. So long as such laws remained on the books, the editor concluded, "so long will we be fitting subjects for assaults on our persons and property, by knavish and brutal white men, who, knowing we have no protection in law, think they can rob and murder us with impunity." Under the leadership of John Jones, a free black businessman, Chicago blacks attacked the "black codes." In 1864, they formed the Repeal Association and soon secured some eleven thousand signatures on a petition urging the legislature to repeal the black codes. The petitioners charged the "black laws" with "our present degraded condition" and demanded, "in the name of the great republic," the same treatment as other citizens of the state.

In Philadelphia, blacks protested racial discrimination on the city's streetcars. During 1861 and 1862, the Philadelphian William Still circulated a petition requesting the Board of Presidents of the city railway company to "rescind the rules indiscriminately excluding colored persons from the inside of the cars." In short, the petition asked officials to stop forcing blacks to ride on the front platform outside streetcars:

> Riding on the platform of a bitter cold day like this I need not say is almost intolerable, but to compel persons to pay the same as those who enjoy comfortable seats inside by a good fire, seems quite atrocious. . . . Before I arrived at my destination it began to snow, which, as I was already thoroughly chilled with the cold, made the platform utterly intolerable.

African Americans waged perhaps their most vigorous fight against restrictions on the vote. In New York, blacks campaigned against the discriminatory property requirement for voting. Whereas white men had unrestricted access to the state's franchise, black New Yorkers had to demonstrate ownership of $250 worth of property. To repeal this restriction, New York blacks formed "suffrage committees" throughout the state. As early as 1860, the New York City and County Suffrage Committee of Colored Citizens urged voters to repeal the property law: "Principles of justice . . . to the state itself, require that the basis of voting should be equal to all." Three years later, Kansas blacks issued a similar appeal to the white citizens of the state:

> We ask you the right of suffrage. . . . This government was founded in the interest of Freedom . . . to deprive any portion of the native population of this country of so essential a right as that of suffrage, is to do violence to the genious of American institutions, and is a departure from the aims of the illustrious founders of the Republic.

Black soldiers fought in about 450 battles during the Civil War. In June 1863 African American soldiers turned back a Confederate assault at Milliken's Bend, located on the Mississippi River just above Vicksburg. *Corbis*

Similarly, in May 1864, five North Carolina free blacks traveled to the White House and delivered a petition to Lincoln. The petition urged the president "to finish the noble work" that he had started with the Emancipation Proclamation. More specifically, the petitioners asked the president to grant "that greatest of privileges . . . the right of suffrage, which will greatly extend our sphere of usefulness." In Louisiana, in September 1862, free blacks established a new bilingual French and English newspaper, *L'Union,* and appealed for full citizenship rights, including the vote. In its inaugural issue, the paper proclaimed "the Declaration of Independence as the basis of its platform" and the fight for "true republicanism, democracy, without shackles" as its primary goal.

Although internal class, color, and cultural conflicts did not disappear during the war years, they were less prominent than before. Louisiana blacks rejected an effort to enfranchise "light-skinned" blacks while leaving darker-skinned people of color "half-free." The *New Orleans Tribune* denounced the effort:

> Colored men desire political advancement and equal rights, but they do not desire the humbling of their brothers to serve as foot-walks for the attainment of privileges that are denied to the men of our race who are presently spilling their blood for the defense of the country.

In October 1864, black representatives from seven southern and eleven northern states met in Syracuse, New York. The convention called for "the elective franchise in all the states now in the Union, and the same in all such states as may come into the Union here after." To coordinate the day-to-day details of the campaign, the attendees also formed the National Equal Rights League.

Under the presidency of John Mercer Langston of Ohio, the Equal Rights League soon established state and local chapters across the country. Strong state units soon emerged in Ohio, Michigan, New York, Pennsylvania, Tennessee, and North Carolina. In early 1865, following a meeting of the Louisiana Equal Rights League, the *New Orleans Tribune* commented on the cross-class nature of the organization:

> There were seated side by side the rich and the poor, the literate and educated man, and the country laborer, hardly released from bondage, distinguished only by the natural gifts of the mind. There, the rich landowners, the opulent tradesmen, recorded motions offered by humble mechanics and freedmen. Ministers of the gospel, officers and privates of the U.S. Army, men who handle the sword or the pen, merchants and clerks, all classes of society were represented; and united in a common thought: the actual liberation from social and political bondage.

The End of the War

Although African Americans served against great odds, their homefront and battlefield activities helped to push the conflict into its final phases. After a brief but solid stand against Union forces, the Confederate army faced increasing reverses on the field of battle. Confederate officials like Secretary of State Judah Benjamin and leading Mississippi planters like J. L. Alcorn suggested the emancipation of enslaved blacks as a wartime measure, designed to secure Confederate independence. Such men expressed a preference for Confederate independence above the institution of slavery per se. As early as January 1864, rebel officers in the Tennessee area recommended the training and use of slaves as soldiers. In a report to their commanding officer, General Patrick R. Claiborne, the Confederate officers concluded: "As between the loss of independence and the loss of slavery, we assume that every patriot will freely give up the latter." Similarly, in a letter to a Confederate senator, General Robert E. Lee urged the government to train and enlist slave soldiers "without delay," even "if it ends in subverting slavery" and freeing the slaves. Thus, in February 1865, for example, under pressure from Robert E. Lee and other Confederate generals, the Confederate congress approved the recruitment of bondsmen into the southern army. The law stipulated that such men would be given their freedom in exchange for military service, but the Union defeated the Confederacy before the plan was put into effect.

The Confederacy degenerated rapidly after the fall of Atlanta to General William T. Sherman's army in September 1864. Sherman's troops marched across Georgia to the sea, taking Savannah and then moving on across South Carolina, exposing the Confederacy to some of its greatest losses of property and slaves as blacks deserted the plantations and followed Sherman's army. Partly out of desperation and partly out of hope, hundreds of blacks abandoned the land and joined Sherman's march. In his own words, Sherman reported that on his arrival "the negroes were simply frantic with joy. Whenever they heard my name, they clustered about my horse, shouted and prayed." As Sherman's troops stormed across the Deep South, Ulysses S. Grant, general in chief of the U.S. Army, pushed the Confederate general Robert E. Lee into the trenches of Petersburg and Richmond, which soon brought the war to a close at Appomattox Court House in April 1865. Over six hundred thousand soldiers had lost their lives in the conflict. When the war finally ended, African Americans had played a major role in their own liberation. By war's end, sixteen black men had received the Congressional Medal of Honor, including four for their services in the U.S. Navy. As Grant put it, "All that have [been] tried have fought bravely."

After Lee's surrender at Appomattox, word spread to enslaved blacks in different and uneven ways. Black soldiers, Freedmen's Bureau officials, army officers, and former slaveholders themselves all informed bondsmen and -women of their new legal status. Even before the end of 1864, Unionist governments in Arkansas, Louisiana, West Virginia, and Maryland had emancipated slaves. Tennessee and Missouri enacted similar measures in early 1865. In Texas, where black people still celebrate "Juneteenth" (June 19) as Emancipation Day, Confederates surrendered two months after Appomattox. In Delaware and Kentucky, loyalist slaveholders resisted emancipation until ratification of the Thirteenth Amendment (December 1865), which stated forthrightly: "Neither slavery nor involuntary servitude, except as a punishment for crime whereof the party shall have been duly convicted, shall exist within the United States, or any place subject to their jurisdiction."

The collapse of slavery also signaled the fall of certain restrictions on the rights of free blacks at the federal, state, and local levels. In March 1865, Congress repealed an early-nineteenth-century law that prohibited blacks from carrying the U.S. mail. In 1864, the United States lifted the ban on blacks testifying against whites in federal courts. In 1863, California repealed its law prohibiting blacks from giving testimony against whites in courts of law. Similarly, by early 1865, Illinois had repealed its black laws, which restricted black settlement in the state and limited their rights before the law. In March of the same year, the District of Columbia outlawed discrimination against blacks on its streetcars. Sojourner Truth, who now lived and worked among freedmen in Arlington, Virginia, soon tested the new law. According to her biographer and friend Olive Gilbert, when Sojourner entered the car,

> the angry conductor told her to go forward where the horses were, or he would put her out. Quietly seating herself, she informed him that she was a passenger. . . . She [also] told him that she was neither a Marylander nor a Virginian to fear his threats; but was from the Empire State of New York, and knew the laws as well as he did. . . . Sojourner rode farther than she needed to go. . . . She left the car feeling very happy.

REHEARSAL FOR RECONSTRUCTION

The Civil War not only resulted in the destruction of slavery and the expansion of civil rights but also set in motion the making of a free black proletariat and the rise of a free black yeomanry. The federal government, military officials, businessmen, churches, and benevolent societies mediated this transformation of enslaved people into free workers and landowners on the one hand, and that of slaveowners into employers and landlords on the other. It was a complicated process. Although northern whites hoped to impose capitalist notions of free, market-driven wage labor on the South, ex-slaveowners hoped to retain as many of the coercive features of bondage as possible. African Americans also had their own ideas about land and labor. They rejected not only slavery but also key features of capitalist ideas of wage labor and landownership. Specifically, they accepted the idea that they should be "free to contract" the terms of their own labor, but like many other workers, they rejected the idea that the "stick of hunger" and the "carrot of property" were sufficient to ensure social justice in the workplace, in the home, or in the community. Freedmen and -women also believed that land could help liberate them from slavery and dependence, but they did not believe that land was an "alienable commodity" subject to market forces. On the contrary, African Americans retained ideas about common uses of land rather than absolute rights of ownership and disposal. They believed that land derived its value from the labor and suffering of those who made it productive. Thus, rather than just any piece of land, blacks hoped to occupy the land of their birth that generations of their families and communities had made productive.

In March 1865, Lincoln signed congressional legislation establishing the Bureau of Refugees, Freedmen, and Abandoned Land (or Freedmen's Bureau) to oversee the transition from slavery to freedom. Although the government charged the agency with distributing food, clothing, and medical supplies to refugees—black and white—it failed to approve a budget for its operations. Consequently, the bureau had to rely on the resources of the War Department for its material base and even the latter's personnel to execute the bureau's mission, which also included support for the educational and religious pursuits of freed people and, above all, the resumption of plantation agriculture on the basis of free wage labor. In addition to the military and the Freedmen's Bureau, the U.S. Treasury Department and northern businessmen and philanthropic societies also played key roles in the transition of previously enslaved blacks into freedmen and -women.

The struggle over the terms of labor and landownership emerged most clearly in the "contraband camps" of the South Carolina Sea Islands and southern Louisiana. Since large numbers of Sea Island planters abandoned their land and slaves in the wake of Union invasion, bondsmen and -women gained extraordinary opportunities to cultivate the land on their own terms. Given the high demand for black men as soldiers and military laborers, black women greatly outnumbered men on some of these establishments. Rather than cultivating the established staple crops, however, black men and women focused on subsistence crops. Their decision displeased federal officials, northern businessmen, and white abolitionists, who hoped to reap private profit and public revenue while demonstrating the "superiority" of "free labor" over "slave labor." In early 1865, the *New York Times* editorialized that "white ingenuity and enterprise ought to direct black labor." More directly, however, the *Times* declared that the production of cotton required "the white brain employing the black labor."

In February 1862, Secretary of Treasury Salmon P. Chase appointed Edward L. Pierce, a Boston attorney, to supervise the cultivation of cotton with free black labor on the Sea Islands. Pierce enlisted the aid of freedmen's societies in New York, Philadelphia, and Boston and appointed some fifty special agents to supervise the plantations. These northerners soon instituted their own version of coerced labor. Instead of the lash, employers denied ex-slaves food, clothing, and other necessities of life. Since Confederates regularly raided the slave-run plantations, demolishing houses and destroying and/or stealing crops, household furnishings, and livestock, federal authorities relocated large numbers of blacks to islands near Port Royal Sound, where bondsmen and -women became dependent on direct government support for subsistence and protection. As enslaved people faced these difficult conditions, they gradually accepted wage labor under the supervision of northern capitalist, philanthropic, governmental, and military organizations.

The coercive features of the new labor system emerged even more clearly in southern Louisiana, where General Nathaniel Banks met with loyalist planters and placed black workers on free labor contracts. In exchange for planter loyalty, Banks promised to use the U.S. Army to discipline and regularize the black labor force. Rather than seeking the consent of blacks, he required all able-bodied men to enter contracts or risk arrest as vagrants. Although the contract specified a 5 percent share of the crop or a wage of $3 per month plus food, housing, and medical care, it also stipulated that blacks could not leave the plantations without the permission of their employers. Backed up by the force of the Union army, understandably, many slaveowners declared loyalty as a means of protecting and recovering their perceived "property right" in slaves. By war's end, some 474,000 blacks had participated in a variety of federally sponsored programs of free labor: in the Upper South, 203,000; in the Mississippi Valley, 125,000; in the South Carolina Sea Islands, the south Atlantic coast, and the Sherman Reserve, 48,000; and in southern Louisiana, 98,000.

Employers, military officials, and benevolent societies soon reported success with "free" black labor. They often compared blacks favorably with white workers. At Fortress Monroe, one supervisor described Irish workers as "crabbed" and willing to work "only so many hours a day," whereas blacks worked "night or anytime and do anything you want done." In the Mississippi Valley, an employer reported that "the lowest estimate is . . . that one negro is [worth] three [white] soldiers if they are decently paid." After a period of using free black labor, authorities like General Saxton of the Sea Islands reported that blacks successfully cultivated the cotton crop and proved that "the negroes will work cheerfully and willingly with a reasonable prospect of reward." Another general said that "the negro may be profitably employed by enterprising men."

Although the emergence of wage labor represented a cut above slavery, it was by no means an equitable arrangement. Under the threat of starvation and exposure to Confederate raids, African Americans reluctantly moved toward the production of traditional cash crops. Black plantation hands also made lower wages than military laborers or black soldiers. In 1863, whereas black soldiers could claim $10 per month, field hands earned from as low as $2 per month in the southern Louisiana district, to $6.50 in the Sea Islands, to a high of $7.00 in the Mississippi Valley. On the Sea Islands, federal authorities and their commercial allies also sought to transform the "task" system into "piece work" and to undercut the autonomy that bondsmen and -women had previously enjoyed under this arrangement. At the same time, in southern Louisiana and the Mississippi Valley, employers retained the "gang system" and employed overseers or foremen. The gang system reminded African Americans of the most detested aspects of chattel slavery. Thus, as part of the new arrangement, they insisted that the whip had to go. Indeed, some blacks assured federal officials that they would even work "without money," but they would not endure the whip, separation from their families, or work under "Secesh overseers." When these conditions were not met, according to one army provost marshal, blacks banned together and laid down "their own rules, as to when, and how long they will work etc. etc. and the overseer loses all control over them." In some cases, the bondsmen and -women drove off the overseers, stating that "they would make Laws for themselves."

Although enslaved blacks made the increasing transition to wage labor, they perceived wage labor as a temporary way station toward landownership. On 12 January 1865, Garrison Frazier, a spokesman for black freedmen in Savannah, declared that "the way we can best take care of ourselves . . . is to have land, and turn it and till it by our own labor . . . until we are able to buy it and make it our own." Although most Unionists resisted the allocation of planters' land to blacks, some northern whites believed that blacks should be compensated with land for their years of uncompensated toil. As one Methodist clergyman on the Sea Islands put it, blacks "had made [the land] what it was and . . . it belonged to them, and them only." In 1862, the U.S. government passed the Direct Tax Act, which provided for the confiscation of land on which owners failed to pay taxes and allowed federal officials to reallocate such land to blacks for lease or purchase. Under the provisions of this law, African Americans gained land in "contraband villages," including "Freedman's Village" in Washington, D.C., and "Point Lookout" on Maryland's western shore. On 31 December 1863, Lincoln authorized the direct tax commissioners "to permit loyal residents of Sea Islands to preempt forty-acre plots on any government-controlled land before it was put up for auction."

African Americans optimistically staked their claims. They invariably turned to land "on the old homestead, where they had been born, & had labored & suffered." As a result of opposition from some tax commissioners, however, the government soon revoked such claims and undercut the most promising avenue for landownership for ex-slaves. Still, compared with other areas of the Union-occupied South, blacks gained their greatest wartime opportunities for landownership on the Sea Islands, where over one hundred families gained estates designated for "charitable" purposes. Even more important, in January 1865, in his "march to the sea," General William T. Sherman enhanced black landownership when he issued Special Field Order #15, which allowed enslaved blacks to occupy and gain "possessory title" to forty-acre plots of land on the coastal islands and mainland rice plantations of South Carolina, Georgia, and parts of Florida. By war's end, some twenty thousand former enslaved blacks had settled on some one hundred thousand acres of land known as the Sherman Reserve.

At Davis Bend, Mississippi, blacks secured leases on six plantations during the Civil War years. Two of these plantations belonged to Jefferson Davis, president of the Confederacy, and a relative, Joe Davis. When Union forces took the area and confiscated the land, African Americans had already taken control of the place and were operating it on their own terms. Under General Grant's command, the federal government decided to transform the area into a refuge for the growing number of fugitives who had followed the Union forces there. The government not only leased parcels of land to groups of blacks but also provided "rations, mules, and tools," which the freedmen agreed to pay for out of the proceeds of their crops. Under the leadership of Benjamin Montgomery, a former bondsman, plantation manager, and store operator, African Americans soon raised nearly two thousand bales of cotton and realized a profit of $160,000 at Davis Bend. The settlement also had its own system of government, including elected judges and law enforcement officials.

Davis Bend demonstrated that African Americans were not uniformly hostile to the market economy. Rather, they were determined to enter freedom on their own terms. Independent black farmers also emerged in coastal North Carolina, parts of Arkansas, and Tidewater Virginia, where federal officials sanctioned the cultivation of land and use of the property "of Rebels in Arms against the Government." Landownership programs nonetheless benefited northern white migrants and ex-slaveowners far more than blacks. The direct tax provision resulted in the sale of nearly 90 percent of available property to northern whites. Although blacks gained substantial holdings in the Sherman Reserve, most of this land reverted to Confederate landowners during the final months of 1865. Moreover, even when the government permitted the confiscation of rebel property in the Confiscation Act of 17 July 1862, Congress amended the measure in accord with the constitutional prohibition of "bills of attainder." In other words, even in cases of forfeiture, on the death of primary offenders, property reverted to their heirs. The children of slaveholders would regain the property that formerly enslaved blacks occupied as a result of sales under the confiscation law. Thus, rather than a prelude to landownership and economic independence, the Civil War offered the most telling rehearsals for the postwar rise of inequitable wage labor and sharecropping systems.

∿

ALTHOUGH WAGE LABOR PLACED SOME AFRICAN AMERICANS on a new economic footing, it was by no means an equitable process. Indeed, the government replaced the whip with the threat of starvation, homelessness, and exposure to Confederate attacks. At the same time, the government facilitated the transition of some blacks from wage earners to landowners, but this was the least successful aspect of the "rehearsal" for freedom. Federal authorities used land and labor policies to win the war, strengthen the Republican Party, and create loyal governments in Confederate territory. As we will see in Part IV, only briefly would blacks gain the franchise and enter the Republican coalition as partners. Thus, before African Americans could fully consolidate their position as workers and citizens, they would experience the onset of a new white supremacist regime. Jim Crow would not only restrict their participation in the polity but also undercut their thrust for landownership and economic independence.

PART IV

Emancipation and the First Generation of Freedom
1865–1915

Following the Civil War, some 4 million African Americans gained their freedom and made the transition from "slave" to "citizen" and "free worker." Although African Americans had sacrificed their lives for emancipation and enabled the Union to triumph over the Confederacy, federal policies nonetheless hampered their passage from enslavement to freedom. President Abraham Lincoln and his successor Andrew Johnson enacted Reconstruction policies favorable to the defeated Confederate states. In rapid succession, southern states enacted the "black codes," which not only deprived blacks of the right to vote and aided and abetted the activities of terrorist groups like the Ku Klux Klan but also authorized the use of police power to coerce blacks into signing unjust labor contracts. African Americans responded to postbellum restrictions on their rights by escalating their protest activities and building alliances with northern Republicans. Between 1867 and the early 1870s, partly as a way to defeat the Democratic Party in southern elections, northern Republicans enacted new legislation extending full citizenship rights to African Americans, including the right to vote, hold public office, and shape Reconstruction policy in their own interests.

Although the demand for full citizenship rights gained the support of northern Republicans, the African American struggle for economic justice received less support from white allies. Blacks believed that they were entitled to a portion of southern agricultural land as just compensation for years of enslavement, but both the Democratic and Republican Parties rejected their claims. Failure to ensure African Americans access to land weakened their position in the political economy and paved the way for the resurgence of the Democratic Party by the mid-1870s and the rise of the segregationist system by the 1890s and early 1900s.

As the promise of freedom faded, some African Americans moved to rural and urban settings outside the South, but most stayed put and intensified their institution-building, cultural, political, economic, and civil rights activities on a national scale. Part IV discusses the economics and politics of emancipation; the rise of Jim Crow; and the emergence of a plethora of new African American strategies for social change during the late nineteenth and early twentieth centuries.

CHAPTER 11

⟞⟝

The Politics of Emancipation: Winning and Losing the Franchise

After a bitter Civil War that claimed the lives of over six hundred thousand Americans, some four million African Americans gained their freedom. Blacks entered perhaps their most optimistic moment in the nation's history. For the first time since the arrival of Africans in the New World, the majority of blacks took the status of free people. Yet the transition from slavery to freedom was fraught with difficulties. From the outset of the emancipation era, a series of political, economic, and social decisions hampered the transformation of enslaved blacks into citizens and workers. Both President Abraham Lincoln and his successor, Andrew Johnson, defined Reconstruction policy as the prerogative of the executive branch of the federal government. They also proposed to reconstruct the nation on terms acceptable to southern whites. As such, their policies encouraged the disfranchisement of blacks, the rise of abusive labor practices, and the spread of racial violence. The emergence of white supremacist groups like the Ku Klux Klan and the passage of infamous "black codes" deprived blacks of their civil rights and set up a system of forced labor.

Although African Americans faced an exceedingly hostile socioeconomic and political environment during the first years of freedom, they did not take limits on their civil rights sitting down. They joined forces with a small group of white Republican allies to demand full citizenship rights, including the franchise and access to land. Their efforts led not only to the enfranchisement of black men with passage of the Fourteenth and Fifteenth Amendments but also to access to public offices, patronage positions, and state support for black education and social welfare services. Nonetheless, despite these achievements, radical Reconstruction governments failed to confiscate rebel land and redistribute it to ex-slaves. Moreover, Republican Party leaders soon turned away from blacks toward southern whites as the mainstay of the party's strength and helped to set the stage for the resurgence of the Democratic Party. The presidential election of 1876 symbolized the downfall of radical Reconstruction, the intensification of racial violence, and the subsequent disfranchisement of blacks through legal and extralegal means. By the early 1890s, African Americans faced a new and more hostile environment in the South and the nation. Accordingly, they would also search for new and more effective strategies for social change.

PRESIDENTIAL RECONSTRUCTION AND THE RADICAL CHALLENGE

From the initial announcement of emancipation in 1863 through the early postwar years, a variety of presidential decisions hampered the transition from slavery to freedom. Lincoln defined Reconstruction policy as the prerogative of the president. Except for certain high-ranking Confederate military and government officials, he pardoned and restored full citizenship rights to all southern whites who took an oath of "future loyalty" to the Union and pledged to abolish slavery. When the number of postwar loyalists amounted to at least 10 percent of the votes cast in the presidential election of 1860, he empowered the state to call a constitutional convention and establish a new government. By war's end, the president had approved the Reconstruction of the border states of West Virginia, Maryland, and Missouri. Although these newly reconstructed governments extended "freedom" to blacks, they denied African Americans full citizenship rights, including the right to vote. The law encouraged southern states to adopt measures toward blacks "consistent . . . with their present condition as a laboring, landless, and homeless class," rather than as free workers and citizens. Although Lincoln cautiously suggested the enfranchisement of the most educated, skilled, and even light-skinned blacks, southern states rejected the idea, and the president dropped the matter. In short, Lincoln hoped to reconstruct the South on terms acceptable to white southerners, ex-slaveholders and nonslaveholders alike.

Johnson and Early Reconstruction

Following Lincoln's assassination in April 1865, his successor, Andrew Johnson, gave even less consideration to African Americans. Johnson, a Tennessean and former owner of five bondsmen, entered politics as a champion of the white yeoman farmer. Early in his career, he had advocated a slave for every "white family" to perform the "drudgery and menial service." As a loyal Unionist, however, he accepted the emancipation of blacks but made his racial sentiments clear. "Damn the Negroes," he said to one Union general, "I am fighting those traitorous aristocrats, their masters." During the early Reconstruction years, Johnson declared his belief that "this is a country for white men, and by God, so long as I am president, it shall be government for white men." In his message to Congress in 1867, he took his disdain of African Americans a step further. He declared that blacks had "shown less capacity for government than any other race of people." Even more so than Lincoln, Johnson hoped to unify the white South against northern whites and free blacks alike. Within less than two years, he had pardoned over seven thousand high-ranking Confederates and property holders.

Beginning in mid-August 1865, southern states met in convention, adopted new constitutions, and regained their place in the Union. Loyalty to the "Lost Cause" and "white supremacy" defined the outcome of the first senatorial and congressional elections in North Carolina, South Carolina, Georgia, and Louisiana, where the Democratic Party advocated a government "for the exclusive benefit of the white race." Accordingly, legislators planned strategies and enacted laws designed to get things back "as near to slavery as possible." In 1865–1866, beginning with South Carolina and Mississippi, southern states enacted a plethora of new laws, called "black codes." Although these codes theoretically accepted the right of blacks to purchase and own property, marry, make contracts, and sue and be sued in courts of law, they identified the control of black labor as the linchpin of economic recovery and political influence for the postwar South. These laws permitted any white person to arrest blacks; authorized the removal of black children from the homes of poor families; and permitted whites to whip black children and adults as a measure of labor or social discipline.

As southern whites regained economic and political power, postbellum blacks joined forces to demand full citizenship rights. Newspapers, mass meetings, and the "Negro Convention Movement" articulated their position. As early as August 1865, the Nashville *Colored Tennesseean* proclaimed: "All we want is the rights of men. . . . We are Americans. . . . Deal justly with us. That's all we want. That we mean to have come what may!" In December of the same year, the black *New Orleans Tribune* urged Congress to end what the editor called the "conservative and exclusively white man loving administration" of Andrew Johnson. In Norfolk, Charleston, and Nashville, "Negro" conventions adopted the rhetoric of the Revolution and protested against "taxation without representation." As one resolution stated: "Representation and taxation go hand in hand and it is diametrically opposed to Republican institutions to tax us for the support and expense of the government, and deny us at the same time, the right of representation." In North Carolina, a group of blacks reminded President Johnson of their recent and past services in defense of the country:

> Some of us are soldiers and have had the privilege of fighting for our country in this war. . . . We want the privilege of voting. It seems to us that men who are willing, on the field of danger, to carry the muskets of Republics, in the days of peace ought to be permitted to carry its ballots; and certainly we cannot understand the justice of denying the elective franchise to men who have been fighting for the country, while it is freely given [to those who have been fighting against it].

Over and over again, such appeals also emphasized citizenship by birth and determination to stay in America and fight. The editor of one black newspaper was direct: "We do not intend leaving this country. . . . We were born here. Most of us will die here."

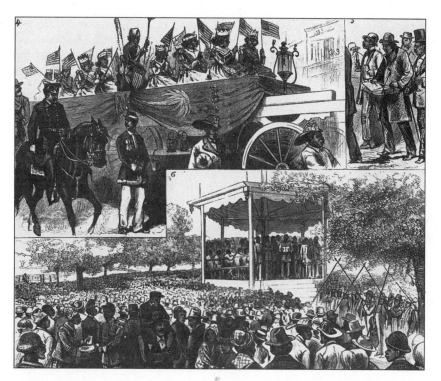

From the initial announcement of the Emancipation Proclamation in January 1863, African Americans regularly celebrated Emancipation Day. These occasions provided African Americans with not only an opportunity to join together for fellowship and thanksgiving for liberation but also a platform for protesting injustices and restrictions on their rights. Here are scenes from Emancipation Day celebrations in Charleston, South Carolina. *Black Charleston Photo Collection, College of Charleston*

"Radical" Republicans Strike Back

African Americans were not entirely alone in their early postbellum civil rights movement. They received support from the radical wing of the Republican Party: in the U.S. Senate, Charles Sumner of Massachusetts, Benjamin Wade of Ohio, and Henry Wilson of Massachusetts; in the U.S. House of Representatives, Thaddeus Stevens of Pennsylvania, George W. Julian of Indiana, and James M. Ashley of Ohio. Although some radicals hoped to pursue a punitive course, punishing ex-Confederates for treason, most envisioned a new nation where a strong national state would ensure "equality before the law" for all citizens. Henry Wilson stated, "I believe in equality among citizens—equality in the broadest and most comprehensive democratic sense." Although radicals like Sumner and Stevens supported black suffrage and rejected the dominant notion of "a white man's government," most Republicans were northern moderates and conservatives who

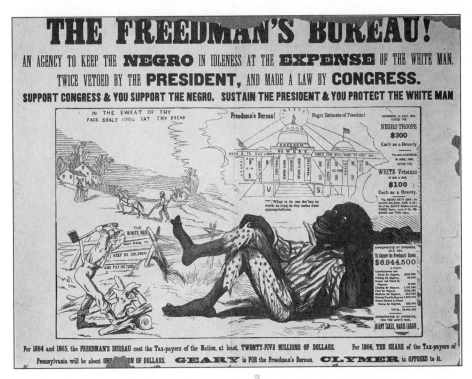

Andrew Johnson and the Democratic Party detested the Freedmen's Bureau and moved to abolish it, as shown in this campaign literature, but African Americans also gradually gained the support of white northern Republican allies such as Pennsylvania congressman Thaddeus Stevens (*opposite*). *Above and opposite: Library of Congress*

hoped to avoid or subordinate the black issue to their own economic and political concerns—that is, northern capitalists' penetration of the southern economy. Passage of the black codes, the growing use of violence, and black activism slowly turned most northern Republicans toward the position that presidential Reconstruction was "no reconstruction at all." By early 1866, radicals and moderates took the position that Congress had the authority to withhold national representation from the South until such states guaranteed the civil rights of freedmen. This position soon clashed with Johnson's idea of Reconstruction as a presidential prerogative and set the stage for the enfranchisement of southern black men as a political expedient. As during the Civil War, when Republicans needed blacks to win the war, they now turned toward blacks to help reconstruct the nation along industrial capitalist lines.

Beginning in early 1866, Congress took a series of steps that culminated in black manhood suffrage. First, in February, Republicans passed the Freedmen's Bureau and Civil Rights Bills. The former aimed to extend the life of the bureau, give it direct funding (that is, remove its reliance on the military budget), and expand the power of agents to judge cases involving black rights. (See the Documents section.) The Civil Rights Bill went even further. It conferred national citizenship on all persons (except Native Americans) born in the United States, without regard to race. Johnson vetoed both measures, describing the Freedmen's Bureau's provisions for black education as an "immense patronage" that gave more to blacks than it did "to our own [white] people." In his veto of the Civil Rights Bill, Johnson's racism was even clearer: "The distinction of race and color is by the bill made to operate . . . against the white race." In April, Congress overrode Johnson's veto and voted the Civil Rights Bill into law. Despite Johnson's opposition, Congress passed the Reconstruction Act of 1867, which divided the eleven Confederate states (except Tennessee, which early on cooperated with radical Republican plans for Reconstruction) into five military districts. Each district had a

Eng.d by G E Perine & Cº N York.

military commander with authority to use the army to ensure the protection of life and property. For national representation, southern states had to draft new constitutions, enfranchise black voters, and ratify the Fourteenth Amendment. The Fourteenth Amendment (approved in 1868) made it illegal for any state (1) to enforce or make any laws abridging the "privileges and immunities" of citizens; (2) to deny "equal protection of the law"; and/or (3) to deprive citizens of life, liberty, or property, without "due process of law." In a follow-up measure, Congress empowered military officials to register voters and organize and oversee elections. Still, the measure requiring black suffrage applied only to ex-Confederate states and not to the nation as a whole. Only in 1870, with passage of the Fifteenth Amendment, would all black men nationwide gain the right to vote.

Advocates of black suffrage had to overcome not only southern resistance but the opposition of white women, who vigorously pushed for the enfranchisement of women along with that of black men. During the Civil War years, northern white women had played a major role in the Union war effort. They had organized hundreds of freedmen's aid societies and fundraising efforts on behalf of Union soldiers. They had also curtailed their agitation for the suffrage. Many believed that their contributions to the abolition of slavery and preservation of the Union would also emancipate women and lead to their enfranchisement. Consequently, in the early postwar years, many white women regrouped their forces and pushed for woman suffrage. The Fifteenth Amendment angered woman suffragists, partly because the original draft inserted the word *male* into the Constitution for the first time, although the final version of the law was silent on sex or gender. As approved by the states, the Fifteenth Amendment outlawed the disfranchisement of men based on "race, color, or previous condition of servitude." White male supporters of black suffrage justified their position on the premise that this was the "Negro's hour," meaning black men.

When it appeared that black men might obtain the vote before white women, the woman suffrage movement split. Although some white suffragists like Lucy Stone supported black male suffrage as the right thing to do in the short run, others like Susan B. Anthony and Elizabeth Cady Stanton opposed black male suffrage. These women not only opposed black male suffrage but also joined the ranks of the Democratic Party and soon offered a racist rationale for their movement. Writing in the *Revolution*, a Democratic Party–supported organ, for example, Anthony declared:

> While the dominant party have with one hand lifted up TWO MILLION BLACK MEN and crowned them with the honor and dignity of citizenship . . . with the other they have dethroned FIFTEEN MILLION WHITE WOMEN— their own mothers and sisters, their own wives and daughters—and cast them under the heel of the lowest orders of manhood.

On another occasion, for her part, Stanton appealed to fears of interracial sexual relations between black men and white women. She charged that the vote would give black men a license to rape: "The Republican cry of 'Manhood Suffrage' creates an antagonism between black men and all [white] women that will culminate in fearful outrages on womanhood in the Southern states."

Black women desired the vote no less than white women, but most perceived their own interests in racial terms and supported black male suffrage. Frances Ellen Watkins Harper articulated their viewpoint. She argued that the primary obstacle in the path of black women was white racism rather than black men and sided with Frederick Douglass when he said that the defeat of black male suffrage would make black women less, rather than more, secure. Supporting Harper and Douglass were women like Caroline Remond Putnam and Lottie Rollin. Moreover, Douglass, Harper, and others agreed that black women suffered special forms of brutality and violations of their rights because they were black, not because they were women. In 1869, in his address to the American Equal Rights League, Douglass declared:

> When women, because they are women, are hunted down through the cities of New York and New Orleans, when they are dragged from their houses and hung upon lamp posts; when their children are torn from their arms, and their brains dashed upon the pavement; when they are objects of insult and outrage at every turn; when they are in danger of having their homes burnt down over their heads; when their children are not allowed to enter schools; then they will have an urgency to obtain the ballot equal to our own.

The fight for black male suffrage divided the predominantly white woman suffrage movement. It also created rifts within the black community. Not all black women supported black male suffrage over their own. Sojourner Truth, for example, joined Stanton and Anthony in opposing black manhood suffrage. As she put it, "If colored men get their rights, and not colored women theirs, you see the colored men will be masters over the women, and it will be just as bad as it was before." Supporting Truth were other black women like Mary Ann Shadd Cary and Hariett Forten Purvis. When the woman suffrage movement split, these women also supported the National Woman Suffrage Association, while Harper, Douglass, and others joined with the American Suffrage Association. Still, despite limitations, the acquisition of black manhood suffrage represented a fundamental break with the past. For the first time, most African American men gained citizenship rights on an equal legal footing with whites. They would soon use these new rights to transform their place in American politics and society.

FROM "RADICAL" TO "REDEEMER" REGIMES

Once African Americans achieved the right to vote, they wasted little time exercising their new power. Groups of blacks and their white Republican allies entered the black belt and set up Union Leagues, which spread the word of new political empowerment and the possible fruits that voting could bring. Contemporary observers frequently commented on the scope and spirit of early black political mobilization. The manager of one southern plantation declared: "You never saw a people more excited on the subject of politics than are the negroes of the South. They are perfectly wild." According to one observer, "It is the hardest thing in the world to keep a negro away from the polls . . . that is the one thing he will do, to vote." In the election of 1868, a northern reporter wrote from Alabama that blacks had defied "fatigue, hardship, hunger, and threats of employers" to stand in line in a "pitiless storm" to cast their votes. In another election, a Tennessee Valley Republican reported that "the negroes . . . voted their entire walking strength—no one staying at home that was able to come to the polls." During election times, southern planters would often declare, "Negroes all crazy on politics again." Recalling the initial impact of the franchise on blacks, one ex-slave later recalled that "politics got in our midst and our revival or religious work for a while began to wane." In some places, the Union League and offices of the Republican Party nearly displaced the black church as the principal communal gathering place.

Black Political Gains

Blacks used the franchise to augment and even to transcend their political strategies of the early emancipation years. Whereas African Americans were excluded from the presidential state conventions, they accounted for over a quarter (265) of the total delegates to the radical state constitutional conventions. They made up a majority of delegates at the Louisiana and South Carolina conventions; 40 percent in Florida; 20 percent in Georgia, Mississippi, Alabama, and Virginia; and 10 percent in Texas, North Carolina, and Arkansas. African Americans helped to draft new

A group portrait of the first African Americans to serve in the U.S. Senate and House of Representatives. Hiram Revels, seated on the far left, was elected to the Senate in 1870. He took the seat previously occupied by Jefferson Davis, president of the Confederacy. *The Granger Collection, New York, #E96.16*

constitutions that not only enfranchised ex-slaves but also initiated reforms that liberalized southern laws and improved the social welfare and legal position of poor whites. The new constitutions set up the South's first state-funded system of free public education, provided for the building of orphan homes, and established institutions for the mentally insane and the poor. Some states like Texas, Mississippi, Louisiana, and especially South Carolina also took limited steps to redistribute land to freedmen and poor whites, particularly up-country whites.

Following the enactment of the new constitutions, African Americans increased their influence on the political process. By the end of Reconstruction, sixteen blacks had served as U.S. congressmen; over six hundred as state legislators; eighteen as lieutenant governors, treasurers, superintendents of education, and/or secretaries of state; and hundreds of others as local justices of the peace, members of school boards, county commissioners, sheriffs, and aldermen. Some had served as mayors of small local municipalities like the towns of Donaldson, Louisiana, and Natchez, Mississippi. African Americans achieved their most impressive political gains in South Carolina. In 1870, blacks captured four of the state's eight executive offices, sent three of their numbers to the U.S. Congress, and elected Jonathan J. Wright to the state's Supreme Court. At the same time, they sent a majority to the state's House of Representatives (and Senate after 1873). Throughout the Reconstruction era, in South Carolina, the palmetto state, blacks controlled the legislature, including its principal committees. Moreover, after 1872, a black also served as Speaker of the House. In 1873, the racist journalist James S. Pike decried this show of black power: "Sambo . . . is already his own leader in the Legislature. . . . The Speaker is black, the clerk is black, the doorkeepers are black, the little pages are black."

Although the black majority states of South Carolina, Louisiana, and Mississippi accounted for the largest numbers of black public officials, Georgia, Florida, Alabama, and other southern states added to the total. Only Texas, Tennessee, and

Arkansas failed to send blacks to the U.S. Congress. As suggested earlier, these developments were closely intertwined with the rise of the Union Leagues, sponsored by the Republican Party. From the outset, the congressional headquarters of the leagues hired over eighty blacks as "itinerant lecturers," including men like William U. Sanders of Maryland, James H. Jones of Virginia, and James Lynch, editor of the African Methodist Episcopal (AME) *Christian Recorder*. These agents frequently received accolades for their ability to hold audiences of as large as three thousand freedmen "spellbound for hours at a time." Reinforcing the work of these paid agents were northern-born blacks like the Ohio-born Civil War veteran William N. Viney, who bought land in South Carolina and soon organized black political gatherings at his own expense. Tunis G. Campbell, a New Jersey–born black, achieved even greater results in McIntosh County, Georgia. More importantly, however, black political activism included growing numbers of ex-slaves. In Bolivar County, Mississippi, Blanche K. Bruce, an ex-slave, spearheaded the formation of a local political organization that enabled him to hold the office of sheriff, tax collector, and superintendent of education. It was this organization, patronage, and political base that allowed Bruce to enter the U.S. Senate in 1875. The former bondsman Henry Demas headed a similar Republican organization in St. John the Baptist Parish in Louisiana.

Each state soon produced its own coterie of grassroots black leaders. These included Alabama's James T. Alston, South Carolina's Alfred Wright, Florida's Calvin Rogers, and Georgia's Thomas Allen. Formerly enslaved blacks valued education and literacy as leadership qualities. A shoemaker, minister, and farmer, Thomas Allen explained the situation in rural Georgia: "In my county the colored people came to me for instructions, and I gave them the best instructions I could. I took the *New York Tribune* and other papers, and in that I found out a great deal, and I told them whatever I thought was right." Educated freeborn blacks and mulattoes took a disproportionate number of leadership positions. Although they made up only about 6 percent of the total black population, freeborn blacks and mulattoes accounted for an estimated 25 to 30 percent of all Reconstruction era black politicians. Few of these leaders claimed jobs as field hands or general laborers. In South Carolina, for example, nearly 85 percent of Reconstruction black politicians owned real or personal property, and 65 percent could read and write. Teachers, preachers, and artisans figured prominently among this group, but education and social standing on white terms did not fully determine former bondsmen's selection and evaluation of their leaders. They often articulated the belief "that what a man does, is no indication of what he is." Blacks frequently described their leaders as "thoroughgoing" men and "stump speakers" who tried to "excite the colored people to do the right thing."

Northern blacks also formed numerous Republican clubs and supported the Republican Party as the party of emancipation and citizenship. Black Republicans sometimes risked bodily harm and defied white Democratic opponents. During the 1880s, for example, a Cincinnati black challenged the illegal voting practices of the Democratic Party. "There upon," as one writer put it, "a gang of older hoodlums pounced upon the challenger, dragged him into the streets and beat him savagely." Other northern blacks also faced harassment and even death when they resolved to vote for the candidate of their choice. In 1871, when Philadelphia blacks promised to help the Republican Party oust the local Democratic machine, local police and the mayor's office fomented an attack on blacks designed to prevent them from voting. Rioting erupted in several wards of the city, and some four blacks lost their lives as a result. Among the dead was the activist school teacher Octavius V. Catto, who was a leader in the black community, an organizer for the Republican Party, and officer in the Pennsylvania Equal Rights League. *Harper's Weekly* later published a photo of Catto, commenting that he was "a worthy colored citizen of Philadelphia [whose murder was] entirely unprovoked."

Although disfranchised along with white women, black women also helped to mobilize the black electorate. They actively participated in political meetings, rallies, and parades. In some cases, they also voted on resolutions at mass meetings. On one occasion, for example, the *New York Times* reported that "the entire colored population [men and women] of Richmond" participated in the selection of black delegates. Moreover, during the state constitutional conventions themselves, black women joined men in the galleries and voiced their opinions during debates on the floor. Recent studies show that black women often accompanied men to the polls and helped to give broader family and communal meaning to the franchise. Along with men, they were also prepared for confrontations with hostile whites. One contemporary observer reported women carrying arms, axes, or hatchets, "their aprons or dresses half-concealing the weapons." These women justified the fight for black manhood suffrage as important to themselves, their families, and their communities.

African Americans expected and received greater consideration of their rights from black than from white elected officials. Whites often complained that black

Although black women were denied the vote along with white women, they were active participants in electoral politics, as depicted in this 1868 illustration. Harper's Weekly, *25 July 1868*

law officers prevented them from executing their usual labor and social practices. In Georgia, one overseer complained that if he proceeded as desired, "I should only get myself into trouble, and have the negro sheriff sent over by Campbell to arrest me." Moreover, when black voters placed whites into office, such recipients of black support also responded much better to the needs of their constituents than they would have otherwise. In North Carolina, one mayor remarked: "They look upon me as a protector . . . and not in vain. . . . The colored men placed me here and how could I do otherwise than to befriend them." In Alabama, one white newspaper reported in 1870 that "there is a vagrant law on our statute books . . . but it is a dead letter because those who are charged with its enforcement are indebted to the vagrant vote for their offices." Indeed, some black elected officials complained that black constituents often expected much more from them than they could reasonably hope to deliver. John R. Lynch said that blacks "magnified" his office of justice of the peace well beyond its importance or potential.

As we will see in Chapter 12, although radical state governments modified some of the harshest features of the black codes, they failed to establish blacks on their own land. At the national level, the government pursued policies that enriched capital over the needs of labor and permitted the proliferation of corrupt financial schemes. Such practices helped to rob the radical regimes of their legitimacy in the eyes of many northerners as well as southerners. Railroad land grants, tax policies, and state aid for a variety of projects entailed substantial fraud, bribery, and embezzlement of funds. To be sure, African Americans participated in these corrupt practices. In Texas, for example, railroad magnates bribed black legislators to enhance the disbursement of state monies for their projects. In other cases, black public officials like the lieutenant governor of Louisiana promoted projects that benefited their own business investments. Still, more often than not, corruption deprived rather than enriched black law makers and their constituents. In 1872, for example, when the South Carolina Republican Robert B. Elliott sought a U.S. Senate seat, his opponents offered him a bribe of $15,000 to withdraw from the race. When he refused, his opponents used money to destroy his campaign. Moreover, black schools suffered mightily from the theft of money earmarked for the education of black children. In Louisiana, for example, several parishes closed their schools because of insufficient funds.

Reaction and Backlash

Only slowly did radicals enact legislation guaranteeing blacks equal access to public accommodations. In 1875, Congress passed the Civil Rights Bill, which called for an end to racial discrimination in the selection of juries and in public accommodations, including theaters, restaurants, railroads, and hotels. Yet before Republicans passed the measure, they deleted the sections calling for an end to racial discrimination in churches, schools, and cemeteries. According to most radicals, the government had a responsibility to ensure blacks equal "political" and "civil" rights, but not "social" rights. As the Pennsylvanian Thaddeus Stevens put it, "Negro equality . . . does not mean that a negro shall sit on the same seat or eat at the same table with a white man. That is a matter of taste which every man must decide for himself." Moreover, Republican state governors often used their appointive powers and access to patronage to attract Democrats to the Republican fold. Such appointments displeased not only blacks but also southern white Unionists (scalawags) who had supported the Republican Party through the war years. In Louisiana, a group of loyalists protested that "it is a shame to erase a radical Republican off the School Board to take a dam rebel."

Republican efforts to woo rebel support failed. Blacks and their white Republican allies soon became the targets of new and more violent attempts to remove them from office, "redeem" the South for the Democratic Party, and promote the forces of white supremacy. As early as 1865, a visitor to Louisiana reported that whites governed "by the pistol and the rifle." As the principal cause, a white Tennessean stressed the postwar decline of a vested property interest in African Americans. As he said, black life was "cheap now. . . . Nobody like 'em enough to have any affair of the sort [murder] investigated." In his testimony, the former bondsman Henry Adams later recalled that whites killed more than two thousand blacks in the area near Shreveport, Louisiana, where he lived. According to Freedmen's Bureau officials, whites frequently shot blacks down "like wild beasts without provocation." In the Sabine River area of Texas, the ex-slave Susan Merritt recalled murdered blacks floating in the river and warned that whites would face numerous "souls crying" out against them on Judgment Day.

Between 1868 and 1871, blacks faced the onset of a new wave of violence. At least seven black members of the radical constitutional conventions were later murdered, and others faced intimidation and beatings. For his work on behalf of the Republican Party and the Georgia Equal Rights Association, Klansmen forced Abram Colby into the woods, stripped him naked, and beat him for nearly three hours. In Eutaw, Greene County, Alabama, a white mob attacked a Republican campaign rally, killing four blacks and wounding over fifty others. Following a loss at the polls of Laurens County, South Carolina, whites drove some 150 freedmen and their families from their homes, killing thirteen people, including a white judge who had gained election on the basis of black votes. As before, black women—mothers, wives, and daughters—not only witnessed these brutal beatings and murders of black men but also were victims. Indeed, some black women were beaten, raped, and murdered because their men "voted the radical ticket" (see box).

Organizations like the Ku Klux Klan, the Knights of the White Camellia, and the White Brotherhood proliferated. These organizations served as paramilitary support groups for the Democratic Party, which aimed to drive blacks and their white allies from office. Formed in Pulaski, Tennessee, in 1866, the Klan would soon become the most infamous of these terrorist groups. As violence escalated against blacks and their white allies, Congress passed the Ku Klux Klan and Enforcement Acts of 1871–1872. These laws empowered the president to appoint election supervisors to prevent intimidation of voters and/or fraudulent voting practices and made it easier for the U.S. district attorney to use federal courts to prosecute state officials as well as individuals for such violations. Prosecutions soon

SOURCES FROM THE PAST

1871

Harriet
Hernandez
Testifies
Before
Congress on
Ku Klux Klan
Violence

Spartanburg, South Carolina

WITNESS: HARRIET HERNANDEZ

Question   How old are you?

Answer   Going on thirty-four years.

Question   Are you married or single?

Answer   Married.

Question   Did the Ku-Klux ever come to your house at any time?

Answer   Yes, sir; twice.

Question   Go on to the second time; you said it was two months afterwards?

Answer   Two months from Saturday night last. They came in; I was lying in bed. Says he, "Come out here, sir; Come out here, sir!" They took me out of bed; they would not let me get out, but they took me up in their arms and toted me out—me and my daughter Lucy. He struck me on the forehead with a pistol, and here is the scar above my eye now. Says he, "Damn you, fall!" I fell. Says he, "Damn you, get up!" I got up. Says he, "Damn you, get over this fence!" and he kicked me over when I went to get over; and then he went to a brush pile, and they laid us right down there, both together. They laid us down twenty yards apart, I reckon. They had dragged and beat us along. They struck me right on the top of my head, and I thought they had killed me; and I said, "Lord o' mercy, don't don't kill my child!" He gave me a lick on the head, and it liked to have killed me; I saw stars. He threw my arm over my head so I could not do anything with it for three weeks, and there are great knots on my wrist now.

Question   What did they say this was for?

Answer   They said, "You can tell your husband that when we see him we are going to kill him."

Question   Did they say why they wanted to kill him?

Answer   They said, "He voted the radical ticket, didn't he?" I said, "Yes, that very way."

Question   When did your husband get back after this whipping? He was not at home, was he?

Answer   He was lying out; he couldn't stay at home, bless your soul! . . . He had been afraid ever since last October.

Question   Is that the situation of the colored people down there to any extent?

Answer   That is the way they all have to do—men and women both.

Question   What are they afraid of?

Answer   Of being killed or whipped to death.

Question   What has made them afraid?

Answer   Because men that voted radical tickets they took the spite out on the women when they could get at them.

Source: Excerpt from *U.S. Congressional Hearings on the KKK,* vol. 5, Gerder Lerner, ed., *Black Women in White America: A Documentary History* (New York: Random House, 1972), pp. 182–185.

took place in North Carolina, Mississippi, and South Carolina, where President Grant sent in the army and forced some two thousand Klansmen to flee the state, but violence continued in Louisiana, Alabama, and Mississippi, all of the so-called unredeemed states. Democratic rifle clubs took to the streets in broad daylight and traveled from place to place disrupting Republican Party meetings, beating and killing blacks. According to one black official, "It was the most violent time that ever we have seen." Encouraged by the surge of white supremacy, Virginia rejected radical Reconstruction and remained under military rule until Ulysses S. Grant took office in the spring of 1869. Only after Grant authorized a vote on the state's constitution, which enfranchised Confederate veterans, did Virginians approve a new constitution. The state then elected a Democratic governor and gave Democrats a majority in the legislature. At the same time, Georgia Republicans remained silent or voted with white Democrats to unseat duly elected black legislators. Democrats retained power in Delaware and regained control of Maryland in 1867; West Virginia in 1870; Georgia in 1870–1871; Alabama in 1874; Mississippi in 1875; and South Carolina, Louisiana, and Florida in 1876.

The so-called redeemer regimes soon worked to dismantle radical achievements. The governor of Georgia, James M. Smith, boasted that the southern states could "hold inviolate every law of the United States and still so legislate upon our labor system as to retain our old plantation system." After regaining the seats of power in the South, redeemers took a series of legislative steps to disfranchise black voters: poll tax requirements in Delaware and Tennessee; property qualifications in Maryland; poll tax and criminal conviction provisions in Virginia; and poll tax and residency requirements in Georgia. In Mississippi, Alabama, and elsewhere, the state instituted gerrymandering schemes that annulled the impact of black majority counties and districts. State and local officials also redefined certain offices from elective to appointive to accomplish the same aim. Moreover, as we will see in Chapters 12 and 13, redeemer governments reinforced ex-slaveholders' control over the black labor force by heightening vagrancy statutes, cutting social welfare and educational expenditures, and deepening the segregation of blacks and whites in the institutional, cultural, and social life of the region. In 1875, a southern newspaper captured the redeemers' intent when the editor declared that the Fourteenth and Fifteenth Amendments "may stand forever; but we intend . . . to make them dead letters on the statute-book."

The presidential election of 1876 symbolized the downfall of radical Reconstruction. In an election marked by violence throughout the South, the Democratic candidate, Samuel J. Tilden of New York, received nearly 4.3 million popular votes, compared with just over 4 million for his Republican opponent, Rutherford B. Hayes of Ohio. The election hinged on the outcome of 20 disputed electoral votes from the states of Oregon, Florida, Louisiana, and South Carolina. These states had sent in two sets of returns, one from the Democratic Party and the other from the Republicans. To resolve the dispute, which inflamed old hostilities growing out of the Civil War, Congress established an Electoral Commission, which consisted of seven Republicans and seven Democrats, plus five justices of the U.S. Supreme Court, one presumably independent (but who was in fact a Republican).

Consequently, the commission, which voted strictly along party lines, awarded all 20 votes to the Republican Rutherford B. Hayes, who won by an electoral vote of 185 to Tilden's 184.

Although the vote appeared strictly a partisan issue, it was more than that. It involved intense negotiations on racial and regional issues. At stake was the ability of the South to craft its own racial policies toward African Americans. Southerners accepted the decision, partly because Republicans and the new president promised a policy of noninterference in southern race relations. Shortly after his inauguration, Hayes ended radical Reconstruction by removing the remaining federal forces from the South and giving southerners a free hand in dealing with the black population. On removing the troops, Hayes declared: "I feel assured that no resort to violence is contemplated in any quarters, but that, on the contrary, the disputes in question are to be settled solely by such peaceful remedies as the Constitution and the laws of the State provide." From the perspective of blacks and their southern Republican white allies, however, the election of 1876 represented "a corrupt bargain" in which Hayes received the southern white vote in exchange for a northern promise of a future lenient hands-off policy regarding black-white relations in the South. The meaning of emancipation and Reconstruction became, and remains, one of the most contested areas in African American and American studies (see box).

LIMITS OF ELECTORAL POLITICS

Despite the downfall of Reconstruction, southern blacks continued to vote and hold public office through the turn of the century. African Americans served in every session of the Virginia Assembly through 1891; North Carolinians sent fifty-two blacks to the state's lower house from the election of 1876 through 1894; South Carolinians elected forty-eight blacks to the state's general assembly from about 1878 to 1902. Moreover, southern states sent ten blacks to the U.S. Congress after the settlement of 1876, the same number as elected before 1876. Blacks also continued to vote and hold office at the county and local levels, particularly in small enclaves like the "black second" congressional district of eastern North Carolina. Still, by 1890, the black vote dissipated in the violent climate of the post-Reconstruction South. Thus, when formal constitutional disfranchisement emerged during the 1890s, it sanctioned a practice that was already well under way in some places.

As redeemer regimes gained power in one southern state after another, blacks sought alternatives to the Republican Party. In 1872, Frederick Douglass, the foremost black Republican spokesperson of the period, had made his famous speech declaring the Republican Party the "deck" and all else "the seas." Now, in the 1880s, Douglass declared that he was "an uneasy Republican." Indeed, according to Douglass, "If the Republican party cannot stand a demand for justice and fair play . . . it ought to go down." In 1876, Senator Bruce of Mississippi criticized the

CHANGING HISTORICAL INTERPRETATIONS

The First Reconstruction

The historiography of slavery framed the first generation of scholarship on the meaning of emancipation in American and African American life. Writers took sides in the anti- and pro-slavery discussions of the antebellum and Civil War years. In 1874, for example, James S. Pike, formerly an antislavery journalist, published *The Prostrate South*. According to Pike, the emancipation and enfranchisement of some 4 million slaves empowered "a mass of black barbarism" and resulted in the rise of "the most ignorant democracy that mankind" ever saw. He emphasized the white South as victims of "Negro Rule," backed up by northern "carpetbag" and southern "scalawag" Republican allies. As such, he helped to set the tone for a "tragic" interpretation of Reconstruction. During the late nineteenth and early twentieth centuries, Columbia University professors John W. Burgess and William A. Dunning helped to perpetuate and popularize the racist view of the post–Civil War years. This perspective—emphasizing Reconstruction as a period of "corrupt," "ignorant," and "black" rule—culminated in the publication of historian Claude Bower's *The Tragic Era* (1927).

Like shifts in slavery studies, emancipation scholarship changed under the impact of the modern civil rights movement of the 1950s and 1960s. As African Americans and their white allies assaulted the bastions of the segregationist order, they also demanded a new look at the history of Reconstruction and the rise of Jim Crow. The new writers also emphasized the "tragic" nature of Reconstruction, but they turned the tables. In their view, Reconstruction was "tragic" for ex-slaves, not for ex-slaveholders and their descendants. It was "tragic" because it missed a unique opportunity to usher in a new multiracial democracy, sketched out by blacks and their white Republican allies. As W. E. B. Du Bois put it in his groundbreaking work of reinterpretation, *Black Reconstruction* (1935), "The unending tragedy of Reconstruction is the utter inability of the American mind to grasp its real significance, its national and worldwide implications. . . . The attempt to make black men American citizens was in a certain sense all a failure, but a splendid failure." Du Bois emphasized not only the failure to extend full citizenship rights to blacks in practice but also the failure to provide economic justice to ex-slaves in the form of land. "To have given each one of the million negro free families a forty acre freehold would have made a basis of real democracy in the United States that might easily have transformed the modern world." Instead, following emancipation, the nation crafted a new system of "white supremacy" under the legal rubric of "separate but equal." By the late 1960s, studies by historians John Hope Franklin, Kenneth Stampp, and Staughton Lynd elaborated on Du Bois's viewpoint.

In the wake of the Black Power movement and growing disappointment with the fruits of the civil rights movement during the mid- to late 1960s, a new generation of scholars highlighted the limitations of existing Reconstruction scholarship, which revolved increasingly around the "tragedy" of race relations and sidestepped important social and political issues. By the 1980s and 1990s, growing numbers of scholars advanced new studies of class formation and gender relations as keys to a fuller understanding of the early emancipation era. In 1987,

CONTINUED

for example, the late historian Armstead Robinson argued that the "Civil War origins of the post war labor system constitute the first line of inquiry that demands attention" in emancipation research. Studies by Thomas Holt, Peter Kolchin, Nell Painter, Gerald David Jaynes, and Julie Saville all emphasize in varying degrees the transition of enslaved blacks to free workers, sharecroppers, and members of a rural wage-earning proletariat. For their part, historians Evelyn Brooks Higginbotham, Tera Hunter, Leslie Schwalm, and Glenda Gilmore, among others, document the gendered as well as class and racial nature of African American life in the post–Civil War rural and urban South. They are sensitive to the ways that ex-slaves built on their cultural experiences in the slave community and influenced their own transformation from slaves into wage earners, commercial farmers, and sharecroppers. As the African Americans and the nation grapple with new labor and social policies in the early twenty-first century, the proliferation of scholarship on the emancipation era offers an extraordinary resource. This scholarship is replete with insights into the vagaries of culture, power, and economics.

Republican Party when the U.S. Senate failed to seat P. B. S. Pinchback of Louisiana. He even advised blacks to divide their vote between the two major parties to secure greater political concessions. In Mississippi and South Carolina, during the 1880s and 1890s, black Republicans affected a fusion arrangement with Democrats whereby they agreed to allow Democrats to obtain a certain number of positions in exchange for a seat in the legislature and a proportion of local offices.

Northern blacks also criticized the party of Lincoln. As early as 1883, George T. Downing, a well-to-do caterer of New York and Newport, Rhode Island, broke with the Republicans and supported the Democratic Party. He urged blacks to split their votes "because division would result in increased support from all quarters." At a convention in Pittsburgh in 1884, blacks refused to endorse either the Democrat or Republican candidate. In Massachusetts, James M. Trotter, a former officer in the state's famous Fifty-Fourth Regiment, deserted the Republican Party, resigned his patronage post, and supported the Democrat Grover Cleveland, who later appointed Trotter recorder of deeds for the District of Columbia. In New York, the Albany lawyer James C. Matthews, and the minister of the AME Bethel Church, T. McCants Stewart, led a group of blacks out of the Republican Party and into the Democratic Party. Black newspaper editors also increasingly criticized the Republican Party, although they did not make the break and join the Democratic Party. These included W. Calvin Chase of the *Washington Bee* and T. Thomas Fortune of the *New York Age*. In 1883, Chase described the Republican Party as "little, if anything, better than the hidebound slave-holding Democratic party." Similarly, Fortune, in 1886, encouraged blacks to split their votes under the motto "Race first: then party."

African Americans also supported independent movements like the Greenback Party, the Readjuster movement, and the Populist Party. In Virginia, for example, blacks supported the Readjuster movement against "redeemer" rule. The Readjusters advocated a partial repudiation of the state's debt to free funds for education and social services. In 1879, black voters helped Readjusters come to power in Virginia and soon gained recognition of black needs. Formed in 1875, the Greenback Party developed a program of "cheaper money and free silver coinage" that also appealed to black farmers. Moreover, some southern Greenbackers articulated a policy of interracial equity. In 1878, the Texas Greenback Labor Party held its first state convention, declaring that the party would "protect alike the rights of every individual in the union, irrespective of section, state, riches, poverty, race, color, or creed." Some seventy black groups claimed affiliation with the state's Greenbacks, comprising 482 local units. Two years later, the Texas Greenbackers denounced "the attempted disfranchisement of citizens as a crime, whether committed by Republicans in Massachusetts and Rhode Island or Bourbon Democrats in Texas."

Following the collapse of the Greenback Party by the mid-1880s, African American farmers gravitated to the emerging Farmers' Alliance movement. This movement coalesced around the national Farmers' Alliance and Industrial Union (called the Southern Alliance) and its northern and midwestern counterpart, the National Farmers' Alliance (called the Northern Alliance). Meeting in Houston, Texas, in 1886, African Americans formed a separate body, the Colored Farmers' Alliance and Cooperative Union (called the Colored Alliance). Although black and white alliance men cooperated on a series of educational, social, and economic programs, they soon parted ways over the question of disfranchisement and strategies for empowering black farm laborers. At its 1890 convention, the Colored Alliance supported the Lodge Federal Election Bill, designed to ensure black voting rights, but the white body staunchly opposed the measure. A year later, black alliance men called a strike of cotton pickers to improve the terms of their labor, but the white alliance men encouraged whites to break the strike of black farmers. Colonel Leonidas L. Polk, president of the Southern Alliance, declared that the strike would benefit blacks at the expense of white farmers. Moreover, the white alliance men hoped to strengthen their hand as owners of land and employers of labor, and avoid capital-labor confrontations and conflict. Predominantly tenants, sharecroppers, and farm laborers, blacks could not afford to take that position. Still, as the presidential campaign of 1892 unfolded, some black alliance men supported the formation of the Populist Party as their best hope for the future.

Although the Readjuster and Greenback movements gained modest support among blacks, the Populist Party emerged as the most promising alternative to southern racism during the 1890s. Tom Watson, the influential Georgia Populist, urged whites to overcome their racism and join forces with the black farmer. On one occasion, Watson declared that "the colored tenant . . . is in the same boat with the white tenant, the colored laborer with the white laborer." Moreover, Watson appealed directly to African Americans: "If you stand up for your rights and for your manhood, if you stand shoulder to shoulder with us in this fight, the people's party will wipe out the color line and put every man on his citizenship irrespective of color." When a white mob threatened to lynch the black Populist Anthony Wilson, who had made over sixty speeches supporting the Populist Party, white Populists responded to Watson's plea that they come to the man's defense as well as his own. Two thousand white farmers stood guard outside Watson's home for two nights. Still, except for parts of Texas and a few Upper South counties, where blacks made up a significant proportion of the electorate, the Populists failed to win over the bulk of black voters. Although Democrats continued to use terrorism against black voters, under the Populist threat they also launched underground appeals for blacks to go to the polls and vote the Democratic ticket. More importantly, however, Populists like Tom Watson soon succumbed to the onset of white supremacy and supported the constitutional disfranchisement of black voters.

Amidst the Populist upsurge of the late 1880s and early 1890s, southern states mobilized to remove the remaining vestiges of black political power. These states now adopted constitutional reforms to supplement the ongoing use of violence and legislative processes to deprive blacks of their civil rights. Mississippi launched the constitutional disfranchisement movement in 1890, followed by South Carolina in 1895 and Louisiana in 1898. By 1902, Alabama, Virginia, and North Carolina had amended their constitutions to disfranchise black citizens. In 1908, Georgia followed suit, and in 1910 Oklahoma became the last state to enact disfranchisement provisions by constitutional fiat. The Populist Tom Watson now took the position that "white men would have to unite before they could divide" along class lines. He now supported any Democratic candidate who would endorse black disfranchisement among other "Populist reforms." Some white conservatives like Alexander Caperton Braxton of Virginia hoped to eliminate poor blacks and some poor whites from the franchise while allowing some educated blacks to vote along with whites, but a new generation of radical white supremacists won the day. These included Governor, and later Senator, James K. Vardaman of Mississippi; Senators Benjamin Tillman of South Carolina, Braxton Cower Bragg of Alabama, and Charles Brantley Aycock of North Carolina; and Congressman Thomas W. Hardwick of Georgia. These men hoped to eliminate "all blacks" from the political process while including all white men.

Although the principal architects of white supremacy, racial violence, and disfranchisement were white men, they were joined by white women. One of the most articulate of these was Georgian Rebecca Latimer Felton, who later became the first woman to serve (although only briefly) in the U.S. Senate. In 1897, in a speech before the State Agricultural Society, she targeted enfranchised black men as a threat to white womanhood. She later recalled:

> I warned those representative men . . . of the terrible . . . corruption of the negro. . . . I told them that these crimes [rape] . . . would grow and increase with every election where white men equalized themselves at the polls with an inferior race.

Felton then justified the growing lynching of black men as a response to the alleged rape of white women. She even urged white men to lynch "a thousand a week if it becomes necessary." Felton was not the only southern white woman to advocate the lynching and disfranchisement of black men. Her ideas gained expression among white women across the South. Middle- and upper-class white women flooded the ranks of the United Daughters of the Confederacy and challenged white men to reclaim the control over black people that their fathers and grandfathers had gained over the slaves. In 1898, in North Carolina, white women joined the White Government Leagues and helped to mobilize votes against the interracial Populist movement. At one Democratic Party rally, a white woman urged white men to remove the "black vampire hovering over our beloved old North Carolina."

Although specific disfranchisement provisions varied somewhat from state to state, Mississippi and other southern states instituted what popular historian Lerone Bennett has described as "a wall with holes in it." Southerners barred blacks from voting by a wall of poll taxes, literacy tests, property qualifications, and moral stipulations, including prohibitions on persons convicted of major crimes like murder and arson, as well as lesser offenses like bribery, burglary, and theft. Even as such walls removed black voters, however, legislators punched holes in the wall for poor whites to qualify. The most famous of these provisions were the "grandfather," "understanding," and "good character" clauses. In other words, if literacy, property, or poll tax laws disqualified whites, they could nonetheless vote by claiming a grandfather who had voted in a previous election; an "understanding" of the contents of the Constitution or any other document that they might be required to read but could not; and/or "good character" despite possible prior criminal convictions. Other states—Florida, Texas, Arkansas, Kentucky, and Tennessee—continued to deprive blacks of the vote through the adoption of legislative mechanisms like the poll tax and the Australian secret ballot, which required a level of literacy that large numbers of blacks and whites lacked. In Louisiana, the number of black voters declined from over 130,300 in 1894 to less than 1,350 by 1900. The number of poor white voters also declined, but disfranchisement was fundamentally a racial movement, designed to remove black voters. Whites also later adopted the "white primary," whereby the Democratic Party allowed only whites to vote for the selection of candidates for public office. Thus, even where small numbers of blacks remained on the rolls, their influence was further diminished.

The disfranchisement movement precipitated a new wave of black activism. As early as September 1883, Frederick Douglass delivered his "Address to the People of the United States." In this speech, he justified "Negro" or "colored" conventions as a necessary step in the struggle for equal rights. As in the struggle against slavery, Douglass urged blacks to agitate for full citizenship rights:

> Until this nation shall make its practice accord with its Constitution and its righteous laws, it will not do to reproach the colored people of this country with keeping up the color line—for that people would prove themselves scarcely worthy of even theoretical freedom, to say nothing of practical freedom, if they settled down in silent, servile and cowardly submission to their wrongs, from fears of making their color visible. . . . Who would be free must strike the blow.

In 1890, black leaders staged several protest meetings in support of the Lodge Elections Bill, which aimed to eliminate racial discrimination in the exercise of the franchise.

In the same year, civil rights activities gained new strength with the formation of the Afro-American League. Formed in Chicago under the leadership of T. Thomas

Fortune, the organization elected the North Carolina educator J. C. Price as president and pushed to end all vestiges of racial discrimination. Later that same year, a group of blacks met in Washington, D.C., and formed the Citizens Equal Rights Association with goals similar to those of the Afro-American League. When these organizations became defunct, they gave way to the Afro-American Council in 1898, under the leadership of T. Thomas Fortune and Bishop Alexander Walters of the AME Zion church. The Afro-American Council retained the same ideological orientation as that of its predecessors but made little headway and gradually faded by 1908.

Despite vigorous protest activities, African Americans failed to stem the tide of white resistance and the weakening of the Republican alliance. From the election of Rutherford B. Hayes through the presidencies of Theodore Roosevelt and William Howard Taft during the early twentieth century, northern Republicans gradually turned their backs on southern blacks. In the *Civil Rights Cases* of 1883, the U.S. Supreme Court pronounced the Civil Rights Act of 1875 unconstitutional. It claimed that the federal government could protect citizens only against the discriminatory activities of the state rather than against the actions of its individual citizens. In the case of *Plessy v. Ferguson* (1896), the U.S. Supreme Court went a step further. It upheld the constitutionality of the "separate but equal" doctrine, accepted the notion of "white supremacy," and fomented the rise of Jim Crow. (See the Documents section.)

Such federal policies mirrored the transition of the Republican Party from what some historians call the "black-and-tan" racially mixed republicanism of the radical era to the "lily-white" republicanism of the 1890s. In the election of 1896, which placed the Republican William McKinley of Ohio in the president's office, the Republican Party sanctioned the separation of blacks and whites in the southern wing of the party and gradually excluded blacks from viable participation in the political arena. In 1901, George White of North Carolina left Washington. He was the last black southern congressman before the modern civil rights era. By 1910, however, some twelve white Republicans had entered Congress from the South, a product of black disfranchisement and exclusion from the political process.

During the early years following the downfall of Reconstruction, blacks had routinely gained key federal patronage positions. These included jobs in the postal service and as customs collectors at various ports. Theodore Roosevelt continued to make a few conspicuous black appointments in the South—Dr. William D. Crom as collector of customs at the port of Charleston, South Carolina, and a black woman as postmistress in Indianola, Mississippi, for example. For his part, although Taft retained black appointees in the capital city (particularly in the Treasury Department and the Office of the Recorder of Deeds) and in a few posts in the West and North, he replaced black appointees in the South with whites and also initiated the segregation of blacks and whites in federal buildings. When the Democrat Woodrow Wilson took office in 1912, he accelerated a process of segregation already set in motion by Republicans. The first southern president since the Civil War, Wilson also went a step further and required applicants for civil service jobs to submit photographs with their applications, which facilitated racial discrimination and the spread of segregation in the federal government.

The gradual disengagement of northern whites from support of black rights is vividly illustrated by the artist Thomas Nast's changing portrayal of blacks in his postbellum political sketches. *Harper's Weekly,* *5 August 1865 (left) and 14 March 1874 (right)*

~

THE TRANSFORMATION OF ENSLAVED BLACKS into citizens and workers was inextricably tied to the actions of the state. With the aid of black people as soldiers and civilians, the Union army had defeated the Confederacy on the battlefield. Blacks now expected to reap the full fruits of their labor. They wanted the federal government to use its authority to intervene, confiscate southern land, and help establish blacks on land of their own. Despite extraordinary efforts on their own behalf, blacks were soon disappointed—not only by the antiblack policies of presidential Reconstruction and the subsequent rise of the Democratic "redeemer" and Jim Crow regimes but also by the narrow class and racial policies of their Republican allies. Political Reconstruction failed to incorporate their hope for land and also frustrated their quest for full citizenship rights and opened the way for the violent resurgence of Confederates and ex-slaveowners to economic, social, and political power. Thus, as we will discuss in Chapter 12, the transition to freedom was complicated not only by the intensification of racist public policies but also by the rise of a new system of economic exploitation and unjust labor practices.

CHAPTER 12

~

Economic Emancipation, Land, and the Search for Industrial Opportunities

T he struggle for political freedom was interwoven with the fight for land, employment, and economic opportunities. Postbellum employers and public officials not only instituted policies and practices that curtailed African American access to the franchise and full citizenship rights but also undermined their quest for economic independence. Planters sought to maintain old forms of labor control, including use of the whip, police, and military authority to force able-bodied men to work. At the same time, they happily transformed prior provisions to the enslaved—food, clothing, housing, medical care, and access to garden plots, hunting grounds, and fishing waters—into purchasable cash items for emancipated blacks. Only a thin line separated such southern labor practices from the free wage labor policies of northern employers and military and government officials. Northerners tied social welfare services and aid to the freedmen and their families to wage labor. They insisted that the freed people assume full responsibility for the care of their own sick, disabled, and indigent. In short, northerners enjoined African Americans to "work or starve." When the spur of hunger and need seemed insufficient, northerners, like southerners, also resorted to various forms of coercion, including the roundup and incarceration of vagrants without visible means of support. For their part, African Americans sided with free labor advocates against planters but resisted the exploitative and unjust practices of both. Formerly enslaved people advocated sharecropping over rural wage labor; landownership over sharecropping; and, increasingly, urban life and labor over work in the countryside. In other words, when the government failed to provide ex-slaves with land, black men and women pooled their resources and worked to protect and advance their own family, class, and racial interests.

RURAL WAGE LABOR AND NEW FORMS OF COERCION

Ex-slaveholders emerged from the Civil War with deep-seated notions about their right to command the labor of blacks. Planters detested the idea of treating ex-slaves as independent agents in the labor market, partly because of the racist heritage of slavery and partly because they lacked the money to pay sufficient wages to attract and retain a free black labor force. According to the *Augusta Transcript*, southern planters believed that the prosperity of the South and their own class interests depended on "one single condition—*the ability of the planter to command [black] labor.*" Over and over again, planters challenged northern victors with the question, Will the Negro work? Overwhelmingly, they concurred that blacks were "naturally lazy" and would not work under any incentive except the lash. In their view, high wages, opportunities for upward mobility, or even kindness would not compel blacks to work. One Louisiana sugar planter concluded in no uncertain terms that "the great secret of our success [as slaveholders] was the great motive power contained in that little instrument [the whip]." A Georgia newspaper made the same point, portraying blacks as "improvident and reckless of the future." Another Louisiana planter was even more direct: the "inborn nature of the negro . . . cannot be changed by the offer of more or less money." When one Alabama slaveowner returned to his plantation after the war, he reported that "Negroes will not work for pay, the *lash* is all I fear that will make them."

Northern employers shared much of the southern perspective on free black labor. Beginning during the war years, northerners purchased their own southern land, leased plantations from southern landowners, or entered partnerships with southern planters. Although northerners envisioned quick riches on cotton plantations "manned" by "cheap" free black labor, they couched their economic motives in a broader reform vision of "industrial progress." From their vantage point, they would bring "free labor" to a land suffering from stagnation and "backwardness" as a result of years of bondage. When blacks resisted the capitalist work regimen, northerners increasingly described black workers as "ignorant," "shiftless," and "unreliable." Harriet Beecher Stowe, who resided on a Florida plantation during the Reconstruction years, criticized the free people as "great conservatives" who failed to adopt northern suggestions for more efficient labor and farming techniques. Henry Lee Higginson, a northern investor in a Georgia cotton plantation, concluded: "It is discouraging to see how . . . much more hopeful they appear at a distance than near to." Other northerners expressed the view that slavery had destroyed the capacity of blacks for "self-directed labor" and advocated the restoration of corporal punishment. On one occasion, the *New York Times* suggested that perhaps freedmen and -women needed "new masters."

During the early post–Civil War years, military authorities, the Freedmen's Bureau, and state and local governments helped to underwrite a new system of coercion. In 1865–1866, military officials continued to aid planters by coercing black workers into signing contracts. When a Virginia couple resisted a whipping by their employer, an army provost marshal used the "wooden horse" to secure the desired result. In South Carolina, a planter expressed surprise when a Yankee officer punished two black men for loitering by hanging them by the thumbs. According to the planters, the men actually pleaded to be whipped instead. In Mississippi, a northern officer gave one black man "twenty lashes, and rubbed him down right smart with salt, for having no visible means of support." A Georgia minister and ex-slaveholder confided to his sister that the northern troops' discipline of black workers created "a remarkable quietude and order in all the region." Another planter was even more emphatic: he said that it is "good they are here."

Unlike the military, the Freedmen's Bureau initially protected black workers from the planters' efforts to reinstitute prewar forms of labor control. Bureau officials informed planters that the notion of "bodily coercion" had fallen with the destruction of slavery. Yet the bureau soon privileged the planters' labor demands over black workers' rights. Oliver O. Howard, bureau head, informed blacks that they must enter labor contracts with the landowners: "A man who can work has no right to support by government. No really respectable person wishes to be supported by others." A Mississippi agent of the bureau put it bluntly: "A man can scarcely be called free . . . who is the recipient of public charity." For its part, the Louisiana bureau not only eliminated the black orphan home and apprenticed black children to white employers but also ordered the arrest of all able-bodied persons without "written proof" of employment.

In their search for new modes of commanding black labor, planters adopted the contract labor agreement, enforceable by law. One planter said, "Let everything proceed as formerly . . . the contractual relation being substituted for that of master and slave." A Mississippi planter explained:

We go on like we always did . . . and I pol'em if they don't do right. This year I says to em, "Boys, I'm going to make a bargain with you. I'll roll out the ploughs and the mules and the feed, and you shall do the work; we'll make a crop of cotton and you shall have half. I'll provide for ye; give ye quarters, treat ye well, and when ye won't work, pole ye like I always have." They agreed to it and I put it into the contract that I was to whoop 'em when I pleased.

In North Carolina, the ex-slaveholder William L. DeRossett wrote to his brother regarding the newly emancipated woman Letitia:

Old Letitia is with me still on the old terms. . . . I notified her when I first saw the order freeing them, that she was, at liberty to go, but that if she staid with me it must be as she had before & if she misbehaved I would not hesitate to flog her. She acquiesced fully & I have had no trouble.

As suggested in Chapter 11, the black codes represented the pivot of southern efforts to coerce black labor. These codes revolved around southern states' definition and punishment of "vagrancy." The Mississippi law defined vagrancy broadly to include "idleness," "disorderly" conduct, and even those who "miss spend what they earn." Persons convicted of vagrancy faced punishment by fines and/or involuntary labor. By New Year's Day, the Mississippi code required blacks to show a written labor contract for the coming year. Law officers could arrest almost anyone without a job. Such persons could be arrested, jailed, fined, placed on a chain gang, or hired out to private employers. Under so-called false-pretense provisions, any workers who deserted their employment before the contract expired forfeited all wages owed up to that moment. For violation of the law, as during bondage, African Americans could also be arrested by any white citizen. Similarly, under "anti-enticement" statutes, any employer who

SOURCES FROM THE PAST

1865

The South Carolina Black Code Addresses Apprenticeship and Vagrancy

Husband and Wife

I. The relation of husband and wife amongst persons of color is established. . . .

Master and Apprentice

XV. A child over the age of two years, born of a colored parent, may be bound by the father, if he be living in the District, or in case of his death or absence from the District, by the mother, as an apprentice, to any respectable white or colored person, who is competent to make a contract—a male until he shall attain the age of twenty-one years and a female until she shall attain the age of eighteen years. . . .

XXII. The master or mistress shall teach the apprentice the business of husbandry, or some other useful trade or business, which shall be specified in the instrument of apprenticeship; . . .

XXIII. The master shall have authority to inflict moderate chastisement and impose reasonable restraint upon his apprentice, and to recapture him if he depart from his service.

XXIV. The master shall receive to his own use the profits of the labor of his apprentice. . . .

Contracts for Service

XXXV. All persons of color who make contracts for service or labor, shall be known as servants, and those with whom they contract shall be known as masters.

XXXVI. Contracts between masters and servants, for one month or more, shall be in writing, be attested by one white witness, and be approved by the Judge of the District Court, or by a Magistrate. . . .

Vagrancy and Idleness

XCV. These are public grievances, and must be punished as crimes.

XCVI. All persons who have not some fixed and known place of abode, and some lawful and reputable employment . . . shall be deemed vagrants, and be liable to the punishment hereinafter provided. . . .

XCVIII. The defendant, if sentenced to hard labor after conviction, may, by order of the District Judge, or Magistrate, before whom he was convicted, be hired for such wages as can be obtained for his services, to any owner or lessee of a farm, for the term of labor to which he was sentenced, or be hired for the same labor on the streets, public roads, or public buildings. The person receiving such vagrant shall have all the rights and remedies for enforcing good conduct and diligence at labor that are herein provided in the case of master and servant.

Source: Acts of the General Assembly of the State of South Carolina, 1864–1865, pp. 291–304.

offered work to a black person already under contract with another could be imprisoned for varying lengths of time and/or fined $500. With minor variations, other states erected similar statutes, including generous provisions for the removal of black children from their homes for apprenticeship with white families (see box).

Although some codes failed to single blacks out by name, everywhere it was understood that the labor contract and vagrancy provisions of southern laws referred primarily to blacks. Early postwar contracts entailed agreements between ex-slaveholders and "large groups" of freedmen. Some contracts provided for "standing wages" paid on an annual basis. This procedure enabled planters to extract the maximum amount of labor from the newly freed people, since workers forfeited their wages if they quit before the expiration of the contract. In reality, however, most contracts provided "share-wages." Because most planters had little cash following the Civil War, they offered former bondsmen a share of the crop as wages, which they often paid collectively to field hands, who then divided the crop among themselves. In these arrangements, planters continued to rely on antebellum methods of grading workers, whereby men as "full hands" received more than women and young workers, who were considered "half" to "three-quarter" hands. Rarely did workers receive as much as 20 percent of the produce. For their part, rural artisans—carpenters, coopers, blacksmiths—usually signed individual monthly wage contracts at higher rates of pay than their field hand brothers and sisters.

LANDOWNERSHIP AND RESISTANCE TO WAGE LABOR

Although some African Americans gave in to the new forms of coercion, most questioned the terms of their labor and frustrated efforts to place their work on an unequal wage basis. According to the editor of an Alabama newspaper, "We have land but can no longer control" the black workers; "hence we want Northern laborers, German laborers, to come down and take their places, to work our lands for ten dollars a month." The wife of one planter expressed the same view: "Give us five million of Chinese laborers in the Valley of the Mississippi . . . and we can furnish the world with cotton and teach the negro his proper place." Several southern states—South Carolina, Louisiana, Arkansas, Alabama, Tennessee, Mississippi, Texas, Virginia, and West Virginia—passed laws encouraging the recruitment of immigrant labor, but these efforts proved futile. European and Asian workers found southern working conditions and labor practices intolerable and thus moved on to other regions and jobs. The failure of these labor schemes forced southerners to recognize their long-term dependence on the labor of black freedmen.

Emancipated blacks knew very well the difference between their free present and their enslaved past. As two black leaders testified in July 1865, "They all knew they were their own men, and women." When asked, "Whose servant are you?" a South Carolina woman responded "that she was her own servant." When her ex-owner threatened to let her go if she refused to accept his terms, she replied, "I'll leave then," which she did. African Americans invariably asked questions about the precise nature of their employers' obligations as well as their own under contracts. Even before the war ended, African Americans on a Louisiana plantation asked: "When will our wages be paid?" "What clothing are we to have?" "What land are we allowed?" "Can we keep our pigs?" Soon after federal occupation of the Sea

Islands, one ex-slave made the point clearly: "I craves work, ma' am, if [I] gets a little pay, but if we don't gets pay, we . . . don't care to work." Frances Leigh, the daughter of the planter Pierce Butler, revealed how blacks responded to contract negotiations in a long description of contract time:

> For six mortal hours I rot in the office without once leaving my chair while the people poured in and poured out, each one with long explanations, objections, and demonstrations. . . . One wanted this altered in the contract, and another that. One was willing to work in the mill but not in the field. Several would not agree to sign unless I promised to give them the whole of Saturday for a holiday. Others . . . "would work for me till they died," but would not put their hand to no paper.

As suggested above, black women no less than men participated in demands for higher pay and better working conditions. According to one observer, Harriet Ware, a group of black women confronted the Boston plantation owner and manager Edward Philbrick:

> The women came up in a body to complain to Mr. Philbrick about their pay—a thing which has never happened before and shows the influence of very injudicious outside talk which has poisoned their minds against their truest friends. The best people were among them, and even old Grace chief spokeswoman.

Philbrick later leased his plantation to another white planter, but blacks soon confronted both men with demands for "a dollar a task: A dollar a task." This represented a substantial increase over their usual pay. On another occasion, Grace led a delegation of some twenty black women to Philbrick's door. She told Philbrick in no uncertain terms that the women were "done working for such agreement. I've done sir." Grace recounted her hard labor and the labor of her children in making two bales of cotton but receiving little in return: "I knows those two bales cotton fetch 'nought money, and I don't see what I'se got for 'em."

African Americans not only participated in individual or small group skirmishes with landowners but also organized statewide "labor conventions" between 1869 and 1871. In Georgia, South Carolina, and Alabama, African Americans called for "intermediary officers" to oversee the contracts and ensure equitable wages, hours, and conditions of labor. Although states largely rejected such proposals, blacks also used the conventions to form independent agricultural labor organizations. In some states, these farm labor organizations developed alongside the Union Leagues. Thus, even as they organized to influence public policy, black farmworkers took steps to set their own pay, hours, and conditions of work. As such, these efforts established precedents for the emergence of the Colored Farmers' Alliance, farmworkers' strikes, and the Populist movement of the late 1880s and 1890s (see Chapter 11).

Until the onset of World War I, African Americans resisted wage labor primarily through a relentless search for their own land. Blacks retained an abiding faith in the possibilities of landownership. On one South Carolina plantation, a black worker rejected wage labor with the comment: "I mean to own my own manhood . . . and I'm goin' on to my own land, just as soon as when I git dis crop in, an' I don't desire for to make any change until den." In Dublin County, North Carolina, a local police chief reported that some blacks, in their words, "intend to have lands, even if they shed blood to obtain them." Some of these North Carolina blacks also demanded "all of the crops" that they had raised on their former master's lands. On one occasion, General U. S. Grant complained that the ex-slaves' belief in landownership "is seriously interfering" with "their willingness . . . to make contracts for the coming years."

It is difficult to exaggerate the importance that ex-slaves attached to land, whether they owned it or rented it. After the Civil War, contemporary observers frequently commented on the enthusiasm of blacks working independently on their own or rented land. A Freedmen's Bureau official stated: "They appear to be willing to work but are decisive in their expressions to work for no one but themselves." One ex-slaveholder and planter had a reputation for treating his black wage laborers "with the utmost kindness." Yet even he reported that "they prefer to get a little patch [of land] where they can do as they choose." Some of this land was so poor that some employers claimed that blacks "could not raise a peck of corn to the acre." Another ex-slave wrote to Abraham Lincoln: "I had rather work for myself and raise my own cotton than work for a gentleman for wages."

Many African Americans believed that they should gain land as compensation for years of enslavement. As early as November 1861, the editor of the New York *Anglo-African,* a black newspaper, had advocated the redistribution of confiscated southern land to newly emancipated blacks:

> The government should immediately bestow these lands upon these freed men who know how to cultivate them, and will joyfully bring their brawn arms, their willing hearts, and their skilled hands to the glorious labor of cultivating as their own, the lands which they have bought and paid for by their own sweat and blood.

A Boston black rebuked the notion that former masters should be compensated:

> Why talk about compensating masters? Compensate them for what? What do we owe them? What does the slave owe them? What does society owe them? Compensate the masters? . . . It is the slave who should be compensated. The property of the South is by right the property of the slave. You talk of compensating the masters who has stolen enough to sink ten generations, and yet you do not prepare to restore even a part of that which has been [stolen from blacks].

In North Carolina, another black wrote that

> if the strict law of right and justice is to be observed, the country around about me, or the sunny South, is the entailed inheritance of the Americans of African

descent, purchased by the invaluable labor of our ancestors, through a life of tears and groans, under the lash and the yoke of tyranny.

The *New Orleans Tribune* also editorialized: "The land tillers are entitled by a paramount right to the possession of the soil they have so long cultivated. . . . Let us create a new class of landholders, who shall be interested in the permanent establishment of a new and truly republican system."

At war's end, the Freedmen's Bureau had embarked on its own land redistribution program for African Americans. In 1865, the bureau controlled some 850,000 acres of abandoned land. In addition to Oliver O. Howard, bureau head, officials like General Fisk in Tennessee, Lieutenant Thomas Conway in Louisiana, and General Rufus Saxton in South Carolina, Georgia, and Florida all worked to settle blacks on their own land as independent producers. In early summer 1865, Saxton initiated plans to settle blacks on forty-acre farms where they could work for themselves and "readily achieve an independence." Saxton expressed his firm belief that blacks could become successful commercial farmers: "Let the world see ere long the fields of South Carolina, Georgia and Florida white with [cotton]." By September 1865, President Johnson had not only ordered Howard and his agents to cease the allocation of land to ex-slaves but also ordered the restoration of all but a small fraction of the blacks' land to the former owners. By the early 1870s, only a few blacks held title to their small plots. In rapid succession, blacks lost land on the South Carolina Sea Islands, in the Sherman Reserve, on Davis Bend in Mississippi, and in southeastern Virginia, where the army evicted nearly twenty thousand blacks from confiscated and abandoned property.

Newly emancipated blacks resisted the reoccupancy of their land by ex-slaveholders. In Norfolk County, Virginia, armed blacks resisted sheriffs as well as federal officers sent to evict them. They even questioned the president's right to pardon the Confederate landowners. At a mass meeting of the group, one black leader, Richard Parker, declared: "We don't care for the President nor the Freedmen's Bureau. We have suffered long enough; let the white man suffer now." Only after a fierce battle with law officers did the blacks vacate the land. In South Carolina, Sea Island blacks also organized along military lines and fought repossession of land by former owners. According to a Bureau officer, "They [the former owners] . . . say openly, that none of them, will be permitted to live upon the Islands." When a group of planters arrived on John's Island in early 1866, African Americans disarmed the group and advised them to leave and never return. A similar force of blacks met and turned whites back on James Island. In the end, however, federal forces sided with ex-Confederates and helped them to recover the land.

Although northern and southern elites had clashed over efforts to liberate blacks and establish a free labor system, they agreed that the distribution of "free land" to ex-slaves violated the principle of "free enterprise" and "private property." They maintained that all "free people" could gain wealth and secure their well-being through industry, frugality, honesty, and ambition. Now that blacks were "free," they must prove themselves capable of functioning in a free society. Underneath the ideological opposition to land redistribution to blacks, as noted earlier, northern whites had their own plans for exploiting free black labor. Their plans were not limited to those who bought land in the South and hired black workers. They also included the designs of northern industrialists who hoped to employ southern blacks to help defeat the rising demands of the northern-based white labor movement. As early as 1866, for example, northern industrialists recruited southern blacks as strikebreakers. Indeed, northern and southern white elites feared that the distribution of land to blacks would disrupt class relations among whites. According to the *Nation*, a leading national publication during the period, "The division of rich men['s] lands among the landless . . . would give to our whole social and political system a shock from which it could hardly recover without the loss of liberty."

THE SHARECROPPING SYSTEM

As African Americans lost their struggle for landownership, particularly in the Deep South, they turned toward sharecropping as an alternative to rural wage labor. Since few blacks had access to capital, they placed a high premium on their labor. In exchange for their labor, African Americans insisted on access to small family plots. They hoped to cultivate this land independently, with their own family members, without strict day-to-day supervision under "overseers" or "foremen." African Americans believed that this arrangement would enable them to enter the landowning class much faster than wage labor. When planters repossessed the land of ex-slaves on James Island, South Carolina, one dispossessed black man remarked: "If I can't own de land, I'll hire or lease land, but I won't contract" (that is, work for wages). In addition to land, African Americans expected to receive access to tools, seed, and fertilizer, plus food, housing, supplies, and a substantial proportion of the final crop. Depending on how much they received from landowners upfront, crop shares might vary from one-third to one-half for the worker, with the remainder going to the landowner to cover supplies, rent, and debts to merchants and bankers.

As black families gained a footing on these small sharecropping units, black women now divided their labor more evenly between the field and household work. One Georgia plantation owner noted the change: "Gilbert will stay on his old terms, but withdrawn Fanny and puts Harry and Little Abram in her place and puts his son Gilbert out to a trade. Cook Kate wants to be relieved of the heavy burden of cooking for two and wait on her husband." On a Louisiana plantation, when planters tried to coerce black women into the field, black men responded that "whenever they wanted their wives to work they would tell them themselves; and if [they] could not rule [their] own domestic affairs on the place [they] would leave it." Although white elites viewed white women who stayed at home as the ideal of "true womanhood," they saw black women who did the same thing "as lazy" and even "ludicrous." Both northern and southern white elites ridiculed these black women as the "female aristocracy" or the people who "played the lady" by imitating white ideals. Although scholars have long noted the "withdrawal" of black women from "field labor" during the postbellum period, recent studies accent their reemployment in black household labor, alongside a persistent pattern of field labor as well. By 1870, although most women reported their occupation to the U.S. Census Bureau as "Keeping House," they were also consistent laborers in the cotton fields as well. Moreover, many women supplemented the family's income with household work for wages or in-kind payments. At the same time, children of various ages were an indispensable part of the family labor force.

The rise of radical Republican governments reinforced the expansion of the sharecropping system. In state after state, Republicans eliminated overt constraints on the free blacks' right to move from place to place; required parental consent before taking black children from their homes; and narrowed the scope of vagrancy laws, including prohibitions on the hiring out of blacks who could not pay fines to private employers. The radical governments also limited efforts to prohibit one employer from hiring workers employed by another. Perhaps most importantly, whereas the Johnson administration had permitted a creditor to place a lien on a planter's crop "superior to all other claims," including the black workers' right to a share of the crop, the new laws gave workers a lien on crops "superior to all other claims," including those of bankers and merchants who made loans or offered credit to landowners. As such, the law defined the sharecropper as "a partner" rather than an employee in the production process. Even in Mississippi, the new

African Americans continued to work on cotton plantations during the early emancipation years. *Valentine Museum*

radical laws instructed law enforcement officers to interpret the law "in the most liberal manner [for] the protection and encouragement of labor." By 1872, some planters complained that most southern states offered "ample protection" to the tenants and "very little" to landlords. By 1880, the total number of southern farms had increased to 1.1 million, but the average size had declined from 347 acres during the 1860s to 156 acres.

Before African Americans could secure their economic footing under radical governments, the Democratic Party replaced the radicals and reinstituted repressive labor legislation. By 1877, contemporary observers stated openly that the new racist governments would go as far as they could go "without actually reestablishing personal servitude." Calling themselves "redeemers" of southern society, southern Democrats strengthened the hand of the landowners and weakened the bargaining position of black workers. They extended or reinstituted the vagrancy, anti-enticement, and convict laws. The redeemer governments also reestablished the "superiority" of landlord and merchant claims to their proportion of the crop over the workers' share. State protection of landowners' rights gained perhaps its most extreme form in North Carolina's Landlord and Tenant Act of 1877. The Tar Heel state placed full authority over the crop and settlement in the hands of the planters. In effect, the state made the planter "court, sheriff, and jury." In short, courts of law redefined the sharecropper as a "wage earner only" rather than a "partner" in the production of the crop.

Whereas sharecropping had emerged as a hopeful alternative to wage labor, it now deteriorated into an exploitative system that undercut blacks' dreams of rising into the yeomanry. Planters regularly "fixed the books" at the end of the year and kept blacks in perpetual debt. Blacks could rarely break even. When they resisted this form of economic injustice by quitting, the vagrancy laws permitted the employment of convicts by private employers. This convict lease system, as it was called, rerouted black workers back into the plantation economy on even worse terms than before. By 1900, blacks owned a smaller percentage of land in the cotton belt than they had owned in 1877, but the amount of land owned by blacks had increased to an estimated 12 million acres. Nearly 80 percent of southern blacks worked as sharecroppers or cash tenants on land owned by whites. Between 1880 and 1910, the number of black sharecroppers increased from 429,000 to 673,000. Moreover, as the nation moved into the second decade of the twentieth century, the spread of the boll weevil increased the riskiness of cotton cultivation and intensified the difficulties of black farm families.

African Americans now sought a way out of the sharecropping system itself. Although the struggle for landownership continued, many blacks now pushed for "the fixed rent" over the "share crop" system. Since landlords invariably shortchanged them at the end of each growing season, they now hoped to pay a "fixed" amount in crops or cash up front for use of the land. Then, at the end of the year, they owned the entire yield and could market their produce as they saw fit. Moreover, they were not bound to the land through a system of debt. Once the rental period expired, they were free to move elsewhere. In 1900, nearly half of black tenants worked on "fixed" rather than share rents. By 1910, however, the percentage had dropped to nearly 43 percent.

Although sharecropping emerged as the dominant labor system in the postbellum cotton South and shaped patterns of black migration, it was by no means universal. Tobacco, sugar, and rice followed different patterns of production and generated different forms of resistance, with different levels of effectiveness. In Virginia and North Carolina, tobacco growers preferred wage labor and offered few opportunities for blacks to gain their own plots of land or work on shares. Only during the early twentieth century, as tobacco prices dropped and the industry declined, did sharecropping gradually spread among Upper South tobacco farmers. In short, compared with their counterparts in the cotton regions, tobacco workers experienced a greater continuity of wage labor throughout the emancipation era. On the other hand, in the sugar district of Louisiana, the centralized system of gang labor persisted well into the emancipation era. Northern capital poured into the sugar industry and enabled planters to concentrate production on a few large units by paying relatively high wages, which attracted black workers into the industry year round, but under strict, clocklike supervision. The sugar industry also lured black workers by the allotment of garden plots, which workers cultivated on their own time, for their own benefit. Still, sugar planters complained of labor shortages. Black workers placed a high priority on their own plots and used harvest time to bargain for higher wages. Consequently, sugar production lagged behind that for cotton and tobacco.

In the postbellum rice fields, landownership and independent production allowed ex-slaves to shape the terms of their labor more so than elsewhere. African Americans retained and strengthened the beneficial aspects of the antebellum "task" system, including access to small plots of land that they worked independently. One group of South Carolina freedmen declared that they hoped "to work just as we have always worked." Planters soon responded by letting rice growers work "as they choose without any overseer." During radical Reconstruction, rice planters also accepted a "two-day" system, whereby blacks agreed to give landowners two days of work per week, leaving the bulk of their time for work on their own land, which some received through the state land commission. Moreover, South Carolina's black majority exercised a great deal of political influence. According to one rice planter, black officials exerted authority at harvest times: "The Negro magistrate . . . tells them that no rice is to [be] shipped until it is all got out and divided according to law." South Carolina blacks also discouraged outside capitalist investments in the area and kept rice production relatively low. As one South Carolina ex-slave recalled, bondage provided "no rest, Massa all work, all de time; plenty to eat but no rest, no respose." Freedom, on the other hand, offered a "chance for [a] little comfort."

Whether blacks worked under a wage, sharecrop, or modified task system, they faced the brunt of economic exploitation in the postbellum South. To improve their position, black farmworkers not only regularly moved from one employer to another within their county of origin but also gradually moved westward. Despite legal restrictions on their movement from place to place, African Americans sought better opportunities on the newer cotton lands of the lower Mississippi Valley, including the states of Louisiana, Texas, Arkansas, and Mississippi. Defying anti-

This 1897 photo shows a group of migrant blacks waiting to board a Mississippi River boat to Kansas. *Library of Congress*

enticement laws, planters and labor recruiters entered the older black belt areas advertising higher wages and better working conditions in the West. As early as winter 1866, the U.S. Commissioner of Agriculture reported that every

> railroad train during this winter has been loaded with negroes going to the West under promise of increased wages. . . . It is estimated that twenty-five thousand negroes have left South Carolina this winter for Florida and the West and the number which have left Georgia is much greater, as for some time [the] average number passing through has been 1,000 daily. This depletion of labor still actively continues, and it is a matter of increasing importance to the planters. They offer ten to twelve dollars per month, besides food, house, firewood, and land for a garden, but the negroes are promised more in the West, and accordingly emigrate.

In 1877, the Civil War veteran and political organizer Henry Adams of Louisiana estimated that some sixty thousand black working people were prepared to leave the South. Adams described the South as an "impossible" place to live, with ex-slaveowners holding the power and enjoying "the right as they enjoy it." Under the leadership of Benjamin "Pap" Singleton, some six thousand blacks left the states of Louisiana, Mississippi, and Texas for Kansas in 1879. The "Kansas Exodus," as this movement was called, reflected the failure of Reconstruction to live up to its promise of citizenship and economic freedom. Although life in Kansas also proved disappointing and some blacks drifted back to the Deep South, most stayed and drew the line even more sharply between their slave past and the hope for a free future for themselves and their families. By 1910, blacks in southern counties with black majorities had dropped from 57 percent in 1880 to 45 percent of the total population.

Reinforcing the westward movement of postbellum blacks were black soldiers and cowhands. Although the federal government had quickly disbanded black units following the Civil War, the U.S. Army maintained four all-black units, the Twenty-Fourth and Twenty-Fifth Infantry and the Ninth and Tenth Cavalry. Some twenty-five thousand black men served in these units between 1866 and the beginning of World War I. Feared by Native Americans as "Buffalo Soldiers," presumably because of their black skin and woolly hair, these black units played a major role in the late-nineteenth-century wars that decimated the Native American population in the West. African American soldiers also participated in the last major U.S. military assault against Indians, the Ghost Dance campaign of 1890–1891, which culminated in the Battle of Wounded Knee Creek in South Dakota. In addition to helping to break Native American resistance, black soldiers also helped to suppress organized white labor in the silver mining strikes of Coeur d'Alene, Idaho. Although the earliest contingents of black soldiers were predominantly young single men or married men without their wives and children present, by the 1880s growing numbers of black soldiers brought their wives and children to western military outposts and facilitated the rise of black settlements in the West.

Along with the Buffalo Soldiers, some blacks entered the West as cowboys and herders in the cattle range industry. By the 1890s, blacks made up about 2 percent of the region's cowboys. They also spread widely throughout the western and southwestern states and territories of Texas, New Mexico, Arizona, Kansas, Wyoming, Montana, California, and the Dakotas, to name a few. Black range workers participated in longhorn cattle drives from central Texas north to railheads at towns like Abilene, Dodge City, Denver, and Cheyenne, among others. In his personal recollections of life as a cowboy, the Texas-born Daniel ("80 John") Wallace described how cowboys "slept on the ground in all kinds of weather with our blankets for a bed . . . a saddle for a pillow . . . and gun under his head." Moreover, Wallace later moved out of the rank of cowhand and became a rancher who owned his own cattle and over ten thousand acres of land in Mitchell County, Texas. Yet until the advent of the modern civil rights movement, African American cowboys and cattlemen were excluded from most popular and scholarly images and accounts of the West. Whether blacks lived in the rural South or on the western frontier, however, they found it exceedingly difficult to make ends meet. Consequently, they moved into the nation's cities in rising numbers before the onset of World War I.

URBANIZATION

From the outset of the emancipation era, blacks believed that "freedom was free-er" in the cities than in the countryside. In 1865, a group of eleven freedmen and -women and their children moved from the rural hinterlands to the outskirts of Macon, Georgia. When queried about their move, an old man spoke for the group: "I wanted to be a free man . . . I likes ter be free man whar I's can go an' cum, an' no-body says not'ing." Another former bondsman made the same connection between the city and freedom. Blacks, he said, wanted "to get closer to freedom, so they'd know what it was—like it was a place or a city." In North Carolina, one man from Warren County walked for miles to get to Raleigh, where he was determined "ter find out I wuz really free." Another man spoke for a group of blacks who had left rural Dinwiddie County, Virginia, for Richmond: "Thar a'n't no chance fo' people o' my color in the country I came from." Rural Alabama blacks headed for Selma "to be free." The belief that freedom was somehow "free-er" in the city persisted through the early twentieth century. In 1908, for example, the scholar and activist W. E. B. Du Bois wrote that the "country was peculiarly the seat of slavery . . . and its blight still rests . . . heavily on the land . . . [but] in cities the negro has had his chance."

Migration to Cities of the South, North, and West

The percentage of U.S. blacks living in cities increased from an estimated 5 to 7 percent in 1860 to over 25 percent in 1910. In the urban South, blacks averaged about one-third of the total black and white population, whereas they rarely made up more than 7 percent of the total in northern and western cities before the onset of World War II. Between 1880 and 1910, Richmond's black population increased from 27,800 to 46,700; Louisville's from 20,900 to 40,500; Savannah's from 15,700 to 33,200; and that of New Orleans from 57,600 to 89,700. For its part, the black population of Washington, D.C., rose from only 11,000 in 1860, to 35,500 in 1870, to 95,000 in 1910, representing the second-largest black urban population in the nation. Baltimore's black population also increased rapidly, rising from about 28,000 during the 1860s to 85,000 in 1910. Moreover, as the nation completed its interregional and national rail connections—particularly the Pennsylvania Railroad, the Illinois Central, and the Southern Pacific—black migrants, who often worked on the rails, used these lines to seek better opportunities for themselves and their families outside the South.

Between the Civil War and World War I, an estimated 400,000 blacks left the South. The percentage of blacks living in the North and West increased from 7.8 percent in 1860 to about 11 percent in 1910. A few East Coast and Midwest cities like Philadelphia, Chicago, Pittsburgh, and New York absorbed the bulk of these newcomers, who came mainly from the Upper South and border states of Tennessee, Kentucky, Missouri, and Virginia. By 1910, New York's black population had risen to 91,700, the largest urban concentration of blacks in the country. Philadelphia's black population reached 84,500, the fifth-largest concentration of blacks in the country, behind the District of Columbia, New Orleans, New York, and Baltimore. Other black migrants gradually moved to West Coast and Pacific Northwest cities like Los Angeles, Seattle, and San Francisco. Western cities attracted a more diverse black population than northern or southern ones. In San Francisco, for example, the migrants included not only both northern- and southern-born blacks but also a substantial number of foreign-born blacks: from Canada, the Cape Verde Islands, and the West Indies, especially Jamaica. In short- and long-distance moves, blacks utilized established transportation, kin, and friendship networks. A Tennessee-born couple later recalled how they migrated to Los Angeles: "We came here in 1902. . . . We were doing pretty well, so we sent back and told cousins to come along. When the cousins got here, they sent for their cousins. Pretty soon the whole community was made up of Tennessee people."

Cities continued to attract disproportionately more women than men. By 1910, there were only 87 black males to every 100 black females in southern cities. The white sex ratio was nearly even. In cities like Nashville, Montgomery, and Charleston, the figure was less than 80 men to every 100 women. Even in the booming industrial city of Birmingham, with its huge demand for male iron- and steelworkers, there were slightly more women than men. Black women also dominated the migration flow to the older northeastern seaport cities of Philadelphia, Boston, and New York, where expanding domestic and personal service sectors offered relatively greater job opportunities for black women than for men. Conversely, young men dominated the migration stream to the newly expanding industrial cities of the Great Lakes. In 1910, for example, there were some 85 to 87 men to every 100 black women in New York and Philadelphia, compared with 105 to 108 men to every 100 women in Chicago, Detroit, Pittsburgh, and Cleveland.

Opposition and Exclusion

Despite the freed people's optimistic turn toward cities, contemporary whites viewed the rising black urban population with alarm. The ex-slaveholder Henry Ravenel of South Carolina lamented that "they all want to go to the cities, either Charleston or Augusta." Another South Carolinian remarked that "our beloved city has become Pandemonium." Freedmen's Bureau officials reinforced alarming images of migration. According to bureau reports, African Americans were "crowd[ing]," "flocking," "overrun[ning]," or "throng[ing]" the cities to "fearful excess." Referring to black urbanites as idle, immoral, criminal, and bearers of disease as well as "vice," public officials took steps to suppress the movement. In Richmond, New Orleans, Savannah, and other southern cities, authorities revived the antebellum pass system and regularly harassed old residents as well as newcomers. In Richmond, one observer complained that "all that is needed to restore Slavery in full is the auction block." In Galveston, Texas, the Union commander ordered blacks without a "home" or "master" to work on city streets or leave the city. The same commander urged the city council and mayor to enact a law punishing "all hired servants" who quit their jobs before the expiration of their contracts. In Mobile, Alabama, a group of freed people exclaimed that it was not the ex-Confederates that they feared, but Union soldiers.

In Meridian, Mississippi, authorities destroyed a black settlement on the edge of the city. Officials justified their actions on the pretext that it represented a public health hazard. Similarly, in Natchez, Mississippi, authorities removed blacks from their homes and destroyed the structures on the premise that they were contaminated with yellow fever. As late as 1900, George Washington Cable, the southern writer, observed that "there is a notion among Southern people . . . that it is highly important that the Negro should be kept on the plantation." In the North, too, whites expressed alarm at the possible in-migration of large numbers of southern blacks. In 1887, a journalist for an African American newspaper, the *New York Freeman*, complained that "the Northern white men knew practically nothing of the Negro; he is looked upon more as a problem than as a factor in the general weal, with the same desires, passions, hopes, ambitions as other human creatures." In 1906, Howard University professor Kelly Miller remarked that whites in New York and other northern cities displayed a "prevailing dread of overwhelming [black] influx from the South."

Southern and northern urbanites backed up their opposition to black settlement by violence. As lynching engulfed blacks in the countryside, urban whites adopted the race riot as their principal form of mob violence. Destructive race riots broke out in New Orleans and Memphis in 1866; in Philadelphia in 1871; in Danville, Virginia, in 1883; in Wilmington, North Carolina, in 1898; in New York in 1900; in Atlanta in 1906; and in Springfield, Illinois, in 1904 and 1908. White mobs entered black communities, destroyed property, and beat, killed, and injured scores of people, forcing many to flee for their lives. Invariably, local police joined the mobs in their attacks, while other officials, including mayors and governors, aided and abetted the violence by overt actions or by inaction as public servants responsible for ensuring public safety. Moreover, some of the violence involved outright lynchings. In Nashville, for example, brutal lynchings of blacks occurred in 1872, 1875, 1877, and 1890 (see Chapter 13).

Champions of white labor made it exceedingly difficult for blacks to make a living in the city. As early as 1865, the *Nashville Daily Press and Times* feared that freedmen and -women "would at once come into rivalry with white labor." Thus, the paper vigorously campaigned for the colonization of ex-slaves elsewhere. In Montgomery, Alabama, white mechanics criticized employers who hired blacks when whites were available "at the same price." In 1885, a racist columnist for the *Atlanta Constitution* protested the employment of blacks as brick masons and carpenters: "Darn this idea of getting indignant at shaking hands with the nigger when you're slapping the quarters and halves and dollars into that same paw." Even in household service, employers frequently advertised for white women over blacks. Southern daily newspapers lodged a growing battery of complaints against black women as workers. In such papers as the *Nashville Daily Press and Times*, the *Richmond Dispatch*, and the *Montgomery Daily Ledger*, employers criticized black women workers and advertised for white ones: "Wanted: a white girl to do general housework for a family of two persons. Irish or German preferred." Other ads stated simply: "Wanted a good white woman as a housekeeper." Although northern industrialists like the steel magnate Andrew Carnegie made generous contributions to black colleges and developed close relations with Booker T. Washington and other elites, they turned to Europeans and American-born whites to fill their labor needs. For their part, western employers often preferred Asian and white workers over blacks. African Americans lost out to Chinese in the railroad construction boom and to white workers of Irish, German, and other backgrounds in skilled trades and general labor jobs.

White workers barred blacks from their unions and reinforced the exclusionary practices of industrialists. According to one white steel unionist, compelling whites to work with black men "was itself cause sufficient to drive . . . [white workers] into open rebellion." The Sons of Vulcan, the Associated Brotherhood of Iron and Steel Heaters, the Iron and Steel Roll Hands Union, the Railroad Brotherhoods, the Boilermakers Union, the International Association of Machinists, and the Plumbers' Steamfitters' Union all restricted membership to white workers either formally or informally. Although the National Labor Union, formed in 1866, and the Knights of Labor (KOL), formed three years later, encouraged the inclusion of diverse ethnic and racial groups, they also permitted white locals to establish segregated bodies that discriminated against black workers. Similarly, when the American Federation of Labor supplanted the KOL after 1886, it initially organized black and white workers together but soon relinquished the fight for racial inclusion and permitted segregation and exclusionary practices.

Although black men had entered a variety of urban occupations as enslaved and free blacks, they now saw their occupational horizons shrinking. Black artisans, for example, were increasingly replaced by whites. On the eve of the Civil War, only about 17 and 21 percent of black men occupied bottom-rung jobs in New Orleans and Charleston, respectively. By 1880, however, nearly 50 percent of black men occupied such jobs in both cities. During the early 1880s, a visitor to Charleston reported that "the master mechanics, builders, carpenters, blacksmiths, etc. are white, while the journeymen and laborers are colured." Although exclusionary practices were less dramatic in the North than in the South, northern blacks also faced displacement from artisan jobs. In Cleveland, the percentage of black men who worked in jobs as blacksmiths, shoemakers, painters, and carpenters dropped from 31.7 percent in 1870 to only 11.1 percent forty years later. At about the same time, the percentage of black men in skilled trades declined from 15 percent to 1.1 percent in Philadelphia. White union members ensured the decline by barring young African Americans from training as craftsmen.

As blacks lost ground in the artisan field, they also faced exclusion from the rapidly expanding industrial sectors. In the postwar South, textile mills rapidly expanded, but employers largely excluded blacks from these new industrial enterprises. As early as 1881, a Nashville cotton manufacturer hired an all-white work force. Blacks, these employers often argued, were incapable of mastering work on machinery. Moreover, one employer argued, the whirring of the machines would put blacks to sleep. Although blacks continued to work in the iron and tobacco industries of Richmond, one of the most industrialized cities of the South, postwar employers narrowed their range of occupations according to certain stereotypes about black character. The Richmond Chamber of Commerce declared: "In temper he is tractable and can be easily taught . . . the negro in the heavier work . . . is a most valuable hand." Accordingly, new South iron and steel men employed blacks for the most difficult jobs in the rolling mills, whereas their tobacco counterparts employed blacks in the production of chewing tobacco. White workers took the more desirable, cleaner, cigar and cigarette production jobs, which utilized new machinery.

Growing numbers of urban black men and women worked as day laborers. By 1890, the percentage of black men in general labor, domestic, and personal service jobs stood at nearly 68 percent in Atlanta, 60 percent in Richmond, and 67 percent in Nashville. In the same cities, at the same time, 92, 81, and 90 percent, respectively, of the black female labor force worked in domestic and personal service occupations. Northern cities followed roughly the same pattern. In 1900, the percentage of black men in these positions exceeded 64 percent in Chicago, nearly 58 percent in New York, 68 percent in Detroit, and 60 percent in Cleveland. An estimated 80 to 90 percent of black women in these cities worked in domestic and personal service occupations. African American women washed, cleaned, and cooked, whereas black men dug ditches, built and repaired roads, and moved tons of freight in railroad yards and on the docks. Such jobs revolved around the arduous tasks of lifting, hauling, cleaning, and cooking, but they were carried out in a variety of settings: in private homes, hotels, factories, department stores, restaurants, theaters, train stations (and on trains), boat ports (and on boats), office buildings, hospitals, schools, churches, and clubhouses. Although some blacks worked in the newest and most fashionable hotels, offices, or bank buildings, with their spacious rooms, high ceilings, marble walls, and overhead fans, most labored in jobs and surroundings with long hours, few amenities, low pay, and close supervision of work routines. Certain descriptions of urban African American work emerged and persisted over the period: "It is the negroes who do the hard work. They handle goods on the levee, and at the railroad; drive drays and hacks; lay gas pipes and work on [and in] new buildings."

Although African Americans took jobs at the cellar of the urban economy, they nonetheless faced difficulties holding on to these positions. Under the impact of hard times, unemployment, technological change, and hardening racial attitudes, white workers coveted certain jobs in the service sector and moved to displace blacks. Black caterers, waiters, and barbers serving a white clientele faced increasing competition from European immigrants. In Louisville, as early as 1885, an Irishman not only exploited prevailing racist ideas about the benefits of racial separation but also reversed the rhetoric. Since black barbers retained wealthy white customers by serving blacks and whites on a segregated basis, the Irishman exclaimed: "It is nothing more or less than selling [their] birthright for a few dollars. If their barbers had race pride at heart they would step down and out of business." According to the black Cincinnati writer Wendell Dabney, African Americans were unprepared for the immigrant assault on their barbering stronghold:

> White men came into the barber business. The Negro barbers laughed. More white men came. Less laughing. The white man brought business methods. . . . He gave new names to old things. Sanitary and sterilized became his great words, the open sesame for the coming generation. . . . Old customers died and then their sons "who know not Joseph." . . . Negro barber shops for white patrons melted as snow before a July sun.

In Detroit, blacks dropped from 55 percent of all barbers serving a predominantly white clientele in 1870 to only 24 percent in 1890. Although blacks made up 17 percent of all barbers in Boston in 1870, by 1900 their percentage had plummeted to only 5 percent. Moreover, as Americans moved toward European-style (that is, modern or formal style) service in barbershops, catering, and restaurants, they increasingly emphasized qualifications, including literacy, training, and expertise, and replaced their black kitchen staffs with whites. In 1906, for example, Milwaukee's prestigious Plankinton House replaced its black waiters with Greeks and other European immigrants. As employers dismissed blacks from such service occupations, they often justified their actions in the language of efficiency as well as racism, suggesting that blacks "did not tend to business."

Opportunities in the New Industrial Economy

Although blacks found it exceedingly difficult to expand their footing in the urban economy, some gradually made inroads on new industrial jobs. In the South, except for textiles, they gained employment in companies producing cotton-related goods and services, such as the Nashville Cotton Seed Oil Company, the Dixie Oil Company, and the Alabama Compress and Storage Company in Montgomery. In South Carolina, some black workers moved from the rice fields into the phosphate pits of Charleston. As the city's phosphate industry developed and expanded after 1867, it employed a predominantly black labor force to dig rock from land-based pits as well as to collect rock from river beds by dredges. Black laborers also transported the rock to railroad lines, where it was then shipped to mills, crushed into fine powder, treated with acid, and transformed into fertilizer. These mill operations also employed a predominantly black work force.

In the rural industrial sectors of the economy, black men worked as coal, lumber, and railroad workers. Railroad expansion and rural industries like coal mining often went hand in hand. In parts of Virginia, West Virginia, and Ohio, for example, many blacks helped to build the Chesapeake and Ohio, Norfolk and Western, and Virginian Railroads. In each case, as they completed laying track, many black workers took jobs in the coal mining labor force of the central Appalachian region. Similarly, as the Birmingham coal and iron district expanded during the late nineteenth and early twentieth centuries, African Americans entered its labor force in growing numbers. Indeed, by the onset of World War I, blacks made up the majority of all coal miners in the Birmingham district. Yet they faced the abusive contract and convict labor systems, discriminatory wage scales that paid whites more than blacks for the same work, disfranchisement, and a brutal system of lynchings and racial violence. Although such labor conditions were more extreme in the Deep South than they were in the urban and industrial districts of the Upper South and border states, such socioeconomic and political conditions helped to prompt a growing number of blacks to seek a living farther north.

Northern blacks gained their most prominent opportunities in the steel, meatpacking, and other heavy industries. As European immigration fueled the rise of a new labor movement, employers reevaluated the potential of black workers. As early as 1881, the steel employers' *Iron Age* commented favorably on the skills of southern black boilers, heaters, and rollers. Less than ten years later, the magazine reported: "Wherever the Negro has had a chance to acquire the necessary skill . . . he has shown himself capable." In rapid succession, as white workers walked out on

African Americans responded to exclusion from white labor unions by forming their own all-black unions. Some of these unions developed affiliations with white bodies, as did this Charleston, South Carolina, bricklayers union (c. 1881). *Black Charleston Photo Collection, College of Charleston Library*

strike, industrial firms employed black strikebreakers. In the Pittsburgh district, steel companies employed black strikebreakers in 1875, 1887–1889, 1892, 1901, and 1909. As labor historians Sterling D. Spero and Abram L. Harris noted: "Almost every labor disturbance . . . saw Negroes used as strikebreakers. . . . In every instance the Negroes brought in were men trained in the mills of the South." Company officials would later refer to black workers as "strike insurance." In the Chicago stockyards strike of 1904 and again in the teamsters' strike of 1905, employers used nonunion black workers as strikebreakers. A mob of about two thousand to five thousand whites stoned about two hundred black workers who entered one plant under "police protection." White workers referred to blacks in derogatory terms as a "scab race" and as "big, ignorant, vicious Negroes, picked up from the criminal elements of the black belts of the country." In New York City, blacks served as strikebreakers in 1895, 1904, 1907, 1910, 1911, and 1912. In western cities, large numbers of Asians and Latino workers complicated the black industrial experience. In 1903, in Los Angeles, for example, nearly two thousand blacks gained jobs with the Southern Pacific Railroad when Mexican American workers walked out on strike. This development ushered in a set of interethnic conflicts that hampered the African American and Latino struggle for social justice.

Strikebreaking was not merely a consequence of employers dividing black and white workers. It also represented black workers' resistance to labor union discrimination. Moreover, in the iron and steel industry, where blacks were used most often and effectively to break the back of white labor, African Americans had developed deep antebellum work traditions that facilitated their responses to inequality in both racial and class terms. The Tredegar Iron Works in Richmond, Virginia, employed large numbers of blacks before the Civil War and nearly one thousand slaves during the war. Although whites stereotyped black workers as lazy, inefficient, and incapable of performing skilled work, black iron- and steelworkers mastered a variety of jobs, including skilled jobs as puddlers and iron and steel heaters. When U.S. Steel took over the Tennessee Coal and Iron Company in 1907, African Americans made up about 25 to 30 percent of the labor force in the Birmingham district of Alabama. Understandably, white workers in northern steel centers like western Pennsylvania feared African Americans as potential competitors.

Still, strikebreaking was not an entirely black affair. When African Americans gained steel industry jobs as strikebreakers, they were usually accompanied by small groups of immigrants and American-born white workers as well. In the Pittsburgh district, for example, when white puddlers struck one company, white heaters and rollers stayed on the job and later cooperated with black strikebreakers and ensured the return of the mills to full productivity. Nonetheless, unlike white immigrant workers who entered industrial jobs as strikebreakers and stayed, blacks often lost their jobs as whites returned to work. By 1910, Pittsburgh's iron and steel mills employed nearly 300,000 workers, but African Americans made up only about 3 percent of the total, compared with 29 percent for American-born whites and 68 percent for immigrants. At the same time, in Chicago, blacks made up fewer than 400 of the city's 16,367 packinghouse workers. Blacks made up an even smaller proportion of the city's steelworkers. In Cincinnati, African Americans made up an estimated 1 percent of the city's metal workers, while the black population in some small northern cities like Evansville, Indiana, either stagnated or declined as a result of limited job opportunities.

Although black workers used strikebreaking as one strategy for improving their economic position, they also gradually formed unions to fight for their rights and humanity as blacks and as workers. They knew that employers were no more likely to support their interests than were white workers. Thus, black workers sought to close ranks with organized white labor. They formed skilled unions of carpenters, barbers, and masons; semiskilled and common labor unions of teamsters, longshoremen, and bar, restaurant, and hotel employees, including bootblacks; and industrial unions of dock-, iron-, and steelworkers. As early as 1869, under the leadership of Isaac Myers of Baltimore, African Americans formed the black National Labor Union and pressed for higher wages, better working conditions, and recognition of their citizenship rights. In 1871, in Nashville, black dock workers went on strike for higher wages. In 1881, black boilers formed the Garfield Lodge No. 92 at the Black Diamond Steel Works in Pittsburgh. Complementing the

Pittsburgh local was the formation of Sumner Lodge No. 3 in Richmond, Virginia. When black workers struck the Black Diamond Works in 1881–1882, white union officials supported their search for work at other mills during the shutdown. When employers turned to Richmond for black strikebreakers, the Sumner Lodge foiled their effort. By gaining jobs in other mills, with the support of white workers and by joining hands with black workers in Richmond, African American workers demonstrated a resolve to organize across geographical as well as race lines, when possible.

When the American Federation of Labor (AFL) supplanted the Knights of Labor during the 1890s, black workers played a crucial role in the rise of the multiracial United Mine Workers of America (UMWA). Although the UMWA was a constituent of the racially exclusive AFL, it represented a radical departure from the parent body's discriminatory policies. Black coal miners became both members and officers of the UMWA. The coal miner Richard L. Davis of Ohio became the most renowned of the black office holders. In 1891, Davis was elected to the executive board of the UMWA District Six (Ohio). He held the Ohio post for six years, and in 1896 and again in 1897 he was elected to the national executive board, the highest position held by an African American in the UMWA. Although he consistently encouraged blacks to join the union (and, at times severely criticized them for their reluctance), he opposed exclusionary hiring practices, advocated the election of blacks to leadership positions in the union, and protested white miners' discriminatory

Black and white miners at Gary, McDowell County, West Virginia, c. 1900. Both black and white miners belonged to the United Mine Workers of America. *United Mine Workers of America Photo Archives*

attitudes and behavior toward black workers. Davis urged white workers to organize against corporate exploitation and confront those who gained unequal benefits from the "sweat and blood" of fellow workers. At a time when African Americans faced increasing restrictions on their civil rights, witnessed the meteoric rise of Booker T. Washington (the ex-slave and founder of the Tuskegee Institute), and turned increasingly toward the ideology of racial solidarity and self-help, black and white workers joined the United Mine Workers of America, an interracial union within the American Federation of Labor. Davis's life symbolized this complicated intertwining of black workers' class and racial identities at the turn of the twentieth century.

African American labor activism included black female household workers, who deployed a variety of strategies for changing the basis on which they lived and labored. Household workers regularly supplemented their meager income by taking food from their employers' cupboards, bringing loads of laundry home and refusing to return them, and quitting their jobs in the midst of their employers' plans to lavishly entertain and impress business and professional guests. Black women also organized collectively and launched strikes against exploitative employers. Black laundry women staged strikes in Jackson, Mississippi, in 1866; in Galveston, Texas, in 1877; and in Atlanta in 1881. The Atlanta strike became one of the most militant labor campaigns of the period. Black women formed the Association of Washer Women, established a strike fund of $300, and struck for higher wages. Within two weeks, the *Atlanta Constitution,* the city's leading newspaper, reported that the strike was "causing quite an inconvenience among our citizens." Only the combined activities of landlords, city council, and local police broke the strike. Before the strike ended, however, the women had defied municipal officials and encouraged the strike's spread to other sectors of the economy. According to a report in the city's leading newspaper, the *Atlanta Constitution,* "Not only washerwomen, but the cooks, house servants and nurses are asking an increase. The combinations are being managed by [the] laundry ladies."

EMERGENCE OF NEW BUSINESSES AND ENTREPRENEURS

As African American workers sought to improve their class position, their efforts coalesced with a rising race consciousness and helped to stimulate the growth of new entrepreneurial activities. As we will see in Chapter 13, these efforts were closely intertwined with a pattern of residential and institutional segregation in the larger community life of the city. From the outset of the emancipation era, blacks demonstrated a determination to accumulate capital, go into business, and create employment and necessary social services for themselves. As early as 1869, blacks from Baltimore, Wilmington, and Washington, D.C., formed the Chesapeake Marine and Dry Dock Company. Capitalized at $40,000, the company employed three hundred black mechanics, paid off its start-up loan in five years, and prospered through the next decade. At about the same time, other blacks placed their hope on the Freedmen's Savings Bank. Chartered in 1865, the Freedmen's bank failed during the economic depression of 1873. Thousands of ordinary blacks lost their life's savings during this crisis. Although many became discouraged and never quite trusted banks again, black banking and insurance institutions soon reemerged and expanded.

The Virginia Building and Savings Company symbolized nascent black capital accumulation and middle-class formation. In 1879, the company advertised that "in union there is strength!" It also made a special appeal to black workers as a cornerstone in black business development: "We desire to encourage and support our mechanics, and to supply capital and business for our merchants." In 1888, Richmond blacks formed the True Reformers Bank, while blacks in Washington, D.C., founded the Capital Savings Bank. In 1890, Alabama blacks formed the Penny Savings and Loan Company. By 1907, the Alabama bank had become the second-largest black bank in capital and deposits, behind the True Reformers. In Durham, North Carolina, considered by some scholars the capital of the black business world, blacks formed the North Carolina Mutual Life Insurance Company under the leadership of John Merrick, a former slave brickmason, hod carrier, and barber. By 1915, Merrick and his partners, Dr. Aaron McDuffie and the grocer Charles C. Spaulding, had not only opened offices in twelve states and the District of Columbia but also established two drugstores, a Mechanics and Farmers Bank, and a real estate company and were preparing to launch a textile mill employing black workers.

In 1900, under the leadership of Booker T. Washington, head of Tuskegee Institute in Alabama, African Americans formed the National Negro Business League (NNBL). The NNBL pledged to provide products, services, and jobs to the black community. Emphasizing self-help and racial solidarity, local chapters soon spread throughout the nation. According to league records, black enterprises in the United States increased by 100 percent between 1900 and World War I—from 20,000 to 40,000: banks increased from 4 to 51; funeral homes from 450 to 1,000; drugstores from 250 to nearly 700; and retail establishments from 10,000 to 25,000. Cosmetic firms also claimed a growing share of black business activities, which provided employment to black workers, particularly women. In Chicago, the Overton Hygienic Manufacturing Company, manufacturer of "High Brown Face Powder," was capitalized at $268,000, employed thirty-two people, and manufactured sixty-two different products, mainly serving the cosmetic needs of black people. By the early twentieth century, pioneering black beauty culturists and entrepreneurs like Annie Turbo Malone, Sarah Spencer Washington, and most notably Madame C. J. Walker successfully marketed skin, hair, and beauty products to black women. Born Sarah Breedlove to sharecropping parents in Delta, Louisiana, Madame Walker made the transition from St. Louis washerwoman to the foremost black female entrepreneur of the period. After working for a brief period for Annie Malone, Walker later moved to Denver and then to Indianapolis. Her cosmetics company employed an energetic black sales staff, which enabled large numbers of black women to escape domestic service. Until recently, Walker (see photo) was widely regarded as perhaps the first self-made African American female millionaire.

Madame C. J. Walker, born Sarah Breedlove, emerged as the most prominent African American businesswoman of the early twentieth century. She successfully marketed a variety of beauty projects designed to enhance the health and condition of black women's hair and skin. *Courtesy of A'Lelia Bundles/ Madame Walker Family Collection*

As we will see in Chapter 14, the black press both mirrored and promoted black business as a vehicle for self-employment and middle-class formation. The number of black weeklies increased from just over two dozen in 1880 to over 150 by the early 1900s. In addition to established papers like the *New York Globe,* the *Indianapolis Freeman,* and the Cleveland *Gazette,* new and more aggressive business-oriented black weeklies also moved to the fore during the early twentieth century—the *Chicago Defender, Pittsburgh Courier,* and *Norfolk Journal and Guide,* to name a few. One editor articulated a common view when he declared: "The men and women who are conducting business houses are worthy of our support. With our help they can develop into powerful institutions that will give employment to thousands of our boys and girls."

Some black business and professional people not only promoted black enterprise as a vehicle for black employment but also encouraged a radical critique of labor and race relations. As early as 1868, middle-class leaders supported the ship caulker Isaac Myers and the formation of the Colored National Labor Union. The labor convention of 1869 endorsed the call for government-funded forty-acre lots for ex-slaves, the right of workers to organize and bargain collectively, and the acquisition of full political and citizenship rights for formerly enslaved people. The convention concluded: "Our mottoes are liberty and labor, enfranchisement and education. The spelling-book and the hoe, the hammer and the vote, the opportunity to work and to rise . . . we ask for ourselves and our children." For their part, black leaders like Frederick Douglass, T. Thomas Fortune of the *New York Age,* and John R. Lynch of Mississippi criticized "wage slavery" and emphasized the unity of interest between black and white workers. During the 1880s, for example, Fortune adopted the "land monopoly" ideas of reformer Henry George and offered a radical class analysis of black life after emancipation. In his view, the same elite control of southern land that had given rise to chattel slavery now gave rise to *"industrial slavery,* a slavery more excruciating in its exactions, more irresponsible in its machinations than any other slavery." Fortune praised the Knights of Labor and urged black workers to join white labor against the "odious and unjust tyranny" of white capital. As Fortune put it, "Since we are largely of the laboring population, it is very natural that we should take sides with the labor forces in their fight for a juster distribution of the results of labor."

Cross-class responses to economic discrimination were by no means unproblematic. They produced tensions and conflicts within the black community even as they forged links across geographical, cultural, and class lines. As we will see in Chapter 14, middle-class and elite black business and professional people established their own institutions and articulated their own ideas and beliefs about the future of blacks in America. Their vision often clashed with the views of working-class and poor blacks. By the 1890s, black elites like Fortune had become disillusioned with the organized labor movement and stepped away from radical class analyses of black life and labor. As black elites abandoned the organized labor movement, some black workers like the coal miner Richard L. Davis sought to strengthen it.

More so than elites, black workers and the poor also retained an abiding interest in migration and possible emigration strategies for social change. Before moving to Kansas in 1879, for example, Henry Adams and others had anticipated emigration in the event the Kansas effort failed. African emigration associations developed throughout the South and even the West as African Americans moved outward. In 1891, the American Colonization Society (ACS) reported that the number of prospective emigrants had become "numerous and urgent." Some blacks expressed the view that "the colored man has no home in America." Two years after the election of 1876, a group of two hundred blacks left South Carolina for Liberia. In South Carolina, Reverend R. H. Cain and Martin R. Delany headed the South Carolina Liberian Exodus Association. Delany again reiterated his belief that Africa represented the best place "to seek new homes." By the 1890s, the African Methodist Episcopal bishop Henry McNeal Turner emerged as the leading advocate of emigration to Africa. A South Carolina–born black, Turner became the first black army chaplain in the U.S. Army during the Civil War. Following the war, he settled in Georgia and became one of the black members expelled from the state's legislature in 1868. By 1876, Turner had become a vice president of the ACS and advocated emigration through the 1890s. In 1892, he advocated Liberia as a place for black "manhood, freedom, and fullest liberty."

Other blacks rejected colonization overseas but sought a territory for an independent black state or nation within the United States. They considered New Mexico, Arizona, Nebraska, and Kansas, which (as noted earlier) soon emerged as a principal target of post-Reconstruction black migration. All-black towns proliferated during the late nineteenth and early twentieth centuries. Beginning with Nicodemus, Kansas (1877), black town building spread rapidly through the trans-Appalachian West: Mound Bayou, Mississippi (1887); Langston City, Oklahoma (1890); Boley, Oklahoma (1904); and Allensworth, California (1908). All-black towns emerged in northern, southern, and western states, including Alabama, Louisiana, Iowa, Illinois, Kansas, New Mexico, and especially Oklahoma, which contained over thirty all-black towns by World War I. Although African Americans provided the labor force of black towns, such towns usually included the investment of white as well as black capital. Some of the most well-known black founders included the northern freeborn black Edward P. McCabe, an early settler of Nicodemus, Langston City, and Liberty, Oklahoma; the former Mississippi bondsman Isaiah T. Montgomery of Mound Bayou; and Allen Allensworth, a formerly enslaved Kentuckian and the highest-ranking black soldier on his retirement from the U.S. Army in 1907. Although many poor and working-class blacks supported out-migration, members of the black upper and middle classes resisted out-migration for poor and working-class blacks. As political leaders, the former hoped to retain the latter as black constituents; as business and professional people, they hoped to retain them as clients; and as landowners and employers, they hoped to retain their labor. For their part, established northern and western black leaders also opposed the mass out-migration of southern blacks, hoping to hold on to the gains they believed small numbers brought to their communities.

∾

THROUGHOUT THE LATE NINETEENTH CENTURY, postbellum blacks retained a vision of landownership as the fundamental route to economic independence and political empowerment. They rejected both northern and southern white notions of wage labor. In their view, white visions of work robbed them of their birthright to a portion of the land that they had worked and enriched as bondsmen and -women. Consequently, they turned toward the sharecropping system as an alternative to rural wage labor. Sharecropping promised access to land, which they could work independently and avoid gang labor and the strict supervision of overseers. Yet the rise of new postwar forms of labor coercion—state laws regulating vagrancy, debt, and credit—compelled blacks to work under repressive conditions that rendered sharecropping far from free. Although blacks defied such restrictions and moved from place to place in search of better working and living conditions within the rural South, their responses also signaled a significant shift in their vision for social change.

Urban wage labor gradually expanded as a new and more promising alternative to both rural wage labor and sharecropping. By the eve of World War I, black men and women had not only engaged in strikebreaking as a means of gaining industrial jobs and counteracting the exclusionary practices of white unions but also formed their own all-black unions, walked out on strike, and challenged the unjust labor and social practices of their employers. At the same time, black workers gradually responded to the appeals of a new generation of black entrepreneurs who promised to help offset economic discrimination by employing black workers within black-owned and operated firms. These workplace struggles and entrepreneurial developments transcended the question of economic freedom. They were also closely related to the cultural, intellectual, and institutional dimensions of emancipation, the rise of Jim Crow, and the transformation of the larger African American community. These issues are examined in Chapters 13 and 14.

PART I	**The African American Experience in Global Perspective: Prelude to a New World** (Chapters 1–2)
3000–2850 B.C.	Upper and Lower Egypt unite into a single kingdom, forming one of the earliest recorded cultures in human history.
1000 B.C.	South of Egypt, the Nubians develop an independent state, known by the Egyptians as Kush.
730 B.C.	Kush invades Egypt and establishes the 25th, or Ethiopian, Dynasty.
146 B.C.	The Romans conquer Carthage, renaming it "Africa," a name that will eventually refer to the entire continent.
A.D. 711	The Arabs gain control of North Africa and Egypt; the Islamic faith gains increasing influence.
A.D. 1000–1591	In succession, the great West African kingdoms of Ghana, Mali, and Songhay reach their peak and gradually decline.
1200–1400	Europeans initiate sugar plantations on the islands of Cyprus and Sicily, and in southern Spain and Portugal, using enslaved European, Arab, and African labor.
1444	The Portuguese reach the Senegal River and establish a fort at El Mina and sugar plantations on the islands of Madeira, Príncipe, and São Tomé.
1492	Christopher Columbus makes his first voyage to the New World. (Some scholars believe that African presence in the New World predates the arrival of Columbus.)

1494	The Treaty of Tordesillas gives to Spain most land in the Americas and to Portugal the territory of West Africa.
1502	Spain imports the first Africans to work on sugar plantations in Hispaniola (later Saint-Domingue, then Haiti).
1516	The king of Benin restricts and later bans slave trade.
1522	The earliest recorded revolt of African captives in the Americas takes place in Hispaniola.
1556	The Angolans defeat the king of Kongo with Portuguese assistance; slave raiding escalates.
1595	The Spanish government gives Portugal a monopolistic license, *asciento*, to provide slaves to Spain's New World colonies.

PART II   Enslavement, Revolution, and the New Republic, 1619– 1820 (Chapters 3–6)

1526	Africans accompany Lucas Vásquez de Ayllón to the future site of South Carolina, where they staged the earliest recorded slave rebellion in North America.
1565	Enslaved Africans help the Spanish establish St. Augustine, Florida, the first permanent non-Indian settlement in North America.
1607	The British establish their first permanent settlement, at Jamestown, Virginia.
1619	The first Africans enter British America at Jamestown, Virginia, via a ship engaged in piracy against Spanish colonies in the Caribbean.
1624	John Phillip, described as "a negro Christened in *England* 2 years since," testifies in the Virginia court against a white man.
1626	The Dutch initiate African bondage in the North, importing blacks from the Dutch West Indian colony of Curaçao.
1630	The Virginia court sentences a white man, Hugh Davis, to a sound whipping "for . . . defiling his body in lying with a negro."
1639	Maryland statute declares: "All the inhabitants of the province of Christian standing (slaves excepted) to enjoy full liberties and rights of Englishmen."
1640	The Virginia court sentences a black runaway to a lifetime of servitude but gives two white runaways only one additional year of service. In Virginia, a white man has "to do penance in church according to the laws of England, for getting a negroe woman with child and the woman whipt."

1641	Massachusetts sanctions the institution of slavery and indentured servitude for blacks and whites in its Body of Liberties.
1656	New England prescribes the death penalty for any slaveowner who "willfully killed his servant or slave."
1661	The Virginia assembly passes a statute mandating the enslavement of Africans *durante vita*—for life.
1662	Chesapeake slave codes redefine offspring by the status of the mother rather than the status of the father.
1664	The Maryland assembly passes a statute pronouncing Africans "slaves for life."
1669	Virginia approves a law permitting masters to kill slaves as a disciplinary measure.
1670	Virginia prohibits blacks from importing white servants. The first Africans enter the colony of South Carolina with planters from the Caribbean island of Barbados.
1676	Enslaved African Americans help lower- and middle-class whites challenge the unjust authority of colonial elites in Bacon's Rebellion in Virginia.
1688	Germantown, Pennsylvania, Mennonites issue their protest against the African slave trade.
1712	New York slaves and some Native Americans set fire to buildings and kill nine whites before authorities put down the revolt.
1718	A French company under the direction of Scotsman John Law lays out the city of New Orleans and encourages the importation of blacks into Louisiana.
1727	Pennsylvania iron masters express their dependence on black labor by petitioning the colonial legislature to reduce tariff duties on slaves.
1728	Boston prohibits blacks from carrying a stick or cane or "any other thing of that nature" that might "be fit for quarrelling or fighting."
1730	Connecticut enacts a law permitting the whipping of blacks for "attempting to strike" a white person.
1733	Spanish officials promise freedom to blacks who desert the plantations of British North America.
1734	South Carolina officials accuse Charleston blacks of cornering the market on certain products through legal and illegal trade.
1735	South Carolina's Negro Act restricts clothing blacks may wear, arguing that slaves wear clothes "much above" their condition.

1735	The First Great Awakening, a new brand of Christianity, attracts the attention of growing numbers of slaves and poor whites.
1750	The British Parliament reverses its prohibition of slave labor in the colony of Georgia.
1754	New Jersey Quaker John Woolman writes antislavery pamphlet *Some Considerations on the Keeping of Negroes*.
1755	Two white Baptists initiate the first evangelical mission among blacks, on William Byrd's plantation in Mechlenburg County, Virginia.
1760	New York slave Jupiter Hammon writes "An Evening Thought," the earliest known poem by an American-born black.
1766	Philadelphia school teacher Anthony Benezet publishes the antislavery pamphlet *A Caution and Warning to Great Britain and Her Colonies*.
1767	In Boston, Senegal-born slave Phillis Wheatley writes "Address to the Atheist," expressing her firm commitment to Christianity.
1770	Runaway slave and sailor Crispus Attucks is the first of four colonials to die in the Boston Massacre.
1772	In the Somerset case, the English Supreme Court declares that the free "law of England" overrules the institution of slavery elsewhere on English soil. Phillis Wheatley writes a poem expressing the hope that the earl of Dartmouth, the king's representative in North America, will fight tyranny.
1773	The *Pennsylvania Gazette* urges colonists to reconcile the contradiction between their fight against England and the continuing enslavement of Africans. A group of Virginia slaves holds a secret meeting to select a leader to guide their participation in the growing conflict between England and the colonies.
1774	The Continental Congress votes to outlaw African slave trade and sanctions a boycott against those who continue the practice. In St. Andrew Parish, Georgia, six black men and four women revolt against their owner and neighboring planters.
1775	Abolitionists form the Society for the Relief of Free Negroes Unlawfully Held in Bondage (April). British officer Lord Dunmore declares freedom for "all indentured servants and negroes" in exchange for taking up arms against the rebel forces (November).
1776	The colonies issue their Declaration of Independence but delete Jefferson's clause condemning England for slave trade and slavery (July 4).

1777	The Connecticut legislature enlists able-bodied soldiers without regard to "color or status." Most northern states pass similar legislation by 1781.
1779	The Continental Congress approves the use of black troops, slave and free.
	The British issue the Philipsburg Proclamation, extending freedom to slaves in exchange for military service.
1781	Maryland authorizes enlistment of slave and free blacks; Virginia bars enlistment of slave blacks but admits free blacks.
	South Carolina and Georgia bar both slave and free blacks from military service but offer slaves as bounties to encourage enlistment of whites.
1782	Black New York minister and writer Jupiter Hammon publishes *A Winter Piece*, a sermon reinforcing the quest for freedom.
1783	The Revolutionary War officially ends with the signing of the Treaty of Paris.
	By war's end, some 5,000 blacks have served in the revolutionary army.
	The Massachusetts Supreme Court concludes in the Quok Walker case that slavery is "inconsistent with our own conduct and constitution."
1785	The Second Great Awakening emerges in the James River, Virginia, area and merges antislavery religious traditions with new revolutionary ideology.
1786	Some blacks join white farmers in Shays's Rebellion; others volunteer to help put down the revolt.
1787	The Articles of Confederation government passes the Northwest Ordinance, which prohibits slavery in the territory north of the Ohio River.
	African Americans gain an English charter for a black Masonic order.
1789	The U.S. Constitution guarantees the extension of slavery until 1807 and mandates the return of fugitives who escape across state lines.
1791	Benjamin Banneker is appointed "scientific assistant" to Major Andrew Ellicott, the presidential appointee to survey the District of Columbia as the location of the nation's capital.
1792	The outbreak of Haitian Revolution sends growing numbers of free black émigrés to the United States.
1793	Congress passes the Fugitive Slave Act, authorizing slaveowners to enter free territory and apprehend runaways.

1794	Under the leadership of Richard Allen, blacks found the Bethel African Methodist Episcopal Church of Philadelphia.
	Eli Whitney invents his cotton gin, resulting in the dramatic expansion of cotton production.
1800	Boston invokes a state law against free blacks and orders the deportation of 240 free blacks from the city.
	Gabriel Prosser and a group of enslaved artisans plan a revolt in Richmond, Virginia.
1804	Beginning with Pennsylvania in 1780, all northern states pass gradual abolition laws; southern states allow manumission by will or deed.
1811	A large slave rebellion erupts in St. John the Baptist Parish in Louisiana; free blacks volunteer to help put down the revolt.
1812–1814	During the War of 1812, free blacks play an important role in the navy and in the defense of New Orleans.
1814	Andrew Jackson's frontier army attacks the Creek nation and forces concessions that enable the expansion of slavery into the southwest.
1817	Influential whites form the American Colonization Society to push resettlement of free blacks on African soil.

PART III   **The Antebellum Era, Expansion of Cotton Culture, and Civil War, 1820–1865** (Chapters 7–10)

1820	Northern and southern states approve the Missouri Compromise, which violates the Northwest Ordinance by extending slavery northwest of the Ohio River.
1821	New York black businessman Allen Royce opens the African Grove, billed as America's first black theater.
1822	Free black carpenter Denmark Vesey plots a rebellion against slaveholders in Charleston, South Carolina.
1823	The U.S. Supreme Court declares unconstitutional the incarceration of free black seamen who enter southern ports; southern states defy the ruling.
1827	Presbyterian minister Samuel Cornish and Jamaican-born teacher John Russwurm found *Freedom's Journal*, the nation's first black newspaper, in New York.
1829	Free black North Carolina carpenter David Walker issues his famous antislavery pamphlet, *Walker's Appeal*.
1830	African Americans hold the first National Negro Convention at Bethel AME Church in Philadelphia, with representatives from eight states.

1831	Slave preacher, carpenter, and carriage driver Nat Turner leads the most renowned slave rebellion in rural Virginia.
	In Boston, William Lloyd Garrison launches the abolitionist newspaper *Liberator.*
1832	The New England Anti-Slavery Society (later renamed the Massachusetts Anti-Slavery Society) is formed in Boston.
1833	The American Anti-Slavery Society is formed in Philadelphia by black and white abolitionists.
	A white mob destroys a school for young black women in Canterbury, Connecticut.
1836	Samuel Cornish, Philip Bell, and Charles B. Ray launch the *Colored American* (originally the *Weekly Advocate*), the longest-running antebellum black publication.
	Washington, D.C., prohibits free blacks or their agents from keeping "any tavern, ordinary, shop, porter cellar, refectory, or eating house of any kind, for profit or gain."
1838	Frederick Douglass escapes from his Maryland owner and moves to New Bedford, Massachusetts.
	Abolitionist David Ruggle initiates the first black magazine, the *Mirror of Liberty*, in New York.
1839	Led by Cinque, 53 enslaved Africans overpower the Cuban slaver *Amistad* and sail into Long Island Sound; they are later freed by the U.S. Supreme Court.
1840	The American and Foreign Anti-Slavery Society is formed, partly as a protest against the women's rights stand of the American Anti-Slavery Society.
1841	One of the most destructive antebellum race riots breaks out in Cincinnati.
	Rev. J. W. C. Pennington writes *A Text Book of the Origin and History of the Colored People.*
1843	Isabella Baumfree changes her name to Sojourner Truth and later becomes one of the most renowned itinerant ministers, antislavery activists, and women's rights advocates.
	At the National Convention of Colored Men in Buffalo, Henry Highland Garnet delivers "An Address to Slaves of the United States."
1845	Frederick Douglass, under pressure from white abolitionists, publishes his *Narrative of the Life of Frederick Douglass.*
	Harriet Jacobs (Linda Brent) escapes from slavery and later publishes her *Incidents in the Life of a Slave Girl: Written by Herself* (1861).

1846	The U.S. Senate rejects the Wilmot Proviso, which calls for a ban on slavery in any territory gained as a result of military conquest.
1847	Richmond's Tredegar Iron Works hires a predominantly slave work force after white workers walk out to protest the training of slaves for skilled jobs.
1848	Frederick Douglass launches a new organ of abolitionism, the *North Star*, which aims to increase the role of blacks in their own liberation.
1849–1850	Harriet Tubman escapes from her master on the eastern shore of Maryland and later makes nearly twenty trips into slave territory to aid fugitives.
1850	The Fugitive Slave Act outlaws the slave trade in Washington, D.C., but strengthens the hand of slave catchers in the free states.
	New York City blacks form the American League of Colored Laborers to organize skilled black workers and stimulate the growth of black business.
1851	In Christiana, Pennsylvania, abolitionists kill one slave catcher and mortally wound another. Participants are later acquitted of treason and murder.
	At the Akron, Ohio, Woman's Rights Convention, Sojourner Truth delivers an address that later becomes famous as the "And Ar'n't I a Woman?" speech.
1852	Harriet Beecher Stowe publishes her influential antislavery novel, *Uncle Tom's Cabin*.
	Martin R. Delany publishes *The Condition, Elevation, Emigration and Destiny of the Colored People of the United States*.
1853	William Wells Brown publishes *Clotel, or, The President's Daughter*, the first novel by an African American.
	Solomon Northrup publishes *Twelve Years a Slave: Narrative of Solomon Northrup, a Citizen of New York*.
1854	The Kansas-Nebraska Act violates the provisions of the Missouri Compromise of 1820 and helps set the stage for the Civil War.
	A national Emigration Convention meets in Cleveland, Ohio, and endorses a plan of African American resettlement in Africa.
1857	The U.S. Supreme Court rules in the Dred Scott case that blacks "were not intended to be included under the word 'citizens' in the constitution."
1859	The *Clothilde*, the last known slave ship to dock in a U.S. port, transports 130 Africans to Mobile, Alabama.
	Harriet E. Wilson writes *Our Nig, or, Sketches from the Life of a Free Black*, the first novel by an African American woman.

1859	John Brown, a white abolitionist minister from Kansas, leads an attack on the federal arsenal at Harpers Ferry, Virginia.
1860	Abraham Lincoln is elected president on the Republican Party ticket, which promises to uphold slavery where it already exists but to block its expansion into the new territories.
1861	Eleven southern states secede from the Union and establish the Confederate States of America.
	Congress passes the First Confiscation Act, which defines slaves as "contraband" of war (August).
1862	General David Hunter defies War Department orders and recruits the First Regiment of South Carolina Volunteers (May).
	Congress passes the Second Confiscation Act, which proclaims all slaves owned by southern rebels "forever free" (July).
1863	President Lincoln's Emancipation Proclamation declares all slaves free, except those in loyal territory (January).
	The New York draft riot results in violent attacks on the black community (July).
	Mary Ann Shadd Cary, a black journalist and antislavery activist, becomes the first official woman recruiter for the Union Army (August).
	Black soldiers of the Massachusetts Fifty-Fourth decide to fight without pay to protest racial inequality between black and white soldiers (September).
1864	Confederate troops massacre black soldiers after they surrender at Fort Pillow on the Mississippi River (April).
	Congress passes legislation equalizing the pay of black and white soldiers (June).
	Blacks from southern and northern states form the National Equal Rights League to protest racial discrimination (October).
1865	Congress establishes the Bureau of Freedmen, Refugees, and Abandoned Land (Freedmen's Bureau) to oversee the transition from slavery to freedom (March).
	The Civil War ends when Confederate general Robert E. Lee surrenders at Appomattox Court House in Virginia (April).
	Abraham Lincoln is assassinated; Andrew Johnson succeeds him as president (April).
	The Thirteenth Amendment outlaws slavery (December).

PART IV	**Emancipation and the First Generation of Freedom, 1865–1915** (Chapters 11–14)
1865–1866	Beginning with South Carolina and Mississippi, southern states pass "black codes," which deny blacks full citizenship rights.
1866	Veterans of the Confederate army form the Ku Klux Klan in Pulaski, Tennessee.
	The Freedmen's Bureau and northern philanthropic and missionary societies establish Fisk (1866), Howard (1866), and Atlanta (1867) Universities.
1867	Radical Republicans pass the Reconstruction Act of 1867 and make Reconstruction a prerogative of Congress rather than the president.
1868	The Fourteenth Amendment provides blacks full citizenship rights under the law.
1869	African Americans form their own National Labor Union under the leadership of Isaac Meyers of Baltimore.
1870	The Fifteenth Amendment enfranchises all men regardless of race, color, or previous condition of servitude.
1871	Congress passes the first of several Ku Klux Klan and Enforcement Acts, outlawing the use of violence to deprive citizens of the right to vote.
1873	The Freedmen's Bureau Bank, chartered in 1865, fails during an economic depression.
1875	Congress passes the Civil Rights Act of 1875, which calls for an end to racial discrimination in public accommodations like theaters, hotels, and restaurants.

1876	The presidential election of Republican Rutherford B. Hayes symbolizes the downfall of Radical Reconstruction.
1879	Some 6,000 blacks leave the Deep South states of Texas, Louisiana, and Mississippi for Kansas.
1880	African Americans form the Knights of Pythias, followed by the United Order of True Reformers (1881) and the Mosaic Templars of America (1882).
1882	Historian and minister George Washington Williams publishes *History of the Negro Race in America: From 1619 to 1880.*
1883	The U.S. Supreme Court strikes down the Civil Rights Act of 1875 and limits federal protection to the activities of states rather than those of individual citizens.
1884	Blacks in Washington, D.C., form the Medico-Chirurgical Society, the earliest black medical society.
1890	Numerous black farmers join whites in the Populist movement, designed to address the issues of class inequality. Mississippi initiates the movement for the constitutional disfranchisement of black voters; other southern states soon follow suit.
1891	Black labor leader Richard L. Davis is elected to the Executive Board of the United Mine Workers of America District Six (Ohio).
1892	The number of recorded lynchings peaks at about 160. Frances Ellen Harper publishes *Iola Leroy, or Shadows Lifted,* the first novel by a postbellum black writer.
1895	Booker T. Washington delivers his famous "Atlanta Compromise" address, urging blacks to push for economic and institutional improvements rather than political rights.
1895–1896	African Americans form the National Medical Association; the National Baptist Convention, U.S.A.; and the National Association of Colored Women.
1898	Four all-black units fight with the U.S. Army in the Spanish-American War.
1899	Charles Chestnut publishes *The Conjure Woman* and the *Wife of His Youth and Other Stories of the Color Line.*
1900	The National Negro Business League is formed under the leadership of Booker T. Washington.
1902	Gertrude "Ma" Rainey, considered the earliest professional black singer, tours Missouri (with the Rabbit Foot Minstrels), where she first hears the blues.
1903	W. E. B. Du Bois publishes *Souls of Black Folk* and becomes Booker T. Washington's leading critic.

1903	Under the leadership of W. E. B. Du Bois, 29 African Americans form the Niagara movement "to complain, and to complain loudly and insistently about racial discrimination."
1905	St. Louis laundress Madame C. J. Walker works for beauty manufacturer Annie Malone before producing her own renowned skin and hair care products for black women. Ferdinand "Jelly Roll" Morton, known as the first true jazz composer, publishes his jazz compositions as *Jelly Roll Blues*.
1906	President Theodore Roosevelt unjustly discharges some 167 black soldiers of the Twenty-Fifth Infantry Regiment.
1908	In his bout with Tommy Burns in Sydney, Australia, Jack Johnson becomes the first black heavyweight champion of the world.
1909–1910	African Americans and their white allies form the National Association for the Advancement of Colored People and the National Urban League. Race riots break out when Jack Johnson knocks out "great white hope" Jim Jeffries to retain his crown as heavyweight champion of the world.
1911	Black women form the Negro Women's Equal Franchise Federation and push for the right to vote.
1912	Woodrow Wilson, the first southern president since the Civil War, takes office and escalates the segregation of blacks and whites in the federal government. W. C. Handy, considered the first person to popularize the blues, publishes his *Memphis Blues*.

DOCUMENTS AND TABLES

THE BLACK POPULATION IN COLONIAL AMERICA, 1630-1780

	1630	1640	1650	1660	1670	1680	1690	1700
North	10	427	880	1,162	1,125	1,895	3,340	5,206
South	50	170	720	1,758	3,410	5,076	13,389	22,611
Total	**60**	**597**	**1,600**	**2,920**	**4,535**	**6,971**	**16,729**	**27,817**

	1710	1720	1730	1740	1750	1760	1770	1780
North	8,303	14,091	17,323	23,958	30,222	40,033	48,460	56,796
South	36,563	54,748	73,698	126,066	206,198	285,773	411,362	518,624
Total	**44,866**	**68,839**	**91,021**	**150,024**	**236,420**	**325,806**	**459,822**	**575,420**

THE ENSLAVED AND FREE BLACK POPULATION IN THE NEW REPUBLIC, 1790-1860

	1790	1800	1810	1820
Slave	697,624	893,602	1,191,362	1,538,022
Free	59,557	108,435	186,446	233,634
Total	**757,181**	**1,002,037**	**1,377,808**	**1,771,656**

	1830	1840	1850	1860
Slave	2,009,043	2,487,355	3,204,313	3,953,760
Free	319,599	386,293	434,495	488,070
Total	**2,328,642**	**2,873,648**	**3,638,808**	**4,441,830**

Source: Both tables from Harry A. Ploski and James Williams, eds., *The Negro Almanac: A Reference Work on the Afro-American,* 4th ed. (New York: John Wiley and Sons, 1983), p. 457.

THE AFRICAN AMERICAN POPULATION AS A PERCENTAGE OF THE TOTAL U.S. POPULATION, 1790–1860

Year	Total Population	Black Population	Percentage
1790	3,929,214	757,208	19.3
1800	5,308,483	1,002,037	18.9
1810	7,239,881	1,377,808	19.0
1820	9,638,453	1,771,656	18.4
1830	12,866,020	2,328,642	18.1
1840	17,069,453	2,873,648	16.8
1850	23,191,876	3,638,808	15.7
1860	31,443,321	4,441,830	14.1

Source: Kenneth Estell, ed., *The African American Almanac,* 6th ed. (Detroit: Gale Research, Inc., 1994), p. 635. Used by permission.

THE DECLARATION OF INDEPENDENCE: THE DELETED SECTION

Thomas Jefferson's original draft of the Declaration of Independence sharply denounced the slave trade. The document also blamed British king George III for the horrors of human bondage, but the founding fathers eliminated this section from the final draft.

He (George III) has incited treasonable insurrections of our fellow citizens, with the allurements of forfeiture and confiscation of our property.

He has waged cruel war against human nature itself, violating its most sacred rights of life and liberty in the persons of a distant people who never offended him, captivating and carrying them into slavery in another hemisphere, or to incur miserable death in their transportation thither. This piratical warfare, the opprobrium of INFIDEL powers, is the warfare of the CHRISTIAN King of Great-Britain. Determined to keep open a market where MEN should be bought and sold, he has prostituted his negative for suppressing every legislative attempt to prohibit or to restrain this execrable commerce. And that this assemblage of horrors might want no fact of distinguished die, he is now exciting those very people to rise in arms among us, and to purchase that liberty of which he has deprived them, by murdering the people on whom he also obtruded them: thus paying off former crimes committed against the LIBERTIES of one people with crimes which he urges them to commit against the LIVES of another.

THE CONSTITUTION OF THE UNITED STATES (1788) COMPARED WITH THE CONSTITUTION OF THE CONFEDERATE STATES (1861)

When the southern states seceded from the Union in 1861, they adopted the provisions of the U.S. Constitution nearly verbatim. Unlike the U.S. Constitution, which referred to blacks in code language such as "three fifths of all other persons," the Confederate Constitution explicitly named blacks as "negroes," "Africans," and "slaves."

THE CONSTITUTION OF THE UNITED STATES	THE CONSTITUTION OF THE CONFEDERATE STATES OF AMERICA
Article I	**Article I**
SEC. 2. . . . Clause 3. Representatives and direct taxes shall be apportioned among the several States which may be included within this Union, according to their respective numbers, which shall be determined by adding to the whole number of free persons, including those bound to service for a term of years, and excluding Indians not taxed, three fifths of all other persons. The actual enumeration shall be made within three years after the first meeting of the Congress of the United States, and within every subsequent term of ten years, in such manner as they shall by law direct. The number of Representatives shall not exceed one for every thirty thousand, but each State shall have at least one Representative; and until such enumeration shall be made, the State of *New Hampshire* shall be entitled to choose three, *Massachusetts* eight, *Rhode Island and Providence Plantations* one, *Connecticut* five, *New York* six, *New Jersey* four, *Pennsylvania* eight, *Delaware* one, *Maryland* six, *Virginia* ten, *North Carolina* five, *South Carolina* five, and *Georgia* three. . . .	SEC. 2. . . . (3) Representatives and direct taxes shall be apportioned among the several States which may be included within this Confederacy according to their respective numbers, which shall be determined by adding to the whole number of free persons, including those bound to service for a term of years, and excluding Indians not taxed, three-fifths of all slaves. The actual enumeration shall be made within three years after the first meeting of the Congress of the Confederate States, and within every subsequent term of ten years, in such manner as they shall by law direct. The number of Representatives shall not exceed one for every fifty thousand, but each State shall have at least one Representative; and until such enumeration shall be made, the State of South Carolina shall be entitled to choose six; the State of Georgia ten; the State of Alabama nine; the State of Florida two; the State of Mississippi seven; the State of Louisiana six; and the State of Texas six. . .
SEC. 9. Clause 1. The migration or importation of such persons as any of the States now existing shall think proper to admit shall not be prohibited by the Congress prior to the year one thousand eight hundred and eight, but a tax or duty may be imposed on such importation, not exceeding ten dollars for each person. . . .	SEC. 9. (1) The importation of negroes of the African race, from any foreign country, other than the slaveholding States or Territories of the United States of America, is hereby forbidden; and Congress is required to pass such laws as shall effectually prevent the same. . . .

THE FUGITIVE SLAVE ACT (1793)

In its first official legislation designed to enable slaveholders to recover fugitives, the U.S. Congress followed the lead of the U.S. Constitution and avoided use of the term SLAVE.

An act respecting fugitives from justice, and persons escaping from the service of their masters

SECTION 1. *Be it enacted by the Senate and House of Representatives of the United States of America in Congress assembled,* That whenever the executive authority of any state in the Union, or of either of the territories northwest or south of the river Ohio, shall demand any person as a fugitive from justice, of the executive authority of any such state or territory to which such person shall have fled, and shall moreover produce the copy of an indictment found, or an affidavit made before a magistrate of any state or territory as aforesaid, charging the person so demanded, with having committed treason, felony, or other crime, certified as authentic by the governor or chief magistrate of the state or territory from whence the person so charged fled, it shall be the duty of the executive authority of the state or territory to which such person shall have fled, to cause him or her to be arrested and secured, and notice of the arrest to be given to the executive authority making such demand, or to the agent of such authority appointed to receive the fugitive, and to cause the fugitive to be delivered to such agent when he shall appear: But if no such agent shall appear within six months from the time of the arrest, the prisoner may be discharged. And all costs or expenses incurred in the apprehending, securing, and transmitting such fugitive to the state or territory making such demand, shall be paid by such state or territory.

SEC. 2. *And be it further enacted,* That any agent, appointed as aforesaid, who shall receive the fugitive into his custody, shall be empowered to transport him or her to the state or territory from which he or she shall have fled. And if any person or persons shall by force set at liberty, or rescue the fugitive from such agent while transporting, as aforesaid, the person or persons so offending shall, on conviction, be fined not exceeding five hundred dollars, and be imprisoned not exceeding one year. . . .

AN ACT TO PROHIBIT THE IMPORTATION OF SLAVES (1807)

In this act outlawing the international slave trade, Congress used the words "negro, mulatto, or person of colour" interchangeably with "slave."

An act to prohibit the importation of slaves into any port or place within the jurisdiction of the United States, from and after the first day of January, in the year of our Lord one thousand eight hundred and eight

Be it enacted by the Senate and House of Representatives of the United States of America in Congress assembled, That from and after the first day of January, one thousand eight hundred and eight, it shall not be lawful to import or bring into the United States or the territories thereof from any foreign kingdom, place, or country, any negro, mulatto, or person of colour, with intent to hold, sell, or dispose of such negro, mulatto, or person of colour, as a slave, or to be held to service or labour. . . .

THE *DRED SCOTT* CASE (1857)

During the late 1830s and early 1840s, Dred Scott, a Missouri slave, spent several years with his owner in the free territories of Illinois and Minnesota. In 1847, when his owner returned him to Missouri and to enslavement, Scott (aided by white supporters) sued for his freedom. The Circuit Court of St. Louis County granted him his freedom, but the Missouri State Supreme Court reversed the decision. The U.S. Supreme Court upheld the ruling of the state court. Chief Justice Roger B. Taney wrote the Court's majority opinion.

The question is simply this: Can a negro, whose ancestors were imported into this country, and sold as slaves, become a member of the political community formed and brought into existence by the Constitution of the United States, and as such become entitled to all the rights, and privileges, and immunities, guaranteed by that instrument to the citizen? One of which rights is the privilege of suing in a court of the United States in the cases specified in the Constitution. . . .

It is difficult at this day to realize the state of public opinion in relation to that unfortunate race, which prevailed in the civilized and enlightened portions of the world at the time of the Declaration of Independence, and when the Constitution of the United States was framed and adopted. But the public history of every European nation displays it in a manner too plain to be mistaken.

They had for more than a century before been regarded as beings of an inferior order, and altogether unfit to associate with the white race, either in social or political relations; and so far inferior, that they had no rights which the white man was bound to respect; and that the negro might justly and lawfully be reduced to slavery for his benefit. . . .

And upon a full and careful consideration of the subject, the court is of opinion, that, upon the facts stated in the plea in abatement, Dred Scott was not a citizen of Missouri within the meaning of the Constitution of the United States, and not entitled as such to sue in its courts; and, consequently, that the Circuit Court had no jurisdiction of the case, and that the judgment on the plea in abatement is erroneous. . . .

. . . Its judgment for the defendant must, consequently, be reversed, and a mandate issued, directing the suit to be dismissed for want of jurisdiction.

THE EMANCIPATION PROCLAMATION (1 JANUARY 1863)

On New Year's Day 1863, President Abraham Lincoln issued his famous Emancipation Proclamation. Although this document symbolized the gradual transformation of the Civil War into a war for the emancipation of slaves, it excluded slaveholding Unionists from its provisions.

Whereas, on the twenty-second day of September, in the year of our Lord one thousand eight hundred and sixty-two, a Proclamation was issued by the President of the United States, containing among other things the following, to wit:

"That on the First Day of January, in the Year of our Lord One Thousand Eight Hundred and Sixty-three, all persons held as Slaves within any State, or designated part of a State, the people whereof shall there be in rebellion against the United States, shall be then thenceforth and FOREVER FREE, and the Executive Government of the United States, including the Military and Naval authority thereof, will recognize and maintain the freedom of such persons, and will do no act or acts to repress such persons, or any of them, in any effort they may make for their actual freedom. . . ."

THE FREEDMEN'S BUREAU ACT (1865)

The short-lived Bureau of Refugees, Freedmen, and Abandoned Lands (1865–1872) provided much-needed emergency food, clothing, health, and education services for black and white victims of war. It also promised blacks a mechanism for purchasing their own land, specifying forty acres as an upper limit.

An act to establish a bureau for the relief of freedmen and refugees

Be it enacted by the Senate and House of Representatives of the United States of America in Congress assembled, That there is hereby established in the War Department, to continue during the present war of rebellion, and for one year thereafter, a bureau of refugees, freedmen, and abandoned lands, to which shall be committed, as hereinafter provided, the supervision and management of all abandoned lands, and the control of all subjects relating to refugees and freedmen from rebel states, or from any district of country within the territory embraced in the operations of the army, under such rules and regulations as may be prescribed by the head of the bureau and approved by the President. The said bureau shall be under the management and control of a commissioner to be appointed by the President, by and with the advice and consent of the Senate, whose compensation shall be three thousand dollars per annum, and such number of clerks as may be assigned to him by the Secretary of War, not exceeding one chief clerk, two of the fourth class, two of the third class, and five of the first class. . . .

SEC. 2. *And be it further enacted,* That the Secretary of War may direct such issues of provisions, clothing, and fuel, as he may deem needful for the immediate and temporary shelter and supply of destitute and suffering refugees and freedmen and their wives and children, under such rules and regulations as he may direct.

SEC. 3. *And be it further enacted,* That the President may, by and with the advice and consent of the Senate, appoint an assistant commissioner for each of the states declared to be in insurrection, not exceeding ten in number, who shall, under the direction of the commissioner, aid in the execution of the provisions of this act; . . .

SEC. 4. *And be it further enacted,* That the commissioner, under the direction of the President, shall have authority to set apart, for the use of loyal refugees and freedmen, such tracts of land within the insurrectionary states as shall have been abandoned, or to which the United States shall have acquired title by confiscation or sale, or otherwise, and to every male citizen, whether refugee or freedman, as aforesaid, there shall be assigned not more than forty acres of such land, and the person to whom it was so assigned shall be protected in the use and enjoyment of the land. . . .

APPROVED, March 3, 1865.

THE THIRTEENTH AMENDMENT (1865)

Shortly after the Confederate army was defeated, the Thirteenth Amendment to the Constitution declared an end to the system of human bondage throughout the nation.

Sec. 1. Neither slavery nor involuntary servitude, except as a punishment for crime whereof the party shall have been duly convicted, shall exist within the United States, or any place subject to their jurisdiction.

Sec. 2. Congress shall have power to enforce this article by appropriate legislation.

THE FOURTEENTH AMENDMENT (1868)

Before southern states could regain their full and legitimate place in the Union, Radicals insisted that they approve the Fourteenth Amendment to the U.S. Constitution, which offered African Americans full citizenship rights and equal protection of the laws.

Sec. 1. All persons born or naturalized in the United States, and subject to the jurisdiction thereof, are citizens of the United States and of the State wherein they reside. No State shall make or enforce any law which shall abridge the privileges or immunities of citizens of the United States; nor shall any State deprive any person of life, liberty, or property, without due process of law; nor deny to any person within its jurisdiction the equal protection of the laws. . . .

THE FIFTEENTH AMENDMENT (1870)

Despite the enactment of the Fourteenth Amendment, southern states continued to obstruct African American access to full citizenship rights. The Fifteenth Amendment dispelled any uncertainty that black men were entitled to vote.

Sec. 1. The right of citizens of the United States to vote shall not be denied or abridged by the United States or by any State on account of race, color, or previous condition of servitude.

Sec. 2. The Congress shall have power to enforce this article by appropriate legislation.

BIBLIOGRAPHY

Research Guides, General Studies, and Document Collections

Reference Guides and Historiography

Gates, Henry Louis, et al. *Harvard Guide to African American Research*. Cambridge: Harvard University Press, forthcoming.

Goings, Kenneth W., and Raymond A. Mohl, eds. *The New African American Urban History*. Thousand Oaks, Calif.: Sage Publications, 1996.

Ham, Debra Newman, ed. *The African American Mosaic: A Library of Congress Resource Guide for the Study of Black History and Culture*. Washington, D.C.: U.S. Government Printing Office, 1993.

Hine, Darlene Clark. *Hine Sight: Black Women and the Re-Construction of American History*. Brooklyn, N.Y.: Carlson, 1994.

———. *The State of Afro-American History: Past, Present, and Future*. Baton Rouge: Louisiana State University, 1986.

Jewsiewicki, Bogumil, and David S. Newbury, eds. *African Historiographies: What History for Which Africa?* Beverly Hills, Calif.: Sage, 1986.

McPherson, James M., et al., eds. *Blacks in America: Bibliographical Essays*. Garden City, N.Y.: Anchor Books, 1971.

Meier, August, and Elliott Rudwick. *Black History and the Historical Profession*. Urbana: University of Illinois Press, 1986.

Neale, Caroline. *Writing "Independent" History: African Historiography, 1960–1980*. Westport, Conn.: Greenwood Press, 1985.

Norton, Mary Beth, and Pamela Girardi, eds. *The AHA's Guide to Historical Literature*. Vols. 1 and 2. 3rd ed. New York: Oxford University Press, 1995.

Walker, Clarence E. *Deromanticizing Black History: Critical Essays and Reappraisals*. Knoxville: University of Tennessee Press, 1991.

Weinberg, Meyer, ed. *Racism in the United States: A Comprehensive Classified Bibliography*. New York: Greenwood Press, 1990.

Documentary Volumes and Anthologies

Adero, Mulaika, ed. *Up South: Stories, Studies, and Letters of This Century's Black Migrations.* New York: W. W. Norton, 1993.

Adler, Mortimer A., Charles Van Doren, and George Ducas, eds. *Great Documents in Black American History.* Chicago: Encyclopedia Britannica Educational Corporation, 1969.

Andrews, William, Frances Smith Foster, and Trudier Harris, eds. *The Oxford Companion to African American Literature.* New York: Oxford University Press, 1997.

Bardolph, Richard, ed. *The Civil Rights Record: Black Americans and the Law, 1849–1970.* New York: Thomas Y. Crowell, 1970.

Berlin, Ira, et al. *Free At Last: A Documentary History of Slavery, Freedom and the Civil War.* New York: New Press, 1992.

Blassingame, John. *The Frederick Douglass Papers.* Vol. 1. New Haven: Yale University Press, 1979.

———. *Slave Testimony: Two Centuries of Letters, Speeches, Interviews, and Autobiographies.* Baton Rouge: Louisiana State University Press, 1977.

Blaustein, Albert P., and Robert L. Zangrando. *Civil Rights and African Americans: A Documentary History.* Evanston, Ill.: Northwestern University Press, 1968.

Carson, Claybourne, et al., eds. *The Papers of Martin Luther King, Jr.* Berkeley: University of California Press, 1992.

Emanuel, James A., and Theodore L. Gross, eds. *Dark Symphony: Negro Literature in America.* New York: Free Press, 1968.

Fishel, Leslie H., Jr., and Benjamin Quarles. *The Black American: A Documentary History.* 3rd ed. Glenview, Ill.: Scott, Foresman, 1976.

Foner, Philip Sheldon, and Ronald L. Lewis, eds. *The Black Worker: A Documentary History from Colonial Times to the Present.* Vols. 1–8. Philadelphia: Temple University Press, 1978–1984.

Frazier, Thomas R., Jr. *Afro-American History: Primary Sources 1970.* Rev. ed. Chicago: Dorsey Press, 1988.

Genovese, Eugene. *In Red and Black: Marxian Explorations in Southern and Afro-American History.* 1971. Reprint, Knoxville: University of Tennessee Press, 1984.

Goodheart, Lawrence B., Richard D. Brown, and Stephen G. Rabe, eds. *Slavery in American Society.* 3rd ed. Lexington: D. C. Heath, 1993.

Hampton, Henry, and Steve Fayer. *Voices of Freedom: An Oral History of the Civil Rights Movement from the 1950s Through the 1980s.* New York: Bantam, 1990.

Harlan, Louis, and Raymond M. Smock, eds. *The Booker T. Washington Papers.* Urbana: University of Illinois Press, 1972.

Hatch, James V., and Ted Shine. *Black Theater, U.S.A.: Forty-Five Plays by Black Americans, 1847–1974.* New York: Free Press, 1974.

Hayes, Floyd W., III. *Turbulent Voyage: Readings in African American Studies.* San Diego: Collegiate Press, 1992.

Hill, Patricia Liggins, ed. *Call and Response: The Anthology of the African American Literary Tradition.* Boston: Houghton Mifflin, 1998.

Hill, Robert, ed. *The Marcus Garvey and University Negro Improvement Association Papers.* Berkeley: University of California Press, 1983–1987.

Holt, Thomas C., and Elsa Barkley Brown, eds. *Major Problems in African-American History.* Vol. 1, *From Slavery to Freedom, 1619–1877.* Boston: Houghton Mifflin Company, 2000.

Kousser, J. Morgan, and James M. McPherson, eds. *Region, Race, and Reconstruction: Essays in Honor of C. Vann Woodward.* New York: Oxford University Press, 1982.

Kusmer, Kenneth L. *Black Communities and Urban Development in America, 1720–1990.* Vols.1–9. New York: Garland, 1991.

Lerner, Gerda. *Black Women in White America: A Documentary History.* New York: Vintage Books, 1973.

Lowenberg, Bert J., and Ruth Bogin, eds. *Black Women in Nineteenth Century American Life: Their Words, Their Thoughts, Their Feelings.* University Park: Pennsylvania State University Press, 1976.

Meier, August, Elliott Rudwick, and Francis L. Broderick, eds. *Black Protest Thought in the Twentieth Century.* Indianapolis and New York: Bobbs-Merrill, 1971.

Meltzer, Milton, ed. *In Their Own Words: A History of the American Negro, 1619–1865.* New York: Thomas Y. Crowell Company, 1964.

Mullane, Deirdre, ed. *Crossing the Danger Water: Three Hundred Years of African-American Writing.* New York: Doubleday, 1993.

Nichols, Charles H. *Many Thousands Gone: The Ex-Slaves' Account of Their Bondage and Freedom.* Bloomington: Indiana University Press, 1963.

Osofsky, Gilbert. *The Burden of Race: A Documentary History of Negro-White Relations in America.* New York: Harper & Row/Harper Torchbooks, 1967.

Rawick, George P., ed. *The American Slave: A Composite Autobiography.* Westport, Conn.: Greenwood Press, 1972–1979.

Ripley, C. Peter. *The Black Abolitionist Papers.* Chapel Hill: University of North Carolina Press, 1985.

Rose, Willie Lee, ed. *A Documentary History of Slavery in North America.* New York: Oxford University Press, 1976.

Sterling, Dorothy. *We Are Your Sisters: Black Women in the Nineteenth Century.* New York: W. W. Norton, 1984.

Weinstein, Allen, and Frank Otto Gatell, eds. *American Negro Slavery: A Modern Reader.* 2nd ed. New York: Oxford University Press, 1973.

General Studies

Asante, Molefi Kete. *African American History: A Journey of Liberation.* Maywood, N.J.: Peoples Publishing Group, 1995.

Bennett, Lerone, Jr. *Before the Mayflower: A History of Black America.* 5th ed. New York: Penguin Books, 1982.

Berry, Mary Frances, and John W. Blassingame. *Long Memory: The Black Experience in America.* New York: Oxford University Press, 1982.

Christian, Charles M. *Black Saga: The African American Experience.* Boston: Houghton Mifflin, 1995.

Cowan, Tom, and Jack Maguire. *Timelines of African American History: 500 Years of Black Achievement.* New York: Roundtable Press, 1994.

Davis, F. James. *Who Is Black? One Nation's Definition.* University Park: Pennsylvania State University Press, 1991.

Foner, Philip Sheldon. *Organized Labor and the Black Worker, 1619–1982.* 2nd ed. New York: International Publishers, 1982.

Forbes, Jack. *Black Africans and Native Americans: Color, Race, and Caste in the Evolution of Red-Black Peoples.* New York: Basil Blackwell, 1988.

Franklin, John Hope, and Alfred A. Moss Jr. *From Slavery to Freedom: A History of African Americans.* 8th ed. New York: McGraw-Hill, 2000.

Giddings, Paula. *When and Where I Enter: The Impact of Black Women on Race and Sex in America.* New York: Morrow, 1984.

Harley, Sharon. *The Timetables of African-American History: A Chronology of the Most Important People and Events in African-American History.* New York: Simon & Schuster, 1995.

Hine, Darlene Clark, Elsa Barkley Brown, and Rosalyn Terborg-Penn, eds. *Black Women in America: An Historical Encyclopedia.* 2 vols. Brooklyn, N.Y.: Carlson, 1993.

Hine, Darlene Clark, William C. Hine, and Stanley Harrold. *The African-American Odyssey.* Upper Saddle River, N.J.: Prentice Hall, 2000.

Hine, Darlene Clark, and Kathleen Thompson. *A Shining Thread of Hope: The History of Black Women in America.* New York: Broadway Books, 1998.

Horton, James Oliver, and Lois E. Horton, eds. *A History of the African People: The History, Traditions & Culture of African Americans.* London: Salamander Books, 1995.

Huggins, Nathan I., Martin Kilson, and Daniel M. Fox, eds. *Key Issues in the Afro-American Experience.* Vols. 1 and 2. New York: Harcourt Brace Jovanovich, 1971.

Hull, Gloria T., Patricia Bell Scott, and Barbara Smith. *But Some of Us Are Brave: Black Women's Studies.* Old Westbury, N.Y: Feminist Press, 1982.

Jones, Jacqueline. *American Work: Four Centuries of Black and White Labor.* New York: W. W. Norton, 1998.

———. *Labor of Love, Labor of Sorrow: Black Women, Work, and the Family from Slavery to the Present.* New York: Basic Books, 1985.

Kelley, Robin D. G., and Earl Lewis, eds. *To Make Our World Anew: A History of African Americans.* New York: Oxford University Press, 2000.

Marable, Manning. *How Capitalism Underdeveloped Black America: Problems in Race, Political Economy and Society.* Boston: South End Press, 1983.

Meier, August, and Elliott Rudwick. *Black History and the Historical Profession.* Urbana: University of Illinois Press, 1986.

———. *From Plantation to Ghetto.* 3rd ed. New York: Hill and Wang, 1976.

Palmer, Colin A. *Passageways: An Interpretive History of Black America.* Vols. 1 and 2. Ft. Worth: Harcourt Brace, 1998.

Smallwood, Arwin D., and Jeffrey M. Elliot. *The Atlas of African-American History and Politics: From the Slave Trade to Modern Times.* New York: McGraw-Hill, 1998.

Smith, Jessie Carney. *Black Firsts: 2,000 Years of Extraordinary Achievements.* Detroit: Visible Ink Press, 1994.

Taylor, Quintard. *In Search of the Racial Frontier: African Americans in the American West, 1528–1990.* New York: W. W. Norton, 1998.

Walker, Juliet E. K. *The History of Black Business in America: Capitalism, Race, Entrepreneurship.* New York: Macmillan Library Reference, 1998.

Walton, Hanes, Jr. *Black Politics: A Theoretical and Structural Analysis.* Philadelphia: J. B. Lippincott, 1972.

PART I: The African American Experience in Global Perspective: Prelude to a New World (Chapters 1–2)

North and East Africa

Abun-Nasr, Jamil M. *A History of the Maghrib in the Islamic Period.* Cambridge: Cambridge University Press, 1987.

Adams, William Yewdale. *Nubia: Corridor to Africa.* 1977. Reprint, Princeton: Princeton University Press, 1984.

Bagnall, Roger S. *Egypt in Late Antiquity.* Princeton: Princeton University Press, 1993.

Bernal, Martin. *Black Athena: The Afroasiatic Roots of Classical Civilization.* Vol. 1. New Brunswick, N.J.: Rutgers University Press, 1987.

Breasted, James Henry. *A History of Egypt: From the Earliest Times to the Persian Conquest.* 1912. Reprint, New York: Scribner's, 1967.

Drake, St. Clair. *Black Folk Here and There: An Essay in History and Anthropology.* 1987. Reprint, Los Angeles: Center for Afro-American Studies, UCLA, 1990.

Grimal, Nicolas. *A History of Ancient Egypt.* Cambridge, Mass.: Blackwell, 1992.

Hodgson, Marshall G. S. *The Classical Age of Islam.* Vol. 1. Chicago: University of Chicago Press, 1974.

———. *The Expansion of Islam in the Middle Period.* Vol. 2. Chicago: University of Chicago Press, 1974.

Levine, Molly Myerowitz. "The Use and Abuse of Black Athena." *American Historical Review* 97, no. 2 (1992): 440–460.

Lewis, Bernard. *The Arabs in History.* 6th ed. New York: Oxford University Press, 1993.

Trigger, Bruce G., et al., eds. *Ancient Egypt: A Social History.* New York: Cambridge University Press, 1983.

West Africa

Connah, Graham. *African Civilizations: Precolonial Cities and States in Tropical Africa: An Archaeological Perspective.* New York: Cambridge University Press, 1987.

Conrad, David C. "Islam in the Oral Traditions of Mali: Bilali and Surakata." *Journal of African History* 26, no. 1 (1985): 33–50.

Dunn, Ross E. *The Adventures of Ibn Battuta, a Muslim Traveler of the Fourteenth Century.* Berkeley: University of California Press, 1986.

Hopkins, A. G. *An Economic History of West Africa.* New York: Columbia University Press, 1973.

Law, Robin C. C. *The Horse in West African History: The Role of the Horse in the Societies of Pre-Colonial West Africa.* Oxford: Oxford University Press and the International African Institute, 1980.

———. *The Oyo Empire, c. 1600–c. 1836: A West African Imperialism in the Era of the Atlantic Slave Trade.* Oxford: Clarendon, 1977.

Levtzion, Nehemia. *Ancient Ghana and Mali.* London: Methuen, 1973.

Lewis, Bernard. *Race and Color in Islam.* New York: Harper & Row, 1971.

Mbiti, John S. *African Religions and Philosophy.* Garden City, N.Y.: Doubleday/Anchor, 1970.

Paulme, Denise. *African Sculpture.* New York: Viking, 1962.

Phillips, William D., Jr. *Slavery from Roman Times to the Early Transatlantic Trade.* Minneapolis: University of Minnesota Press, 1985.

Saad, Elias. *Social History of Timbuktu: The Role of Muslim Scholars and Notables, 1400–1900.* Cambridge: Cambridge University Press, 1983.

Sanneh, Lamin O. *West African Christianity: The Religious Impact.* Maryknoll, N.Y.: Orbis, 1983.

Smith, Robert S. *Kingdoms of the Yoruba.* 3rd ed. Madison: University of Wisconsin Press, 1988.

Verger, Pierre. *Trade Relations Between the Bight of Benin and Bahia from the Seventeenth to Nineteenth Century.* Ibadan, Nigeria: Ibadan University Press, 1976.

Vogel, Susan, ed. *For Spirits and Kings: African Art from Paul and Ruth Tishman Collection.* New York: Harry N. Abrams, 1981.

Vogt, John. *Portuguese Rule on the Gold Coast, 1469–1682.* Athens: University of Georgia Press, 1979.

Slave Trade and Slavery

Curtin, Philip D., ed. *Africa Remembered: Narratives by West Africans from the Era of the Slave Trade.* Madison: University of Wisconsin Press, 1967.

——. *The Atlantic Slave Trade: A Census.* Madison: University of Wisconsin Press, 1969.

Davidson, Basil. *The African Slave Trade.* Rev. ed. Boston: Little, Brown, 1970.

Davis, David Brion. *The Problem of Slavery in Western Culture.* New York: Oxford University Press, 1966.

Ewald, Janet. "Slavery in Africa and the Slave Trades from Africa." *American Historical Review* 97, no. 2 (1992).

Inikori, Joseph E., and Stanley L. Engerman, eds. *The Atlantic Slave Trade: Effects on Economies, Societies, and Peoples in Africa, the Americas, and Europe.* Durham: Duke University Press, 1992.

——. *Forced Migration: The Impact of the Export Slave Trade on African Societies.* New York: Africana, 1982.

Miers, Suzanne, and Igor Kopytoff, eds. *Slavery in Africa: Historical and Anthropological Perspectives.* Madison: University of Wisconsin Press, 1977.

Patterson, Orlando. *Slavery and Social Death: A Comparative Study.* Cambridge: Harvard University Press, 1982.

Robertson, Claire C., and Martin A. Klein, eds. *Women and Slavery in Africa.* Madison: University of Wisconsin Press, 1983.

Rodney, Walter. *How Europe Underdeveloped Africa.* Rev. ed. Washington, D.C.: Howard University Press, 1982.

Thomas, Hugh. *The Slave Trade: The Story of the Atlantic Slave Trade: 1440–1870.* New York: Simon & Schuster, 1997.

Thornton, John. *Africa and Africans in the Making of the Atlantic World, 1400–1680.* Cambridge: Cambridge University Press, 1992.

Latin America and the Caribbean

Beckles, Hilary McD. *White Servitude and Black Slavery in Barbados, 1627–1715.* Knoxville: University of Tennessee Press, 1989.

Berlin, Ira, and Philip D. Morgan, eds. *Cultivation and Culture: Labor and the Shaping of Slave Life in the Americas.* Charlottesville: University Press of Virginia, 1993.

Blakely, Allison. *Blacks in the Dutch World: The Evolution of Racial Imagery in a Modern Society.* Bloomington: Indiana University Press, 1993.

Bovill, E. W. *The Golden Trade of the Moors.* 1963. Reprint, with additional material by Robin Hallet, ed., London: Oxford University Press, 1968.

Bush, Barbara. *Slave Women in Caribbean Society, 1650–1838.* Bloomington: Indiana University Press, 1990.

Conrad, Robert. *The Destruction of Brazilian Slavery, 1850–1888.* Berkeley: University of California Press, 1972.

Cox, Edward L. *Free Coloreds in the Slave Societies of St. Kitts and Grenada, 1763–1833.* Knoxville: University of Tennessee Press, 1984.

Craton, Michael. *Sinews of Empire: A Short History of British Slavery.* Garden City, N.Y.: Anchor, 1974.

Degler, Carl N. *Neither Black Nor White: Slavery and Race Relations in Brazil and the United States.* New York: Macmillan, 1971.

De Montillano, Bernard Ortiz, et al. "They Were Not Here Before Columbus." *Ethnohistory* 44 (Spring 1997).

De Queirós Mattoso, Katia M. *To Be a Slave in Brazil, 1550–1888.* New Brunswick, N.J.: Rutgers University Press, 1986.

Foner, Laura, and Eugene D. Genovese, eds. *Slavery in the New World: A Reader in Comparative History.* Englewood Cliffs, N.J.: Prentice Hall, 1969.

Gaspar, David Barry, and Darlene Clark Hine, eds. *More Than Chattel: Black Women and Slavery in the Americas.* Bloomington: Indiana University Press, 1996.

Genovese, Eugene. *From Rebellion to Revolution: Afro-American Slave Revolts in the Making of the Modern World.* Baton Rouge: Louisiana State University Press, 1979.

Herskovits, Melville J. *The Myth of the Negro Past.* Boston: Beacon Press, 1958.

Hoetink, H. *Slavery and Race Relations in the Americas: Comparative Notes on Their Nature and Nexus.* New York: Harper & Row, 1973.

Klein, Herbert. *African Slavery in Latin America and the Caribbean.* New York: Oxford University Press, 1986.

Knight, Franklin W. *Slave Society in Cuba During the Nineteenth Century.* Madison: University of Wisconsin Press, 1970.

Lockhart, James, and Stuart Schwartz. *Early Latin America: A History of Colonial Spanish America and Brazil.* Cambridge: Cambridge University Press, 1983.

Mintz, Sidney. *Sweetness and Power: The Place of Sugar in Modern History.* New York: Viking, 1985.

Mintz, Sidney W., and Richard Price. *The Birth of African-American Culture: An Anthropological Perspective.* Boston: Beacon, 1992.

Palmer, Colin A. *Slaves of the White God: Blacks in Mexico, 1570–1650.* Cambridge: Harvard University Press, 1976.

Palmié, Stephan, ed. *Slave Cultures and the Cultures of Slavery.* Knoxville: University of Tennessee Press, 1995.

Price, Richard, ed. *Maroon Societies: Rebel Slave Communities in the Americas.* Garden City, N.Y.: Anchor Books, Doubleday, 1973.

Rout, Leslie B., Jr. *The African Experience in Spanish America, 1502 to the Present Day.* Cambridge: Cambridge University Press, 1976.

Schwartz, Stuart B. *Slaves, Peasants, and Rebels: Reconsidering Brazilian Slavery.* Urbana: University of Illinois Press, 1992.

Stein, Stanley J. *Vassouras: A Brazilian Coffee County, 1850–1900.* 1957. Reprint, Princeton: Princeton University Press, 1985.

Thompson, Vincent Bakpetu. *The Making of the African Diaspora in the Americas, 1441–1900.* New York: Longman, 1987.

Van Sertima, Ivan. *They Came Before Columbus: The African Presence in Ancient America.* New York: Random House, 1976.

General Studies

Ajayi, J. F. Ade, and Michael Crowder, eds. *History of West Africa.* Vol. 1. 2nd ed. New York: Columbia University Press, 1976.

Collins, Robert O. *African History: Text and Readings.* 1971. Reprint, New York: M. Wiener, 1999.

Curtin, Philip D., et al. *African History.* Boston: Little, Brown, 1978.

Fage, J. D., and Roland Anthony Oliver, eds. *The Cambridge History of Africa.* Vol. 2, *From c. 500 B.C. to A.D. 1050.* New York: Cambridge University Press, 1977.

July, Robert W. *A History of the African People.* 5th ed. Prospect Heights, Ill.: Waveland Press, 1998.

Shillington, Kevin. *History of Africa.* London: Macmillan, 1995.

PART II: Enslavement, Revolution, and the New Republic, 1619–1820
(Chapters 3–6)

The Colonial South and North

Berlin, Ira, and Philip D. Morgan, eds. *The Slave's Economy: Independent Production by Slaves in the Americas.* London: Frank Cass, 1991.

Breen, T. H., and Stephen Innes. *"Myne Owne Ground": Race and Freedom on Virginia's Eastern Shore, 1640–1676.* New York: Oxford University Press, 1980.

Corkran, David H. *The Cherokee Frontier: Conflict and Survival, 1740–62.* 1962. Reprint, Norman: University of Oklahoma Press, 1966.

———. *The Creek Frontier, 1540–1783.* Norman: University of Oklahoma Press, 1967.

Craven, Wesley Frank. *White, Red, and Black: The Seventeenth-Century Virginian.* New York: W. W. Norton, 1977.

Greene, Lorenzo Johnston. *The Negro in Colonial New England, 1620–1776.* 1942, Reprint, New York: Atheneum, 1968.

Hall, Gwendolyn Midlo. *Africans in Colonial Louisiana: The Development of Afro-Creole Culture in the Eighteenth Century.* Baton Rouge: Louisiana State University Press, 1992.

Hatley, M. Thomas. *The Dividing Paths: Cherokees and South Carolinians Through the Era of Revolution.* New York: Oxford University Press, 1993.

Jordan, Winthrop D. *White Over Black: American Attitudes Toward the Negro, 1550–1812.* Chapel Hill: University of North Carolina Press, 1968.

Klein, Herbert S. *Slavery in the Americas: A Comparative Study of Virginia and Cuba.* Chicago: University of Chicago Press, 1967.

Kulikoff, Allan. *Tobacco and Slaves: The Development of Southern Cultures in the Chesapeake, 1680–1800.* Chapel Hill: University of North Carolina Press, 1986.

Landers, Jane. *Black Society in Spanish Florida.* Urbana: University of Illinois Press, 1999.

Littlefield, Daniel C. *Rice and Slaves: Ethnicity and the Slave Trade in Colonial South Carolina.* 1981. Reprint, Urbana: University of Illinois Press, 1991.

Menard, Russell R. "The Maryland Slave Population, 1658 to 1730: A Demographic Profile of Blacks in Four Counties." *William and Mary Quarterly* 1, no. 32 (1975): 29–54.

Morgan, Edmund S. *American Slavery, American Freedom: The Ordeal of Colonial Virginia.* New York: W. W. Norton, 1975.

Piersen, William D. *Black Yankees: The Development of an Afro-American Subculture in Eighteenth-Century New England.* Amherst: University of Massachusetts Press, 1988.

Silver, Timothy. *A New Face on the Countryside: Indians, Colonists, and Slaves in South Atlantic Forests, 1500-1800.* New York: University of Cambridge Press, 1990.

Tate, Thad W. *The Negro in Eighteenth-Century Williamsburg.* 1965. Reprint, Williamsburg, Va.: Colonial Williamsburg Foundation for the University Press of Virginia, 1985.

Usner, Daniel H., Jr. *Indians, Settlers, and Slaves in a Frontier Exchange Economy: The Lower Mississippi Valley Before 1783.* Chapel Hill: University of North Carolina Press for the Institute of Early American History and Culture, 1992.

Wood, Betty. *Slavery in Colonial Georgia, 1730–1775.* Athens: University of Georgia Press, 1984.

Culture, Resistance, and Abolitionism

Andrews, William L. *To Tell a Free Story: The First Century of Afro-American Autobiography, 1760–1865.* Urbana: University of Illinois Press, 1986.

Aptheker, Herbert. *Negro Slave Revolts in the United States, 1526–1860.* New York: Columbia University Press, 1943.

Creel, Margaret Washington. *A Peculiar People: Slave Religion and Community-Culture Among the Gullahs*. New York: New York University Press, 1988.

Davis, Thomas J. *A Rumor of Revolt: The "Great Negro Plot" in Colonial New York*. Amherst: University of Massachusetts Press, 1990.

Equiano, Olaudah. *The Life of Olaudah Equiano, or, Gustavus Vassa, the African*. 1837. Reprint, edited by Paul Edwards, New York: Negro Universities Press, 1969.

Essig, James D. *The Bonds of Wickedness: American Evangelicals Against Slavery, 1770–1808*. Philadelphia: Temple University Press, 1982.

Frey, Sylvia R. *Water from the Rock: Black Resistance in a Revolutionary Age*. Princeton: Princeton University Press, 1991.

Gomez, Michael A. *Exchanging Our Country Marks: The Transformation of African Identities in the Colonial and Antebellum South*. Chapel Hill: University of North Carolina Press, 1998.

Hine, Darlene Clark, and Earnestine Jenkins, eds. *A Question of Manhood: A Reader in U.S. Black Men's History and Masculinity, 1750–1870*. Vol. 1. Bloomington: Indiana University Press, 1999.

Lampe, Gregory P. *Frederick Douglass: Freedom's Voice, 1818–1845*. East Lansing: Michigan State University Press, 1998.

McManus, Edgar J. *Black Bondage in the North*. Syracuse: Syracuse University Press, 1973.

Melish, Joanne Pope. *Disowning Slavery: Gradual Emancipation and "Race" in New England, 1780–1860*. Ithaca: Cornell University Press, 1998.

Mullin, Michael (Gerald W.) *Africa in America: Slave Acculturation and Resistance in the American South and the British Caribbean, 1736–1831*. Urbana: University of Illinois Press, 1992.

———. *Flight and Rebellion; Slave Resistance in Eighteenth-Century Virginia*. New York: Oxford University Press, 1972, 1979.

Nash, Gary B. *Forging Freedom: The Formation of Philadelphia's Black Community, 1720–1840*. 1988. Reprint, Cambridge: Harvard University Press, 1991.

Sobel, Mechal. *Trabelin' On: The Slave Journey to an Afro-Baptist Faith*. Princeton: Princeton University Press, 1988.

Soderlund, Jean R. *Quakers and Slavery: A Divided Spirit*. Princeton: Princeton University Press, 1985.

White, Shane. *Somewhat More Independent: The End of Slavery in New York City, 1770–1810*. Athens: University of Georgia Press, 1991.

Zilversmit, Arthur. *The First Emancipation: The Abolition of Slavery in the North*. Chicago: University of Chicago Press, 1967.

Revolutionary and Early National Era

Berlin, Ira, and Ronald Hoffman, eds. *Slavery and Freedom in the Age of the American Revolution*. 1983. Reprint, Urbana: University of Illinois Press and the United States Capitol Historical Society, 1986.

Davis, David Brion. *The Problem of Slavery in the Age of Revolution, 1770–1823*. Ithaca: Cornell University Press, 1975.

Hoffman, Ronald, and Peter J. Albert, eds. *The Transforming Hand of Revolution: Reconsidering the American Revolution as a Social Movement*. Charlottesville: University Press of Virginia, 1996.

Johnston, James Hugo. *Race Relations in Virginia and Miscegenation in the South, 1776–1860*. Amherst: University of Massachusetts Press, 1970.

Lynd, Staughton. *Class Conflict, Slavery, and the United States Constitution: Ten Essays*. 1967. Reprint, Indianapolis: Bobbs-Merrill, 1968.

Macleod, Duncan J. *Slavery, Race, and the American Revolution.* London: Cambridge University Press, 1974.

McColley, Robert. *Slavery and Jeffersonian Virginia.* 2d ed. Urbana: University of Illinois Press, 1973.

McDonald, Roderick A. *The Economy and Material Culture of Slaves: Goods and Chattels on the Sugar Plantations of Jamaica and Louisiana.* Baton Rouge: Louisiana State University Press, 1993.

Mellon, Matthew T. *Early American Views on Negro Slavery: From the Letters and Papers of the Founders of the Republic.* 1934. Reprint, New York: Bergman, 1969.

Quarles, Benjamin. *The Negro in the American Revolution.* 1961. Reprint, New York: W. W. Norton, 1973.

Robinson, Donald L. *Slavery in the Structure of American Politics, 1765–1820.* 1970. Reprint, New York: W. W. Norton, 1979.

Walker, James W. St. G. *The Black Loyalists: The Search for a Promised Land in Nova Scotia and Sierra Leone, 1783-1870.* 1976. Reprint, Toronto: University of Toronto Press, 1992.

Wiecek, William M. *The Sources of Antislavery Constitutionalism in America, 1760–1848.* Ithaca: Cornell University Press, 1977.

Wright, Donald R. *African Americans in the Early Republic, 1789–1831.* Arlington Heights, Ill.: Harlan Davidson, 1993.

General Studies

Berlin, Ira. *Many Thousands Gone: The First Two Centuries of Slavery in North America.* Cambridge: Harvard University Press, 1998.

Boles, John B. *Black Southerners, 1619–1869.* Lexington: University of Kentucky Press, 1984.

Duignan, Peter, and Clarence Clendenen. *The United States and the African Slave Trade, 1619–1862.* California: Stanford University Press, 1963.

Ferguson, Leland. *Uncommon Ground: Archaeology and Early African America, 1650–1800.* Washington, D.C.: Smithsonian Institution Press, 1992.

Higginbotham, A. Leon, Jr. *In the Matter of Color: Race and the American Legal Process.* New York: Oxford University Press, 1978.

Huggins, Nathan Irvin. *Black Odyssey: The Afro-American Ordeal in Slavery.* New York: Vintage Books, 1977.

Kolchin, Peter. *American Slavery, 1619–1877.* New York: Hill and Wang, 1993.

Morton, Patricia, ed. *Discovering the Women in Slavery: Emancipating Perspectives on the American Past.* Athens: University of Georgia Press, 1996.

Scherer, Lester B. *Slavery and the Churches in Early America, 1619–1819.* Grand Rapids: Eerdmans, 1975.

Williams, Eric. *Capitalism & Slavery.* Chapel Hill: University of North Carolina Press, 1944.

Williams, William Henry. *Slavery and Freedom in Delaware, 1639–1865.* Wilmington: SR Books, 1996.

PART III: The Antebellum Era, Expansion of Cotton Culture, and Civil War, 1820–1865 (Chapters 7–10)

Social Conditions, Culture, and Community Life

Abrahams, Roger D. *Singing the Master: The Emergence of African American Culture in the Plantation South.* New York: Pantheon, 1992.

Bay, Mia. *The White Image in the Black Mind: African-American Ideas About White People, 1830–1925.* New York: Oxford University Press, 2000.

Blassingame, John W. *The Slave Community: Plantation Life in the Antebellum South.* Rev. ed. New York: Oxford University Press, 1979.

Botkin, B. A. *Lay My Burden Down: A Folk History of Slavery.* Chicago: University of Chicago Press, 1945.

Cornelius, Janet Duitsman. *"When I Can Read My Title Clear": Literacy, Slavery, and Religion in the Antebellum South.* Columbia: University of South Carolina Press, 1991.

Escott, Paul D. *Slavery Remembered: A Record of Twentieth-Century Slave Narratives.* Chapel Hill: University of North Carolina Press, 1979.

Frazier, E. Franklin. *The Negro Church in America.* New York: Schocken, 1974.

———. *The Negro Family in the United States.* 1939. Reprint, Chicago: University of Chicago Press, 1966.

Fredrickson, George M. *The Arrogance of Race: Historical Perspectives on Slavery, Racism, and Social Inequality.* Middletown, Conn.: Wesleyan University Press, 1988.

———. *The Black Image in the White Mind: The Debate on Afro-American Character and Destiny, 1817–1914.* 1972. Reprint, Middletown, Conn.: Wesleyan University Press, 1987.

Genovese, Elizabeth Fox. *Within the Plantation Household: Black and White Women of the Old South.* Chapel Hill: University of North Carolina Press, 1988.

Gutman, Herbert G. *The Black Family in Slavery and Freedom, 1750–1925.* New York: Vintage Books, 1977.

Harris, J. William, ed. *Society and Culture in the Slave South.* London: Routledge, 1992.

Joyner, Charles. *Down by the Riverside: A South Carolina Slave Community.* Urbana: University of Illinois Press, 1984.

King, Wilma. *Stolen Childhood: Slave Youth in Nineteenth-Century America.* Bloomington: Indiana University Press, 1995.

Levine, Lawrence W. *Black Culture and Black Consciousness: Afro-American Folk Thought from Slavery to Freedom.* New York: Oxford University Press, 1977.

Lincoln, C. Eric. *The Black Church Since Frazier.* New York: Schocken Books, 1974.

Malone, Ann Patton. *Sweet Chariot: Slave Family and Household Structure in Nineteenth-Century Louisiana.* Chapel Hill: University of North Carolina Press, 1992.

Mintz, Steven, ed. *African American Voices: The Life Cycle of Slavery.* St. James, N.Y.: Brandywine Press, 1993.

Owens, Leslie Howard. *This Species of Property: Slave Life and Culture in the Old South.* New York: Oxford University Press, 1976.

Painter, Nell Irvin. *Sojourner Truth: A Life, A Symbol.* New York: W. W. Norton, 1996.

Perdue, Theda. *Slavery and the Evolution of Cherokee Society.* Knoxville: University of Tennessee Press, 1979.

Raboteau, Albert J. *A Fire in the Bones: Reflections on African-American Religious History.* Boston: Beacon Press, 1995.

———. *Slave Religion: The "Invisible Institution" in the Antebellum South.* New York: Oxford University Press, 1978.

Salvatore, Nick. *We All Got History: The Memory Books of Amos Webber.* New York: Random House, 1996.

Savitt, Todd L. *Medicine and Slavery: The Diseases and Health Care of Blacks in Antebellum Virginia.* Urbana: University of Illinois Press, 1978.

Savitt, Todd L., and Ronald L. Numbers, eds. *Science and Medicine in the Old South.* Baton Rouge: Louisiana State University Press, 1989.

Scarborough, William K. *The Overseer: Plantation Management in the Old South.* 1966. Reprint, Athens: University of Georgia Press, 1984.

Schwarz, Philip J. *Twice Condemned: Slaves and the Criminal Laws of Virginia, 1705–1865*. Baton Rouge: Louisiana State University Press, 1988.

Stuckey, Sterling. *Slave Culture: Nationalist Theory and the Foundations of Black America*. New York: Oxford University Press, 1987.

Tadman, Michael. *Speculators and Slaves: Masters, Traders, and Slaves in the Old South*. Madison: University of Wisconsin Press, 1989.

Van Deburg, William L. *The Slave Drivers: Black Agricultural Labor Supervisors in the Antebellum South*. 1979. Reprint, New York: Oxford University Press, 1988.

Webber, Thomas L. *Deep Like the Rivers: Education in the Slave-Quarter Community, 1831–1865*. New York: W. W. Norton, 1978.

Weiner, Marli F. *Mistresses and Slaves: Plantation Women in South Carolina, 1830–80*. Urbana: University of Illinois Press, 1998.

White, Deborah Gray. *Ar'n't I a Woman? Female Slaves in the Plantation South*. New York: W. W. Norton, 1985.

Woodson, Carter G. *The History of the Negro Church*. 1921. Reprint, Washington, D.C.: Associated Publishers, 1985.

Resistance, Abolitionism, and the Law

Barnes, Gilbert Hobbs. *The Antislavery Impulse, 1830–1844*. 1933. Reprint, Gloucester, Mass.: P. Smith, 1973.

Belz, Herman. *Abraham Lincoln, Constitutionalism, and Equal Rights in the Civil War Era*. New York: Fordham University Press, 1998.

Bracey, John H., Jr., August Meier, and Elliott Rudwick, eds. *American Slavery: The Question of Resistance*. Belmont, Calif.: Wadsworth Publishing, 1971.

Campbell, Stanley W. *The Slave Catchers: Enforcement of the Fugitive Slave Law, 1850–1860*. Chapel Hill: University of North Carolina Press, 1970.

Cheek, William F., and Aimee Lee Cheek. *John Mercer Langston and the Fight for Black Freedom, 1829–1865*. Urbana: University of Illinois Press, 1989.

Dillon, Merton L. *Slavery Attacked: Southern Slaves and Their Allies, 1619–1865*. Baton Rouge: Louisiana State University Press, 1990.

Douglass, Frederick. *Narrative of the Life of Frederick Douglass: An American Slave*. Edited by Houston A. Baker. New York: Penguin, 1982.

Fehrenbacher, Don E. *Slavery, Law, & Politics: The Dred Scott Case in Historical Perspective*. New York: Oxford University Press, 1981.

Finkelman, Paul. *Dred Scott v. Sandford: A Brief History with Documents*. Boston: Bedford Books, 1997.

———. *An Imperfect Union: Slavery, Federalism, and Comity*. Chapel Hill: University of North Carolina Press, 1981.

Fladeland, Betty. *Abolitionists and Working-Class Problems in the Age of Industrialization*. Baton Rouge: Louisiana State University Press, 1984.

Friedman, Lawrence J. *Gregarious Saints: Self and Community in American Abolitionism, 1830–1870*. New York: Cambridge University Press, 1982.

———. *The Inner Civil War: Northern Intellectuals and the Crisis of the Union*. 1965. Reprint, New York: Harper & Row, 1968.

Harrold, Stanley. *The Abolitionists & the South, 1831–1861*. Lexington: University Press of Kentucky, 1995.

Jacobs, Harriet A. [Linda Brent]. *Incidents in the Life of a Slave Girl: Written by Herself*. Edited by Jean Fagan Yellin. Cambridge: Harvard University Press, 1987.

Jones, Norrece T. *Born a Child of Freedom, Yet a Slave: Mechanisms of Control and Strategies of Resistance in Antebellum South Carolina.* Middletown, Conn.: Wesleyan University Press, 1990.

Kraditor, Aileen S. *Means and Ends in American Abolitionism: Garrison and His Critics on Strategy and Tactics, 1834–1850.* 1969. Reprint, Chicago: Dee, 1989.

Lofton, John L. *Denmark Vesey's Revolt: The Slave Plot That Lit a Fuse to Fort Sumter.* Rev. ed. Kent, Ohio: Kent State University Press, 1983.

McFeely, William S. *Frederick Douglass.* New York: W. W. Norton, 1991.

McKivigan, John R. *The War Against Proslavery Religion: Abolitionism and the Northern Churches, 1830–1865.* Ithaca: Cornell University Press, 1984.

McLaurin, Melton Alonza. *Celia, a Slave.* Athens: University of Georgia Press, 1991.

McPherson, James M. *The Struggle for Equality: Abolitionists and the Negro in the Civil War and Reconstruction.* Princeton: Princeton University Press, 1964.

Oates, Stephen B. *The Fires of Jubilee: Nat Turner's Fierce Rebellion.* 1975. Reprint, New York: Harper & Row, 1990.

———. *To Purge This Land With Blood: A Biography of John Brown.* 1970. Reprint, Amherst: University of Massachusetts Press, 1984.

Pease, William Henry, and Jane H. Pease. *They Who Would Be Free: Blacks' Search for Freedom, 1830–1861.* 1974. Reprint, Urbana: University of Illinois Press, 1990.

Quarles, Benjamin. *Black Abolitionists.* New York: Oxford University Press, 1969.

Richards, Leonard L. *Gentlemen of Property and Standing: Anti-Abolition Mobs in Jacksonian America.* New York: Oxford University Press, 1970.

Starobin, Robert S. *Denmark Vesey: The Slave Conspiracy of 1822.* Englewood Cliffs, N.J.: Prentice Hall, 1970.

Ullman, Victor. *Martin R. Delany: The Beginning of Black Nationalism.* Boston: Beacon, 1971.

Walters, Ronald G. *The Antislavery Appeal: American Abolitionism After 1830.* 1978. Reprint, New York: W. W. Norton, 1984.

Yellin, Jean Fagan. *Women and Sisters: The Antislavery Feminists in American Culture.* New Haven: Yale University Press, 1989.

Free Blacks and Urban and Industrial Bondage

Alexander, Adele Logan. *Ambiguous Lives: Free Women of Color in Rural Georgia, 1789–1879.* Fayetteville: University of Arkansas Press, 1991.

Berlin, Ira. *Slaves Without Masters: The Free Negro in the Antebellum South.* New York: Oxford University Press, 1974.

Brown, Letitia W. *Free Negroes in the District of Columbia, 1790–1846.* New York: Oxford University Press, 1972.

Curry, Leonard P. *The Free Black in Urban America, 1800–1850: The Shadow of the Dream.* Chicago: University of Chicago Press, 1981.

Finkelman, Paul. *Free Blacks in a Slave Society.* Vol. 17. New York: Garland Publishing, Inc., 1989.

Franklin, John Hope. *The Free Negro in North Carolina, 1790–1860.* 1943. Reprint, New York: W. W. Norton, 1971.

Goldin, Claudia D. *Urban Slavery in the American South, 1820-1860: A Quantitative History.* Chicago: University of Chicago Press, 1976.

Horton, James Oliver. *Free People of Color: Inside the African American Community.* Washington, D.C.: Smithsonian Institution Press, 1993.

Jackson, Luther P. *Free Negro Labor and Property Holding in Virginia, 1830–1860.* 1942. Reprint, New York: Russell & Russell, 1971.

Johnson, Michael P., and James L. Roark. *Black Masters: A Free Family of Color in the Old South.* New York: W. W. Norton, 1984.

———. *No Chariot Let Down: Charleston's Free People of Color on the Eve of the Civil War.* New York: W. W. Norton, 1994.

Johnson, Whittington B. *Black Savannah, 1788–1864.* Fayetteville: University of Arkansas Press, 1996.

Landers, Jane G. *Against the Odds: Free Blacks in the Slave Societies of the Americas.* Portland: Cass, 1996.

Lebsock, Suzanne. *The Free Women of Petersburg: Status and Culture in a Southern Town, 1784–1860.* New York: W. W. Norton, 1984.

Lewis, Ronald L. *Coal, Iron, and Slaves: Industrial Slavery in Maryland and Virginia, 1715–1865.* Westport, Conn.: Greenwood Press, 1979.

Litwack, Leon F. *North of Slavery: The Negro in the Free States, 1790–1860.* Chicago: University of Chicago Press, 1961.

Phillips, Christopher. *Freedom's Port: The African American Community of Baltimore, 1790–1860.* Urbana: University of Illinois Press, 1997.

Powers, Bernard E., Jr. *Black Charlestonians: A Social History, 1822–1885.* Fayetteville: University of Arkansas Press, 1994.

Starobin, Robert. *Industrial Slavery in the Old South.* New York: Oxford University Press, 1970.

Taylor, Henry Louis, Jr., ed. *Race and the City: Work, Community, and Protest in Cincinnati, 1820–1970.* Urbana: University of Illinois Press, 1993.

Trotter, Joe W., Jr. *River Jordan: African American Urban Life in the Ohio Valley.* Lexington: University Press of Kentucky, 1998.

Wade, Richard C. *Slavery in the Cities: The South, 1820–1860.* New York: Oxford University Press, 1964.

Wikramanayake, Marina. *A World in Shadow: The Free Black in Antebellum South Carolina.* Columbia: University of South Carolina Press, 1973.

Civil War and Early Emancipation

Berlin, Ira, Joseph P. Reidy, and Leslie S. Rowland, eds. *The Black Military Experience.* New York: Cambridge University Press, 1982.

Berlin, Ira, et al., eds. *The Destruction of Slavery.* New York: Cambridge University Press, 1985.

———. *The Wartime Genesis of Free Labor: The Lower South.* New York: Cambridge University Press, 1990.

Bernstein, Iver. *The New York City Draft Riots: Their Significance in American Society and Politics in the Age of the Civil War.* New York: Oxford University Press, 1990.

Cox, LaWanda. *Lincoln and Black Freedom: A Study in Presidential Leadership.* 1981. Reprint, Urbana: University of Illinois Press, 1985.

Crofts, Daniel W. *Reluctant Confederates: Upper South Unionists in the Secession Crisis.* Chapel Hill: University of North Carolina Press, 1989.

Faust, Drew Gilpin. *The Creation of Confederate Nationalism: Ideology and Identity in the Civil War South.* Baton Rouge: Louisiana State University Press, 1988.

Glatthaar, Joseph T. *Forged in Battle: The Civil War Alliance of Black Soldiers and White Officers.* New York: Free Press, 1990.

McPherson, James M. *Battle Cry of Freedom: The Civil War Era.* New York: Oxford University Press, 1988.

———. *The Negro's Civil War.* New York: Random House, 1965.

Quarles, Benjamin. *The Negro in the Civil War.* 1953. Reprint, New York: Da Capo, 1989.

Rose, Willie Lee, ed. *Rehearsal for Reconstruction: The Port Royal Experiment.* 1964. Reprint, New York: Oxford University Press, 1976.

Savage, Kirk. *Standing Soldiers, Kneeling Slaves: Race, War, and Monument in Nineteenth-Century America.* Princeton: Princeton University Press, 1997.

State, Regional, and General Studies

Berwanger, Eugene H. *The Frontier Against Slavery: Western Anti-Negro Prejudice and the Slavery Extension Controversy.* Urbana: University of Illinois Press, 1967.

Campbell, Randolph B. *An Empire for Slavery: The Peculiar Institution in Texas, 1821–1865.* Baton Rouge: Louisiana State University Press, 1989.

David, Paul A., et al. *Reckoning With Slavery: A Critical Study in the Quantitative History of American Negro Slavery.* New York: Oxford University Press, 1976.

Elkins, Stanley. *Slavery: A Problem in American Institutional and Intellectual Life.* 1959. 3rd ed. Chicago: University of Chicago Press, 1976.

Fields, Barbara J. *Slavery and Freedom on the Middle Ground: Maryland During the Nineteenth Century.* New Haven: Yale University Press, 1985.

Fogel, Robert W. *Without Consent or Contract: The Rise and Fall of American Slavery.* New York: W. W. Norton, 1989.

Fogel, Robert W., and Stanley L. Engerman. *Time on the Cross: The Economics of American Negro Slavery.* 1974. Reprint, New York: W. W. Norton, 1989.

Foner, Jack D. *Blacks and the Military in American History.* New York: Praeger, 1974.

Genovese, Eugene. *Roll, Jordan, Roll: The World the Slaves Made.* 1974. Reprint, New York: Vintage Books, 1976.

Harding, Vincent. *There Is a River: The Black Struggle for Freedom in America.* New York: Vintage Books, 1983.

Kolchin, Peter. *Unfree Labor: American Slavery and Russian Serfdom.* Cambridge: Harvard University Press/Belknap Press, 1987.

Lane, Ann J., ed. *The Debate Over Slavery; Stanley Elkins and His Critics.* Urbana: University of Illinois Press, 1971.

Moore, John Hebron. *The Emergence of the Cotton Kingdom in the Old Southwest: Mississippi, 1770–1860.* Baton Rouge: Louisiana State University Press, 1988.

Oakes, James. *The Ruling Race: A History of American Slaveholders.* New York: Vintage Books, 1983.

———. *Slavery and Freedom: An Interpretation of the Old South.* New York: Alfred A. Knopf, 1990.

Rose, Willie Lee, ed. *Slavery and Freedom.* New York: Oxford University Press, 1982.

Smith, Julia Floyd. *Slavery and Plantation Growth in Antebellum Florida, 1821–1860.* Gainsville: University of Florida Press, 1973.

———. *Slavery and Rice Culture in Low Country Georgia, 1750–1860.* Knoxville: University of Tennessee Press, 1985.

Stampp, Kenneth M. *The Peculiar Institution: Slavery in the Ante-bellum South.* 1956. Reprint, New York: Vintage Books, 1989.

Woodward, C. Vann. *American Counterpoint: Slavery and Racism in the North-South Dialogue.* 1971. Reprint, New York: Oxford University Press, 1983.

PART IV: Emancipation and the First Generation of Freedom, 1865–1915
(Chapters 11–14)

Institutions, Culture, and Politics

Abbott, Richard H. *The Republican Party and the South, 1855–1877: The First Southern Strategy.* Chapel Hill: University of North Carolina Press, 1986.

Anderson, James D. *The Education of Blacks in the South, 1860–1935.* Chapel Hill: University of North Carolina Press, 1988.

Blackett, R. J. M. *Beating Against the Barriers: Biographical Essays in Nineteenth-Century Afro-American History.* Baton Rouge: Louisiana State University Press, 1986.

Bowen, David Warren. *Andrew Johnson and the Negro.* Knoxville: University of Tennessee Press, 1989.

Brodie, Fawn M. *Thaddeus Stevens: Scourge of the South.* 1959. Reprint, New York: W. W. Norton, 1966.

Brown, Elsa Barkley. "'What Has Happened Here': The Politics of Difference in Women's History and Feminist Politics." *Feminist Studies* 18 (Summer 1992).

Current, Richard N. *Those Terrible Carpetbaggers.* New York: Oxford University Press, 1988.

Donald, David. *Charles Sumner and the Rights of Man.* New York: Knopf, 1970.

Du Bois, W. E. B. *The Autobiography of W. E. B. Du Bois: A Soliloquy on Viewing My Life from the Last Decade of Its First Century.* New York: International Publishers, 1968.

———. *Darkwater: Voices from Within the Veil.* 1920. Reprint, New York: Schocken, 1969.

Duster, Alfreda M., ed. *Crusade for Justice: The Autobiography of Ida B. Wells.* Chicago, Ill.: University of Chicago Press, 1970.

Dvorak, Katherine L. *An African-American Exodus: The Segregation of the Southern Churches.* Brooklyn: Carlson, 1991.

Fields, Mamie Garvin, and Karen Fields. *Lemon Swamp and Other Places: A Carolina Memoir.* New York: Free Press, 1983.

Fierce, Milfred C. *The Pan-African Idea in the United States, 1900–1919: African-American Interest in Africa and Interaction with West Africa.* New York: Garland, 1993.

Fitzgerald, Michael W. *The Union League Movement in the Deep South: Politics and Agricultural Change During Reconstruction.* Baton Rouge: Louisiana State University Press, 1989.

Gaines, Kevin K. *Uplifting the Race: Black Leadership, Politics, and Culture in the Twentieth Century.* Chapel Hill: University of North Carolina Press, 1996.

Gatewood, Willard B. *Aristocrats of Color: The Black Elite, 1880–1920.* Bloomington: Indiana University Press, 1993.

Gilmore, Glenda Elizabeth. *Gender and Jim Crow: Women and the Politics of White Supremacy in North Carolina, 1896–1920.* North Carolina: University of North Carolina Press, 1996.

Harlan, Louis R. *Booker T. Washington: The Making of a Black Leader, 1856–1901.* New York: Oxford University Press, 1972.

———. *Booker T. Washington: The Wizard of Tuskegee, 1901–1915.* New York: Oxford University Press, 1983.

Henderson, Alexa Benson. *Atlanta Life Insurance Company: Guardian of Black Economic Dignity.* Tuscaloosa: University of Alabama Press, 1990.

Higginbotham, Evelyn Brooks. *Righteous Discontent: The Women's Movement in the Black Baptist Church, 1880–1920.* Cambridge: Harvard University Press, 1993.

Holt, Thomas. *Black Over White: Negro Political Leadership in South Carolina During Reconstruction.* Urbana: University of Illinois Press, 1977.

Jones, Jacqueline. *Soldiers of Light and Love: Northern Teachers and Georgia Blacks, 1865–1873.* 1980. Reprint, Athens: University of Georgia Press, 1992.

Kaczorowski, Robert. *The Politics of Judicial Interpretation: The Federal Courts, Department of Justice, and Civil Rights, 1866–1876.* Dobbs Ferry, N.Y.: Oceana Publications, 1985.

Lewinson, Paul. *Race, Class, & Party: A History of Negro Suffrage and White Politics in the South.* New York: Grosset and Dunlap, 1965.

Lewis, David Levering. *W. E. B. Du Bois: Biography of a Race, 1868–1919.* New York: Henry Holt, 1993.

McFeely, William S. *Yankee Stepfather: General O. O. Howard and the Freedmen.* New Haven: Yale University Press, 1968.

McMurry, Linda O. *George Washington Carver: Scientist and Symbol.* New York: Oxford University Press, 1981.

Meier, August. *Negro Thought in America, 1880–1915: Racial Ideologies in the Age of Booker T. Washington.* Ann Arbor: University of Michigan Press, 1963.

Montgomery, David. *Beyond Equality: Labor and the Radical Republicans, 1862–1872; with a Bibliographical Afterward.* 1967. Reprint, Urbana: University of Illinois Press, 1981.

Moses, Wilson Jeremiah. *Alexander Crummell: A Study of Civilization and Discontent.* New York: Oxford University Press, 1989.

Neverdon-Morton, Cynthia. *Afro-American Women of the South and the Advancement of the Race, 1895–1925.* Knoxville: University of Tennessee Press, 1989.

Nieman, Donald G. *To Set the Law in Motion: The Freedmen's Bureau and the Legal Rights of Blacks, 1865–1868.* Millwood, N.Y.: KTO, 1979.

Ovington, Mary White. *Black and White Sat Down Together: The Reminiscences of an NAACP Founder.* New York: The Feminist Press at the City University of New York, 1995.

Perman, Michael. *Reunion Without Compromise: The South and Reconstruction, 1865–1868.* Cambridge: Cambridge University Press, 1973.

———. *The Road to Redemption: Southern Politics, 1869–1879.* Chapel Hill: University of North Carolina Press, 1984.

Redkey, Edwin S. *Black Exodus: Black Nationalist and Back-to-Africa Movements, 1890–1910.* New Haven: Yale University Press, 1969.

Render, Sylvia Lyons, ed. *The Short Fiction of Charles W. Chesnutt.* Washington, D.C.: Howard University Press, 1981.

Ripley, C. Peter. *Witness for Freedom: African American Voices on Race, Slavery, and Emancipation.* Chapel Hill: University of North Carolina Press, 1993.

Roberts, John W. *From Trickster to Badman: The Black Folk Hero in Slavery and Freedom.* Philadelphia: University of Pennsylvania Press, 1989.

Robinson, Cedric J. *Black Marxism: The Making of the Black Radical Tradition.* Atlantic Highlands, N.J.: Zed Books, 1983.

Rudwick, Elliott. *W. E. B. Du Bois: Voice of the Black Protest Movement.* Urbana University of Illinois Press, 1982.

Singletary, Otis A. *Negro Militia and Reconstruction.* 1957. Reprint, New York: McGraw-Hill, 1969.

Smith, Gerald L. *A Black Educator in the Segregated South: Kentucky's Rufus B. Atwood.* Lexington: University Press of Kentucky, 1994.

Smith, J. Clay, Jr. *Emancipation: The Making of the Black Lawyer, 1844–1944.* Philadelphia: University of Pennsylvania Press, 1993.

Stepto, Robert B. *From Behind the Veil: A Study of Afro-American Narrative.* 2nd ed. Urbana: University of Illinois Press, 1991.

Stuckey, Sterling. *Going Through the Storm: The Influence of African American Art in History.* New York: Oxford University Press, 1994.

Terborg-Penn, Rosalyn. *African American Women in the Struggle for the Vote, 1850–1920.* Bloomington: Indiana University Press, 1998.

Thornbrough, Emma Lou. *T. Thomas Fortune: Militant Journalist.* Chicago: University of Chicago Press, 1972.

Toll, Robert C. *Blacking Up: The Minstrel Show in Nineteenth-Century America.* New York: Oxford University Press, 1974.

Walker, Clarence E. *A Rock in a Weary Land: The African Methodist Episcopal Church During the Civil War and Reconstruction.* Baton Rouge: Louisiana State University Press, 1982.

Wells-Barnett, Ida B. *Crusade for Justice: The Autobiography of Ida B. Wells.* Chicago: University of Chicago Press, 1972.

Wheeler, Edward L. *Uplifting the Race: The Black Minister in the New South, 1865–1902.* New York: University Press of America, 1986.

White, John. *Black Leadership in America from Booker T. Washington to Jesse Jackson.* 2nd ed. New York: Longman, 1990.

Woodson, Carter G. *The Mis-Education of the Negro.* New York: Associated Publishers, 1977.

Economic Emancipation and the Sharecropping System

Cohen, William. *At Freedom's Edge: Black Mobility and the Southern White Quest for Racial Control, 1861–1915.* Baton Rouge: Louisiana State University, 1991.

Glymph, Thavolia, and John J. Kushma, eds. *Essays on the Postbellum Southern Economy.* College Station: Texas A&M University Press for University of Texas at Arlington, 1985.

Higgs, Robert. *Competition and Coercion: Blacks in the American Economy, 1865–1914.* New York: Cambridge University Press, 1977.

Jaynes, Gerald David. *Branches Without Roots: Genesis of the Black Working Class in the American South, 1862–1882.* New York: Oxford University Press, 1986.

Magdol, Edward. *A Right to the Land: Essays on the Freedmen's Community.* Westport, Conn.: Greenwood Press, 1977.

Mandle, Jay R. *Not Slave, Not Free: The African American Economic Experience Since the Civil War.* Durham: Duke University Press, 1992.

Oubre, Claude F. *Forty Acres and a Mule: The Freedmen's Bureau and Black Land Ownership.* Baton Rouge: Louisiana State University Press, 1978.

Powell, Lawrence N. *New Masters: Northern Planters During the Civil War and Reconstruction.* New Haven: Yale University Press, 1980.

Ransom, Roger L., and Richard Sutch. *One Kind of Freedom: The Economic Consequences of Emancipation.* Cambridge: Cambridge University Press, 1977.

Saville, Julie. *The Work of Reconstruction: From Slave to Wage Laborers in South Carolina, 1860–1870.* Cambridge: University of Cambridge Press, 1994.

Schwalm, Leslie A. *A Hard Fight for We: Women's Transition from Slavery to Freedom in South Carolina.* Urbana: University of Illinois Press, 1997.

Schweninger, Loren C. *Black Property Owners in the South, 1790–1915.* Urbana: University of Illinois Press, 1990.

Migration, Cities, and Wage Labor

Arnesen, Eric. *Waterfront Workers of New Orleans: Race, Class and Politics, 1863–1923.* New York: Oxford University Press, 1991.

Crew, Spencer R. *Black Life in Secondary Cities: A Comparative Analysis of the Black Communities of Camden and Elizabeth, N.J., 1860–1920.* New York: Garland, 1993.

Daniels, Douglas Henry. *Pioneer Urbanites: A Social and Cultural History of Black San Francisco.* Philadelphia: Temple University Press, 1980.

Du Bois, W. E. B. *The Philadelphia Negro: A Social Study.* 1899. Reprint, Philadelphia: University of Pennsylvania Press, 1996.

Fink, Gary, and Merl E. Reed. *Race, Class, and Community in Southern Labor History.* Tuscaloosa: University of Alabama Press, 1994.

Hamilton, Kenneth Marvin. *Black Towns and Profit: Promotion and Development in the Trans-Appalachian West, 1877–1915.* Urbana: University of Illinois Press, 1991.

Hunter, Tera W. *To 'Joy My Freedom: Southern Black Women's Lives and Labors After the Civil War.* Cambridge: Harvard University Press, 1997.

Johnson, Whittington B. *Black Savannah, 1788–1864.* Fayetteville: University of Arkansas Press, 1996.

Katz, Michael B., and Thomas J. Sugrue, eds. *W. E. B. Du Bois, Race, and the City: The Philadelphia Negro and Its Legacy.* Philadelphia: University of Pennsylvania Press, 1998.

Katzman, David M. *Seven Days a Week: Women and Domestic Service in Industrializing America.* New York: Oxford University Press, 1978.

Letwin, Daniel. *The Challenge of Interracial Unionism: Alabama Coal Miners, 1878–1921.* Chapel Hill: University of North Carolina Press, 1998.

Painter, Nell Irvin. *Exodusters: Black Migration to Kansas after Reconstruction.* Kansas: University Press of Kansas, 1976.

Rabinowitz, Howard N. *Race Relations in the Urban South, 1865–1890.* Urbana: University of Illinois Press, 1980.

Rachleff, Peter J. *Black Labor in the South: Richmond, Virginia, 1865–1890.* Philadelphia: Temple University Press, 1984.

Tripp, Steven Elliott. *Yankee Town, Southern City: Race and Class Relations in Civil War Lynchburg.* New York: New York University Press, 1997.

Weare, Walter B. *Black Business in the New South: A Social History of the North Carolina Mutual Life Insurance Company.* Urbana: University of Illinois Press, 1973.

Wright, George C. *Life Behind a Veil: Blacks in Louisville, Kentucky, 1865–1930.* Baton Rouge: Louisiana State University Press, 1985.

Social Conditions, Lynchings, and Race Riots

Brundage, W. Fitzhugh, ed. *Under Sentence of Death: Lynching in the South.* Chapel Hill: University of North Carolina Press, 1997.

Downey, Dennis B., and Raymond M. Hyser. *No Crooked Death: Coatesville, Pennsylvania, and the Lynching of Zachariah Walker.* Urbana: University of Illinois Press, 1991.

Ingalls, Robert P. *Urban Vigilantes in the New South: Tampa, 1882–1936.* Knoxville: University of Tennessee Press, 1988.

Lane, Roger. *Roots of Violence in Black Philadelphia, 1860–1900.* Cambridge: Harvard University Press, 1986.

Royster, Jacqueline Jones, ed. *Southern Horrors and Other Writings: The Anti-Lynching Campaign of Ida B. Wells, 1892–1900.* Boston, Mass.: Bedford, 1997.

Trelease, Allen W. *White Terror: The Ku Klux Klan Conspiracy and Southern Reconstruction.* Westport: Greenwood Press, 1979.

State, Regional, and General Studies

Ayers, Edward L. *The Promise of the New South: Life After Reconstruction.* New York: Oxford University Press, 1992.

Berwanger, Eugene H. *The West and Reconstruction.* Urbana: University of Illinois Press, 1981.

Cobb, James G. *The Most Southern Place on Earth: The Mississippi Delta and the Roots of Regional Identity.* New York: Oxford University Press, 1992.

Dittmer, John. *Black Georgia in the Progressive Era, 1900–1920.* Urbana: University of Illinois Press, 1977.

Du Bois, W. E. B. *Black Reconstruction in America.* 1935. Reprint, New York: Atheneum, 1992.

Foner, Eric. *Nothing but Freedom: Emancipation and Its Legacy.* Baton Rouge: Louisiana State University Press, 1983.

———. *Reconstruction: America's Unfinished Revolution, 1863–1877.* New York: Harper & Row, 1988.

Franklin, Jimmie Lewis. *Journey Toward Hope: A History of Blacks in Oklahoma.* Norman: University of Oklahoma Press, 1982.

Franklin, John Hope. *Reconstruction After the Civil War.* Chicago: University of Chicago Press, 1961.

Kolchin, Peter. *First Freedom: The Response of Alabama's Blacks to Emancipation and Reconstruction.* Westport, Conn.: Greenwood Press, 1972.

Litwack, Leon F. *Been in the Storm So Long.* 1979. Reprint, New York: Vintage Books, 1980.

———. *Trouble in Mind: Black Southerners in the Age of Jim Crow.* New York: Vintage Books, 1998.

Logan, Rayford W. *The Betrayal of the Negro: From Rutherford B. Hayes to Woodrow Wilson.* New York: Collier, 1965.

McMillen, Neil R. *Dark Journey: Black Mississippians in the Age of Jim Crow.* Urbana: University of Illinois Press, 1990.

Savage, W. Sherman. *Blacks in the West.* Westport: Greenwood Press, 1976.

Stampp, Kenneth M. *The Era of Reconstruction, 1865–1877.* 1965. Reprint, New York: Vintage Books, 1967.

Williamson, Joel. *The Crucible of Race: Black-White Relations in the American South Since Emancipation.* New York: Oxford University Press, 1984.

Woodward, C. Vann. *Reunion and Reaction: The Compromise of 1877 and the End of Reconstruction.* 1951. Reprint, New York: Oxford University Press, 1991.

———. *The Strange Career of Jim Crow.* 1955. 2nd ed. rev. New York: Oxford University Press, 1966.

Wright, Gavin. *Old South/New South: Revolutions in the Southern Economy Since the Civil War.* New York: Basic Books, 1986.